The End of the
Spanish Civil War
Alicante 1939

The End of the Spanish Civil War Alicante 1939

Jonathan Whitehead

First published in Great Britain in 2023 by
Pen & Sword History
An imprint of Pen & Sword Books Limited
Yorkshire – Philadelphia

Copyright © Jonathan Whitehead 2023

ISBN 978 1 39906 391 3

The right of Jonathan Whitehead to be identified as
Author of this Work has been asserted by him in accordance
with the Copyright, Designs and Patents Act 1988.

A CIP catalogue record for this book is
available from the British Library

All rights reserved. No part of this book may be reproduced or
transmitted in any form or by any means, electronic or mechanical
including photocopying, recording or by any information storage and
retrieval system, without permission from the Publisher in writing.

Typeset by Mac Style
Printed in the UK by CPI Group (UK) Ltd, Croydon, CR0 4YY.

Pen & Sword Books Limited incorporates the imprints of After the Battle, Atlas, Archaeology, Aviation, Discovery, Family History, Fiction, History, Maritime, Military, Military Classics, Politics, Select, Transport, True Crime, Air World, Frontline Publishing, Leo Cooper, Remember When, Seaforth Publishing, The Praetorian Press, Wharncliffe Local History, Wharncliffe Transport, Wharncliffe True Crime and White Owl.

For a complete list of Pen & Sword titles please contact

PEN & SWORD BOOKS LIMITED
47 Church Street, Barnsley, South Yorkshire, S70 2AS, England
E-mail: enquiries@pen-and-sword.co.uk
Website: www.pen-and-sword.co.uk
or
PEN AND SWORD BOOKS
1950 Lawrence Rd, Havertown, PA 19083, USA
E-mail: Uspen-and-sword@casematepublishers.com
Website: www.penandswordbooks.com

Alicante, July 1936

It began in the second fortnight of July. Heat, sun, crowds of people at the seaside, open-air dances, outings, glorious holidays ... the gardens on the outskirts of the town were filled with music and laughter, the fragrant jasmine and the bougainvillea, heavy with flowers ...

Ángel Pascual Devesa

Contents

Translation and Place Names   x
Maps   xii

Part One – 1936–1938   1

Chapter 1   **A threatening tide of history**   3
Introduction: the Civil War in Spain

Chapter 2   **Akra Leuké**   11
The outbreak of war in Alicante

Chapter 3   **José Antonio ¡presente!**   22
The case of the leader of the Falange, imprisoned in Alicante, and the violence in the Republican zone

Chapter 4   **Your children will be next**   30
Alicante and the air war

Chapter 5   **Malditos, malditos, malditos los causantes de tanto dolor …**   38
25 de Mayo 1938

Part Two – 1939

Chapter 6   **Bullets hurt, corpses stink**   51
The defeat of the Republican Army: the Ebro and Catalonia

Chapter 7   **An ocean of darkness and death, but an infinite ocean of light and love**   63
Humanitarian aid in Alicante

Chapter 8	Cerca del agua perdida del mar *The arrival of Negrín in Alicante after the debacle in Catalonia*	70
Chapter 9	Stay out of the range of the artillery fire *Non-Intervention: the effects of British and French foreign policy*	77
Chapter 10	The end may justify the means as long as there is something that justifies the end *The role of the Spanish Communist Party*	83
Chapter 11	Red sunset *The situation in Alicante*	89
Chapter 12	One Munich was not enough *Britain and France recognise Franco*	94
Chapter 13	The quickest way of ending a war is to lose it *Differing views on how to end the war*	102
Chapter 14	El olvido es peor que los recuerdos *Negrín moves his government to Elda-Petrer (Alicante)*	108
Chapter 15	His last ounce of courage *The battle for Cartagena and the Republican Navy*	115

Part Three – The End		123
Chapter 16	Usted haga como yo, no se meta en política *The second coup d'état*	125
Chapter 17	El destino infortunado de España, derrotada y maltrecha *The flight of the government*	132
Chapter 18	Written in the blood of a Spanish soldier *The civil war within the civil war*	138

Chapter 19	El abrazo de Vergara *Peace negotiations with the Nationalists*	146
Chapter 20	Una gota de pura valentía vale más que un océano cobarde *Evacuation*	154
Chapter 21	Wo bleibt Gambara? *The tragedy of the port*	162
Chapter 22	And the almond tree shall flourish *Campo de los Almendros*	174
Chapter 23	En el yermo de la historia *The Albatera concentration camp*	180

Part Four – Aftermath   189

| Chapter 24 | No ha llegado la paz; ha llegado la victoria | 191 |

Dramatis Personae   204
Glossary   206
Chronological Table   212
Presidents of Government/Prime Ministers of the Republic during the Civil War   214
Epigraphs and chapters   216
Acknowledgements   220
Notes   222
Bibliography and sources   253

Translation and Place Names

All translations into English that appear in this book are by the author unless cited from English-language editions.

I avoid using English translations of areas and towns, with one exception, Cataluña/Catalunya, where the population has become accustomed to using the English name Catalonia. The multiple official languages in Spain make place names a source of both confusion and political and linguistic dispute. The first language of most of the Spanish population is known to non-Spaniards as Spanish, while most Spanish people tend to call it *castellano* (with lower-case 'c'), which translates into English as Castilian. For consistency and expediency, I use the Castilian Spanish names for towns and regions, rather than the names in local languages (Catalan, Valencian, Basque or Galician). In most cases, with the first reference, I include the name in the local language in brackets. For example: *Gerona (Girona)*.

Under the terms of clause 3.2 of the Constitution (1978) and clauses 6.1 and 6.2 of the Statute of Autonomy of the Community of Valencia (1982), Alicante town and province have two official languages: Spanish (Castilian) and Valencian. On my first visit in 1980, as we entered the town by road, there was a sign that said 'Alicante/Alacant'. In other words, the local authorities had equitably chosen to put the name of the town in both languages. Right-wing opponents of the new democracy had nevertheless painted 'Alicante' over the name in Valencian, while defenders of the local language had painted 'Alacant' over the name in Spanish. Neither of the groups that defaced the sign appeared to have realised that the sign still said Alacant and Alicante, just not as neatly. To add to the confusion, there is a long-standing political and linguistic debate on whether the local language should be recognised as Catalan. The Statute uses the name Valencian. The use of *valenciano* as a first language is widespread in many rural areas of the province, and in major towns like Elche, Alcoy and Denia.

The name 'Alicante' can refer to the province and the town that is the capital of the province. Where necessary I follow the local protocol and distinguish between 'Alicante capital' and 'Alicante province'.

When I use a Spanish word as an adjective (e.g. *franquista, falangista*), I respect Spanish protocols and use lower-case first letters.

All Spanish people have two surnames: their father's and their mother's. Of those in the public eye, some become known with both: *Largo Caballero, Martínez Barrio*; but many are widely known with only one: *Franco, Negrín, Azaña*, etc. I use one or two according to common practice.

For the sake of consistency, wherever the first reference to an institution appears in Spanish, I give a translation in English either in brackets or as a footnote, however obvious that translation may seem. When quoting or giving book titles in Spanish, I respect Spanish language protocols. In other words, I only use upper-case letters where appropriate in Spanish.

The head of government in Spain is known as the 'President of the Government' or the 'President of the Council of Ministers'. To avoid confusion with the head of state, the 'President of the Republic', I use 'Prime Minister'.

The forces that rallied to the military insurgency in 1936 labelled themselves '*nacionales*', translated literally as 'nationals'. However, given the substantial number of North Africans, Italians and Germans in their ranks, and the fact that the name implies that the Republicans were somehow not national/Spanish, most modern historians writing in either Spanish or English avoid the term. I have therefore chosen to follow the practice of most English-language Hispanists and use 'Nationalist'.

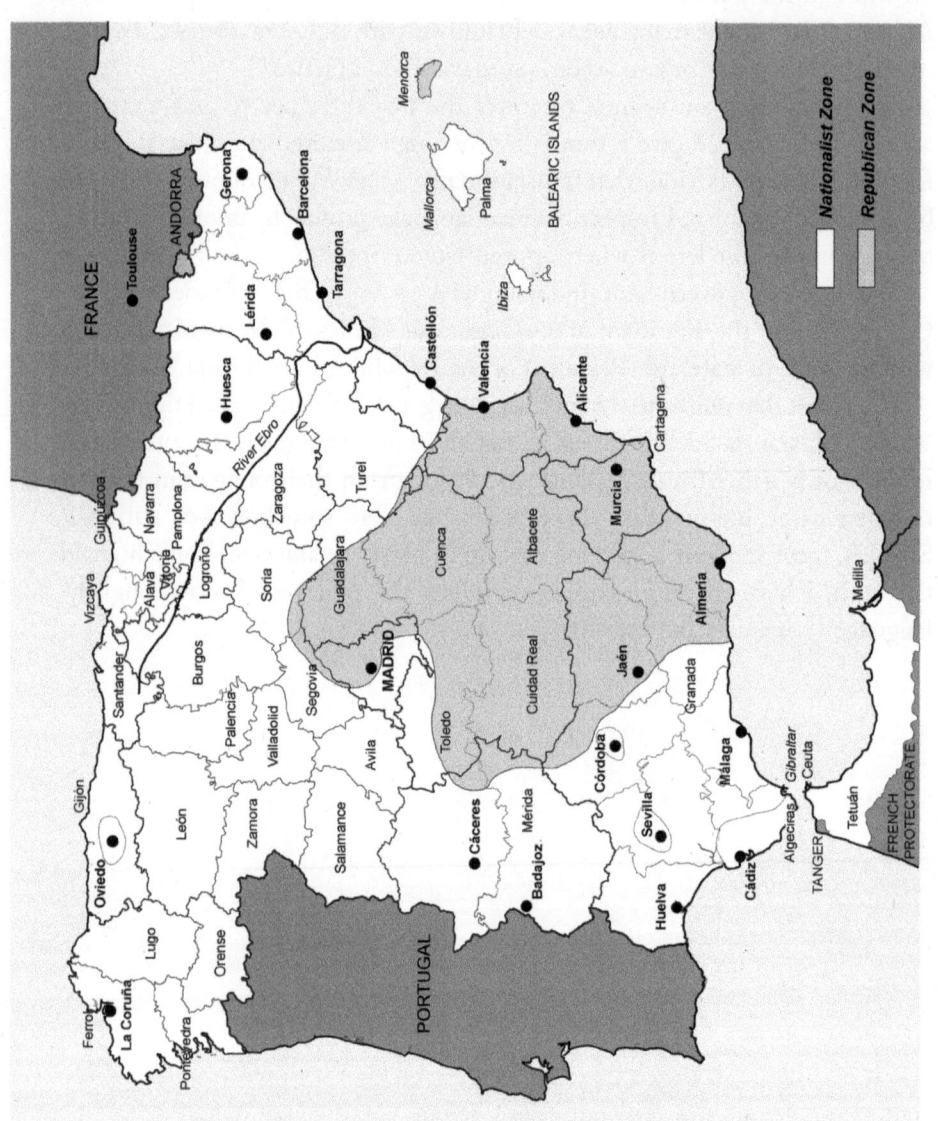

Map 1. Spain, March 1939. (*Pen & Sword*)

Map 2. Alicante Province. (*Pen & Sword*)

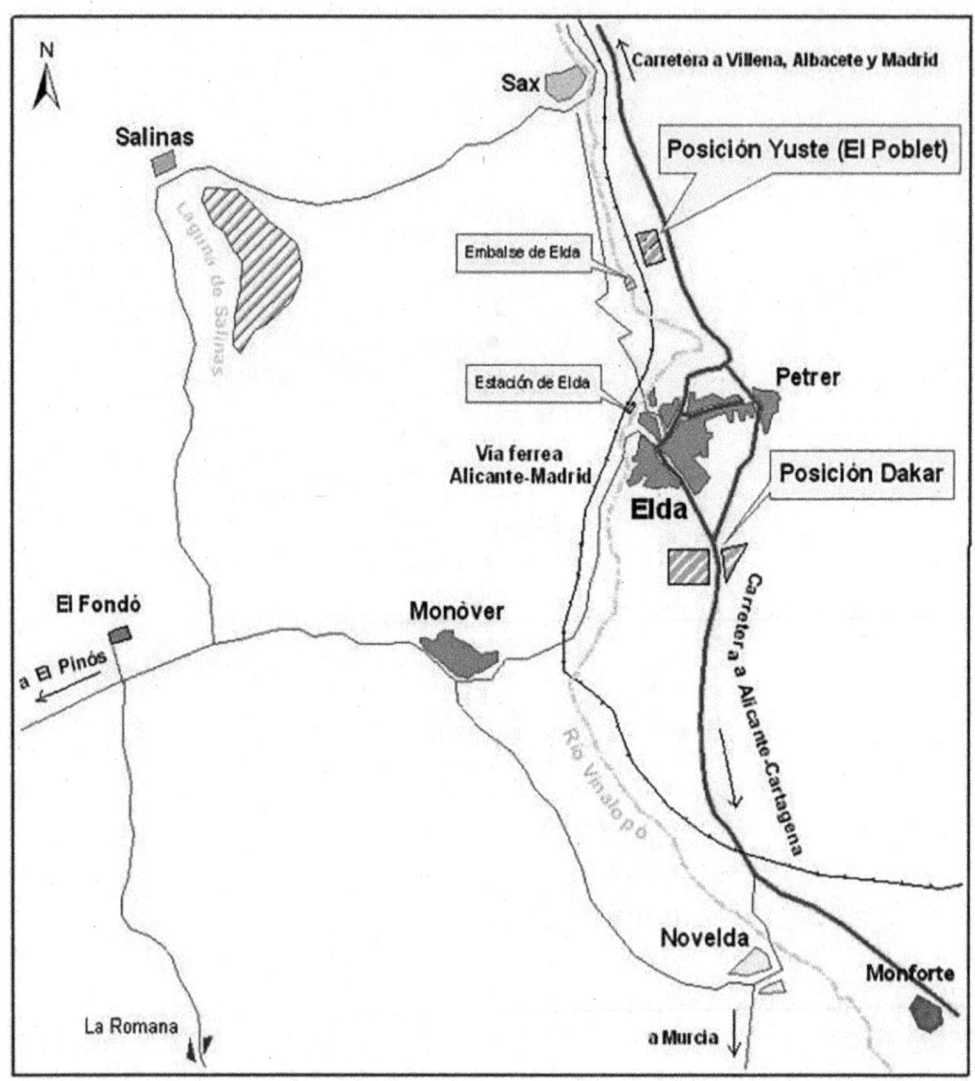

Map 3. Elda-Petrer. (*Courtesy of José Ramón Valero Escandell*)

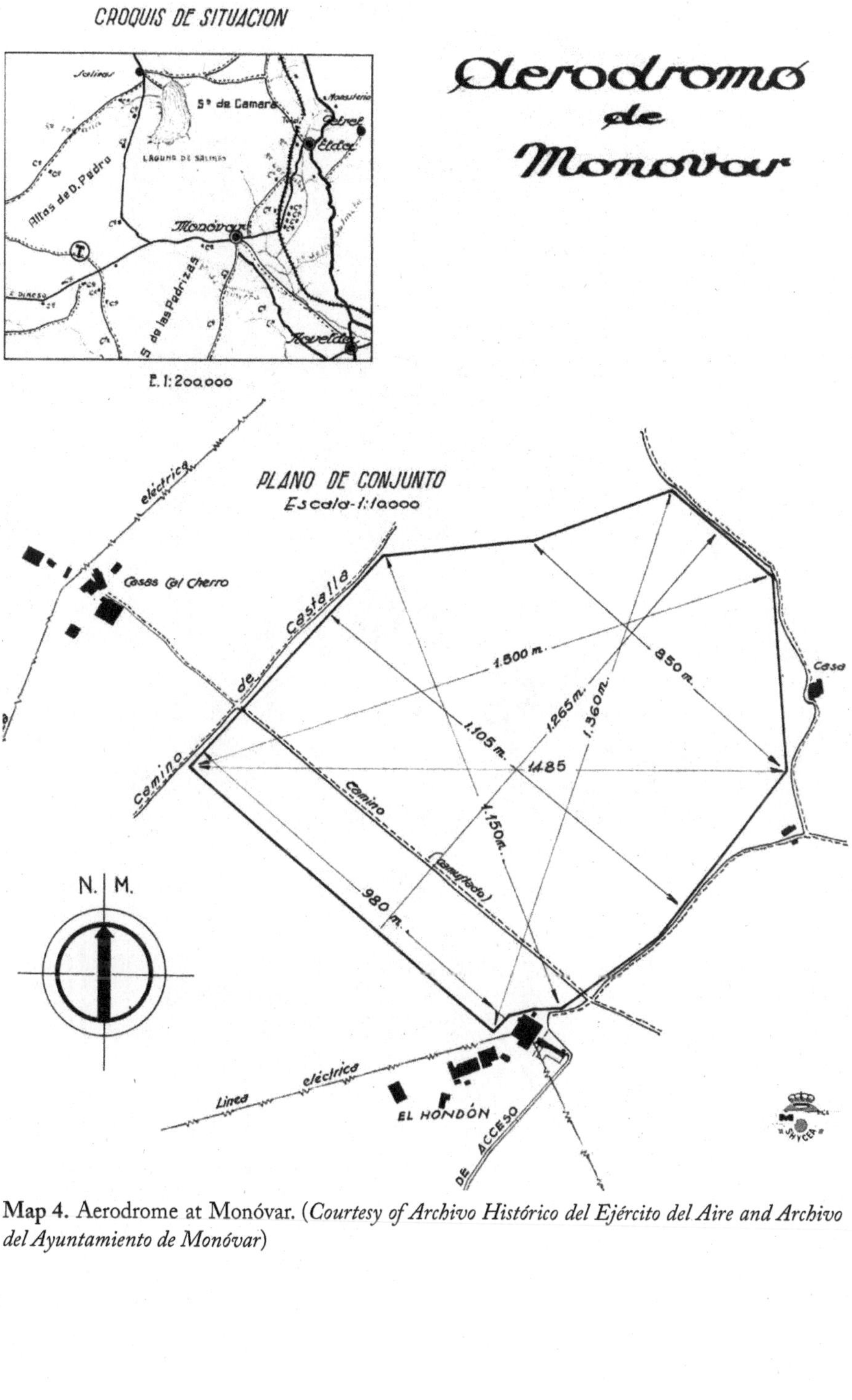

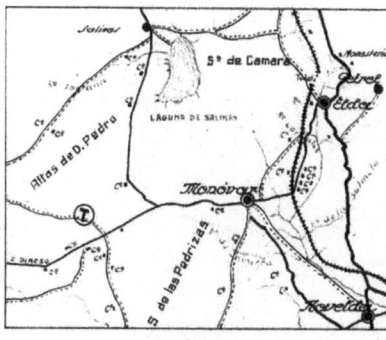

Map 4. Aerodrome at Monóvar. (*Courtesy of Archivo Histórico del Ejército del Aire and Archivo del Ayuntamiento de Monóvar*)

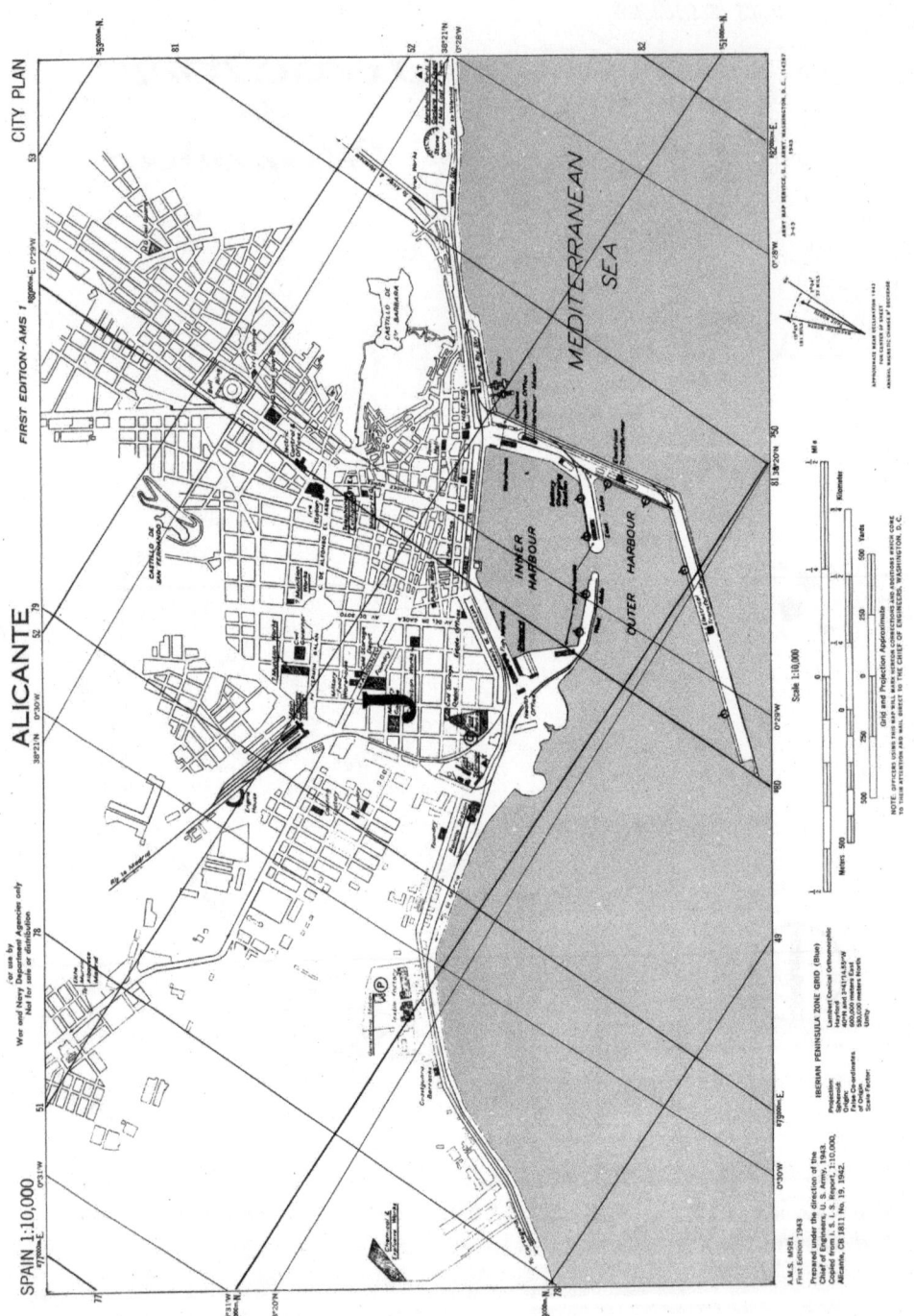

Map 5. Alicante (1942). (*Courtesy of the University of Texas*)

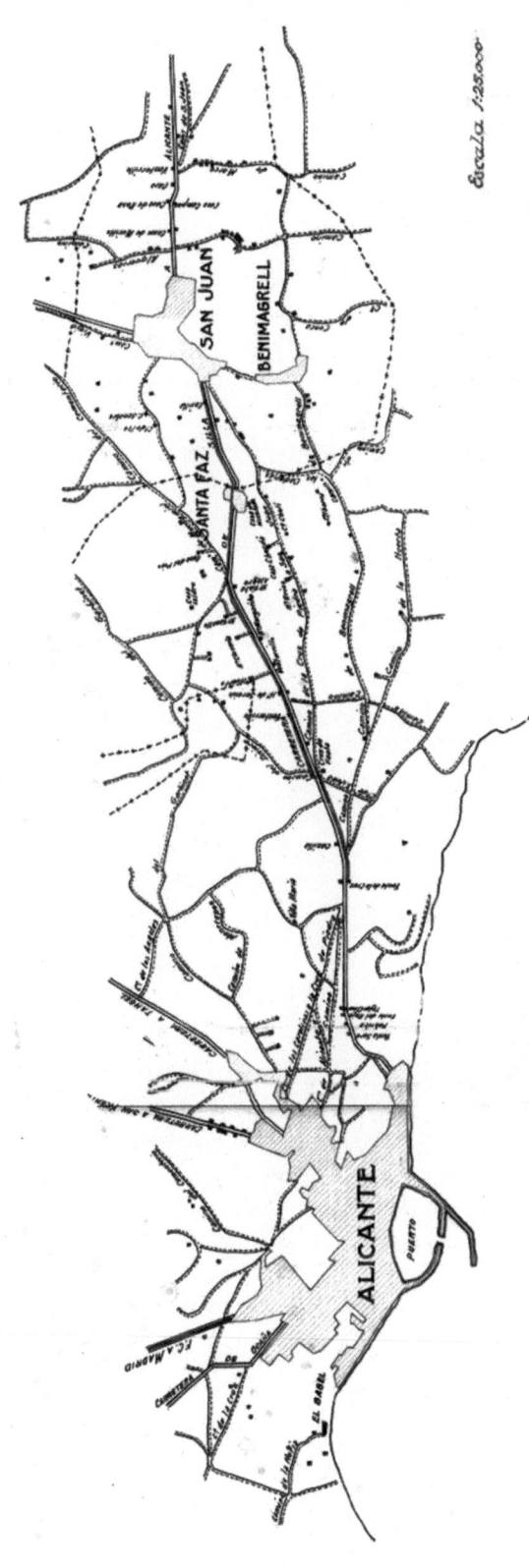

Map 6. Wartime project to supply San Juan with drinking water, showing area between Alicante and the village. (*Courtesy of Archivo Municipal de San Juan*)

Part One

1936–1938

Chapter 1

A threatening tide of history

Introduction: the Civil War in Spain

In the early spring of 1939 the Second Spanish Republic teetered on the brink of defeat and extinction. That it had not already fallen was due mainly to the strategies of two men: Doctor Juan Negrín López, President of the legitimate government of the Republic, and *Generalísimo* Francisco Franco, undisputed leader of the military insurgency that followed the unsuccessful coup d'état of July 1936. However, the final phase of the Civil War was to be defined by the intervention of the far less well-known Colonel Segismundo Casado, a career officer who had remained loyal to the Republic and risen to the post of Commander of the Army of the Centre.

For the Spanish Republicans, the European war against fascism began three years before Britain and France declared war on Germany and almost four years before the *Wehrmacht* occupied France. Indeed, many, including Negrín, rejected the label 'Spanish Civil War' and referred to the conflict as the 'Spanish War', the first military front in the international struggle against the forces of Hitler and Mussolini. The Second Spanish Republic had been proclaimed in April 1931 when, in the face of growing popular hostility towards the monarchy, King Alfonso XIII chose to abandon the country rather than abdicate the throne. In Alicante, when the new Mayor, Lorenzo Carbonell Santacruz, addressed the council that had just elected him unanimously, he made the optimistic and grandiose claim, befitting perhaps the enthusiasm of so many, that 'The Republic, founded by Republicans, with the sacrifice made by our fallen, is not a Republic only for Republicans, it is a Republic for all Spaniards.'[1]

In the early years (1931–33), centre-left coalition governments in Madrid introduced a series of political and social reforms that on paper threatened the traditional structures and value systems upon which Catholic, conservative Spain was based. British historian Raymond Carr defined the task undertaken by Republicans as: 'the liquidation of the institutional hindrances to a progressive, democratic society – notably an influential state church, a powerful army, *latifundismo*.'[2] Between October 1931 and September 1933, under the leadership of Manuel Azaña, the government introduced changes that included: new labour laws; a huge educational programme that prioritised the construction of thousands of new schools and excluded religion from the compulsory curriculum; an overhaul of the armed forces (especially measures to reduce the senior officer corps); and land reform designed to create an agrarian system based on smallholdings. The government in Madrid also took measures to secularise the State, to extend the franchise to women and to legalise divorce.

Nevertheless, the new authorities failed in their attempts to implement far-reaching reform or to satisfy the expectations of the popular classes. They lacked the means, or the political dexterity, to enforce measures that met with the resistance of powerful economic and social forces. In the words of the Spanish activist and writer Constancia de la Mora, 'Reforms cannot take place on paper alone.'[3] It is also possible that precisely by seeking simultaneously to introduce sweeping changes in all the bastions of the most conservative sectors of society, the government simply overestimated its capacity to impose change and enabled the right to mount a coordinated defence of their interests. British historian Helen Graham described the Republican agenda as 'an immensely ambitious programme of structural reform':

> Indeed, it was almost certainly too ambitious to attempt so much at one time. Even worse, the attempt was being made at a time of world economic depression. [...] The inherent complexity of structural reform [...] only added to the problems rapidly gathering on the new political horizon.[4]

The error of many of those on the left was to believe that the Republic was more than a political system; they assumed that the overthrow of the monarchy would automatically lead to an irrevocable transformation of Spain and thus raised the expectations of a population impatient for radical change. The failure of the first Republican governments was not for want of purpose or enthusiasm but was due precisely to the reality that those in power were culpable of political over-reach: they had set themselves a target that was beyond them.

Regardless of the shortcomings and the lack of substantial progress towards structural change, the ambitions of the government enraged the right and led to a conservative backlash. A right-wing coalition comfortably defeated a divided left at the elections of 1934 and embarked on a course of reconfirming the authority of the traditional centres of power. The *bienio negro* (black biennium) that followed was a period of repression and economic hardship during which many on the left lost faith in the Republic. Employers took advantage of the victory to cut wages and sack troublesome workers. Landowners raised rents and evicted impoverished tenants. The government undertook the task of dismantling the social reform of the previous two years. However, at the beginning of 1936, in the last democratic elections in Spain in more than forty years, the left agreed on an electoral alliance, the *Frente Popular*,* which fought on a platform of the 'reassertion of the reformist impulse of the Republic',[5] and won a narrow victory. Manuel Azaña, leader of the Republican Left Party†, was thus able to form a centre-left government, with the parliamentary support of the Socialists‡ and Communists§. Unfortunately, the apparently irreconcilable antagonism between left and right was exacerbated by increasing disenchantment with the democratic process on both extremes and an upsurge in street violence in many towns.

The Church, the army, the landowners, the industrialists and the bankers refused to make any concessions to the landless rural population and the urban proletariat. Those that demanded, supported or implemented reform were conveniently labelled the anti-Spain, the exponents of a vast international Jewish–masonic–Communist conspiracy.[6] In the face of the challenge to their own interests and privileges, leading representatives of the right resolved that only military intervention could save the eternal values of Spain from subversion and sedition. On 19 July General Francisco Franco arrived in Tetuán and took command of the Spanish African Army that had mutinied two days before. Meanwhile, General Emilio Mola, '*el director*' and architect of the *golpe de estado*¶, had issued orders for military insurrection across mainland Spain.

However, the coup failed. Although the insurgents were able to seize control in the Spanish Protectorate, Pamplona, Zaragoza, Sevilla and the northwest, they were defeated by loyalist forces and popular uprisings in the major cities of Madrid, Barcelona, Bilbao and Valencia. Refusing to stand down, the rebels triggered a vicious, bloody civil war, the effects of which are still felt today in the politics of modern, democratic Spain. Pro-Franco British historian Sir Arthur Bryant denied media suggestions that the war was 'a heroic struggle for liberty by an oppressed people against a treasonable clique of military adventurers, reactionary aristocrats and corrupt priests'. The description, though, is remarkably accurate; considerably more so than his surreal portrayal of Franco as 'a man of liberal sympathies and an advocate of social reform'.[7]

---

* Popular Front.
† Izquierda Republicana (IR).
‡ Partido Socialista Obrero Español (PSOE): The Workers' Socialist Party.
§ Partido Comunista de España (PCE): The Communist Party of Spain.
¶ coup d'état.

The Republican war effort was substantially defensive, and after initial breakthroughs, the three major counter-offensives – Brunete, 1937; Teruel, 1937–8; and the Ebro, 1938 – all ended in failure. The greatest triumph was the defence of Madrid. Despite a massive frontal attack against the capital in the autumn of 1936, and the relentless aerial bombardment of the civilian population, the rebel army was unable to take the city until the final days of the conflict, when the fronts had disintegrated across Spain.

Former Prime Minister Manuel Azaña had become President of the Republic in May 1936, and in May 1937 he appointed Doctor Juan Negrín (PSOE) as President of the Government. Negrín was more pragmatic than the outgoing leader, Francisco Largo Caballero (PSOE), and prioritised military objectives over social reform. He sought to restrain the revolutionary violence of the Anarchists and POUM (*Partit Obrer d'Unificació Marxista* – Workers' Party of Marxist Unification) in Aragón and Catalonia, who argued that the war and revolution were indivisible.[8] He contended that disruptions in industry and agriculture and the attacks on the Catholic Church[9] were both undermining the war effort and alienating foreign governments and public opinion. Negrín remained in power virtually until the end of the war.

General Mola and the other leaders of the coup on the mainland took the precaution of forming a seven-man *Junta de Defensa Nacional* (National Defence Committee), which was later extended to include Franco.[10] It was designed to consolidate military authority over self-serving civilian politicians, and, in theory, to contain the over-ambitious by implementing a collegial command. Nonetheless, it took General Francisco Franco a mere two months to establish his complete political and military control. His dominance of the Nationalist movement, as it became known, was enhanced by the fortuitous deaths of several of his closest rivals or potential dissidents. General Sanjurjo, leader of an unsuccessful coup in 1932, died in the early days of the revolt when the aircraft bringing him back from Portugal crashed on take-off. General Goded, a hero of the Rif War and a key figure in the conspiracy, was executed when the uprising in Barcelona was defeated by the Republican militia. José Antonio Primo de Rivera, founder of the *Falange Española*,* was executed by the Republican authorities in Alicante in November 1936. And the original leader of the coup against the Republic, General Emilio Mola, was killed in another fortuitous aircraft accident in June 1937.

Of Franco, Constancia de la Mora later wrote: 'General Goded was more intelligent; General Mola a better soldier; but Franco was the most ambitious.'[11] Crucially for his own personal objectives, it was Franco who made first contact

---

* Literally *Spanish Phalanx* – The Fascist Party.

with Hitler and Mussolini. By petitioning the two dictators to provide transport aeroplanes to shuttle the African Army across the Straits of Gibraltar to mainland Spain, he established himself as their link with the insurgency. When they elected to deal with a single interlocutor rather than a committee of generals, there could be little argument that Franco was the obvious choice. Given the dependency of the Nationalist cause on German and Italian logistical support and weaponry, his position became virtually unassailable.

For two and a half years, sustained by North African volunteer troops and the Italians and Germans, the Nationalists slowly advanced across the peninsula until they had occupied the western half of Spain and most of the north. In response to the involvement of the fascist dictatorships, the USSR agreed to supply weapons to the Republic, but fewer and many of far lower quality than those bestowed on Franco by the Germans and Italians.[12] At this stage the British and French governments were engaged in honing their policy of appeasement. In London, many of those prowling the corridors of power publicly defended a policy officially designed to avoid the 'internationalisation' of the conflict, while in private they acknowledged the strategy as an expression of their greater fear of social revolution than of Hitler. They subsequently backed the French proposal for non-intervention, an agreement by which both sides should be prevented from acquiring weapons from abroad. The embargo thus made no legal distinction between the democratically elected and friendly government in Madrid and a military junta that sought to overthrow the same legitimate, and internationally recognised government. The agreement did little more than offer the British and French diplomatic cover for their pusillanimous efforts to mollify the governments in Berlin and Rome. Hitler and Mussolini both continued to arm the Nationalists, just as Stalin continued to supply the Republic. Von Ribbentrop, German Ambassador to the UK, later suggested that the Non-Intervention Committee that was set up in London to administer and monitor the pact should have been named the Intervention Committee, 'for the whole activity of its members consisted in explaining or concealing the participation of their countries in Spain'.[13] According to Civil War expert Michael Alpert, in the course of the war the Italians contributed:

70,000 men (of whom nearly 4,000 were killed)
759 aircraft
157 tanks
6,797 other military vehicles
1,801 cannon, 1,426 mortars, 3,436 machine-guns
320 million cartridges
7.7 million shells

The German contribution was calculated at:

14,000 men (approximately 300 dead)
840 aircraft
200 tanks
30 anti-tank companies

On the Republican side, by the time the supply of Soviet weapons dwindled after Munich, the USSR had delivered an estimated:

806 aircraft
482 tanks and armoured cars
1,555 cannon
862 million cartridges
3.5 million bombs and shells[14]

Winston Churchill registered his support for neutrality in the conflict, but dismissed Non-Intervention as 'an elaborate system of official humbug'.[15] In an article published in the *Daily Herald* weeks after the military uprising, the Labour peer Lord Strabolgi described the policy of the British government towards the Republic as 'malevolent neutrality'.[16] At the end of the conflict, in the editorial of the March 1939 edition of *Popular Flying*, author W. E. Johns went further: 'Of all the foul and craven hypocrisy of which those in power in Britain had been guilty during the past decade – and nowhere in history will you find such a sequence of faint-hearted perfidiousness – this Spanish business is the worst.'[17]

Almost as a prelude to the calamitous devastation and suffering of the Second World War, the Spanish Civil War dragged on for two and a half years of brutal fighting, extreme heroism, unspeakable atrocities, remarkable examples of personal sacrifice and compassion, aerial bombardments of the civilian population, extraordinary resilience and desperate hardships. The fratricidal nature of the struggle was immediately exacerbated by the international dimension provided by the direct intervention of the great dictators.

The Germans and Italians became increasingly frustrated with their protégé Franco. They invested an impressive array of cutting-edge weaponry and expected a swift return in results. But rather than deal the Republic a series of rapid knock-out blows, Franco's strategy was based on a ruthless ambition that extended beyond regime change. In the autumn of 1936, he took the bizarre military decision to delay the advance on Madrid in order to relieve the siege of the Alcázar (citadel) of Toledo. The base had been occupied by Nationalist officers, families and cadets who valiantly resisted the increasingly desperate attempts of the Republican authorities in the town to force their surrender. By diverting his army from its triumphant march on the capital and investing time on essentially a symbolic victory designed to enhance his own prestige, he allowed the people and authorities in Madrid time to prepare defences and integrate Soviet weapons and the newly arrived international brigades.

Having failed to take the capital, Franco then resolved on a military strategy that would better serve his political objective. In the spring of 1937, he told the Italian ambassador in Burgos (where the Nationalists established their capital) that the war aim of 'capitulation and pacification' would take time, but otherwise military occupation of the country would serve no purpose. He continued: 'I will occupy Spain town by town, village by village, and city by city, railway by railway.'[18] He spurned modern theories of dynamic warfare and showed no qualms at prolonging the war as a means not only to defeat the Republican army but also to facilitate his quest to eliminate as many of the enemy (military and civilian) as possible. While many craved peace, the *Caudillo*,* as he was now known, was set on total victory. In an interview with the Havas News Agency in November 1937, he boasted, 'I will impose my will by victory and will not enter into discussion [...] The war is already won on the battlefields [...] I will only agree to end it militarily [...] The choice for the enemy is fight or unconditional surrender.'[19]

On the other hand, the Prime Minister of the Republic, Dr Juan Negrín, was committed to what his Chief of General Staff defined as *'la doctrina de resistencia a ultranza'* (the doctrine of resistance at any cost).[20] He was fully aware that Franco had no desire and no need to negotiate and would show the vanquished no mercy. He was, however, also convinced that Hitler's ambitions would eventually force a European war in which the British and French would at last embrace the Spanish Republic as a vital ally and the Spanish war would become a crucial front, engulfed within the wider struggle. Even after Munich, when it became impossible to uphold faith in the western democracies, and when Catalonia fell to the Nationalists in the winter of 1938–39, Negrín nonetheless continued to urge his armies to resist in order to secure a coastal redoubt from which to evacuate as many Republicans as possible. Despite the military setbacks, at this stage the Republic still occupied 30% of the Spanish mainland, and crucially controlled the coast from Valencia to Almeria, including Alicante and the naval base at Cartagena (Murcia).

---

* The Spanish equivalent of *Duce* and *Führer*. According to the Dictionary of *the Real Academia de la Lengua*: absolute chief of an armed group or political dictator (usually military).

The human cost of the war is difficult to quantify. Indeed, in his seminal work, *The Spanish Holocaust*, British Hispanist Paul Preston suggests: 'The statistical vision [...] is not only flawed, incomplete and unlikely ever to be complete. It also fails to capture the intense horror that lies behind the numbers.'[21] Nevertheless, after extensive demographic research, Javier Silvestre (University of Zaragoza) and José Antonio Ortega (University of Salamanca) concluded that the conflict produced an 'excess' mortality (*sobremortalidad*) of 540,000 men, women and children. The figure includes those who died in action and civilian victims of military operations, those executed in acts of repression and reprisals, and those whose death through illness and malnutrition were the direct result of the fighting.[22] The eminent historian Enrique Moradiellos puts the figure somewhat higher, at between 650,000 and 735,000 – 2.63% to 2.97% of the population (24.69 million) registered in 1936.[23]

And so, as the end approached, in addition to the hundreds of thousands of Republicans who had already fled Catalonia into France, many more remained trapped in Spain. In the final weeks of the conflict, General Franco seemed satisfied to remain in the background while the final acts of the drama played themselves out. And yet, despite his relatively minor role in this narrative, his war aims are of fundamental significance. He scorned the idea of reconciliation. His goal was ideological cleansing, and whatever promises he might make, the only concession he made to the vanquished was redemption through labour.

Chapter 2

Akra Leuké

The outbreak of war in Alicante

Alicante, a provincial town in a country where for so long the populations outside the big cities had been denied social, cultural and educational resources, proved its unwavering loyalty to the new Republic in the elections of 1931, 1933 and 1936. When the Second Republic was proclaimed in 1931 the town had a population of just over 70,000 inhabitants. Of these, more than one third of the adult population were considered functionally illiterate. Less than half the child population received schooling.[1] The situation was far worse in the rural areas. Alicante's status as capital of the province was reflected in the socio-economic structure: 53% of the working population were employed in the service sector (essentially commerce and transport), 35.22% in industry (construction, metallurgy and timber) and only 11.78% in the primary sector (agriculture and fishing).[2]

The town itself was a peaceful, almost lethargic, haven, and relatively prosperous compared to many other areas of Spain. It enjoyed a privileged quality of life guaranteed by natural conditions: the climate (mild in winter, hot in summer), and its fortuitous setting on the Mediterranean. Two British visitors in the decade before the outbreak of civil war recalled their impressions:

> To the east lies the older part of the Port clambering up the rugged side of the steep rock, at the top of which lies the castle. [...] Through steeply sloping streets we came to the beach. Here were Mediterranean fishing-boats drawn up in ranks; then we returned towards the harbour, more open beach covered with people in gay dresses and children playing on the sands. Then came the bathing establishments built out on piles over the tideless sea. [...] We came back to the broad double avenue of palm trees which faced the more luxurious hotels and cafés. Night came softly on, and one by one amongst the palms the lights of the town threw beams over the chattering people who strolled in ever-thickening processions to and fro beneath the palm trees.[3]

In the critical general elections of February 1936 the Alicante city and province constituency voted massively for the pro-Republican Popular Front candidates. Under the complex rules of the electoral system of the Republic, the province returned the eight members of the open list of the *Frente Popular* and only two of the Conservative list. The *Frente Popular* candidates obtained 54% of the votes cast, which, under the electoral law, precluded the need for a second round.[4] The Socialists (PSOE) won four seats, the Republican Left three and Republican Union one. The right-wing coalition *CEDA** won two and the last seat was taken by an independent.

So clear was the victory that Alicante avoided the controversies that accompanied the election results in many parts of Spain, where the right made (and continue even today to make) claims of widespread *pucherazo* (electoral fraud). The returning officers for the province did, however, highlight two anomalies. In Villajoyosa (La Vila Joiosa), it was reported that some voters had been given transparent ballot papers, which was a clear infringement of the principle of the secret vote as the intentions of the electors were clearly visible to those supervising the poll. The votes were considered invalid.[5] In the second case, in Castell de Castells, the representative of the *Candidatura Contrarrevolucionaria* (Counter-revolutionary Front), Miguel de Cámara, won 425 votes in a town where there were only 407 voters. The results were also declared null and void.[6]

The province was not immune to the street violence that afflicted the country through the short months between the victory of the *Frente Popular* and the outbreak of war. In March, during a demonstration in Torrevieja, which was accompanied by the municipal band, a group of men on the balcony of the Hotel Gómez opened fire on the crowd. The right-wing owner of the hotel, a priest and his two brothers, and a local schoolteacher were later arrested. Meanwhile, the demonstrators retaliated by burning down a number of buildings in the town, including the hotel itself and the local church (*Iglesia de la Inmaculada*). The intervention of the Civil Governor from Alicante and the new police force set up by the Republic, the *Guardia de Asalto*†, was enough to restore order, although all the adjacent towns were put on alert in case of renewed violence.[7]

The coup of 17–18 July galvanised local support for the Republic. Under the military reforms of the Azaña government of 1931, the division of

---

* *Confederación Española de Derechas Autónomas*. Spanish Confederation of Autonomous Right-wing Parties.

† Literally Assault Guard, the special police unit set up after the fall of the monarchy to maintain public order. More loyal to the Republic than the officers of other military and police corps.

Spain into military regions, or captaincies-general, had been scrapped and the structure replaced by 'organic divisions' under the command of a major-general. However, Alicante remained within the same region/division (III) as before, and therefore dependent on the military authorities in Valencia. The commander, Fernando Martínez Monje, appeared at first to waver, but was in turn influenced by the defeat of General Goded's rebellion in Barcelona and declared for the democratically elected government in Madrid. In August, in light of his perfunctory support for the Republic, he was relieved of his post and replaced by José Miaja Menant, a man who would play a significant role both in the battle for Madrid and in the final days of the Civil War. The failure of the mutiny in Valencia was crucial in determining the attitudes of senior officers in Alicante.

At eleven o'clock on the morning of 18 July 1936, the local radio station interrupted its broadcast with a short announcement: '*Muy importante. Dentro de breves momentos comunicarán desde el Ministerio de Gobernación noticias muy importantes para todos los españoles.*' (Very important. In a few short moments, the Ministry of the Interior will issue a communiqué with important news for all Spanish people). The diaries of Emilio Gómez Serrano, the Republican Left *Diputado** for Alicante, provide invaluable insights into life in Alicante during the Civil War. Warned by party colleagues that something was afoot, he immediately assumed the worst. When no details of the uprising were forthcoming, he decided to make for the *Gobierno Civil* (civil government offices) to consult with colleagues of the *Frente Popular*. However, as a self-respecting *alicantino*†, he first sat down to have lunch with his family. He ate, he wrote later that day, 'hastily'. He then joined the representatives of the other parties and set about implementing measures to thwart an insurrection in Alicante.[8]

Pro-insurgency agents, meanwhile, sought to dictate their own strategy. Captain José Meca (11th Tarifa Infantry Regiment) and Lieutenant José Estañ of the *Guardia Civil* (Civil Guard)‡ attempted to persuade the Civil Governor, Francisco Valdés Casas, to declare an *estado de guerra* (state of war – martial law) and thus transfer his power to the Military Governor of the province, General José García Aldave. Valdés Casas refused, and in light of events in Valencia, García Aldave himself chose to prevaricate.[9] He declared that the infantry troops under his command would remain 'neutral' – an act that was, nevertheless, enough to violate his oath of loyalty to the Republic.

---

* Deputy: Member of Congress.
† Demonym for someone from Alicante (feminine: *alicantina*).
‡ Police force with military organisation and discipline.

On the evening of 20 July, Diego Martínez Barrio, the President of the Cortes* and the man who had been Prime Minister for a few hours between 18 and 19 July, arrived in Alicante to hold talks with García Aldave. The governor reiterated his loyalty to the Republic but stated that he would not employ violence against his brothers-in-arms if they pursued their plan to overthrow the left-wing government.[10] On his orders, the troops of the 11th Infantry Regiment were confined to barracks in the Benalúa district and denied any information of developments at a national or local level. Given the dubious loyalty of many senior military and police officers, the civil authorities were aware they could only count on the relatively small force (between seventy and eighty men) of the local *Guardia de Asalto*. The captain of the unit, Eduardo Rubio Funes, played a vital role in organising resistance and led his men in the fighting at the Barraco de las Ovejas on 19 July, where a raiding party of *falangistas*† from the Vega Baja region in the south of the province were halted and forced to surrender (see Chapter 3). However, given that pro-Republic forces would be hugely outnumbered if those sympathetic to the insurrection were to order the men under their command to intervene, it became imperative to mobilise the local population in the form of militia.

Meanwhile, on 22 July, the destroyer *José Luis Díaz* arrived at the port with Republican reinforcements. The ship had been undergoing a refit in Cartagena when its captain, Casimiro Carre Chicarro, had sought to disarm the crew and declare for the insurrection. However, he and his staff were overpowered by his men and put under arrest.[11] Orders were now given to bombard military installations in Alicante should the rebel sympathisers fail to stand down. The next day, the *José Luis Díaz* was joined by the cruiser *Lepanto*, carrying a unit of marines. Nevertheless, fears persisted that troops of the 11th Regiment might be used to occupy the city and depose the Republican authorities. When thousands of *alicantinos* took up position and raised barricades around the barracks, General García Aldave was forced to acknowledge defeat and allow his troops to abandon the base and fraternise with the local population. García Aldave was subsequently placed under arrest and held in relative luxury at the Hotel Samper on the corner between the Explanada and the present-day Rambla. Twenty other members of his staff were held in custody on board the two naval steamships *Rey Jaime II* and *Sil* that had docked in Alicante and were being used as floating prisons.[12] Together with eight other officers,

---

* The equivalent of the Speaker of the House of Commons. Under the Republic, the Parliament was unicameral.
† Members of the Falange.

including Captain José Meca, Aldave was later condemned to death by a Popular Tribunal in Alicante, and executed on 13 October 1936.[13]

Despite their success in stabilising the situation in Alicante, the Republican authorities were becoming increasingly concerned at events in the province of Albacete. The Military Governor, Lieutenant-Colonel Enrique Martínez Moreno, had declared for the insurgency. Under the command of Lieutenant-Colonel Fernando Chápuli (a native of Alicante), rebel units of the *Guardia Civil*, reinforced by *falangistas* and other pro-insurrection elements (approximately 700 men), had taken control of Albacete capital and cut road and train links between Madrid and the east coast. The insurgents were also able to gain control of other towns including Almansa, Hellín, Villarrobledo and La Roda. On 21 July a column of some 500 *milicianos** and an indeterminate number of *guardias de asalto* set out from Alicante by train to stifle the insurrection. Referring to the firearms they had managed to assemble, Gómez Serrano expressed concern that several looked as though they might represent a greater threat to those who carried them than to the enemy.[14]

The first part of the operation centred on Almansa, where fighting continued between rebel *guardias civiles* and local militia. Despite *falangista* and *guardia civil* reinforcements dispatched from Albacete, the insurgents were heavily outnumbered by the column of loyalist *guardias civiles, guardias de asalto* and militia troops from Alcoy (Alcoi), Alicante, Elche (Elx), Elda, Sax and Villena, and eventually surrendered on 22 July. The Alicante column then advanced on Albacete, and having taken the town of Chinchilla, linked up with another unit from Murcia on 24 July. After an aerial bombardment of defensive positions by Republican aircraft, flying out of their base at Los Alcázares in Murcia, and skirmishes with pockets of insurgents, the Republicans entered Albacete on 25 July and re-established communications between Madrid and Alicante, Murcia and Cartagena. The rebel leader Chápuli is generally believed to have committed suicide.[15]

According to Mexican-Spanish writer Max Aub, the victory at Albacete was one of the most significant among the few offensive successes of the Republic.[16] Indeed, in general terms, the Republic's greatest military triumphs were defensive (Madrid, Jarama, Guadalajara, etc.), and even though some offensives did win early successes (Teruel, Ebro, Extremadura), the gains were eventually lost to Nationalist counterattacks. Albacete, on the other hand, remained in the loyalist camp until the end of the war. The triumph was also significant because it was achieved mainly by militia forces, some time before the creation of a regular army.

---

* Members of the militia.

The next major challenge to the legal authority of the Republic in Alicante came on 5 August from its own 'camp', when Anarchists of the CNT-FAI* raided the unguarded military installations at Benalúa and Rabasa and appropriated weapons and supplies. Having witnessed civilians patrolling the streets of Alicante armed with rifles and machetes and dressed in random military apparel, Gómez Serrano described the scene in his diaries as both 'alarming and picturesque'.[17] The struggle for control between those who sought to uphold the legitimacy of the institutions and those who advocated revolution as a political response to the uprising, had begun. When the American journalist Jay Allen arrived in Alicante at the beginning of October, he was told (presumably by the Anarchists who accompanied him), 'how the Civil Governor, don Francisco Valdés, had no authority, how Anarchists were bosses, how Valdés hardly dared stir from his office lest he should be shot'.[18]

At the end of August 1936, the Nationalists launched air attacks against Madrid in preparation for an eventual land offensive, and plans were made to evacuate as many children as possible. By this stage, Constancia de la Mora, the aristocratic granddaughter of Antonio Maura (conservative Prime Minister on five occasions between 1903 and 1922) and wife to Ignacio Hidalgo de los Cisneros, had taken the initiative in setting up homes for young children who had been orphaned or simply abandoned in the capital. She subsequently proposed to officials that the 650 children in the care of these new institutions be moved to Alicante – 'the beautiful seashore resort town in the southeast'.[19] When she first arrived in early September to carry out initial fieldwork on behalf of the *Consejo Superior de Menores* (High Council for Minors), she was 'astonished to find the war had hardly touched the little town. The Republicans had defeated the fascist coup in the early days and then settled down to wait for the end of the rebellion.'[20] After some investigation, she elected San Juan de Alicante (Sant Joan d'Alacant), a village some 5km to the north of Alicante, as an ideal place to set up the *colonias* (retreats or camps).

According to de la Mora's account, the population immediately rallied to the cause. Properties deserted by fleeing Nationalist sympathisers were requisitioned[21] and supplies of beds, linen and food liberally provided. When the first group of 200 children later arrived at the end of the month, they were greeted by a brass band ('slightly off-key') and a parade of schoolchildren. The Mayor, Emilio Urios Cortés, began a short address to welcome the 'little *madrileños*†' but was unable to complete it. De la Mora believed he was unused

---

* Confederación Nacional del Trabajo (National Confederation of Labour) and Federación Anarquista Ibérica (Iberian Anarchist Federation).
† Demonym for people from Madrid.

to making speeches and was overcome with emotion, but another version suggests that as a Valencian speaker he was simply unused to public speaking in Spanish (*castellano*).[22]

It is not easy to calculate how many children were given refuge in San Juan. Various organisations and government agencies (including the UGT and Ministries of Education and Justice) were involved in evacuation schemes and few records appear to remain. In February 1937 a request was made to the provincial health inspector to provide typhus vaccines for 500 children.[23] In February 1938 one report suggested there were 877 evacuees and another 45 refugees from war zones.[24] Four and a half months later, the total of evacuated children living in the various centres was given as 411.[25]

While on a visit to her husband at the Albacete Aerodrome, de la Mora was also encouraged to open a *Hospital de Convalecientes de Aviación* (Air Force Convalescent Hospital) in the same village, at the *Finca La Concepción*. According to an official request for milk from the director of the clinic in September 1937, there were thirty people at the centre, including sick, wounded and staff.[26]

Despite the warm welcome, and the obvious delight of the children at escaping the war and the miserable conditions of church-run orphanages, problems arose when Alicante first began to undergo shortages. Although the people gave generously to the children, food supplies became increasingly meagre. The situation was somewhat alleviated by the arrival of the Russian freighter *Neva* in October. The people of Odessa had made their own contributions to the Republican war effort by donating money and food, and when the ship docked in Alicante, in addition to the provision of vital supplies, it also proved a boost to morale. In the words of de la Mora:

> The townspeople of Alicante knew nothing of the Soviet Union until the *Neva* steamed into the harbour. No 'agents of Stalin' roamed the streets. And yet the people wept with joy in the harbour and we all cheered until we were hoarse, crying '*Viva la URSS.*' One people in all the world had not deserted us.[27]

The cargo unloaded at the docks included: 1,900 tons of wheat, 323 tons of animal fat (lard), 125 tons of condensed milk, 75 tons of tinned meat, 281 tons of pork and ham.[28] Surprisingly, Constancia de la Mora seemed most delighted at the 124 tons of butter, especially as there was no suitable transport available to ship it to Madrid: 'We ate butter at three meals a day for months.'[29]

At a council meeting in San Juan in November 1936, councillors debated changing the overtly religious name of the village. The Socialists proposed

Villa Pablo Iglesias (after the founder of the PSOE) and the Anarchists countered with Villa Ascaso (in honour of a local anarchist hero). Instead, the council elected to adopt a more transversal solution and to rename the village Villa Rusia (literally Russia Town) as a gesture of gratitude towards the USSR.[30] However, custom is indeed compelling, and most people in the province paid no heed and continued to use San Juan (or Sant Joan).

Initially, de la Mora had been assisted in her work by Indalecio Prieto's two daughters, Blanca and Concha, and Dolores Rivas Cherif, the wife of President Azaña. She was deeply indignant when Prieto and Azaña used their personal safety as an argument to oblige the three women to abandon their work in San Juan. According to her own version, the Civil Governor took personal responsibility for removing them from the children's *colonias*, and then escorting them to the airport. Apart from the disappointing attitude of the two men, the decision appears to have been based on a false premise; the women were not in any imminent danger, both city and province were to remain far behind the frontlines for the duration of the Civil War, and San Juan was spared the air raids that the population of Alicante was forced to endure. It must be recorded that de la Mora allowed her own daughter Lourdes (*Luli*) to be evacuated to the USSR during the fighting. However, it is equally true that the circumstances were somewhat different as she was no more than a young child.

There were many who resented the privileges enjoyed by those on the east coast. In March 1937, at a rally in Alicante's main theatre, the *Teatro Principal*, the writer and activist Margarita Nelken insisted on the unity of the struggle and urged a greater commitment to the defence of Madrid. She remonstrated with those living at a safe distance from the front, who believed they could fulfil their duty by making donations to help those suffering directly from fascist aggression or by donning a bright new uniform 'in the tranquillity that reigns in the privileged towns of Levante'.[31]

On the other hand, this view of life in Alicante was distorted. In his description of events at the end of the war, when so many Republicans fled to Alicante, anarchist writer Eduardo de Guzmán cites the words of a comrade who admonished those descending on the town who still believed it had not suffered: 'I can assure you that Alicante was not the happy place that the people on the front or in Madrid thought.'[32] In the war, the city suffered seventy-two air raids, and the urban population endured the same hardships and severe food shortages that civilians underwent throughout Republican Spain. Furthermore, while it is true that Alicante did remain at a safe distance (a minimum of 150km) from the combat zones and that not a single land battle was fought within the boundaries of the province, this did not exclude the male population from active service.

Once the situation in the province appeared to have been stabilised, various militia columns were deployed to reinforce Republican loyalists in other campaigns.

In the last week of July, a unit of 117 Socialist, Communist and anarchist *milicianos* escorted supplies to Madrid, while supporters of other Republican parties began enlisting in their own militia, the *Balas Rojas* (Red Bullets). On 7 August 270 anarchists set out for the Guadix/Granada front. The 5th Regiment recruited men to join the 'Stalin' and 'Francisco Galán' columns preparing the defence of Madrid. A substantial number of *ilicitanos** joined the Alicante column and other militia forces with such compelling names as *Tigres Rojos* (Red Tigers).[33] According to eminent local historian Vicente Ramos, one corporal from the army in North Africa who joined the Elche Battalion was so confused to find his new comrades speaking Valencian (instead of Castilian Spanish) that he assumed he had been transferred to a Russian unit.[34]

Nor was the focus exclusively on the enlistment of combatant militia. The Popular Front parties and unions also recruited voluntary medical units, consisting of a small fleet of ambulances, a doctor, assistants, stretcher-bearers and nurses. However, the most famous unit of *alicantinos* was recruited by the *Juventudes Socialistas Unificadas* (JSU – Unified Socialist Youth). More than 500 young men from Alicante, Altea, Aspe, Benidorm, Benissa, Calpe, Elda, Finestrat, Monóvar, Pego, Relleu, Sella and Villajoyosa gathered in the town to form the *Batallón Alicante Rojo* (Red Alicante Battalion) and subsequently departed on 26 September for Alcalá de Henares, some 40km east of Madrid.[35]

In October 1936 the Republican authorities eventually resolved to introduce conscription and to develop a Popular Army, designed to mould the militia into a more orthodox force, with greater emphasis on military discipline and a unified command and strategy. According to historian James Matthews, the formation of the Popular Army and the decision to introduce conscription were part of the same process, designed 'to secure two very conventional military aims; an adequate and rational supply of manpower, and the necessary control over it'. The Republic required more soldiers and greater efficiency, and therefore 'the government was forced to demand service from its male citizens and assert itself as the sole authority within the disjointed armed forces.'[36] The Alicante Red Battalion was subsequently integrated in the 71st Mixed Brigade† of the 12th Division, under the command of Eduardo Rubio Funes,

---

* Demonym for people of Elche.

† The mixed brigade was designed as the basic combined-arms unit of the Republican army. Sometimes described as a 'pocket division': including infantry, artillery, motorised infantry (cavalry), engineers, etc. It was designed to encourage greater autonomy. For more detail, see: Engel: *Historia de las Brigadas Mixtas* (Madrid, 2005) p.8.

the chief of the *Guardia de Asalto* during the early days of the insurgency in Alicante.

After the battle for Albacete, the next critical Nationalist threat to the security of the province of Alicante came at the Battle of Jarama. Having failed in their assault on the capital, the insurgents opted to complete the encirclement of Madrid through a pincer movement from the north and south that would cut communications with Aragón and the eastern coast. In February 1937 Franco launched the first stage of the operation across the Jarama River against the Madrid–Valencia highway. As in the fighting on the outskirts of Madrid, Soviet weapons, and in particular the T-26 tanks and the Polikarpov fighter planes – the I-15 '*Chato*' and the I-16 '*Mosca*' – played a key role in defending Republican positions. At the same time, the newly formed International Brigades of anti-fascist volunteers from around the world incurred huge losses in the desperate fighting. According to British historian Richard Baxell, of the 500 men of the British Battalion of the XV Brigade who went into action on the first day of the battle, 136 were killed and a similar number wounded fighting to hold what became known as 'Suicide Hill'. Thirty members of a machine-gun unit were captured.[37]

In the meantime, a combined force of Franco's southern army and Italian 'volunteers' of the *Corpo Truppe Volontarie* (CTV), supported by the *Aviazione Legionaria*,* had forced the Republicans to retreat from Málaga. However, fortunately for the Republican cause, by the time the Italians were ready for deployment north of Madrid in support of the rebel troops in the Guadalajara offensive (the second stage of the pincer movement), the Republican army had managed to contain the enemy and stabilise the front at the Jarama River. The vital road link with the east coast was kept open until the bitter end. The 71st Mixed Brigade and the *Alicante Rojo* Battalions subsequently played a key role on the new Guadalajara front, where the Republicans were able to inflict a humiliating defeat on the *CTV*. However, losses were so high that the brigade was eventually withdrawn and deployed in a more static role in the defence of the capital itself.[38]

In an article published in the pro-PCE/UGT *Bandera Roja* in April 1937, the prolific Russian writer Ilya Ehrenburg described Alicante as a place of 'palm trees, holiday-makers, a wine that is strong and sweet, anaemic English women, deep blue seas, just like in the postcards', but insisted that far from this 'warm and carefree' town, the *Alicante Rojo* had been fighting the Italians in unfamiliar icy, mountain conditions, where at night the temperatures fell to minus ten degrees. He quoted one volunteer: 'We only got proper footwear

---

* The Corps of Volunteer Troops and the Legionary Air Force. The Italian expeditionary corps.

five days ago. Until then, we had to brave the snow in *alpargatas**, but we still beat the Italians.'³⁹

The failure to take Madrid led the Nationalists to reappraise their strategy. The prospect of a protracted conflict encouraged the extensive deployment of Italian and German air power behind the Republican lines. Over the next two years this development made Alicante a major target. Apart from the port, the town had a number of significant facilities vulnerable to attack from the air: industrial plants (including the CAMPSA oil storage facility), railway stations, military barracks and two aerodromes. However, the use of air power was not directed exclusively against infrastructures and the armed forces. Indeed, the intervention of the German Condor Legion and the Italian Legionary Aviation was to introduce a new dimension to European warfare, in which intimidatory and indiscriminate attacks on civilians were as instrumental as targeted bombing of military objectives.

---

* *Espadrilles*, or rope-soled sandals.

Chapter 3

José Antonio ¡presente!

The case of the leader of the Falange, imprisoned in Alicante, and the violence in the Republican zone

The earliest reference to Alicante in most histories of the Spanish Civil War involves the death of José Antonio Primo de Rivera. Son of Miguel Primo de Rivera, the dictator who ruled Spain between 1923 and 1930, and co-founder of the fascist party *Falange Española*, José Antonio, as he became known to friend and foe alike, was a brilliant, sophisticated and charismatic leader who, to some extent, embarked on a political career to defend the memory of his father. At the presentation of the new party at the Teatro de la Comedia in Madrid in October 1933, he denounced democracy, 'The most noble calling of all ballot boxes is their destruction', and defended the use of violence, 'when justice and the fatherland are attacked, the only acceptable response is the recourse to fists and guns'.

José Antonio was returned to Parliament in the elections of 1933 as one of the members for Cádiz, but three years later his party polled less than 1% and failed to win a single seat. The electoral defeat and the triumph of the *Frente Popular* led to an upsurge in *Falange** membership. However, having lost his parliamentary immunity, the leader was arrested for a series of relatively minor offences under the Law of Public Order.[1] José Antonio had developed a close relationship with several disaffected army officers (including Sanjurjo). He met with Franco days before the general departed to 'internal exile' in the Canary Islands, where the government had ordered his transfer in an attempt to isolate him from the temptation of military conspiracy. He also remained in contact with General Mola. In a letter, delivered by hand, he famously reminded the man who was the driving force behind the conspiracy that, 'in the end, civilisation has always been saved by a band of soldiers'.[2]

---

* After merging with another extreme-right group, the Falange was now officially known as: *Falange Española de las Juntas de Ofensiva Nacional Sindicalista* (FE de las JONS – Spanish Phalanx of the Juntas of National Syndicalist Offensive).

In June the Republican government deemed it wise to transfer José Antonio, with his brother who had also been detained, to the relative isolation of the provincial prison in Alicante. Jay Allen, the American correspondent of the *News Chronicle*, was allowed to interview the prisoner in October. He confessed in the article published on 24 October that he 'rather liked José Antonio as a person – however frivolous, wrong-headed and dangerous I thought his politics'. During the meeting, the prisoner described his distrust of the ultra-conservative nature of the military leadership of the insurgency and his disillusionment with their unreceptive approach to social questions. He told Jay, 'I do know that if this movement does win and it turns out to be nothing but reaction, then I'll withdraw my Phalanx and I'll … I'll probably be back here in this or another prison in a very few months.'[3]

Of the several attempts to achieve his release or escape, the most famous came in the immediate aftermath of the coup of 18 July when a unit of *falangistas* from Callosa de Seguro and Rafal, led by Antonio Maciá Rives, embarked on a mission to liaise with the authorities in the Benalúa barracks to rescue their chief, and to take control in the capital of the province. According to Vicente Ramos, the detachment consisted of one car and two lorries, the second of which broke down on the road to Alicante. The handful of men who were left behind were subsequently spared the fate of their comrades. Unfortunately for the other participants in the operation, the Republican authorities in Alicante received intelligence of the plan. The *falangistas* were met by *guardias de asalto*, *guardias civiles* and members of the militia as they approached the southern outskirts of the town, at the Paraje de los Doce Puentes, next to the Barranco de las Ovejas. In the short but intense firefight that followed, four *falangistas* were killed and four (plus one *guardia de asalto*) were wounded. While some of the insurgents did manage to escape, fifty-two of the party quickly surrendered, amid shouts of '¡*Nos han engañado!*' (We've been tricked). According to a report that appeared the next day in the local, pro-Republican Left newspaper *El Luchador*,[4] as they were disarmed, the Republican police forces registered a total of seven shotguns, six pistols, four revolvers, an axe and a barber's razor.[5] Other detachments of *falangistas* (from Crevillente and Orihuela), which had travelled by car and train, did reach the barracks in Benalúa and the Rambla, but in light of the failure of the main thrust of the operation, chose caution over valour and withdrew.[6] The men captured in the fighting were subsequently held in the *Reformatorio de Adultos* (Adult Reformatory) pending trial.

In the weeks that followed, the new conditions imposed by war and the legal vacuum caused by the breakdown of the police and judicial structures encouraged left-wing revolutionary groups to take the law into their own hands.

The most notorious expression of this revolutionary justice were the *'checas'*, premises where suspected insurgency sympathisers were interrogated, tortured, brought before a revolutionary tribunal, and executed by non-sanctioned thugs carrying out what British historian Anthony Beevor describes as criminal acts 'under political flags of convenience'.[7] One such operation was based in the Santa Faz monastery, next to the village of San Juan, and some sources suggest that as many as twenty-two right-wing supporters were murdered there between August 1936 and April 1937.[8] Vicente Ramos reported that at the end of the war, the new Nationalist authorities discovered eighteen bodies in the monastery.[9] In its report to the *Causa General* (the inquiry ordered by Franco into Republican violence behind the lines during the Civil War) the *Guardia Civil* alleged the discovery of 'countless bodies' on the site.[10] However, in a separate section, another report claimed a total of twenty-one victims, only five of whom were identified.[11]

It should be emphasised that the findings of the *Causa General* are not exactly reliable as a source. Helen Graham describes the inquiry as 'a sort of untruth and non-reconciliation commission', based on 'lurid denunciation', with no 'evidential guarantees'. It was designed to legitimise the new dictatorship 'through the creation of a Manichaean narrative of the Civil War', which concluded that 'atrocities had been committed only by Republicans and endured only by Franco supporters.'[12] In its report to the commissioners, the local *Guardia Civil* included the Hotel Samper in the list it drew up of eight *checas* in Alicante.[13] Their premise was that as the Military Governor, General García Aldave, had initially been detained there (in comfortable accommodation befitting his rank)*, the hotel could be classified as a clandestine prison.

Nonetheless, and notwithstanding the 'shortcomings' of the *Causa*, there were many examples of heinous acts of violence against defenceless civilians. The practice of the *paseo*, by which victims were dragged from their houses, 'taken for a walk'[14] to a secluded spot and murdered, became commonplace on both sides of the conflict. Alicante did not escape the extra-judicial violence against both sympathisers (and suspected sympathisers) of the rebellion and social elements categorised as counter-revolutionary or capitalist. In July the Civil Governor issued an edict in which he threatened the perpetrators of criminal acts of aggression against individuals and property with the death penalty and described them as 'rebels in the service of the enemies of the Republic'.[15] To little avail. According to Paul Preston:

---

* The brackets are the author's.

the round-up of local right-wingers began immediately after the defeat of the uprising in the city [...] Corpses began to appear on beaches and in the fields. Many house searches were merely an excuse for robbery. Militia groups, and among them recently released common criminals, were largely responsible for the wave of killings and other abuses.[16]

The conservative-leaning local newspaper, *El Día*, published an emotional appeal for common sense and order:

> Let he who must fall, fall; but let him fall in the light of day as an example and lesson to all, with full disclosure, without covert actions, so that the implacable justice of the people be seen to be done. Without vengeance, without hatred, without petty acrimony, let justice be done, but as we said, in the light of day.[17]

In October, Valdés authorised the creation of the *Brigada de Investigación y Vigilancia* (Investigation and Surveillance Brigade) to fill the vacuum caused by the redeployment of *guardia civil* and *guardia de asalto* officers to other fronts and the transfer of the garrison (11th Regiment) to the Murcia region. The brigade was made responsible to the *Comisión Provincial de Orden Público* (Provincial Commission of Public Order), which had been set up in July under the presidency of Vicente Alcalde Butler (PCE).[18] Nonetheless, it proved difficult to overcome the influence of the armed militia that had readily occupied the vacant role of law (their own law) enforcement. On the other hand, the power and authority vacuum stretched beyond policing and defence; it became clear that Alicante was facing extensive new political and administrative demands, and that the 'legitimacy' of the Republic depended to a large extent on the capacity of its agents to provide the conditions and services required by the military and civilians alike. It thus became imperative to establish appropriate new structures to deal with the changing circumstances.

On 25 September an ad hoc committee of forces loyal to the *Frente Popular* imposed the dismissal of the Mayor of Alicante, Lorenzo Carbonell, on the grounds that he had failed to take the measures required in the 'revolutionary reality that the nation was undergoing'.[19] Four days later, Valdés Casas, the Civil Governor, approved the creation of the *consejo municipal* – a municipal or town council comprising those local parties and trade unions opposed to the *golpe*, which had contributed to the defence of the town through the organisation of militia. The seats were allocated according to the influence of each party/union and the need to establish a balance among the groups. Those forces represented were:

- UGT, the Socialist Union (6 seats)
- CNT, the Anarchist Union (6)
- PSOE, the Socialist Party (2)
- PCE, the Communist Party (2)
- IR, Republican Left (2)
- FAI, Anarchist Federation (1)
- UR, Republican Union (1)
- PS, Syndicalist Party (1)[20]

The CNT put forward a plan for a rotating presidency to prevent the accumulation of power in a single group or coalition, but the proposition was rejected in favour of stability and good governance. Rafael Millá Santos (PCE) was subsequently elected President of the council (Mayor) with the votes of the UGT, and the anarchists responded by walking out.

At the provincial level, the *Comité Popular Provincial de Defensa* (Popular Provincial Defence Committee) was set up at the beginning of November to provide a wider political structure. The new body was given responsibility for public order, defence, social care, health and economic affairs.[21] However, the initial relative predominance of the anarchist group CNT-FAI (50% of the seats) undermined attempts to stabilise the political conditions and to control the violence.

Although the killings continued, it is true that the level of revolutionary violence in the city of Alicante did not match the brutality and bloodshed unleashed in Madrid, Barcelona, and other areas where Franco's armies posed a real and imminent danger. The insurrection was stifled with relative speed and efficiency. The town was under no immediate danger of land attack from the Nationalists and most of those who sympathised with the rebels understandably adhered to the principle that discretion is the better part of valour. It should be noted that the expression 'fifth column', used to define supporters of the military insurgency behind Republican lines, was not coined until November. According to Australian journalist Noel Monks (*Daily Express*), when General Mola convened a conference of correspondents at the gates of Madrid, he outlined the positions of the four columns poised to make the final assault on the capital. Unwisely, he then boasted that 'in Madrid, I have a fifth column:– men now in hiding who will rise and support us the moment we march.'[22] His ill-advised comments led to a further purge of Nationalists in the capital, which culminated in the massacre of prisoners at Paracuellos.[23] In a personal interview, the Spanish general invited Monks to accompany his army in the impending conquest of Madrid and to join him for coffee in the Puerta del Sol, the symbolic central square of the capital. Mola never made it into Madrid, though to be fair, as Monks points out, the fifth column did indeed take the capital, just not for another twenty-nine months.[24]

In their synthesis of the findings of the *Causa General*, historians Miguel Ors Montenegro and José Miguel Santacreu Soler found references to a total of 1,005 victims throughout the province of Alicante (988 men and 17 women). Of these, a total of 662 were victims of *paseos* and *sacas*,[*] six were lynched, 209 prisoners died at the front and another 128 were sentenced to death by popular tribunals. They also quote the figures compiled by Valencian historian Vicent Gabarda, in his research into violence throughout what is known today as the Community of Valencia (i.e. the provinces of Alicante, Castellón and Valencia). According to his findings, the number of casualties was 840. He also breaks down the figures and reports that seventy-six people lost their lives in the municipal area of Alicante and the same number in Elche. The town registering the highest number of victims was Alcoy with 124. Orihuela and Callosa de Segura recorded seventy-four and sixty-seven respectively. The majority of those who died were industrialists, traders, members of the armed forces and representatives of the church.[25]

In addition to the personal revulsion that the bloodletting caused many Republican leaders, it also became evident that the unsanctioned violence was causing serious damage to the image of the Republic abroad. President Azaña thus took the lead in the re-establishment of due legal process through the setting-up of the *tribunales populares* (popular tribunals). Azaña had been shocked by the lynching of prisoners in the inaptly named *Modelo* prison in Madrid by anarchist forces on 22 August, in open defiance of the authority of the government. He reportedly told a confidant, 'the bloodshed disgusts me. I can't go on. It will drown us all.'[26] The new courts consisted of three professional judges loyal to the Republic and a jury of fourteen men and women designated by parties and unions that defended the *Frente Popular*. Writing in late 1937, Churchill, a ferocious critic of the Republic in the early months of the conflict, generously conceded that the government in Valencia was not 'a mob of savage Bolsheviks'. He concluded:

> during the past year, a marked advance towards an ordered system of government and war has [...] produced itself in the character of the Republican Government. The shameful wholesale atrocities which the extremists committed in the days when the Communists and Anarchists ruled the tragic scene, have been repressed.[27]

---

[*] The word was coined in the Civil War. It can only be translated as the 'removal of random prisoners from prison and their execution'.

The Vega Baja *falangista* prisoners who had sought to liberate José Antonio and had been captured in the skirmish on 19 July were the first to stand trial before a *tribunal popular* in Alicante. They were found guilty of military rebellion, sentenced to death, and executed by firing squad on 13 September. A driver who had been forced to participate in the raid and nine minors were absolved.

There were other efforts to rescue José Antonio. In mid-September Agustín Aznar Gerner, the commander of the *Falange* militias who was engaged to José Antonio's cousin, Dolores Primo de Rivera y Cobo de Guzmán, reached Alicante with a plan to bribe Anarchist sentries, and having released the prisoner, to smuggle him on board a German ship waiting in the port. However, Aznar was discovered and although he escaped, the operation was aborted. In October he tried again, with the collaboration of the German consul, Hans-Joachim Kindler von Knobloch, but, unable to find personnel willing to accept bribes, they were forced to abandon the mission. Stories of German and Italian submarines that were waiting off the coast to pick up the prisoner in the autumn of 1936 still abound today, but it is difficult to assess how seriously the Germans took the rescue plans. At a 'diplomatic' level, there were moves to arrange a prisoner exchange, most significantly with the son of Largo Caballero, the Republican Prime Minister. There are also suggestions that Mussolini and Spanish philosopher Ortega y Gasset offered to act as intermediaries and that the authorities in London and Paris were willing to intervene to obtain his release. Whatever efforts were made, they were in vain.

José Antonio appeared in court on 16 and 17 November accused of conspiracy and military rebellion. He denied all charges and argued that he had been in prison at the time of the coup. He was found guilty by the *tribunal popular* and sentenced to death. The origin of the order to carry out the sentence remains unclear. It is believed that the Civil Governor, Valdés Casas, was unwilling to endorse the court ruling. It is also unclear whether the government, which had now fled Madrid and installed itself in Valencia, had time to consider the sentence. On the other hand, the theory that it was Prime Minister Largo Caballero alone who gave the order is implausible given the fact that his own son was in the hands of the enemy. The two most likely scenarios are that it was the Provincial Commission of Public Order that sought to avoid the prevarication of a higher authority, or that anarchist militia members believed the diligence of the court was sufficient to warrant the immediate application of the sentence. José Antonio was executed in the prison grounds on the morning of 20 November. According to the testimony of Lieutenant Juan José González Vázquez, who was in charge of the militia firing squad, Primo de Rivera gave the fascist salute and shouted '¡*Arriba España!*' ('Up with Spain' – the *Falange* slogan).[28] At his own court martial after the war, and in his own defence, González Vázquez insisted that he had not given the order to shoot. It was, he claimed, the over-excited anarchist (FAI) *milicianos* in the squad who opened fire before he had time to give the command.[29]

The execution was a serious miscalculation. Rather than release him into the hands of the Nationalists as a loose cannon, capable of undermining Franco's authority and destabilising the unity of the Nationalist movement, the Republic had gifted the insurgency a martyr. There were widely held suspicions that Franco could have done much more to save José Antonio, but that the reservations about his reliability, and fear that he was a potential dissident, discouraged anything more than token support for plans to exfiltrate him from enemy territory. In his memoirs, Ramón Serrano Suñer, Franco's brother-in-law and chief of the *Falange* between 1939 and 1942, denied the *Caudillo*'s 'guilt by deliberate omission'.[30] However, José Antonio was clearly of more use to Franco dead than he was alive. Mythicised as '*el ausente*' (the absent one), within the dialectic of the *Movimiento Nacional* (National Movement) he symbolised the 'revolutionary' idealism of the early fascists, in contrast to Franco's archconservative authoritarianism. Henceforth the *Caudillo* was able to invoke his spirit whenever he wished to make emotional appeals to those on the right whose hopes of social and economic reform and a more equitable national resurgence had been quashed, while diluting his rival's legacy and tightening his own grip on power. In April 1937, by a decree of unification, Franco ordered the merger of the *Falange* with the 'traditionalist' Carlists and thus founded his own version of a single fascist party (*Falange Española Tradicionalista y de las Juntas de Ofensiva Nacional Sindicalista**), of which he proclaimed himself the national chief.

On 28 November 1936, in reprisal for the execution of José Antonio, a squadron of sixteen Junker 52/3s carried out an air raid against Alicante. The next night, in the worst *saca* of the war in Alicante, forty-nine right-wing 'hostages' were dragged from prison, taken to the municipal cemetery and shot.[31] One of the victims was José Maria Maciá Rives, the provincial chief of the *Falange* who had spent time in prison with José Antonio. His brother Antonio had led the failed operation of the Vega Baja *falangistas* to rescue their leader and was one of the fortunate members of the mission to avoid capture. In his last will and testament, witnessed in Alicante on 18 November 1936, José Antonio begged forgiveness for his part in causing the bloodletting that afflicted Spain and wrote, 'If only mine could be the last Spanish blood spilled in civil strife.'[32]

---

* FET de las Jons – Traditionalist Spanish Phalanx of the Councils of the National Syndicalist Offensive.

Chapter 4

Your children will be next

Alicante and the air war

To a certain extent, the notoriety of the German Condor Legion, and in particular the raid on Guernica, have obscured the role of the Italian air force in the Spanish war. In fact, according to the eminent Hispanist Hugh Thomas, who based his figures on reports from the leading press agency in Rome (*Agenzia Stefani*), the Italian Royal Air Force deployed 5,699 air force officers, 312 non-military personnel and about 660 aircraft. They flew 5,318 air raid missions (logging a flight time total of 135,265 hours), delivered 11,524 tons of bombs, and destroyed 903 enemy aircraft and 224 ships. They lost 171 aircrew, 74 fighters, eight bombers, and two close support and two reconnaissance aeroplanes.[1] Although Italian fighters (particularly the Fiat CR.32) played a significant role in the fighting around Madrid, their greatest impact in Franco's cause was to be achieved in the campaign against the Mediterranean coastal cities by the Fiat BR.20, Savoia-Marchetti SM.79 and Savoia-Marchetti SM.81 bombers. Historians Solé i Sabaté and Vollaroya indicate that the greatest number of raids on urban areas, and therefore of those that caused most civilian casualties, were carried out by the Italians.[2]

The *Regia Aeronautica* (Royal Air Force) had unveiled its expertise against civilian populations in the Abyssinian War (1935–37). The time had now come for the expeditionary force in Spain, the *Aviazione Legionaria* (Legionary Air Force), to demonstrate its capacity on the Iberian Peninsula – although the Italians did not replicate the use of chemical weapons (principally sulphur mustard) that had proved so effective in the Horn of Africa. The continual aerial bombardment of Madrid and the air raids on Basque towns awakened Europe to the implications of this new dimension in modern warfare. Non-combatants had long since been identified as military targets, but the war in Spain allowed the Germans and Italians to develop, showcase and enhance new military technologies that extended their capability to wreak havoc and destruction not only on enemy forces but also on infrastructures and civilian populations.

With the collusion of Franco, *Reichsführer* Göring was also able to use the conflict as a training ground for *Luftwaffe* pilots, to test his hardware (including the new Junkers Ju 87 '*Stuka*' dive-bomber prototype), and to develop the strategy of indiscriminate bombing of enemy towns as a means to undermine the popular will to resist. The Germans also developed their expertise in radio communications, reconnaissance and meteorological analysis. They developed new air combat tactics, and, crucially, learnt the importance of coordinating air offensives with armoured and infantry campaigns on the ground.[3]

By the spring of 1938, after eighteen months of war, and with stalemate on the Madrid front, it was clear that the outcome would be decided in the east. After an initial breakthrough, the Republic's 1937–38 winter offensive in Teruel had failed, and in April, having captured what remained of Aragón, the Nationalists had launched the Levante campaign, primarily against Valencia. In mid-May, in a final, desperate roll of the dice, the Republic began preparations for the Ebro counter-offensive – an audacious (and hazardous) plan to cross the river westwards and take the Nationalists by surprise.

By this stage, the Italian squadrons enjoyed the use of three bases on Mallorca: Son Bonet, Son San Juan and Pollensa. From the safety of the Balearic Islands, they were within 115 nautical miles of Barcelona and 150 nautical miles of Valencia and were able to launch a series of low-risk bombing raids against the two cities. According to Count Galeazzo Ciano, Minister of Foreign Affairs and Mussolini's son-in-law, the function of these aerial attacks was quite simple: 'to terrorise Valencia and Barcelona'.[4] But nor did the *Aviazione Legionaria* ignore the smaller towns. Alicante lay a little more than 160 nautical miles to the south-west of Mallorca and comfortably within the range of the Italian aircraft.

In itself the town did not appear to have any strategic significance; it was completely isolated from the ground war and was so far from the front that it was neither vulnerable to attack by land forces, nor in any way a useful base for future counter-offensive operations. However, the town was a railway hub (with three separate stations), and had vital CAMPSA oil storage installations, a gas works and a fertiliser plant (Cros). In military terms, it had two bases – Rabasa and the San Fernando infantry barracks – and two aerodromes. Most important was the role of the port of Alicante in the supply chain of the Republic. According to Soviet secret agent Walter Krivitsky, Stalin was loath to use Barcelona as a point of entry for weapon supplies. While he had established his influence in, and over, the central government, he distrusted the autonomy and political unreliability of the authorities in Catalonia and was determined that they exercise no control over the armaments that were of such crucial importance to the Republic. George Orwell's descriptions of Barcelona in 1937 offer graphic details of the strength of anti-Stalinist feelings in the capital.[5] The Anarchist movement and the POUM were not only dangerously revolutionary, they were also rigorously opposed to the ideology, policies and authoritarianism of the Russian leader. In short, Barcelona was an independent hotbed of heretics that appeared to Stalin as dangerous to his long-term plans as the Nationalists.

Krivitsky offers an extraordinary account of an incident in the autumn of 1936, even before the tragic events in Barcelona of May 1937. He had been put in charge of a consignment of fifty pursuit aircraft and bombers and had arranged for their shipment aboard a Norwegian freighter. He was given orders to deliver the cargo to Alicante, but the ship's master found the port blockaded by Franco's navy. The *comisario político* (political commissar) on board refused to sanction plans to unload the cargo in Barcelona, and as 'the shipload of aircraft plied back and forth in the Mediterranean [...] loyalist Spain was fighting desperately and was woefully short of planes.'[6] After a stop-over in Marseille, the captain did eventually manage to elude the blockade and dock in Alicante.

The town provided a politically dependable alternative access to the Republic and eventually became the established gateway for Soviet aircraft (particularly the legendary I-15 and I-16 Polikarpovs, which had played such a crucial part in the defence of Madrid). In the meantime, the Republican government had also chosen to transfer production of the military aviation section of the prestigious *Hispano-Suiza* company, now in the hands of the unions, from its plant in Guadalajara. Machinery and labour force were transferred by rail to Alicante in September 1936 to continue the manufacture of the French Nieuport-Delage NiD 52 under more secure conditions. The plant was installed at Rabasa, adjacent to San Vicente del Raspeig (known during the war as Floreal del Raspeig), and, at least officially, came under the protection of troops belonging to the Republican air force.

According to the testimony of 15-year-old apprentice Mariano González de Pablo,[7] the installations were surrounded by anti-aircraft batteries, but they appeared to be unmanned. On one occasion, in response to an air raid siren, he rushed out to see the guns in action but found himself alone. He concluded that either there were no troops available to operate the defences or they had taken refuge in the air raid shelter. He also observed that so long as a squadron of fighters had been stationed at the base, the town was spared the relentless bombing that later did so much to damage civilian morale. He further describes the efficiency of the fifth column intelligence services, claiming that air attacks quickly followed the redeployment of the fighters.[8]

As well as production, the facilities at Rabasa also undertook repairs. González de Pablo recalled work not only on the legendary '*Chatos*' (Polikarpov I-15), the tiny Soviet fighters, which proved more effective than the relatively antiquated Nieuport-52, but also on the Focke-Wulf Fw 56 Stösser. He describes how in the early days of the war, Republican agents had successfully negotiated the purchase (probably in Austria) of three German-built aircraft and how they were employed in the training of fighter pilots.

However, the most significant work of the aviation industry in Alicante was based on the assembly of the Soviet Polikarpovs, routinely shipped to Alicante in crates. Hispano-Suiza eventually amalgamated with the Madrid-based Aeronáutica Industrial S.A. (AISA) to form the SAF-15 (Servicios Aéreos de Fabricación – Air Manufacturing Services). The staff were entrusted with the task of collecting the crates containing the parts of the Russian aircraft from the port in Alicante and delivering them to the various installations where they were to be assembled. The Polikarpov I-16 became known as the '*Mosca*' (Fly) because the crates were marked with the point of origin, Москва (Moscow), and the men unloading the ships at the docks in Alicante simply referred to them by using the closest approximation in Spanish.[9] The aircraft was known to the Soviets as the '*Donkey*' and to the Finns as the '*Flying Squirrel*'. In Spain, Franco's Nationalists christened it the '*Rat*'.

Given the dangers posed by enemy incursions, the SAF-15 dispersed its activities across the province. According to González de Pablo's account, the management and administrative services were based first in the convent of the Santa Faz, 8km from Alicante, and then in early 1938 they were moved to an estate next to the village of Villafranqueza, approximately 5km from the town centre. The fuselages, wings and wooden components were conveyed to Agost. The engines, on the other hand, were transported inland and assembled in the Canelobre Caves, near Busot, which provided protection from incursions by German and Italian bombers. Fitters and turners were recruited from the local textile industry, explosives were used to open a tunnel through the rock needed to provide adequate access, and a workshop was constructed by building platforms at the narrowest parts of the cavern. Unfortunately, a number of the vast stalagmites and stalactites, which are the feature of the caves, were shattered during the erection of the plant. As scientists calculate that the speleothems will grow at a rate of one centimetre per hundred years, the damage done to the natural beauty of the caves was extensive.

In mid-July 1938 González de Pablo was transferred to the warehouse where the final fittings and settings were made to the aircraft, at Onil. Of the staff, he later remembered a furniture dealer from Elda, named Vicente, who presented him with a domino set made of scraps from a *Mosca* fuselage, and a young Frenchwoman, Gillet, who was in charge of the paperwork and gave him a French encyclopaedia as a present. Work continued until the very end of the war, although in the last weeks, the lack of engines caused the stockpiling of fuselages, wings and cabin equipment; enough, González de Pablo calculated, for another thirty aircraft if the motors had arrived.

Alicante suffered its first air raid at the beginning of November 1936 when a detachment of three enemy planes (one bomber and two fighter escorts) dropped ten bombs on the town centre and port area, killing two people and injuring another. The German and Italian ships at anchor in the harbour kept their lights on throughout the raid.[10] In his diaries, Gómez Serrano wrote:

> We were woken at four or just after by the noise of terrible explosions. [...] You could hear the roar of the engines and the increasingly intense noise of gunfire. A little later we heard enormous explosions, obviously bombs that had fallen nearby. The terror of the people who had sought refuge in the hallway mounted. Little by little the shooting moved away, and we could no longer hear the planes. The danger had passed, but the fear remained.[11]

The second air attack came three weeks later, on 28 November, in reprisal for the execution of José Antonio. Lasting between 1930 and 0300 the next morning, the attack came to be known as '*el bombardeo de las 8 horas*' (the eight-hour raid). Waves of Heinkel 59s and Savoia S-81s flying out of Mallorca attacked military and civilian targets and caused significant damage to the CAMPSA storage tanks. Three people were killed and twenty-six injured.[12]

It had now become essential to provide the people of Alicante with adequate protection lest the enemy embark on a full-scale air offensive. Construction began on a raft of air raid shelters, both public and private, throughout the town. In July 1937 the town council approved plans to set up a *Junta Local de Defensa Pasiva* (Local Passive Defence Board) designed to raise funds for the building and upkeep of the refuge centres. More than ninety were finally completed; several, including the largest under the Plaza Séneca, have recently been restored and can be visited by the public. By the end of the war there was room in the network of shelters for 38,000 people.[13]

The military authorities also set up the *Defensa Contra Aeronaves* (DECA – Anti-Aircraft Defence) and installed anti-aircraft batteries on the Santa Barbara and San Fernando castles, the Sierra Grossa hilltop and on the Agua Amarga and Babel beaches.[14] Franco's intelligence service also reported guns on the docks, at the CAMPSA depot, and the airport, and searchlights installed on Santa Barbara and in the town centre (Avenida de Maisonnave).[15]

Unfortunately, the defences proved insufficient. Local author Miguel Ángel Pérez Oca reports that the entire system comprised four 76.5mm Skoda guns (manufactured in 1919), three Russian pieces of a similar calibre (1915 and 1930), three 44mm Bofors, and an unknown number of 20mm Oerlikons – installed on rooftops around the town.[16] In the war, not a single enemy aeroplane was shot down. Before to the introduction of radar and given the Republic's limited access to fighter aircraft, it appeared that Baldwin's notorious warning that 'the bomber will always get through'[17] remained chillingly accurate, at least in Alicante. However, little could be done to prevent the dissemination of the rumour that in Alicante the anti-aircraft batteries were manned by fifth columnists.[18] The purchase of additional, more efficient defensive armaments was prevented by the exponents of non-intervention. In a letter home from her base at the *Hospital Inglés de Niños* (English Children's Hospital) in Murcia, the New Zealand nurse Dorothy Morris wrote that this was, 'the direct work of the British who pride themselves on "fair play". I do so hope I live just long enough to be in at the day of retribution for all this.'[19] She later worked in London during the Blitz, first in an aircraft factory and then as welfare officer.

Although the numbers of victims might appear relatively low in comparison to later conflicts, in his study of the impact of air raids in Barcelona, the journalist and humanitarian John Langdon-Davies wrote, 'The aim was not casualties, but the creation of panic. The technique employed was designed to nullify existing Defence measures against panic. It succeeded.'[20] In Alicante the shortage of fighters and the lack of an effective defensive shield against bombers meant it would soon become customary for substantial sections of the population to abandon their homes in the centre of the town in the evenings and to spend the night in second homes or the houses of relatives either inland or along the coast. The nightly exodus became known as the *'columna del miedo'* (the column of fear).

However, the town enjoyed a respite until the autumn of 1937, with only sporadic and relatively minor air raids. In part, this was because the Nationalists had prioritised the battle for the north, but it was also due to the fact that Alicante had become the final link in an escape route for supporters of the insurgency trapped in hostile territory (who were then usually able to finalise their evasion on board Argentinian merchant vessels or Italian and British warships).[21] Historian Peter Anderson details how diplomats working out of the British Embassy were able to persuade the Republican authorities to provide transport to ferry Francoist supporters to the east coast. He also describes the assistance offered by Foreign Minister Julio Álvarez del Vayo in securing the safe passage of the refugees once they arrived at the port in Alicante.[22]

Anderson further reports that by November 1936, the British government had invested £40,000 in the evacuation (from all Republican ports) of 11,095 pro-Franco refugees in 220 voyages (over a total of 75,724 miles).[23] The only substantial assistance to pro-Republican refugees seeking to escape the Nationalists came via arrangements made by Dr Junod of the International Red Cross.[24] In the summer of 1937 the Treasury sanctioned the expenditure of £15,000 on the extraction of refugees from the Republican zone. The Royal Navy provided the British hospital ship HMS *Maine,* and the government authorised the chartering of SS *Gibel Zerjon*. The Treasury later authorised the expenditure of another £10,000, and between June and October it was reported that 7,500 people had been rescued (mostly from Madrid). Before his work for the KGB at GCHQ, a certain young Foreign Office civil servant, Mr John Cairncross, was appointed to the Spanish Section of the Western Department, 'to handle the release of British or British-protected people detained by the Franco authorities in exchange for right-wing persons held by the Republicans'.[25] He drafted a memorandum in November 1937 that admirably exemplified the Foreign Office art of understatement: 'It is probable that the occasions on which H.M. Representatives and Consular Officers in Spain have been of assistance to Spanish nationals are more numerous in the case of insurgent sympathisers than in that of supporters of the other side.'[26]

Captain Edwin Christopher Lance, an ex-army officer and civil engineer, and honorary attaché in Madrid, was one of the more active agents in unauthorised extractions. It is true that the casual indifference to historical truth and accuracy of his biographer, C.E. Lucas Phillips, does undermine the integrity of the story of an undoubtedly brave man. Nevertheless, Lance's version of his involvement in extricating British nationals and Franco sympathisers from Madrid via the Mediterranean ports does offer an interesting picture of wartime Alicante. He refers to the 'fierce heat', the 'parched and whitened hills dominated by the high hill of Santa Barbara crowned with its ancient fort', the 'profound blue sky and sea', the 'genial air' and 'diamond luminosity', the 'splendid double avenue of palm-trees that swept round the entire front, making dark green tunnels to give cool shade by day'. However, civil war and control by Communists and Anarchists had made it 'drab and dreary', a 'grim contrast to the bright and sociable town he [...] had known in happier days'.[27] His admiration for Alicante was also extended to the Royal Navy. The author offers a particularly graphic description of Lance's arrival in the town during one rescue mission:

> After the tension that these convoys imposed, how heart-warming it was at the end of the journey to behold the trim, grey shape of the British

warship riding in the bay and to experience the exhilaration with which the vision of the White Ensign always suffused him! There under her sway dwelt sanity, cleanliness. trust and efficiency.[28]

Lance was eventually accused of working as a Nationalist agent and arrested in October 1937. He spent a year and a half in appalling conditions in a series of detention centres in the Republican zone.

In Alicante the lull in aerial bombardments was ended on the first anniversary of José Antonio's execution when on successive nights Italian aircraft launched attacks on the port area and the town centre. On 21 November, thirty-six people were killed and sixty wounded in a raid that caused the destruction of an improvised shelter in the Calle* de la Huerta in the San Antón district. The prelude to the intensive campaign that was to be initiated in the spring of 1938 also included an attack by the Nationalist navy designed to disrupt trade with North Africa. At mid-afternoon on 10 December, a small task force of four warships under the command of Admiral Francisco Moreno captured the crew of a trawler fishing off the Cabo de la Huerta (a few kilometres from the centre of Alicante) and set fire to the boat. They then took up position five miles offshore and opened fire on the port and town.

In a fifteen-minute attack the *Canarias* discharged thirty-seven shells, the *Baleares* thirty-two and the *Almirante Cervera* sixteen. According to one report, two shells fell on San Juan, the only direct act of aggression against the village during the entire war. There were no casualties.[29] Although little damage was done to the town of Alicante, the raid caused panic among the population. Nine people lost their life. The Republican navy responded by deploying six destroyers from their base at Cartagena, which failed to prevent Moreno launching a similar attack on Valencia but did discourage a second attack on Alicante. However, given the proximity of the base, observers considered it a missed opportunity to inflict a serious blow to Nationalist sea power: 'The republican fleet either lacked a capable information service or did not want to take advantage of this opportunity to mount an attack with all the forces it could muster.'[30] The immediate result of the raid on Alicante was a rapid fall in the volume of merchant shipping using the docking facilities. A few days later, the port was reported to be empty.[31]

As if following a schedule, the Nationalists then launched one air raid a month until May when the *Aviazione Legionaria* gave notice of a new air offensive with four bombardments in ten days (on 13, 17, 18 and 22). Nevertheless, neither the authorities nor the population were prepared for the scale of the events that followed.

---

* *Calle* means street, as in Cabo de la Huerta Street.

Chapter 5

Malditos, malditos, malditos los causantes de tanto dolor ...

25 de Mayo 1938

Most of what we know today about the attack of 25 May 1939 is based on the stories of those who survived the raid, and whose testimonies survived both the dictatorship and the enforced indifference of the democratic transition (1976–1981).[1] Military defeat in 1939 and the ruthless political repression of the new rulers of Spain led to the disappearance of archival references, the institutionalised fear of the vanquished, system justification and, eventually, political resignation. Even when Franco died in 1975, the relatively peaceful dismantlement of the dictatorship came at a price. The *quid pro quo* in the democratic transition was the pact of directed or motivated forgetting, which required Spanish society to overlook the crimes of those who had installed the tyranny and those who had maintained it. The most significant documentary evidence is the Register of the Municipal Cemetery, which lists most of the names of those buried in a mass grave.[2]

In 1974, Vicente Ramos, probably the most prestigious of modern Alicante historians, described 25 May 1938 as:

> The worst day of grief and horror in this sad story [*the Civil War in Alicante*]. At about eleven o'clock in the morning, a squadron of nine[*] aeroplanes, as always from the base in the Balearic Islands, made several passes over the town-centre and released ninety bombs, some of which fell on a packed marketplace and caused some 300 deaths – it is not possible to know the exact number – and more than 220 other casualties.[3]

In a more recent work by Miguel Pérez Oca, the journalist provides a synthesis of the official Italian version of the attack, which was published in the Alicante newspaper *Información*:

---

[*] There is disagreement among witnesses and historians. Some say there were seven aircraft, others claim there were nine.

The operation was carried out by two formations: the first, flying at a height of 4,000 metres, comprised four Savoia 79 "Sparviero" of the 19th squadron, under the command of Captain Zigiotti; and the second, flying at 4,200 metros, comprised three aircraft of the 10th squadron, under the command of Captain De Prato. They took off from Mallorca at 08.10 and returned at 10.50. Total explosives dropped on Alicante: fifty-six 100 kg bombs, eight 20 kg bombs, and twenty 15 kg incendiary devices designed to cause fires in the affected buildings.[4]

The Savoia SM-79 '*Sparviero*' (Sparrowhawk) was later described as, 'Arguably one of the finest torpedo bombers of World War II'. Initially designed as a transport plane, it was then developed as a 'medium-range reconnaissance bomber' powered by three Alfa-Romeo 126 radial engines, with a top speed of 430kph.[5] The aircraft was also equipped with three Breda Safat 12.7mm machine guns and one Breda 7.7mm. Combined with its speed, the defence system allowed it to operate without fighter protection.[6]

In all likelihood, the Italians flew along the shoreline, north to south, or even crossed the coastline north of Alicante and approached the town from the west, to avoid detection by the coastal defences at the port of Alicante. A compilation of the evidence[7] provided by those who witnessed the attack suggests the air raid siren on the front of the central market failed to work, while others suggest it did not give any warning until the aircraft were overhead. There were even unsubstantiated rumours that it had been sabotaged by fifth columnists. The alarm, together with the market clock, is now on display in a glass cabinet at the left-hand entrance to the *Mercado Central* in the avenida de Alfonso el Sabio.

All oral testimonies do agree that it was a typical, clear Alicante day – '*Serían las once y el sol brillaba muy alto*' (It was about eleven and the sun was high in the sky).[8] It is also generally believed that the aircraft were flying well below the 4,000m claimed in the official versions. The British Commission of Investigation (see below), visiting Alicante some months after the raid, was unable to establish specific details and simply included the note: 'Height of attack *reported** to be 4,000 metres.'[9] Some observers, unable to conceive the possibility that the bombing was intentional, looked for alternative hypotheses: that the attack was random or the result of miscalculation, or that the appearance of a Republican fighter might have persuaded the pilots to jettison the payload and return immediately to base. However, given the perfect climatic conditions, the considerable distance between the market and

---

* My italics.

any military, industrial or port facility, and the absence of fighters in the area, the theories lack plausibility.

On the other hand, in terms of competence and valour, it is also true that the Italian air crews operating out of Mallorca did not cover themselves in glory. The British consul in Mallorca claimed they 'were not conspicuous for their courage'.[10] After a Republican air raid on Palma in May 1937, he reported that fighter aircraft did not take off to provide protection until twenty minutes after the siren. He concluded that in all likelihood this was because the pilots were 'in a stupor after a night of revelry'.[11] In a later dispatch to the Foreign Office, he wrote:

> In my last memorandum I reported that three planes bombed Alicante on 20 October (1937). This should be qualified to read: "On 20 October three bombing planes went to the westward with a full load of bombs and returned 4½ hours later without their bombs. They claimed to have bombed Alicante."[12]

I have been unable to find any records of an air raid on Alicante on that date.

Some survivors say that on the morning of 25 May 1938, the marketplace was full because rumours had spread of a fresh delivery of artichokes from the Vega Baja; others say they had heard that the fish stalls had received a consignment of sardines.[13] Whatever the case, the square behind the main market building was full of hungry and anxious women and children searching for food supplies. The Irish nurse and aid worker Mary Elmes was working in a small children's hospital sponsored by Sir George Young and Jesús Monzón. In a letter written in 1998, she recalled one particular victim of the raid, a young girl named Palmira:

> She was a pretty child of twenty-one months, wounded in the bombing of Alicante market in 1938. Her mother was holding her in her arms at the time. In the confusion that followed she lost her child. Very badly injured in the left leg, with her foot hanging on by a few shreds of skin. The overworked surgeons wanted to cut off her foot. Fortunately, the doctor from our little hospital, a paediatrician [Dr Blanc], was against this and took her to our place where she was immobilized on a plank for three months, at the end of which she could stand and eventually walk normally. It was a triumph for Dr Blanc and the English nurses, whose devotion and patience is to be admired. Being so young she couldn't tell us who she was and her family didn't find her for several days – oh such tears of joy when her father finally found her.[14]

Most of the bombs delivered hit the market and surrounding area. The latest consensus suggests that 300 people were killed, many of them children.[15] Gómez Serrano describes scenes of devastation: bodies piled onto lorries; trails of blood; the panic-stricken walking wounded invading the *Casa de Socorro*[*] and the local hospital where bodies were stacked a metre high against the walls. When the *Casa de Socorro* proved unable to accommodate all the victims, staff opened up the adjacent *Teatro Principal*. The dead were buried in a mass grave in the municipal cemetery. The diarist concluded:

> It was a splendid morning, the sky was a transparent blue, cloudless, with perfect visibility. No error was possible, the purpose of the despicable enemy was clear […] One day soon, they will pay for their crimes and suffer in their own cities the same destruction that they cause, and others tolerate, in ours.[16]

Ángel Pacual Devesa was an eminent writer and physician, who worked in the *Casa de Socorro* and was a colleague of Gómez Serrano in *Izquierda Republicana*. His brother, Andrés, was one of the victims of the air raid. He later wrote:

> The bombs began to rain down upon the town, streets, hospitals, schools, markets … The alarms remained silent, the unsuspecting "targets" did not seek shelter, and monstrous numbers were struck down. […] The medical centres, the usual ones, those opened in response to the war, and those improvised that day were inadequate. The care staff could not cope … Few families were not left to grieve […] I too felt the bitter "enemy" shrapnel that dealt me a direct blow to the heart, and my home was overcome by the shadow of mourning.[17]

Of his friend Andrés Pascual Devesa, Gómez Serrano wrote that he was hardly ever at home, but had arrived ten minutes before the building where he lived was hit. He was, Gómez continued, 'so good, so cheerful, such an excellent friend, such a fervent antifascist! Now he will not see the end of the war. Now nothing matters to him, lost as he is to oblivion and mystery.'[18]

The foreign consular diplomatic corps[†] in Alicante immediately dispatched a missive to Civil Governor Jesús Monzón, in which they expressed their collective condolences and added, 'The fact that the attack tragically took place on the town centre, far away from military targets, and therefore caused

---

[*] Literally 'House of Help'. Aid or relief centre.
[†] *Cueroo Consular Extranjero*.

numerous victims among the civilian population, will only deepen Your Excellency's grief.'[19]

Nevertheless, for half a century the fate of the victims was forgotten or at least ignored by all but their families. The massacre receives little attention in the Civil War histories of the prestigious British Hispanists.[20] Hugh Thomas refers to attacks on Valencia and Alicante, and in passing mentions a raid at the beginning of June in which 'the houses of the British Vice-Consul and US Consul in Alicante escaped being hit by a half mile.'[21] Henry Buckley, of the *Daily Telegraph*, does include a reference to the air raid (which he dates 24 May): 'The centre of Alicante which had no war industries of importance or any real objectives had been murderously bombed on several occasions. On May 24th, 300 people were killed.'[22] Otherwise, there are no references to the operation in the major works on the Civil War.

Three days after the raid, the Spanish Ambassador in London, Pablo de Azcárate, delivered a written protest to the Foreign Office in which he conveyed 'the profound indignation experienced by the Spanish people', and complained 'that the bombing of Alicante has not merited so far a single word of condemnation on the part of those [the British authorities] who formerly urged them [the Nationalists] to cease their bombarding open towns'.[23] The bombing of civilian populations by the Germans and Italians did eventually force Lord Halifax, the British Foreign Secretary, to agree to a two-man fact-finding tour to Spain. Wing Commander J.R.W. Smythe-Pigott and Major F.B. Lejeune of the Royal Artillery were dispatched to examine the nature and effects of the attacks and to gather intelligence that would prove useful in the case of a war against Germany.

The Commission of Investigation report (3 September 1938)[24] advised that in most of the cases that had been examined, the bombing was directed at non-military targets. Of the six attacks on Alicante investigated by the commission, they concluded that: one targeted the railway station; another was against the port and railway station; two were clearly aimed at residential areas; one was either an intentional attack on a civilian area or the result of incompetence and poor training; and one was probably an attack on the port and rail depot, in which the crews were surprised by anti-aircraft fire and chose to release their payload over a residential area on the outskirts of the town.[25]

Alicante now became a regular target not only for the Italians but also for the Heinkel He-59s of the Condor Legion. In the month of June four merchant ships sailing under the British flag – *English Tanker* and *St Winifred* (06/06/1939), *Thorpeheaven* (10/06/1939), and *Farnham* (27/06/1939) – were either sunk or wrecked in the harbour.[26] Neither was Alicante the only coastal town in the province to undergo air raids. From the summer of 1938 the town of Villajoyosa underwent a series of relatively desultory attacks that produced two deaths, but further to the north, Denia was the target of thirty-seven raids, which caused thirty-two deaths, hundreds of wounded and significant damage to buildings.[27]

To the south, on 25 August 1938, Torrevieja suffered a particularly brutal attack when the Italians targeted queues that had formed at the fish stalls on the docks to buy the sardines that were being unloaded by local trawlermen. In this case, the investigation commission were on the site within three days of the attack and were able to file the following report:

> The raid was made at about 10.15 a.m. on 25.8.38 by a formation of 5 aircraft in two patrols in line ahead, there being two machines in the leading patrol. It is reported that the formation approached over the sea from the east; to attack the town they altered course and flew N.N.E., dropped their bombs and disappeared from view. No attack was made with machine guns by the aircraft. There being no A.A. defence in the town the formation was not fired upon from the ground. The bombs were dropped from a height variously reported as being between 700 and 1,000 metres, but not in excess of the latter. The accuracy of the height and courses cannot be vouched for as there was nobody with a knowledge of aviation in the town. The visibility according to "Air France, Alicante," Meteorological report taken at 9.50 a.m., 25.8.38, was 50 kilometres; the sky was 8/10ths clear of clouds, the few clouds being at a height of 1,000 to 1,500 metres. About 30 bombs were dropped, of which 4 fell in the harbour, 6 on the beach and the remainder on the town. Approximately 50 houses were damaged or destroyed. Casualties stated to be 17 dead, 70 (approx.) wounded. The Mission consider that—
>
> (a) The attack was not directed against the railway station, salt factories or light railway leading therefrom to the harbour under any misapprehension that these were military objectives.
> (b) In view of the low altitude from which the attack was made and of the perfect weather conditions, the target hit by the bombs was the objective intended for attack.
>
> The Mission find that, though they have had no opportunity of examining—
>
> (a) The Nationalist intelligence reports on Torrevieja,
> (b) The orders issued to the pilots,
> (c) The pilots' reports on the raid,

the raid on Torrevieja on 25.8.38 was a deliberate attack on a defenceless civil population.²⁸

There appear to be no records of the raid in the Torrevieja Municipal Archives.

In response to the findings of the commission, and despite the fact that Franco had declined their offer to investigate Republican targets located in the Nationalist zone, the Undersecretary of State for Foreign Affairs, R. A. Butler, informed the House of Commons that the British government had appealed to *both** sides in the conflict 'to practise more humane methods of warfare'. He added that his hope was that the publicity generated by the commission (a copy of the report had been sent to the League of Nations) would, 'deter *both*† sides from making unjustifiable attacks on civilian populations'. The Labour MP Mr Ernest Thurtle subsequently asked whether there were allegations that the Republic had targeted non-military objectives. Otherwise, he continued, 'May I ask the hon. Gentleman, as he says that the Commission reports that the Spanish Government have not committed any of these offences, why he should appeal to the Spanish Government to desist from doing so?' Butler replied, 'I am not making accusations, but stating facts.'²⁹

In fact, while it is indeed true that it was not the policy of the Republican air force to target civilian populations, it should not be forgotten that it did nevertheless attack urban targets, albeit on a far more modest scale, and it did therefore endanger civilian lives. When the war broke out, in addition to the outdated French Breguet 19 light bombers, the Republicans were forced to adapt their Fokker F.VIIs and Douglas DC-2s as an improvised rudimentary bomber command. The aircraft were capable of carrying only a reduced payload of small-calibre bombs and the initial raids were rendered ineffectual by poor accuracy. Before non-intervention, the government in Madrid was able to purchase a number of French Potez 54s, 540s and 542s, but they proved no match for the Italian and German machines that Mussolini and Hitler were supplying to the Nationalists. Balance was restored with the arrival of the fearsome Soviet Tupolev SB-2s, one of the most advanced light bombers in the world in the second half of the 1930s. The '*Katiuska*', as it became known in Spain, was heavily armed and at altitude could outfly the Fiats and Messerschmitts.

At the outbreak of fighting, the improvised bombers were used mainly against Nationalist military installations in North Africa (Ceuta and Melilla) and insurgent positions in Madrid (the Montaña barracks), Barcelona and Albacete. On the other hand, at the beginning of August 1936, a single Fokker

---

* The italics are mine.
† Ditto.

dropped three bombs on the Basílica de Nuestra Señora del Pilar in the centre of Zaragoza, one of the most sacred sites of the Catholic church in Spain. The bombs failed to explode.

As the war continued, the Republican air force focused on military resources, infrastructures and bases. They bombed enemy positions, aerodromes (Sevilla, Mallorca), naval and port bases (Ferrol and Palma de Mallorca) and railway stations (Segovia). The towns most affected were the two Nationalist enclaves, Oviedo and Granada, but Valladolid and Palma also underwent extensive aerial bombardment. The bombing of urban centres inevitably led to significant civilian casualties. In April 1937 an attack on the railway station and cavalry school in Valladolid caused thirty deaths, including children in an adjacent school.

The most notorious incident occurred in the village of Cabra (province of Córdoba) in November 1938, at the height of the controversy over the bombing of civilians and as the Republican army withdrew across the Ebro. Three Tupolev SB-2s operated by Spanish crews were dispatched to attack the town on the basis of false intelligence that a contingent of Italian troops had been temporarily posted there. As they flew over the town, the pilots detected what they believed to be tents in a central square, and without confirming the target, released some twenty bombs. For reasons unknown, the anti-aircraft defence systems did not respond to their presence. The 'tents' were in fact food stalls in the marketplace, which was already full of peasants selling their wares, and local residents. There were no Italian troops in the town, only members of the 34th Transport Division and a battalion of prisoners of war. On the 80th anniversary of the attack, the town council unveiled a plaque that reads: 'At 7.30 on the morning of 7 November 1938, four months from the end of the Spanish Civil War, three bombers of the F.A.R.E.* dropped 2,000 kilos of bombs and shrapnel on Cabra, causing 109 deaths and more than 300 other casualties.'

The official report of the Republican air force reads:

At 7.27 three B. K. took off to carry out reconnaissance duties and to bomb Cabra. The mission was successful, explosions were observed in the centre of the village. Photographs of the front were obtained. No enemy fighters were observed nor was there anti-aircraft fire. The three machines returned without incident.[30]

---

* *Fuerzas Aéreas de la República Española*. Air Force of the Spanish Republic.

Isolated though the event was, it was potentially extremely damaging to the Republican cause. Although they give slightly different figures for the casualties, Spanish historians Josep Maria Solé i Sabaté and Joan Villaroya describe the raid as 'the most deadly of those carried out by the Republic in the course of the war.'[31] One can only assume, therefore, that if the Nationalist propaganda services did not make a greater issue of the slaughter, particularly abroad, it was because they deemed it wiser not to become engaged in an international dialectic, from which they feared they would unavoidably emerge the losers.[32]

Indeed, supported by Hitler and Mussolini, the Nationalists had imposed their control in the air war and were able to exercise their dominance to spread terror and undermine civilian morale in the main towns of the uninvaded zone. For all the criminal negligence of the Republican crews, the bombing of Cabra was an anomaly. As the Republic became increasingly defenceless against Nationalist attacks, so the capability of its air force to respond was also diminished. On his arrival in Burgos in early 1939, the new Embassy Secretary, Michael Cresswell, prepared a memorandum for the Foreign Office on the situation in the capital of the recently recognised Francoist government, in which he reported:

> There have been no considerable air-raids in Burgos for at least eighteen months, and the German anti-aircraft guns in the neighbourhood are being moved elsewhere; in Burgos itself they still remain, as do the air-raid shelters, but there is little prospect of their being used. The local battery-commander who has held his post for over a year is apt to complain of his lot; only once did he receive news that an identified and therefore presumably hostile aeroplane was heading for Burgos, and he immediately got all his guns ready and looked forward to a little activity. A few minutes before the machine was due to appear he received a telephone call telling him not to shoot, as the machine had been identified as the one specially chartered by Mr. Francis Hemming; so with great regret, and cursing the telephone system, he ordered the dust-covers to be put back on his guns.[33]

While the mandarins of Whitehall persisted in their campaign to tar both sides with the same brush, Butler did at least have the good grace to acknowledge that ultimate responsibility for the bombings by the Italian and German air forces lay with Franco: 'we must hold General Franco responsible for the action of the forces under his command.'[34]

In their response to the commission's findings, the Council of the League of Nations condemned the 'recourse to methods which are contrary to the conscience of mankind and to the principles of international law'.³⁵ Unfortunately, by this stage, the words of the league carried little weight: Japan and Germany had abandoned the organisation in 1933, and Italy left in 1937. Franco announced his decision to withdraw within five weeks of the end of the Civil War – the USSR would be expelled in December 1939.

The nightmare of Guernica was revealed to the European public through the work of such journalists as George Speer, and the vast painting by Pablo Picasso, first displayed at the 1937 Paris International Exhibition.* However, Alicante had neither an eminent *Times* foreign correspondent nor the greatest artist of the twentieth century to immortalise the horror of the attack on its marketplace. At the annual event to commemorate the attack, one survivor later recalled the deafening crash of the bombs and the next fifty years of silence as the incident was erased from history. Only in recent years have the activities of such groups as the *Asociación para la Recuperación de la Memoria Histórica* and the *Comisión Cívica de Alicante*† forced local authorities to engage with the dark chapters of the Civil War. Bomb shelters have been opened to the public under Plaza Séneca and Plaza Balmis to remind the curious about the experiences of the Alicante population during the conflict, and memorials have been placed at the marketplace and the municipal cemetery in remembrance of the victims. The square itself has been renamed Plaza 25 de Mayo.

---

* Now on display at the *Museo Reina Sofía* in Madrid.
† *Association for the Recuperation of Historical Memory* and the *Alicante Civic Commission*.

Part Two

1939

Chapter 6

Bullets hurt, corpses stink

The defeat of the Republican Army: the Ebro and Catalonia

By February 1939 the war in Spain was all but decided. Notwithstanding the obvious military reality that only sides that continue to fight can hope for ultimate victory, by this stage few members of the Republican government, diplomatic corps or armed forces genuinely wished to prolong the struggle or even believed long-term resistance was viable. The army of Catalonia had been disarmed. People in the diminishing Republican zone were suffering severe hardship. At the front and in the civilian population there was increasing disillusionment. Furthermore, Chamberlain and the French had slammed the diplomatic door by making a deal with Hitler at Munich. Nevertheless, Franco had still not won, and two questions remained. The first was how long could or would the Republic continue to resist. The second was whether the *Caudillo* would contemplate making any concessions, indeed negotiate peace terms, if his victory were postponed by Republican resilience, or pressure were brought to bear by foreign governments.

At the Battle of the Ebro (July - November 1936), the Negrín government had made a last perilous attempt to truncate the Nationalist advance, and to persuade the governments in London and Paris that the Republic remained a viable military force. It appeared that Republican leaders were unwilling to assimilate or accept that the strength of their armies lay in defence. Spectacular early successes were negated by Nationalist superiority in artillery and in the air. Franco's troops counterattacked and after months of brutal fighting the Republican armies were forced to retreat across the river, leaving behind them vast numbers of casualties and arms that could not be replaced. In the aftermath of this, the greatest battle of the war, the Nationalists launched the decisive campaign in Catalonia and quickly overran Republican positions. To relieve the pressure in the east, General Vicente Rojo, Chief of General Staff, ordered two major diversionary offensives in the zone where the Nationalist army was most vulnerable. The first was an attack on the Extremadura front, where Rojo hoped the Republican Army would break through to the Portuguese border, and the second involved a combined land–sea operation at

Motril, south of Granada. In the first case, General Antonio Escobar's Army of Extremadura launched an offensive in the first week of January 1939, and in the single most successful counter-attack of the entire war, the Republicans took 500km^2 of territory in three days.[1] In the second case, General Miaja, the commanding officer of Army Group Centre, and his Chief of Staff Matallana declined to act on Rojo's orders and Admiral Miguel Buiza was forced to abort plans for a landing on the coast of Andalucia. Matallana then ordered the army in Extremadura to take up defensive positions and eventually to withdraw to their original positions. It is certainly true that the troops were suffering the same problems confronting the Republicans across Spain: inadequate weapons and supplies, and a lack of air cover. In addition, the weather conditions were unfavourable – heavy rainfall caused artillery and tanks to become trapped in the mud. Nonetheless, Matallana's 'defensive insubordination'[2] and his failure to implement the plans for the Motril offensive, which exposed Escobar's troops to the undivided attention of Franco's southern legions, raised vital questions as to his competence and loyalty. Had Rojo's diversionary plans been undone by his high command's caution, faint-heartedness, or more sinister motives? Hugh Thomas concluded that 'Possibly the reluctance of Matallana derived from treachery.'[3]

A third disastrous operation was launched on 13 January 1939 at the second battle of Brunete, approximately 30km west of Madrid. The first battle had taken place in July 1937, and after three weeks of brutal fighting in extreme heat, had ended in stalemate[4]. Now, Colonel Segismundo Casado was ordered to direct another diversionary attack against the Nationalist army. In poor weather conditions, the Republican offensive was rapidly driven back, but not before 500 Republican soldiers had been sacrificed. In the words of archaeologist Alfredo González-Ruibal, 'The war landscape had changed dramatically since 1937: [the area] was by then heavily fortified with concrete pillboxes and this sealed the fate of the Republicans.'[5] Impenetrable defensive positions, highly effective anti-tank artillery, and relentless mortar and machine-gun fire on the advancing infantry forced Casado to abandon the assault. Given the fact that Franco's 20th Division facing the Republicans had been reinforced and supplied with new weaponry shortly before the offensive, it is unlikely that the outcome was not influenced by the presence in Casado's staff of fifth columnists.[6] In his memoirs, the colonel avoids any details of his own involvement in the operations. He describes Rojo's plans as a 'magnificent idea' but irrelevant, given the fact that, in the bigger picture, there was nothing that could be done at this stage to avoid the final defeat of the Republic.[7]

In November 1936, in light of the Nationalist advance on Madrid, Largo Caballero had moved the capital east to Valencia. A year later, Negrín transferred the seat of government north to Barcelona. Franco's army occupied the city on 26 January 1939 and provoked a mass exodus of refugees (civilians and military personnel) towards the Pyrenees. It appeared that the Second Republic had exhausted the supply of viable capital cities. On 1 February 1939, as they were driven northwards by Franco's army, fifty-five of the original 473 deputies[8] held a last desperate parliamentary session in the castle of Figueras (Figueres), a little over 20km from the French border[9]. The Republican Left deputy for Alicante, Gómez Serrano, did not attend the sitting. In a laconic note in his diary, he wrote, 'I do not think getting to Catalonia is a problem. What I find less clear, is how easy it would be to get back.'[10]

In Figueras, the President of the Cortes, Martínez Barrio, found Prime Minister Negrín waiting alone, 'silent and sombre, shrouded in the smoke of the cigarettes he chain-smoked'. Desperate and indignant, the Prime Minister reminded him of Prometheus Bound.[11] Suffering from extreme physical and mental exhaustion, Negrín delivered a rambling statement to the assembled deputies, in which he outlined the military situation and the government's strategy of determined resistance. In April 1938 the Prime Minister had drafted a list of thirteen war objectives.[12] At Figueres, he outlined a streamlined three-point manifesto or peace plan:

First: the guarantee of national independence and freedom from any type of foreign interference [...]

Second: the guarantee that it be the right of the people to decide their own system of government and destiny [...]

Third: [...] once the war is over, for the sake of the patriotic task of reconciliation, all reprisals and persecution must cease.[13]

According to Foreign Minister Julio Álvarez del Vayo, the government understood that any pledges made on the first two conditions would be empty promises. However, they were determined to obtain a commitment against vengeful retribution, which meant:

no execution or imprisonment of Republicans because of their ideals and because of their defense [sic] of a legal government against rebellion – and, along with such guarantees, facilities for evacuating from Spain all those for whom existence under the rebel régime would be materially impossible and morally a torture – then the cessation of hostilities could be considered. But if these guarantees were refused, then the struggle would continue to the last man and the last cartridge.[14]

In a message to the wider world, Negrín declared: 'in our own struggle in Spain, we are not only defending the interests of Spain, but also those of other countries which not only have failed to help as they should have, but have proved to be one of the main obstacles in our fight.'[15]

In the final months of the war almost half a million civilian and military refugees fled the advancing Nationalist army and crossed the Pyrenees into France. Many of them endured extreme cold, hunger, and sporadic attacks from Franco's pilots ordered to perfect the strafing of defenceless evacuees. Once the mass of those seeking refuge were 'safely' across the border, the Republican leaders followed. On 6 February Negrín accompanied the ageing Manuel Azaña into France, where the President took up residence in the Spanish Embassy in Paris and refused to return to Spain. The relations between the two men had been deteriorating over the previous months. Martínez Barrio described them as *'nieve y fuego'* (snow and fire – chalk and cheese seems inadequate). Azaña's disdain towards others was born of shyness; Negrín refused to be constrained by social or moral barriers. Azaña became immersed in complex dilemmas while Negrín prioritised practical necessity. The idealism of the President of the Republic contrasted with what he saw as Negrín's cynical realism. The President's intellectual scruples were scornfully dismissed by the Prime Minister. Azaña symbolised the legality of the Republic, Negrín its executive powers. When the moral authority of the former and the material authority of the latter failed, there was little left of the Republic.[16]

As the Prime Minister recrossed the border into Spain, he recognised José Antonio Aguirre (*Lehendakari* – President of the Basque government) and Lluis Companys (President of the *Generalitat* – the Catalan government) as they made their own way into France and exile. According to his companion, Julian Zugazagoitia, former Minister of the Interior and Secretary of National Defence in the last Republican government, Negrín was in a good mood and remarked that with Aguirre and Companys out of the way he would at least have one less thing to worry about. He had expressed his own determination not to leave Catalonia until the last Republican soldier had crossed the border.[17] He thus entered France on 9 February when General Rojo informed him that the final detachment of men had reached France, and as Figueras was occupied by the Nationalists.

The war had now reached the final watershed. There would be no more major offensives, and such was the superiority of his armed forces that Franco apparently had no need to deal with his enemy. On the other hand, if the Republic was beaten, the *Generalísimo** had still to conquer the capital and the Zona Centro-Sur (Centre-South Zone) – basically the area between Madrid, Valencia, Almeria and the bulge that stretched west into Extremadura. On 14 January the ambassador in London, Pablo de Azcárate, met the British Foreign Secretary and urged him to bring pressure on the insurgents to offer terms for a conditional surrender based on the conditions set out by Negrín at Figueras – and specifically a guarantee there would be no further reprisals against the vanquished Republicans. He reminded Lord Halifax that the Republic still had authority over the ten provinces of the Centre-South Zone (with a population of ten million), a number of important cities, including the capital and four ports (Alicante, Valencia, Cartagena and Almeria), an army of 500,000 men, and a navy that consisted of three cruisers, three destroyers, seven submarines, five torpedo boats and two gunboats.[18]

Regardless of whatever diplomatic initiatives might be taken, the reality facing Negrín was that the military situation was critical, and that the Republican authorities were confronted by a nightmarish dilemma: to resist or yield, to prolong the bloodshed and suffering in a desperate attempt to win concessions and evacuate those most at risk, or to submit unconditionally to the tyranny that awaited, and thus to put an end to the fighting. The question, then, was to determine, as far as was feasible within their powers, the nature of their defeat. It was a dispute that divided leaders and supporters, led to vicious recriminations, and eventually played a huge part in defining the last weeks of the Republic.

President Manuel Azaña, from his refuge in the Paris Embassy, ignored appeals to fly back to Spain and resolutely refused to move. He had long since given up all hope and now argued that were he to return to Spain, it would be interpreted as a public display of support for the futile government policy of resistance. Álvarez del Vayo spent time with him in Paris, trying desperately to persuade him that as President, his place was in Madrid or Valencia. Azaña told the Minister of Foreign Affairs, 'My duty is to make peace. I refuse to help, by my presence, to prolong a senseless struggle.'[19] He also denied his actions undermined the international status of the Republic. In a letter to Negrín, he wrote: 'It is not true that my presence in Paris will cause or trigger the recognition of Franco. They will recognise Franco because we have lost the war.'[20] Del Vayo disagreed; among the papers of the ambassador in Paris there is a hand-written note from the Secretary of State in which he complains, 'International situation deteriorating by the minute as result of absence of Head

---

* Title bestowed on Franco as supreme military commander.

of State from loyal territory. On him will fall (exclusively) (all) responsibility.' He concluded that the recognition of Franco was inevitable, unless Azaña returned immediately to the Central Zone.[21]

The President was not alone in his desire for a swift cessation of hostilities. He consulted a number of army commanders, including General Rojo, the Chief of General Staff, hero of the defence of Madrid, architect of the Teruel offensive and the Ebro campaign, and among the most prestigious soldiers of the Republic. Although the military leaders declined the invitation to present a written report, it is clear they provided an honest and deeply pessimistic outline of the military situation. Nevertheless, Rojo later denied telling Azaña at this stage that the war was lost.[22]

In any case, Azaña's argument missed the point. Even though, at this late stage, it is unlikely that a forlorn Negrín harboured any lingering hope of a shift in British policy or an early outbreak of war in Europe, his priorities nevertheless lay elsewhere. He was perfectly aware of the desperate plight of his armies, but his resolve to continue the struggle was motivated primarily by a determination to evacuate the maximum number of Republicans, and, if possible, to obtain tangible guarantees from Franco and the international community that the Nationalists would not wreak revenge on those who could not escape. To this end, he needed time and leverage. Hence the Foreign Minister's reminder to Azaña that the success of negotiations 'largely depended on our being able to give the impression that we were ready – if the essential peace guarantees were refused – to continue resistance.'[23]

However, General Rojo would later demand to know, 'What were we supposed to resist with?'[24] According to the American Hispanist Gabriel Jackson, at the outset of the campaign in December 1938, Franco's army in Catalonia consisted of approximately 280,000 troops, 1,000 field guns and 500 aircraft.[25] On the other hand, the Republic had sacrificed its army in the Ebro offensive.[26] In 113 days of fighting the loyalists had lost 75,000 men (30,000 dead) and the weapons and armoury required for the defence of Catalonia. By this stage, Constancia de la Mora was working at the government Foreign Press Bureau in Barcelona. Although zealous in her defence of the official line, she also had a gift for graphic description. At the end of the Ebro campaign, she complained, 'We fought the last part of that battle with our fists and the fascists fought it with heavy artillery.'[27]

Analysts of the military strategy of the Republic were not overexaggerating when they argued that Barcelona had fallen at the Ebro. The defence force that faced the Nationalist advance through Catalonia had approximately half the number of troops that Franco could deploy, fewer than 150 aircraft and no artillery. And by the end of the Catalan campaign, a catastrophic situation had become even worse. According to Colonel Casado, chief of the Army of the Centre, in Catalonia the Republic had lost 50% of the production capacity of its arms industry.[28] Furthermore, when the remnants of the Republican Army of Catalonia were forced to retreat across the border, they were disarmed by the French police authorities and confined in hastily improvised internment camps.[29] An embittered General Rojo later wrote:

> Our army was herded together in concentration camps [...] with a total lack of facilities, crushed without the remotest suggestion or possibility of reorganisation. Our war materiel was appropriated by the French authorities, along with the weapons and vehicles [...] No Spanish civil authority provided management or imposed proper responsibility. [...] Among us, the Spanish, there reigned complete disorder and a complete lack of authority.[30]

On 12 February he ignored a direct order to return to Spain. Instead, he protested at the conduct of the war and the lack of government initiatives to alleviate the suffering of the officers under his command who were now incarcerated in French camps, hungry and cold, and with inadequate sanitary and health facilities. In a letter to Negrín he gave vent to bitter recriminations against the civilian authorities. While steps had been taken to ensure the safe passage of the President of the Republic, President of the Cortes, the Presidents of Catalonia and the Basque Country, and of cabinet ministers, neither the government nor the ambassador in France had taken measures to negotiate with the French authorities the treatment of the Republican rank and file. He concluded, 'The government has abandoned us.'[31] He then told Zugazagoitia (the Secretary General of National Defence) that the duty of obedience did not oblige him to throw himself out of a window simply because a superior ordered him to.[32] The Socialist leader then pondered what might have happened if Republican troops had been allowed to apply this doctrine at Brunete, Belchite, Teruel or the Ebro.

It is certainly true that Negrín's insistence on continued resistance imposed an unbearable strain on the Republican army, and every setback intensified the pressure on those still in active service. In 1938, to cover the losses of two years of brutal fighting, the Republic ordered the draft of 30,000 males born between 1920 and 1921. The ages of men serving in the ranks now ranged from 17 to 45. According to Captain Antonio López Fernández, a member of General Miaja's staff, those called up even included fathers and sons.[33] Anarchist leader Federica Montseny christened the youngest conscripts the '*quinta del biberón*' – literally the 'baby bottle draft'. So many young men had been thrown into battle and slaughtered on the Ebro and in Catalonia that the extension of the bloodshed was a question that raised unavoidable ethical concerns.

Furthermore, there was another factor that had an impact on morale and discipline: the geographically imposed territorial or accidental allegiance that had required officers to declare loyalty to whichever cause controlled the zone in which they were serving. The only alternatives were desertion, imprisonment or death. Indifferent 'geographical' Republican officers were clearly less committed and more reluctant to urge young men to lay down their lives for a cause that they considered at best futile, and at worst mistaken. Many of these officers were also more concerned about their own future should the Republic lose the war, and should they be forced to justify their behaviour and decisions to the Nationalists.

Besides, draftees also varied in their commitment to the cause; again, conscription was based on geography, not on ideology. George Orwell's 'memoirs' are among the most famous works in English on the Civil War. Unfortunately, they are based on a limited perception of events in Aragón and Catalonia. Moreover, they are misleading in the overwhelming significance that the author appears to give to the dispute between those who prioritised social revolution and those who prioritised military efficiency and the war effort, without offering background within the much wider and more complex context of the war.[34] However, the great strength of his work was the portrayal of the reality of the often romanticised struggle of the Civil War: the sufferings and privations of infantrymen in the trenches. In his own words: 'a soldier anywhere near the front line is usually too hungry, or frightened, or cold, or, above all, too tired to bother about the political origins of the war.' He continued, 'A louse is a louse and a bomb is a bomb, even though the cause you are fighting for is just.'[35]

Spanish writer Antonio Muñoz Molina has described conversations with Civil War veterans who insisted they had fired on the enemy with their eyes closed: 'If the man out there on the other side was someone I had never met, and had never done me any harm, why should I want to kill him?' They also recalled playing football matches against troops from the trenches opposite and exchanging tobacco (from the Nationalist zone) for cigarette papers (produced in the Republican zone). Officers on both sides made the mandatory attempts to contain fraternisation, but were frequently ignored. James Matthews quotes reports of a pact between troops stationed on either side of the Ebro, to desist from shooting at each other: '[the men] strolled and washed on both banks of the river'; others 'lay in the sun on the riverbank'.[36] Muñoz Molina concluded:

Normal people are disinclined to kill or die, unless they have been brutalized by fanaticism. War is noble only for the unhinged, and for glib-talking sofa samurais who send poor men off to the slaughter while they sit comfortably in the rear, finding safe office jobs for their friends.[37]

Beyond the demands of military discipline, to combat the lack of enthusiasm for the cause, the Nationalists had chaplains, and the Republicans had political commissars.[38] The task of the former proved relatively easy; the religious unity of Spain, forged over centuries by a militant, obscurantist Catholic church, left no space for debate – dissidence was heresy. The political commissars, on the other hand, had to deal with the substantial ideological and political divisions that plagued the Republic. In his analysis of life in the trenches, Matthews references 'primary group cohesion'[39] and suggests that in conventional warfare the greater loyalty is often to the men and women of the unit to which a soldier belongs and on whom he or she ultimately depends for his survival, rather than to some wider, less tangible collective or ideal.

The growing demoralisation in the Republican Army was exacerbated by inadequate rations, sickness and the lack of medical supplies, irregular pay (a particular problem for their families), poor uniforms, the shortage of weapons and the lack of artillery and air cover – after the collapse in Catalonia, the Republican air force consisted of approximately 100 serviceable aircraft, while Franco could count on almost 1,500.[40] Morale among the Nationalists was understandably higher than in the Republican camp, and, for many, victory proved as strong an incentive as an end to the fighting. However, the defeatism and yearning for an armistice on the Republican side was compounded by the awareness that however much longer and harder they might fight, and whatever sacrifices they and their comrades might make, they could not avert defeat.

While it is easy to question the moral legitimacy of Negrín's willingness to expose those who bore arms for the Republic to further misery and danger, it would be invidious to ignore his commitment to the well-being of those who had remained loyal to the Republic. In his memoirs, Zugazagoitia, Secretary of National Defence, describes how Negrín made it known to the British and French intermediaries that he was prepared to give himself up to the Nationalist authorities in Burgos and sacrifice his own life as a symbolic punishment in return for guarantees that the new regime would offer clemency to the mass of defeated Republicans.[41] In February he also set up the *Servicio de Evacuación**

---

* Sometimes referred to as Emigración rather than Evacuación. See government archives: http://pares.mcu.es/ParesBusquedas20/catalogo/autoridad/122873

de Republicanos Españoles (SERE – Spanish Republicans Evacuation Service) to provide assistance to those exiles seeking to make a new life in the Americas. Nonetheless, the Republican leaders had to deal with a terrible equation, how to balance and justify the sacrifices required of the army against the need to protect the future well-being both of those soldiers who survived and of the civilian population.

After his dismissal of Indalecio Prieto as Minister of War in April 1938, Negrín had taken responsibility for the ministry and chosen to bear direct responsibility for the conduct of the war. This was not his only burden. As Prime Minister, he had faced a continuous struggle to uphold democratic principles and institutions within the Republic against pressure from the CNT-FAI, POUM and members on the left of his own party, the PSOE. It was not until 24 January 1939 that he yielded to the pressure of circumstances and declared a state of war (martial law)†. The proclamation was greeted with resigned indifference. In Alicante, Gómez Serrano watched the ceremony outside military headquarters to mark the occasion. The event was attended by various representatives of the armed forces and a military band consisting of trumpets‡ and drums. The few curious passers-by who paused to watch offered no comments.

Together with his Foreign Minister, Álvarez del Vayo, Negrín also undertook the deeply frustrating task of convincing the world, and specifically the governments in London, Paris and Washington, that Non-Intervention was both a breach of established international protocols and a deeply flawed and ill-advised approach to dealing with German and Italian ambitions in Europe. Addressing the Assembly of the League of Nations in September 1937, he told the delegates that Non-Intervention:

> arose out of the false hypothesis that, if the Spanish Government were allowed to exercise its unquestionable right to buy arms, this would lead to war. All the mistakes of non-intervention are to be traced to that perverted conception out of which it arose. The Spanish Government has never believed that a policy based upon respect for treaties and international obligations could lead to war. We have always considered that the greatest risk of the Spanish Civil War becoming a European conflagration lay, and still lies, in the fact that international law instead of being applied, has been sacrificed to the demands of those who have made blackmail by war an instrument of their foreign policy.[42]

---

† The *Nationalists* had declared a state of war in July 1936.
‡ Ramos specifies *bugles* (*La Guerra Civil, Vol III*. Alicante 1974, p.131).

He also reminded the assembly of the words used by Álvarez del Vayo twelve months earlier, when he warned the League that, 'The blood-stained soil of Spain is already, in fact, the battlefield of a world war.'

The reckless offensive across the Ebro had been designed in part to demonstrate to the world the fighting capacity of the Republic; to convince the western democracies that the Republic was a viable and valuable ally should they finally come to terms with the need to challenge Italy and Germany. It also had the effect of further undermining the confidence of Franco's allies in Rome and Berlin. It took the Nationalists three and a half months to regain what the Republican army had taken in a week. Mussolini, who had made a huge investment in Franco, was becoming increasingly impatient with the strategy and incompetence of the *Generalísimo*. In August he told his son-in-law: 'I predict the defeat of Franco. That man either does not know how to make war or does not want to.'[43] Ciano himself claimed that Franco would have made a good lieutenant-colonel, but that, as a general, he was obsessed with occupying territory rather than defeating the enemy.[44]

Notwithstanding the question of Franco's ability as a military strategist, it should be remembered that his war aims went beyond victory on the battlefield. In his conversation with the Italian Ambassador in Burgos in the spring of 1937, he had already warned his allies: 'I can assure you that I have no interest in territory, but rather in the population. The reconquest of territory is the means, the surrender of the population is the end.'[45] However, he chose to ignore, or at least failed to appreciate, Italian concerns precisely about his strategy and these 'means'.

Nevertheless, in the long run, Franco's shortcomings or ulterior motives did not determine the result of the fighting. On this at least, Orwell was right: 'The outcome of the Spanish war was settled in London, Paris, Rome, Berlin – at any rate not in Spain.'[46] As Hitler and Mussolini continued to supply the Nationalists, Edouard Daladier, the French Prime Minister, had closed the border with Spain in June, and armaments that the Republic so desperately needed were stockpiled north of the Pyrenees. Negrín maintained until the very end that resistance was a perfectly viable option if the Republic could only obtain delivery of these last arms shipments. Again, the sacrifices and achievements of the Republican army were neutralised by the short-sightedness of the leaders in Britain and France. Any advantage gained by demonstrating the fighting spirit of the Republican army was undone by Chamberlain's understanding with Hitler at Munich. The consummation of the policy of appeasement both confirmed that Chamberlain would not shift his policy on Spain and averted the immediate threat of war. The promise of 'peace in our time' was as empty to the Spanish government as it was to the Czechoslovakians.

In addition to the multiple military and diplomatic misfortunes haunting Negrín, the greatest immediate threat to his leadership of the Republic was political. Just as the international isolation imposed from London and Paris forced the dependence of the Republic on the Soviet Union for weapon supplies, so at home Negrín's determination to resist led him to depend increasingly on the Spanish Communist Party (PCE), the only political force with a similarly single-minded determination to fight on. His tactical proximity to the party made him vulnerable to insinuation of ideological affinity and the suggestion that he was a fellow traveller. Within a context in which anti-Communism had a powerful energy among many on the left as well as the right, his dependence on the PCE was a cause of resentment that those who opposed further resistance were now ready to weaponise.

Chapter 7

An ocean of darkness and death, but an infinite ocean of light and love

Humanitarian aid in Alicante

Meanwhile in Alicante, the situation of the civilian population was becoming critical. For the Republic the issue of feeding both troops and non-combatants was a primary factor in the struggle for survival. In the early months of the war food production in the province developed into a source of contention among the Popular Front parties. Anarchist influence, exercised through the powerful *Sindicato Único del Ramo de la Alimentación* (Single Union of the Food Sector – SURA), and their plans for collectivisation of both production and distribution led to open disputes with Socialists and Communists.[1]

In October 1936, acting on the orders of the Ministry of Agriculture, the new town council set up the *Comité Agricola de Alicante* (Agricultural Committee of Alicante) to implement the government policy of expropriation (without compensation) of those rural properties belonging to supporters of the military rebellion. The Welsh-born Hispanist Burnett Bolloten later pointed out that, in fact, much of the land had already been seized by agricultural workers and tenant farmers, and that in many cases the decree was a simple 'seal of legality'.[2] Nevertheless, the new minister, Vicente Uribe, one of the key Communist figures both inside government and within the party, was determined to push through land reform and encouraged the founding of cooperatives as an alternative to the anarchist policy of collectivisation, which he believed would alienate many agricultural small holders. A *Colectividad Cooperativa Confederal* (Confederal Cooperative Collective) was set up in the province of Alicante to coordinate the plan, and only 20% of agricultural land was collectivised (under the control of the UGT and the Anarchist CNT).[3] At the same time, the Civil Governor created a *Comisión Provincial de Abastos* (Provincial Board of Supplies). In December, Federica Montseny (CNT), the first female minster* in Spanish history, visited Alicante and addressed

---
* Minister of Health and Social Policy.

an anarchist rally in the *Cine Monumental*. Having herself ignored anarchist 'protocols' when she accepted office in Largo Caballero's cabinet, Montseny urged those assembled to embrace the unity of all anti-fascists: CNT-FAI, UGT, PSOE, PCE and the Republican parties alike. Victory in the life and death struggle that faced them, she insisted, was contingent on a united front. She concluded: 'the war is between a past that is dead and buried, a present that is being born, and a future that is upon us.'[4]

A month later, in the same venue, José Díaz, Secretary-General of the Communist Party, made another appeal for unity; of unions, parties and regions. He defended the need to overcome rivalries and to centralise the war effort and the economy. He urged the unions to support the economic policies of the government and to avoid initiatives that would undermine the authority of the Popular Front and the military capacity of its armed forces.[5] Following a demonstration of housewives against shortages and rising prices, the town council assumed responsibility for provisions. Mayor Ricardo Millá set up a new *Consejería Local de Abastos* (Local Department of Supplies) in May 1937,[6] and rationing was introduced the following month.

Although disagreements over land reform and agrarian policy undermined coordination and cooperation and prevented a unified, more efficient agricultural sector, political divisions were not the only problems facing those responsible for providing the civil population and the army with sufficient food. The problem of supply could not be solved through administrative restructuring at the municipal level alone. The impact of traditional wartime strains on food production had been further compounded by a number of factors: droughts plagued Spain throughout the conflict; the supplies of seeds and fertilisers were inadequate; shortages of fuel disrupted deliveries; the naval blockade imposed by Nationalist warships prevented food imports – although it did at least encourage local agriculturalists to switch from export crops to the production of food sources for domestic consumption; the theft of vegetables from small holdings and gardens discouraged local production.

The crisis in Alicante was exacerbated by a population surge as the Nationalists advanced in the south, occupied Málaga, and drove desperate refugees north towards Murcia and beyond. In particular, the town of Alcoy received some 3,000 evacuees and Alicante between 12,000 and 16,000. In response to the humanitarian crisis in Andalucía an international, non-governmental team of aid-workers arrived in Almeria in the second half of February. The mission was initially inspired by Sir George Young, a baronet and retired diplomat who had lived in Spain, was an authority on Spanish history and politics, and became known to those he helped as '*el hidalgo inglés*'.*

---

* The *English hidalgo*, or the *English nobleman*.

He did not enjoy the unanimous support of the National Joint Committee for Spanish Relief (NJCSR), the umbrella organisation set up in London to coordinate the aid effort for Republican Spain. In a letter to Honorary Secretary Wilfrid Roberts MP, the secretary of the organisation, Mary M. Miller, complained the aristocrat was 'huffy' and 'infuriating'. She also claimed his attitude made him a 'hopeless' and 'aggravating person to work with', and expressed the wish that he would be forced to stand down.[7] His mission quickly became dependent on the support (economic, logistic and moral) of the Quakers in the form of the American Friends Service Committee (AFSC) whose contribution to Spanish relief both during and after the Civil War was critical in providing medical care and food to the most vulnerable. Young's plan centred on the development of a service named the University Ambulance Unit (in honour of its academic sponsors). He arrived in Almeria in early 1937 with an ambulance and in the company of four nurses, including Dorothy Morris, a nurse from Christchurch (New Zealand).[8] They were joined by Mary Elmes, a volunteer from Cork, who abandoned her academic career and accompanied Lady Young on her own voyage to Spain aboard the HMS *Boadicea*. With them they brought a cargo of 6½ tons of rice, potatoes, beans, flour, soup, bandages and disinfectants.[9]

Faced with the catastrophic situation in Almeria, their first act was to set up kitchens to provide some basic sustenance to the victims of the Nationalist aggression. Young was then persuaded by the local authorities that rather than set up field hospitals close to the front, his team could best serve the needs of the Republic by the provision of care for the thousands of children suffering from wounds inflicted by enemy aircraft and warships, disease, and malnutrition. With funds dwindling, he was easily convinced of the wisdom of the new plan and transferred the ambulance unit to the AFSC. A children's hospital was opened in Almeria with a small nursing staff, which included both Elmes and Morris. Other hospitals were then opened in Murcia and Alicante (in September 1937) – both sites at a relatively safe distance from the Nationalist armies.

The team was also joined by Frida Stewart and Francesca Wilson. Stewart was an anti-fascist activist who, on behalf of the NJCSR, travelled the length of England, France and Spain in an ambulance that, for reasons unknown, had been christened 'the white elephant'.[10] She had met Young at meetings of the Committee and described him and his colleague Sir Peter Chalmers as 'the two Grand Old Men of the movement [...], white-haired and fine-featured democratic aristocrats'.[11] She spent time in Murcia and Madrid, and on her return to Britain worked for the committee in fund-raising and in support of the Basque children who had been evacuated in May 1937.[12] At the end of the war she volunteered to work with Spanish refugees in the south of France. Wilson was a Quaker, a schoolteacher and a writer from Newcastle, who had worked in refugee relief in France, North Africa, Serbia and Austria and supported the Save the Children Fund. She played a huge part in setting up the children's hospitals and was instrumental in encouraging Young to extend the relief programme.[13]

Mary Elmes was put in charge of the new hospital in Alicante and relief centres were opened throughout the province. The local authorities in Crevillente, Elche and Benidorm provided facilities for a number of school camps and Francesca Wilson, who had set up a camp in Murcia, also founded a centre in Benidorm in August 1937.[14]

In the capital of the province, Elmes received the support of Jesús Monzón, the Communist Civil Governor and a friend of Sir George Young. The new centre also enjoyed the active participation of a paediatrician, Dr Manuel Blanc, a Catholic and a conservative, whose brother had been murdered in the early days of the war and whose political allegiances provoked the distrust of the local medical authorities.[15] There are suggestions that the doctor may have treated Monzón's young son and thereby earned the governor's protection in the form of a vital posting to the children's hospital.[16] Monzón was himself a member of a prosperous family from Navarra, and it was partly his relationships with the wealthy and members of the upper classes that later brought him under suspicion when his policies conflicted with the interests of certain luminaries in the Communist Party.

By the late spring of 1938, the hospital staff were expressing concern at the effects on children of the constant air raids. Francesca Wilson wrote:

> The town is half-paralysed [...] The sirens scream and the whole town disappears underground for an hour or two [...] People wait patiently until it's over, but they look strained and anxious. Every crash they hear may mean their home in ruins. I was eager to get children away, and much as Spanish mothers hate to part with them they were eager, too.[17]

It was therefore decided to move the hospital to the Playa San Juan, a few kilometres along the coast, and then to Polop, a small village in the mountains, about 50km from Alicante, and 10km north and inland from the tiny fishing village of Benidorm.[18] Of the new facilities, for thirty children, another member of the nursing staff, Dorothy Litten, wrote:

> the summer residence of a rich man who has fled to a more suitable spot for rich men [...] the house stood empty and makes a surprisingly good

hospital. The rooms are a bit crowded but that does not matter now that the children are out all day, and perhaps before winter it will be possible to return to Alicante.[19]

After one visit to the hospital, Dorothy Morris described the location as:

> cut by ravines of mountain streams so that at all angles one can see the terraces with the neat rows of glossy green trees studded with the brilliant spots of oranges hanging in thousands [...] and now in the last few days all the bare almond trees over the whole countryside have covered themselves with the most delicate blossom pink and white.[20]

On a separate occasion, Morris stopped on the journey back to Murcia to visit Francesca Wilson's camp in Benidorm, which provided for another thirty-five children. It appears she may have foreseen future developments in the tourist industry:

> We bathed in glorious sparkling blue sea from a heavenly beach – behind us the high yellow hills and in the foreground a medley of palms and pinos and old fig trees and cactus [...] The coast has never been known much to the outside world – why I can't imagine. To me it is the most glorious coast almost in the world – far, far more so than the Riviera – and with perfect bathing beaches.[21]

The Polop hospital remained open until the very end of the Civil War. Morris then lived and worked in Britain throughout the Second World War. During the miserable London winter of 1940–41 at the height of the Blitz, she wrote, 'I'm haunted all the time by visions and remembrances of Mediterranean Springs [sic] – ever since January, when I knew there would be great masses of almond blossom on the bare hills & they would be picking oranges in heavenly sunshine in Spain.'[22]

Nevertheless, the situation in the province was far from idyllic and in 1938 Alicante capital was facing a winter of severe shortages and hardships. In his diaries, Gómez Serrano writes that by Christmas the townspeople were fortunate to obtain a daily ration of 100g of black rye bread. On days when none was available, they received 50g of rice. There had been no cooking oil for two months and there were days when, however long customers queued at the market, the only products available were chard, *pencas** and mouldy

---

* The ribs or stems of the chard leaves.

oranges.²³ On 2 February 1939 Gómez Serrano reports there was nothing at all on sale in the central market in Alicante, not even oranges. In response there was a violent demonstration of enraged housewives outside the civil government buildings.²⁴

The situation in other parts of the Republican zone was even worse. By this stage, in Madrid, the daily ration per person had been reduced to 55g of rice or legumes (plus an intermittent supply of such luxuries as sugar and salted fish). Lentils became known as *píldoras de la resistencia* (resistance pills) or *píldoras del Doctor Negrín* (Dr Negrín's pills)*. The population spent much of their time hunting and scavenging for food. *Algarrobas* (carob beans) became a staple, and no part of any vegetable was wasted. Potato peelings were used to make crisps, a Civil War delicacy, or if no oil was available, they were mixed with flour, yeast, vinegar and salt to make an egg-free *tortilla* (omelette).²⁵ There were reports that 400 people a week were dying of the effects of malnutrition.²⁶ In the final months of the war, the population in the capital was surviving on an average intake of 944 calories per day.²⁷ Pioneering oral historian Ronald Fraser quotes a report by the Quaker International Commission for the Assistance of Child Refugees from the winter of 1938–39, which warned that the capital 'could not support life for another two or three months at the existing levels of food supplies'.²⁸

Diet-related conditions were rife. Apart from the generalised inanition, many of the population suffered from pellagra, nutritional neuropathies, optic and auditory neuritis, glossitis and oedema.²⁹ The hunger, illness and desperation bred ever greater disaffection and encouraged an expanding, more active and more confident fifth column. One *falangista* who spoke to Fraser claimed: 'So many doctors joined [the fifth column] that Madrid's health services were virtually in our hands. The recruiting centres were infiltrated by our men. Even some Communist organizations like Socorro Rojo ended up in fifth column hands.'³⁰

When, at the end of the Catalan campaign, the last soldier had escaped the advancing Nationalist army and crossed the border into France, Zugazagoitia heard Negrín say to himself, 'Now let's see how we cope with part two. That's going to be more difficult.'³¹ The Secretary of National Defence understood the comment to mean that Negrín's next goal was to arrange a new rescue plan, this time for Republicans in the Centre-South Zone. On 9 February 1939, in the company of Álvarez del Vayo, the Prime Minister travelled to

---

* The head of the government was also an eminent physician who had trained in both Germany and Spain.

the consulate in Toulouse where he held talks with Captain Antonio López Fernández, the emissary of General Miaja. López Fernández described the mood of the conference as more appropriate to a wake than a cabinet meeting. He further claims that he warned Negrín, del Vayo and Méndez Aspe (Minister of Finance) that further resistance was impossible and that, given Republican Spain was now under martial law, the only solution was for the government officially to delegate authority in an army officer to negotiate the terms of surrender. He described the Centre-South Zone as an aircraft whose engines had failed and insisted that the fate of the passengers now depended on the skill of the pilot. He informed Negrín that a consensus existed in the army that said pilot could only be General Miaja. In his biography of Miaja, López Fernández describes his conviction that Negrín was still committed to 'criminal resistance, ordered beyond any doubt, by the Kremlin'.[32]

The next day, the Prime Minister left the President of the Republic, the President of Congress and the chief of general staff behind in France, and, accompanied by his Foreign Minister, caught one of the last regular Air France flights to the Republic for the short journey to Alicante.[33] Álvarez del Vayo described the trip as 'a splendid flight', and continued, 'As we flew over Barcelona – the city lights shining with a brightness to which we were unaccustomed after two and a half years of war – the feeling of her nearness was so intense as to waken us from sleep.' As they approached Alicante, he recalled 'the fair countryside of the Levant, all the more beautiful in our eyes for being still part of our own Spain'.[34]

The return to Spain of the Prime Minister and his Secretary of State confirmed their intention to continue the struggle. However, it also raised the question of exactly how they intended to resist the enemies of the Republic long enough to implement plans for mass evacuation and to force concessions. Less obvious, but no less significant, was how they would deal with their enemies within the Republic, those civilians and army officers who were set on a course that would undermine, if not sabotage, the entire strategy.

Chapter 8

Cerca del agua perdida del mar

The arrival of Negrín in Alicante after the debacle in Catalonia

After twenty-four hours spent in exile between the French border and Toulouse, Negrín arrived in Alicante early in the morning of 10 February. Perhaps the most damaging of the Prime Minister's qualities as a leader was his inability or unwillingness either to share his intentions or communicate his strategies even to his friends and colleagues. His closest ally at the end, Álvarez del Vayo, described him as 'a humanist and a progressive', 'affable and generous', a man of 'irreproachable loyalty' with 'an almost religious love of his county', and 'more initiative, more energy intelligently applied, and more courage than all his detractors put together'. He concluded, 'above all he is a statesman', and yet even del Vayo conceded, 'he is a man at times almost impossible to work with in joint political action.'[1] On the other hand, it is absurd to expect war leaders to embrace democratic transparency and accountability or to share their purpose and strategies. Fifteen months later in the House of Commons, Churchill condensed his war aim into a single word: 'Victory'. Negrín had chosen to define his own policy with equally unambiguous succinctness: 'Resistance'. He might not have clarified that his aim was to save whomever he could from the ruins of the Civil War, and yet by mid-February 1939 the very nature of the military collapse and the developments in the international arena precluded any suggestion his mission might be different.

For the Nationalists, it appeared the final act of the war had already been written; what remained was a formality, the ratification of victory. On the other hand, for Republican leaders there remained a huge drama to be played out. Negrín's return to the Central-South Zone sent a message of defiance not only to the enemy, but equally importantly to those in the Republic who rejected his agenda of coninued resistance. The alacrity with which he flew back to Spain was highlighted in his speech to the Permanent Delegation of the Cortes in Paris at the end of March. He told the delegates, 'I arrived in Alicante as the newspapers published the news that our Army had completed the evacuation of Catalonia.'[2]

Del Vayo's first impression of the town was the state of the harbour: 'a truly desolate scene [...] The whole port seemed to have been stripped bare by machine-gun fire. A ship with French colours painted on her funnel, to all appearances deserted, lay forlorn at the quayside surrounded by grisly reminders of the enemy bombardments.'³ Negrín and del Vayo were then driven to the headquarters of the Civil Governor where they contacted Generals Miaja and Matallana, and the other field army and navy chiefs, to inform them of their return and of their intention to fix the seat of government in Madrid. In the Spanish version of his memoirs, published in 1968, Colonel Casado reported the call he received in his office in the capital and transcribed from memory the conversation:

> 'Colonel Casado? This is Negrín speaking from Alicante. How are you and how are things there?'
> '*Señor Presidente*: Welcome. All is quiet.'
> 'Do you think I can make it to Madrid without any problems?'
> 'Everything is under control, and I assure you that you can get to Madrid without the slightest difficulty.'
> 'So, that's perfect. I will reach Madrid the day after tomorrow, the 12th, before midday.'
> 'Very well, at your orders, s*eñor Presidente*.'

Negrín later recalled that he had been shocked at the 'cold and dry' tone of the conversations with the army leaders and claimed that he had a 'premonition' that his return 'was a cause of displeasure as if it interfered with something that had been agreed'.⁴ At this point, British Chargé d'Affaires Stevenson telephoned Sir George Mounsey at the Foreign Office to inform him of Negrín and del Vayo's departure for Spain – he supposed their destination was either Madrid or Valencia. He quoted a French colleague who insisted, 'they will get no encouragement to continue the war', and concluded that Negrín was 'finished'.⁵

At midday, the visit to the Governor's offices was aptly interrupted by an air raid. The Prime Minister's party was then escorted to the *Diputación* (Provincial Council). Gómez Serrano described the arrival of Negrín and Álvarez del Vayo as 'unexpected'. News was in short supply and much of what was reported lacked credibility. In his diaries, Gómez Serrano had expressed his understanding that the government had already flown to Madrid on 5 February. He also recorded a story circulating in Alicante that Negrín had arrived in Cartagena on board a submarine.

The Prime Minister and Foreign Minister inspected the premises of the *Diputación* and Gómez Serrano interpreted their interest as part of a design to decentralise government structures and to establish ministerial offices in the town. Negrín then set off for Valencia, stopping *en route* for lunch at a restaurant next to the Peña de Ifach in Calpe. In his entry for 10 February, having described the Prime Minister's visit, Gómez Serrano also refers to the death of Pius XI, the Pope who had strongly condemned the anti-clericalism of the Republic and the secularising policies of the first government. Although he had declared his support for the Nationalist cause and lamented the desecration of churches and the violence against ecclesiastics in the Republican zone, he declined to use the expression 'crusade' to define the Nationalist rebellion. The Vatican had also sought to mediate in Bilbao, where Franco's victorious army wrought vengeance on the clergy who had remained loyal to the Republic. Having first come to an accommodation with both Mussolini and Hitler, Pius later denounced their authoritarianism and racial policies, and in 1938 ordered the preparation of the *Humani generis unitas* encyclical, which denounced antisemitism. He was succeeded by Pius XII who chose not to promulgate the draft.[6] In response to a note from Franco congratulating him on his election, the new Pope expressed 'wishes for further successes befitting your glorious and catholic traditions and with cordial blessing to beloved Spain'. He concluded his message by promising to 'invoke the Divine assistance on your behalf'.[7]

Once in Valencia, Negrín and those members of his cabinet still in Spain held talks with Lieutenant-General Miaja (Commander of the Armed Forces), General Matallana (Commander of the Centre-South Army Group) and local civilian authorities. Uribe, the Minister of Agriculture, reports that Miaja greeted Negrín in his pyjamas.[8] After the meeting, Álvarez del Vayo delivered a statement to the press in which the Prime Minister referred to 'everyone's high morale and determination to resist'.[9] In an aside to his Foreign Minister, Negrín said, 'Did you see that? The rebels don't need motorised divisions against people with such [low] morale. A few bicycles would be enough to break through.'[10]

On 12 February Negrín travelled to Madrid, a city which at times appeared an abandoned outpost and which had not been the seat of government since the autumn of 1936. Nevertheless, it retained a huge symbolic and strategic importance in the '*España no invadida*' (non-invaded Spain), as the Prime Minister was inclined to call it.* The next day Negrín presided over a meeting

---

* A vital part of his discourse was that the war in Spain was not a civil war; the country had been invaded by hostile foreign powers.

of the cabinet and held talks with Colonel Segismundo Casado, the man destined to have a huge but tragic impact in the last weeks of the Republic. Casado had been appointed Chief of the Army of the Centre in May 1938, and in light of Rojo's effective desertion and refusal to return to Madrid, Casado's authority and influence were crucial factors in the 'resist or yield' dialectic. In a new press release, the government made an appeal to the 'Army, men, women, Unions, parties, Press"* to unite in a final effort to prevent Spain 'sinking into a sea of blood, hatred and persecutions' that would condemn future generations to a country united only by 'foreign domination, violence and terror'.[11] Official statements no longer made references to a final victory.

In the meantime, while Franco considered his next move in the ground war, his air force intensified operations on the Valencia front and bombed Valencia, Sagunto, Gandia and Denia. At 1130 on the day that Negrín arrived in Madrid, an Italian squadron of Savoia-Marchetti SM.79s of the XXVII group of the *Aviazione Legionaria delle Baleari* flying out of the base at Son San Juan dropped twenty 250kg bombs on the railway station at Xàtiva (Játiva) at the very moment that a train entered the depot. Passengers included men of the 49th Mixed Brigade on leave after service in the counter-offensive in Extremadura. The explosions caused a giant mushroom cloud. The 109 victims of the raid included eighty-three soldiers, six railway workers and three children. Another 300 people were wounded. The timing of the attack and the fact that a senior staff officer had left the train at an earlier station led to conjecture that the fifth column had been involved in the planning of the mission. What remained of the 49th was disbanded and the survivors redeployed in other brigades.[12]

The next day, at question time in the House of Commons, the Prime Minister and the Undersecretary of State, R. A. Butler, were asked about British operations in Menorca, the only Balearic Island that had remained in the hands of the Republic. The fall of Barcelona had cut the supply route to the island, and its position became unsustainable. Furthermore, there were fears in Nationalist Spain, France and Britain that the Italians were harbouring ambitions to occupy the island and establish a base for their air force and the *Regia Marina Marina* (Italian Royal Navy) as part of their grand design to make the Mediterranean 'an Italian lake'. An agreement was reached between the British Vice-Consul in Mallorca, Captain Alan Hillgarth, and the Nationalist air chief in the Balearics, the Conde de San Luis, whereby HMS *Devonshire* would convey San Luis to Mahon to negotiate the rendition of the Republican forces on the island and thus avoid further bloodshed and

---

* The capitals are in the original.

pre-empt Italian plans. On 7 February the Military Governor, Luis González de Ubieta, was invited aboard the British warship to receive an ultimatum from San Luis.

In spite of the presence of the Royal Navy, or in response, the Italians continued their aerial attacks on the island, and fighting broke out in Ciudadela and Mahon as Nationalist supporters attempted to seize control. González de Ubieta was unable to communicate with Negrín or Miaja, although from the base at Cartagena the Commander of the Navy, Miguel Buiza, gave him instructions to proceed as he saw fit. The terms of the surrender were agreed on 8 February. At first light the next day, before the fifth column and reinforcements from Mallorca took over the island, HMS *Devonshire* put out to sea with 450 Republican refugees and set a course for Marseille.[13]

The answers given by the government to the House of Commons go some way to clarifying their attitude and actions over the following weeks. When asked if the Spanish government had been notified before to the operation, Chamberlain gave the not unreasonable response that Republican authorities were now so 'scattered' that it was not easy to locate the appropriate officers in time. However, he could not offer a satisfactory reply to the question why they had failed to inform the Spanish Ambassador in London, whose address, we can assume, the Foreign Office did have. The Prime Minister also informed the House that no protests had been made to the government in Rome, but that the Nationalist authorities had expressed their regret at the bombardment of the island by Italian aircraft during the negotiations. Crucially, he also announced that an eventual recognition of Franco's regime would be determined if and when deemed appropriate by the government without prior consultation with Parliament. Finally, when asked whether the Royal Navy would offer its protection to Republican leaders, R. A. Butler, spokesperson for the Foreign Office, replied, 'I can say that such facilities as have previously been given for the evacuation of Spanish subjects of both sides in His Majesty's ships will, if circumstances permit, continue to be granted.'[14] It was precisely the rescue of so many Republicans from Menorca that persuaded many on the opposition benches to dilute their criticism of an operation that was seen as intervention on behalf of the Nationalist cause by the most fervent sponsors of Non-Intervention.

Two days later the Duque de Alba, Franco's agent in London, delivered a message to Lord Halifax, via a conversation with Sir George Mounsey, an assistant undersecretary, expressing gratitude for British collaboration in the 'reconquest of Menorca'. In addition, he suggested that 'Franco hoped that he would some day be permitted to recompense the officers of HMS *Devonshire* in recognition of the services rendered to him.'[15] Azcárate, still the Spanish

Ambassador in London, was less enthused. He delivered an 'energetic protest' to Halifax, in which he wrote:

> The British government cannot conceal from themselves that by the mere fact of transporting a rebel emissary on board a ship of the Royal Navy, all the moral weight of the United Kingdom was openly placed at the service of the cause of surrender. The Spanish Government consequently consider that the surrender of the island of Minorca to the Spanish rebels has been entirely, or at least for the most part, the result of the initiative and direct intervention of the Government of the United Kingdom.[16]

On 13 February the Nationalist authorities in Burgos published the *Ley de Responsabilidades Políticas* (Law of Political Responsibilities),[17] which had been approved on 9 February and which set out a judicial framework both for the punishment and repression of those (individuals and collectives) that had remained loyal to the Republic, and for the expropriation of their assets. The law was a jurisprudential infamy. It was made retroactive to October 1934, and could thus be used to prosecute those who had obeyed the laws of the legally established governments of the Republic. In typically convoluted language, it made those who had resisted the military insurrection liable to prosecution on charges of aiding subversion and military rebellion (Articles 1.1.1 and 2.4.A). In other words, those who opposed the military rebellion were guilty of military rebellion. It was, in the words of Ramón Serrano Suñer, brother-in-law of Franco, chief of the *Falange* and a member of Franco's government from 1938–42, *'justicia al reves'* (back to front justice).[18] Nevertheless, the Law was hugely significant as it laid bare Franco's intentions for the new Spain. From this stage on, it became impossible to suggest that the outcome of unconditional surrender to the Nationalists could be anything but submission to a ruthless regime set on revenge and ideological cleansing. Notice had been given: 'Franco was whetting his knife.'[19]

If there was a pivotal event in this phase of the war (between the fall of Catalonia and Franco's proclamation of victory), it was the meeting at Los Llanos, convened by Negrín after preliminary talks in Madrid with Colonel Casado. The Prime Minister discussed the military situation and options with army, navy and air force commanders. The venue, next to an aerodrome 5km south of Albacete, was described by Álvarez del Vayo as 'a splendid country-house and game reserve'.[20] Despite its use as quarters for Republican pilots, it had escaped Nationalist raids, presumably because it belonged to the Marques de Larios. The five-hour-long conference was attended, among others, by General Miaja, Colonel Casado, Rear Admiral Buiza and General Matallana.

No official records or minutes of the meeting are available, although Negrín made a report to the Permanent Parliamentary Delegation at the end of March[21] and Colonel Casado later published his own account.

As a genre, memoirs are not characterised by humility, respect for the truth or balanced descriptions of friend and foe alike. Nevertheless, Casado's *The Last Days of Madrid* (1939) and *Así cayó Madrid* (1968) exude arrogance, ignore reality and pour scorn on his peers. The reliability of his own version of the meeting at Los Llanos is further undermined by the fact that in the original edition, written a month after his arrival in Britain and published in English, Casado claimed the meeting took place at the end of February[22]. Nevertheless, as a historical document, his writings cannot be disregarded. It is clear that Negrín was given a hostile reception, and was warned that morale had reached a new low point and that further resistance was futile.[23] Admiral Buiza, whose ships at the Cartagena base were especially vulnerable to air attacks, threatened to remove the fleet from Spanish territorial waters unless a peace settlement was negotiated immediately.[24] Inexplicably, given later events, General Miaja was the lone military voice in support of the policy of resistance at all costs. In response, Casado was compelled to argue that if Miaja's argument prevailed 'in the true military spirit as indicated in Army Orders, we should be the last to leave'.[25]

Negrín later reported that his interlocutors had little interest in discussing military questions and were more preoccupied with political issues.[26] If López Fernández's version of his meeting with the Prime Minister in early February is reliable, then Negrín had been forewarned of military attitudes. Nor had General Rojo disguised his own conviction that further resistance was futile. Whatever Negrín's expectations, the outcome of the conference was clear: the government had lost the confidence of the army. Most members of the High Command rejected the doctrine of resistance at all costs in favour of peace at any cost, and Negrín could have little doubt that defiance was a viable policy only in the extremely short-term.

In Alicante, unaware of developments in Albacete, but fearful of what lay ahead, Gómez Serrano was coming to terms with the idea of exile. In his diary he wrote a reminder to apply for passports. He concluded, 'What is there left for us to do? The government is a shadow. The administration was destroyed at Barcelona. The State is creaking. This is only held together by a miracle.'[27]

Chapter 9

Stay out of the range of the artillery fire

Non-Intervention: the effects of British and French foreign policy

Months later, when Negrín's supposition that war would eventually break out across Europe had been confirmed, Álvarez del Vayo wrote: 'We did not want an endless and blind struggle, but we were not willing to die a dishonourable death without so much as attempting to secure a peace guaranteeing the lives of those who had committed no other crime than that of defending their country's independence.'[1] When he left the meeting at Los Llanos, Negrín was clearly aware that his policy of resistance and his own political future were in the balance. The Republic was in a state of war in which democratic structures had exhausted their viability. The President was skulking in Paris, Parliament had neither role nor form. The deputies were dispersed throughout Spain and France. Negrín had lost the confidence of the President and many in his own party, particularly since the declaration of martial law. His only active constituency was the military, and the High Command had expressed their opposition to his strategy. Although the Prime Minister later claimed he had been heartened by the response of combat troops, he was also aware that the loss of support among the civilian population must also undermine morale in the trenches.

If the Prime Minister were to secure any concessions from the Nationalists, he required diplomatic initiatives from the liberal democracies and the continued military discipline and will to resist of the Communist movement. In the first case the *Caudillo* had not indicated the slightest inclination to negotiate with an enemy that he wished to annihilate and was now at his mercy. Peace and reconciliation were not on his agenda, only victory and vengeance. Negrín knew that there was little chance of wringing meaningful guarantees of clemency from Franco without foreign intercession and that he was, therefore, dependent on the British and French. Furthermore, he argued that to force Franco to accept mediation, he needed to persuade his enemy and the neutrals that the Republic was willing and able to fight till the end. Unfortunately, he could not fail to see that his greatest asset, the support of the Communist Party, was also his greatest liability. The influence of the PCE in the fragmented remains of the *Frente Popular* alienated those who patrolled the corridors of power in London, and many Spaniards who had originally supported the alliance, including powerful forces in Negrín's own Socialist Party (PSOE). It also gave ammunition to those determined to bring about his downfall.

According to his own account,[2] Negrín outlined his efforts to achieve an end to the war to the General Staff at Los Llanos, but insisted that, without a manifest resolve to fight on, 'to sue for peace would cause a catastrophe'. He also informed them that he had opened channels with British and French diplomats in pursuit of foreign commitments to an 'honourable' peace settlement.

In 1938 the British government had instituted a prisoner exchange mission under Field Marshal Sir Philip Chetwode, which had significant success in arranging for the release of Nationalists held by the Republic and in encouraging Negrín to maintain a moratorium on executions. Unfortunately, the mission had considerably less success in their dealings with the authorities in Burgos, which prevaricated, reneged on *quid pro quo* exchanges, and continued to execute enemy prisoners tried by summary courts martial.[3] Marcel Junod of the International Red Cross had experienced the same problems on the northern front in 1936–7. On one occasion, having secured the release of 130 women ('all of whom belonged to the Spanish aristocracy') from the Basque authorities in Bilbao, on the word of one Count Vallelliano (the head of the Red Cross in the Francoist zone) that the action would be reciprocated, Junod was unable to persuade the Nationalists to respect the agreement. At a gala dinner to celebrate the rescue of the women from Bilbao, the Swiss doctor demanded to know when he could expect to receive the Basque women in exchange. When it became clear that Vallellanio had no intention of complying with the terms of the arrangement, in front of the illustrious guests, the following dialogue ensued:

'Am I to understand that you have no word of honour?'
'We have, but the Reds haven't.'
'I am beginning to believe that the real caballeros [gentlemen] are at Bilbao and not at Burgos.'[4]

The British Chargé d'Affaires in Barcelona, John Leche, who had been responsible for arranging prisoner exchanges, was equally disgusted by the failure of the Nationalists to honour promises made, and by their indifference to the well-being of the mass of their own followers trapped in the Republican zone. In a memorandum to Lord Halifax, he wrote of his 'regret' that he had been invariably disappointed by those 'who doubtless pride themselves on their superior education and gentlemanly qualities'. In conclusion, he suggested the Foreign Office might invite the Nationalists to 'Treat me with the same courtesy and consideration as that which I get at the hands of the "Reds" and exercise a little humanity in favour of their supporters.'[5]

The behaviour of the rebels throughout the negotiations on the mutual release of prisoners was simply a reflection of the sense of entitlement of those who had ruled the country for so long. Spain was their property, and they were not bound by the same standards that they demanded of others. Junod also recalled a meeting with the Nationalist high command when he first broached the idea of an exchange of hostages. A tight-lipped General Mola responded rather bizarrely, 'How can you expect us to exchange a caballero for a red dog?'[6]

Quite apart from the ethical conduct of the two sides in the conflict, it is clear that the Republicans felt compelled by their international isolation to respond more positively to initiatives from London or Paris, while the Nationalists, who enjoyed the material support of the Italians and Germans, felt no such pressure. Attitudes to prisoner exchanges mirrored the reactions to Anglo-French calls via the Non-Intervention Committee for the withdrawal of foreign troops from Spain. While the Republicans disbanded the International Brigades in the autumn of 1938, the Italians continued to deploy replacements for troops lost in action. In an unfortunate intervention on 19 December 1938, Prime Minister Chamberlain told the House of Commons, 'it cannot be denied that, according to the information of the Government, a certain amount of assistance has been given in men and material to *both** sides in recent months, and on General Franco's side some of this assistance appears to have come from Italy.'[7] Following a visit from Spanish Ambassador Pablo de Azcárate the next day, the Undersecretary of State for Foreign Affairs was forced to issue a rectification in the House, and to admit that he was 'glad' to confirm that the government side at least was complying with the agreement.[8]

The aristocratic Chetwode, a highly decorated officer who may have been expected to sympathise with the military rebellion, was dismayed by the brutality of the Nationalists and informed Lord Halifax: 'I can hardly describe the horror that I have conceived of Spain since my interview with Franco three days ago. He is worse than the Reds.' He also complained that Franco failed to keep his word, and when he finally conceded to Chetwode's demands that he honour an agreement to release Republican prisoners in exchange for insurgent sympathisers already transferred to the Nationalist zone, 'nearly half of them

---

* Once more, the italics are mine. Chamberlain cynically refused to distinguish between *both* sides, regardless of the evidence before him.

were not the people he had promised to release but criminals who had been in jail, many of them since before the war started.'[9] Constancia de la Mora, of the Foreign Press Bureau, was given the responsibility of entertaining Lady Chetwode, who had accompanied her husband. De la Mora claims her guest appeared surprised that they had been lodged in extremely elegant quarters in Barcelona rather than in a tent; that 'our ruffians had not stripped the palace where she was staying of all its valuables'; and that the Republican officers who had received these honoured British visitors spoke excellent English and 'had good manners'.[10]

The commission was compelled to ask the Republic not to publicise its own clemency lest the 'comparison of Republican liberality and nationalist brutality' undermine the public relations exercise.[11] On the other hand, its liaison officer with the Republicans, Denys Cowan, was able to open a new channel of communication with the Negrín government, which might be used to orchestrate some type of mediation. Over the following months he also held meetings with Casado and his entourage.

British Ambassador Sir Henry Chilton, a sympathiser with the Nationalist cause, having left Madrid in the summer of 1936, had then refused to return to the capital and had taken up residence in Hendaye on the French border. In the months leading up to his retirement he took personal leave, and in his absence it was left to Chargé d'Affaires Ralph Skrine Stevenson to liaise with the Republican authorities. In the first ten days of February 1939 there were significant contacts between the Republican government and British diplomats on the border between Spain and France. On 2 February Stevenson held talks with Dr Negrín, at which the Prime Minister reiterated his demand for a guarantee based on his three conditions for peace. Crucially, he added that 'said guarantee should be that of the United States of America, France and the United Kingdom.' He further added that since Franco would reject any offer made by the Republican government, it would be necessary for London (or Paris) to put forward the proposal. Stevenson concluded his report to the Foreign Office with a warning that, 'unless some considerable effort for peace is made now the last stage of this war will be one of horror and tragedy.'[12]

Four days later Stevenson met with del Vayo and Jules Henry, the French Ambassador. The British diplomat informed the Spanish minister that the British agent in Burgos had approached Franco with a plan for the cessation of hostilities based on the guarantees required by Negrín. Del Vayo responded with a promise to consult Negrín on the initiative and raised the issue of the evacuation of Republican leaders whose lives would be in danger should they surrender. In his account of the meeting, Stevenson wrote, 'French Ambassador and I both said the Governments which we represented would consider the matter sympathetically.'[13] Ten days later, in a conversation with Ambassador Azcárate in London, the Permanent Undersecretary, Sir Alexander Cadogan, contradicted this report. Arguing diplomatic complications arising from the fact that Negrín and del Vayo had met with Stevenson on French soil, that the Spanish government was dispersed and that the President had taken refuge in France, he claimed that the British 'had hesitated to pass on the conditions to Burgos' until some days later.[14] Azcárate appeared to accept this justification for the standard Foreign Office policy of prevarication.

In a feature article in April 1938, the *Manchester Guardian* identified Franco's three great allies as 'Germany, Italy and non-intervention'.[15] Apart from the brave, if necessarily limited, contribution of Mexico, the Republic could only count on the assistance of the Soviet Union. And Stalin's support had come at a price. From the mid-1930s he had backed the political strategy of the Popular Front as part of his foreign policy aim of collective security against Germany and had instructed national Communist leaders to form alliances with 'bourgeois' parties to demonstrate his commitment to the defence of democratic systems against the Nazi threat. With the outbreak of the Civil War in Spain, and to counter the intervention of Hitler, Mussolini and the authors of Non-Intervention, he supplied weapons and military experts, but insisted the Madrid government transfer its gold reserves to Moscow as payment/collateral. At the end of October 1936 the Republic subsequently delivered approximately 510 tons of gold to a value of $518 million (75% of its reserves – the fifth largest in the world).[16]

Meanwhile, as a select team of expert pilots, tank crews and military training staff joined the Republican war effort and made a crucial difference at Madrid, the Third International (*Comintern*) also organised the recruitment of the International Brigades. However, in return, Stalin treated Spain as if it were a Soviet front. Russian secret service agents were allowed extensive authority within the Republic to purge anti-Stalinists, who were unwaveringly denounced as both fascists and Trotskyists. The activities of such NKVD and GRU* operatives as Alexander Orlov and Walter Krivitsky (who both later defected to the West) caused bitter resentment. The most high-profile cases involved the abduction, torture and elimination of Andreu Nin (leader of the anti-Stalinist POUM and former Councillor for Justice in the Catalan government)[17] and the disappearance of José Robles, which led to the famous rift between his friend and colleague, John Dos Passos, and Ernest Hemingway.[18]

As the Republic sank inexorably towards defeat, so Stalin's commitment to the cause waned. He had failed to achieve his political and strategic aims, and

---

*   Soviet secret intelligence services.

after his defection, Krivitsky wrote of the Soviet leader, 'He played his game boldly against the independence of the Spanish people, but feebly against Franco. He succeeded in murderous intrigue, but failed in waging war [...] All he got out of the adventure was a pile of Spanish gold.'[19]

The closure of the French border and the Nationalist blockade of the Republican ports exacerbated the supply crisis, and by the winter of 1938–39 Negrín was left to bemoan what might have happened had Soviet weapons been available at the Ebro or in Catalonia. At the national level, as the unity of Negrín's Socialist Party (PSOE) was tested by his determination to continue the struggle, it was the PCE that provided him with the assistance and structure, without which he had no authority. Nevertheless, Communist support was a double-edged sword.

Chapter 10

The end may justify the means as long as there is something that justifies the end

The role of the Spanish Communist Party

On 17 November 1938 the Civil Governor of Alicante, the Socialist Ricardo Mella, informed the chief of the *Carabineros* (the elite frontier and coastal police force) of an impending Communist uprising and requested the support of the corps in the defence of the Republic. He also notified the military authorities, which subsequently confined all troops to barracks. On the other hand, and for obvious reasons, he did not share his intelligence with the Communist officers in command of the Assault Guards and the Coastal Service. In Elche, there were three arrests of members of the PCE and in Novelda machine-gun posts were set up to defend an armaments factory.[1]

Mella was the victim (or perpetrator) of a hoax. There was no evidence of Communist plans to seize power, and more significantly, neither Stalin nor the PCE had any interest in destabilising the Negrín government. The ploy was, however, symptomatic of a new climate of anti-Communism that would prove to be a vital factor in the final disintegration of the Republic. The ideologically consistent and coherent fear of Communism by the right needs no explanation. On his attitude to the Spanish Civil War, Churchill wrote, 'Naturally I was not in favour of the Communists. How could I be, when if I had been a Spaniard they would have murdered me and my family and my friends?'[2]

The more complex issue was the anti-Communism of the left and the divisions that it caused. The theory and practice of the Communist Party and its unswerving loyalty to Stalin automatically alienated the libertarian Anarchist movement. The CNT-FAI did not disguise their resentment at the suppression of the militia in favour of a Popular Army that was based on conventional military protocols and discipline, and a hierarchical unified command. The divisions were exacerbated by the repression of revolutionary politics in Aragón and Catalonia in 1937, in particular the dismantlement of the *Consejo de Aragón* (Council of Aragón)*, the most revolutionary of the social experiments in Republican territory in the first months of the war, and the suppression of the POUM amid the street fighting in Barcelona in May. The breach was consolidated by the impunity with which Stalin's agents ruthlessly repressed 'unreliable' elements on the left.

The distrust towards the Communist Party was shared by liberal Republicans and many in the PSOE who defended social reform within the context of western democratic principles as laid out in the constitution of 1931. Their willingness to work with the PCE was based on an awareness that in the second half of the 1930s, the greater enemy was fascism. Nevertheless, as the situation in the Republic deteriorated, so resentment against Communist influence grew. On the same day that the Civil Governor ordered measures to pre-empt a fictional Communist coup d'état, Gómez Serrano wrote in his diary: 'We are fed up with the communist tyranny and its proselytising in all social areas, and in all branches of the state, especially in the armed forces.' He complained that the Communists harassed those who resisted their interpretations of history and were a danger both to well-meaning citizens whose only aim was to be loyal servants of the Republic, and to the political cohesion of those who defended it. He insisted, 'For these people, anyone who has an attitude to war policy that differs from that of those who bear the hammer and sickle are capitulators.'[3]

However justified the acrimony of some, and legitimate fear of others, they should not detract from the contribution of the PCE to the war effort. Regardless of the attitudes and machinations of Soviet leaders and agents, the bravery and discipline of the Communist rank and file had been decisive in the defence of the Republic. It was the legendary 5th Regiment, built around volunteers from the PCE and JSU, that inspired the creation of a Popular Army to militarise the groups of *milicianos* and which produced such inspirational leaders as Juan 'Modesto' Guilloto León, Enrique Líster and Valentín González ('*El Campesino*' – 'the Peasant'). In the early months of the war, party membership rose dramatically among those who may not have identified with its Marxist ideology and goals but nonetheless recognised that the Communists were the most resolute and organised in their resistance to the Nationalists. The PCE also gained the unlikely support of small businessmen and farmers who rallied to their defence of personal property against the revolutionary collectivisation/socialisation strategies of the anarcho-syndicalists, supported by a significant sector of the UGT. In the words of Burnett Bolloten:

---

* The correct/complete name of the Council was *Consejo Regional de Defensa de Aragón* – Aragón Defence Regional Council.

the Communist Party appeared before the distraught middle-classes not only as a defender of property, but as a champion of the Republic and of orderly processes of government [...] They were ready to support it as long as it offered them protection and helped to restore to the government the power assumed by revolutionary committees.[4]

By March 1937 Secretary-General José Díaz was able to claim the number of affiliates had risen to a quarter of a million (not including the autonomous PSUC* in Catalonia) and that more than 50% of the members were serving in the armed forces of the Republic.[5] According to Viñas, from a pre-war figure of 22,500, membership had risen to almost 350,000 by the end of 1937.[6] Historian Mary Vincent described the development of the PCE as a mass party, 'through an avowed and public policy of shoring up the Popular Front, emphasising the legal basis of the Republic, and defending private property, particularly in the countryside'.[7] The party thus gave hope to those who wished to recover the parts of the economy that had come under the control of revolutionary committees, particularly (but far from exclusively) in Aragón and Catalonia. In Alicante, apart from agriculture, the most affected sectors were the textile and metal industries in Alcoy and the shoe-making industry throughout the province.

Díaz had indeed renounced the dictatorship of the proletariat and social revolution, and instead had advocated for a modest political programme of 'democracy with a social content', which envisaged the dismantlement of semi-feudal economic and social structures in rural Spain, the revocation of the remaining privileges enjoyed by the Catholic Church, military reform, and the regulation of the financial oligarchies. Crucially, against the background of civil war, he warned against experiments that sought 'to build the future, while ignoring the present'. His resolve that all social reform be subordinated to military priorities carried the warning that any achievements of the left would otherwise be destroyed 'like a house of cards under the jackboot of militarism and fascism'.[8]

Quite apart from the support of the USSR (the International Brigades, Polikarpov fighters, '*Katiuska*' bombers and the legendary T-26 tanks), the contribution of the Communist Party to the war effort was vast. It played a huge role in the formation of the Popular Army and in transforming the fighting capacity of the Republic from highly effective but anti-militarist urban guerrilla units into a conventional army that defied Franco, Hitler and

---

* Partit Socialista Unificat de Catalunya (Unified Socialist Party of Catalonia). In effect, the Communist Party of Catalonia.

Mussolini for two years. Even Churchill was impressed. In an article published in 1937, he wrote: 'Communists, Anarchists and ordinary folk who support the government alike have been woven into a disciplined army [...] which has a coherent entity, a strict organization and a hierarchy of command.'[9]

Some 50,000 members of the Communist Party were lost in the battles for Málaga, Santander and Asturias. A quarter of the members of the party in Madrid (between 17,000 and 20,000 of a total of approximately 70,000) disappeared at the Ebro and in Catalonia.[10] And yet it was precisely the identification of the Communists with Negrín's policy of resistance at all costs that proved so reciprocally damaging to both the strategy and the party. 'Communist' or 'Communist lackey' became a slur applied to anyone on the left whom opponents wished to discredit, and, in particular, who was in favour of prolonging the war.

The argument that Negrín was a Communist fellow traveller focused essentially on his dependency on the PCE and the impact this had on his leadership. The most damaging argument against him in left-wing circles was the fact that he had turned a blind eye to the activities of Soviet NKVD agents, sanctioned the suppression of the anti-Stalinist POUM and overlooked the ruthless murder of Andreu Nin (or at the very least blithely accepted the implausible Stalinist version of the episode).

Of special interest in this case is the testimony of Jesús Hernández Tomás, Minister of Education and Health until May 1938, then political commissar of the Centre-South army group, and leading member of the PCE in the capital, and eventually 'premature' anti-Stalinist. His memoirs reveal a deep personal antagonism towards the hierarchy of the PCE following his failure to succeed as Secretary-General when José Díaz died in 1942, and his eventual expulsion from the party. Nevertheless, his account of Nin's abduction, torture and murder, and the fatuous attempts at a cover-up, is undoubtedly more accurate than other, more official versions that suggested that Nin had been kidnapped by the Gestapo. He concluded: 'Orlov's men had set up a police apparatus as if they were the lords of a conquered territory.'[11] However, despite Negrín's enforced inclination to excuse Soviet transgressions in the interests of a bigger picture, Hernández claims that the new Prime Minister was in fact extremely anxious to discover the fate of the POUM leader and complained himself that the 'Soviet Police [...] behaved as if they were on home soil, and lacked the courtesy even to inform the Spanish authorities of the detention of Spanish citizens.'[12]

The anti-Negrín lobby also encouraged conspiracy theories involving his appointment as Prime Minister in May 1937. Although the decision was the responsibility of the President, Manuel Azaña (Republican Left), who at no point was suspected of any sympathy towards Marxism or the USSR, it is widely believed that Azaña would have chosen Indalecio Prieto, had the latter not acknowledged that he lacked support from the left of his own party and outside the PSOE. Furthermore, Preston suggests, the Communists had made it known they preferred Negrín.[13] Hernández went so far as to describe the doctor as the 'Kremlin's candidate'.[14] According to the Soviet intelligence officer Walter Krivitsky, he had been told the previous November by Arthur Stashevsky, the 'Commercial Attaché' at the Soviet Embassy in Moscow, that Negrín would be the next Prime Minister. After his defection, Krivitsky wrote that unlike Largo Caballero, who was 'a genuine radical, a revolutionary idealist', Negrín 'had all the makings of a bureaucratic politician [...] just the type to suit Stalin's need'. He also saw the new Prime Minister as 'a good façade to show to Paris and London and Geneva*', and a man who would 'impress the outside world with the "sanity" and "propriety" of the Spanish republican cause; he would frighten nobody by revolutionary remarks'. Most importantly, having come to terms with the calamitous Anglo-French policy of Non-Intervention, Negrín was aware he could not indulge personal qualms or misapprehension about dealing with the Soviet dictator: 'He was ready to go along with Stalin in everything, sacrificing all other considerations to secure [Soviet] aid.'[15]

Nor did his detractors overlook the fact that Negrín spoke Russian and was married to a Russian. In 1914 he had married Maria Fidelman Brodsky Mijailova, the daughter of a Jewish Ukranian businessman, who had fled the pogroms and settled in Germany. Nevertheless, they had separated in the mid-1920s, long before Negrín's involvement in government (divorce was only legalised under the Republic).

Finally, Negrín's opponents pointed to his role in the transfer of the gold reserves to Moscow during his term as Minister of Finance in the Largo Caballero government (July 1936–May 1937). However, the government was collectively aware of the conditions imposed by Non-Intervention and collectively responsible for the decision. In Negrín's own words: 'Negrín proposes the sending; Caballero orders it; Prieto executes the order; Azaña sanctions it.'[16]

Negrín was not a Communist; he was not even on the left of his own Socialist party. Nor was he an 'agent of Moscow'. He was a liberal and a democrat. He was also an eminent scientist, a polyglot, urbane and charming, dynamic and steadfast in his approach to challenges facing the Republic. He did not choose either the Soviets or the PCE as his allies, but above all else

---

* i.e. the League of Nations.

he was aware that the survival of the Republic depended on their support. Analysing the role of the Communists, Hispanist Gerald Brenan later wrote: 'Thanks to the Anglo-French policy of non-intervention they had in the Russian arms a lever which never failed, for whatever private inclinations the Socialist and Republican ministers might have, they knew that a breach with Stalin would mean the rapid loss of the war.'[17] On the other hand, it is also true that while Negrín understandably blamed the Paris and London governments for his reluctant dependence on the USSR, he also freely acknowledged the decisive contribution of the PCE to the defence of the Republic and in the restructuring of its military forces.

In October 1938 Negrín held a dinner for Ralph Skrine Stevenson (the new British Chargé d'Affaires in Barcelona), John Leche (his predecessor), and Howard Denys Russell Cowan (liaison officer of the Chetwode Commission).

According to Stevenson's report of the evening, the Prime Minister gave a 'frank exposition of his attitude in regard to communism', and argued that it 'was not an ideology which suited the Spanish people'. On the other hand, he argued that 'the Government had had to rely to a considerable extent on the Communist Party, not only because it was the best organised force in the early stages of the civil war but because Russia had been the only country which had given the Spanish Government really effective assistance.' He further argued that 'he could and would suppress [the influence] of the Communist Party in a week if he could obtain requisite supplies from France and England.'[18] His guests were equally aware that this was an easy challenge to make; a hypothesis that Negrín knew could never be tested. Nonetheless, he later affirmed that in his capacity as Minister of Defence (5 April 1938–6 March 1939), he was the only minister who did not appoint a single Communist to the command of armies or army groups. Instead, he selected military professionals – including Casado.[19] He further asserted that he appointed fewer Communists to positions of authority within the armed forces than either of his predecessors (Largo Caballero and Prieto) and dismissed the accusations of the latter that he handed over the most important resources of power to the PCE as 'gratuitous and unbecoming'.[20]

In February 1939 the Republic was facing military meltdown. Resistance was a short-term strategy that could only be sustained with the support of the Communists. Crucially, at the meeting with the High Command at Los Llanos, it was abundantly clear that the military leaders were both anti-Negrín and anti-Communist. Furthermore, they saw no need to make a distinction.

Chapter 11

Red sunset

The situation in Alicante

The fall of Barcelona increased the strategic importance of Alicante, and, more ominously, released the Italian air force to extend its operations on the coastal area between Valencia and Almeria. As the cordon tightened on the Centre-South Zone, so the population of Alicante became fractured between the unconditional supporters of the Republic, which included the Communists, the non-communist anti-fascists who maintained their loyalty to the Republic but were unhappy with the role of the Communist Party, the fifth column that was preparing for the day of 'liberation' but maintained a loosely veiled anonymity, and a huge number of people who understood that Franco's victory would not bring peace, but nonetheless yearned for an end to the fighting and the hunger, and many of whom would become last-minute fifth columnists.

On 1 February, for some undisclosed motive, General Miaja, the highest military authority in the Valencia zone, had used his powers under martial law to order the collection (removal) of radio sets from private homes. It was assumed by Gómez Serrano that the measure was designed to prevent people from listening to enemy broadcasts. However, given the shortage of paper and consequent reduction in the size (one or two pages) and circulation of newspapers, it also meant that the population was starved of news in general and denied access to war bulletins from the Republican government. The immediate effect would be to increase the spread of rumours and misleading fifth column–inspired propaganda. The radios were returned to their owners a fortnight later.[1]

Even in the face of impending defeat, life managed to retain a level of normalcy. The bars and restaurants remained open, though only until 7pm. Shops and offices were forced to adopt a more northern European timetable and close at 5pm. The power supply was erratic. In some towns and villages, households enjoyed electricity for only two hours a day. In Alicante, Governor Ricardo Mellá prohibited the use of electrical appliances (including heating) and ordered the restriction of domestic consumption to lighting. Given the lack of coal and other fuels, people first chopped down pines, and then olive and almond trees. For much of the war, the town had resolutely maintained its entertainment sector (nightclubs, music halls, cabaret, theatres), but energy restrictions eventually reduced the leisure options. The concerts of the municipal band were curtailed by conscription.

In September 1938 the *Teatro Principal*, the administration of which had been taken over by the Socialist Union UGT on the outbreak of war, abandoned its programme of reviews and *zarzuelas* (light operas) and operated exclusively as a picture house.[2] Four cinemas (*Central, Monumental, Salón España* and the *Teatro Principal*) did manage to continue showing films. Deprived of other amusements, the audiences were at least able to enjoy such Hollywood classics as *Doorway to Hell* (1930) starring James Cagney, *Now I'll Tell* (1934) with Spencer Tracy, *Enter Madame* (1935) with Cary Grant and *Wedding Night* (1935) with Gary Cooper.[3] Over the war, the vast majority of films shown in Alicante were feature films, mostly from the US. Distribution was dominated by the Hollywood giants: MGM, Hispano Fox, Paramount, Universal, Warner Bros., Columbia, United Artists. In the period 1938–39, Alicante cinemas showed more than 200 US productions and only forty-one Spanish films.[4]

Churches, on the other hand, were still closed. Some were used as warehouses, and those practising Catholics who wished to attend mass had no choice but to arrange private, clandestine services. A particular ramshackle property used by one priest, Father Belda, to receive his congregation became known as the *Catedral de la Rambla.*[*]

As the black market prospered, legal action was brought against individuals speculating in diverse products: vegetables (especially onions and chard), oil, *alpargatas*, cement and indigo.[5] The tram and local rail services were also severely restricted and streetlighting suspended.[6] There was a chronic scarcity of basic resources such as petrol, medicines and medical supplies in general. However, the most difficult hardship for the population to endure was the continuing shortage of food; by the end of March, refugees swelled the population to 100,000. Cooking oil had long since been a luxury, and meat was virtually unobtainable. In the first three months of the year, a total of two cows, twelve pigs and 193 horses were slaughtered at the municipal abattoir.[7]

Prices rose dramatically, even for the ubiquitous lentils. The only compensation for those being overcharged was that the Republican paper money would soon be worth little more than the paper it was printed on. When Gómez Serrano drove to Santa Pola to buy fish from the local trawlermen, he found abundant supplies but no one willing to sell them for Republican

---

[*] The Rambla is the street running from the market area of the town down to the port.

cash. Instead, he had to barter with cigarettes.[8] The popular unrest at the inadequacy, poor quality and erratic supply of bread rations was intensified when Nationalist pilots dropped loaves of white bread on the town instead of bombs.[9] The loaves were wrapped in bags decorated with the colours of the monarchist/Nationalist flag and carrying a message to the population: 'This is the daily bread in Franco's Spain'.[10]

There is evidence that, in relative terms, the war industry fared better in the province than agriculture. Apart from the obvious relocation of plants from areas close to the frontlines to the comparative safety of Alicante, some local manufacturers also helped the war effort by switching from their traditional production lines to weapons, ammunitions and parts that were crucial to maintaining a military capability. Reports compiled by historians José Miguel Santacreu Soler and Fernando Quilis Tauriz suggest that, at the turn of the year, the local arms industry employed nearly 10,000 people and was turning out 1,824,000 Mauser bullets a day, 876,000 cartridges, 5,000 grenades or 650 anti-tank shells. One former toy factory in Ibi produced 115,000 7.62mm and 30,000 9mm bullets per day and had a stockpile of more than two million when Franco's army arrived. The plant in Rabasa was still producing Hispano-Suiza E34 aircraft.[11] Nonetheless, it was clear to all that the domestic weapons industry had little more than a symbolic value while the Republic remained unable to access the consignments of weapons blocked by the French government. Despite Negrín's insistent references to these supplies, it was also evident to all that no further arms supplies would be forthcoming.

The diminishing number of targets also meant the *alicantinos* had to deal with the increasing frequency of air raids. On 4 February they suffered the first night-time attack in seven months. There were another thirteen attacks over the next seven weeks. In total, over the entire war, there were between seventy and seventy-three recorded air raids,[12] which made Alicante the fourth most frequently targeted city after Madrid, Barcelona and Valencia. Approximately 400 people lost their life, the majority of them in the attack on the marketplace in May 1938.

The fighting was over in more than 60% of the national territory. Much of the population had by now become accustomed, or was at least adapting, to the reality of the 'New Spain'. Tens of thousands of Republican supporters or soldiers had been executed, incarcerated, or put to work in forced labour camps. Many of those in the occupied or 'invaded' zones whose dubious political past placed them in imminent danger took the precaution of joining the Nationalist army or the *Falange*. By the end of the war nearly a million adult and adolescent females had joined the *Sección Feminina* (Women's Section of the *Falange*), the aim of which was to train young ladies to be good patriots, good Christians and good wives. Those Basque and Catalan children who spoke Euskera or Catalan at home were learning not to speak their native language in front of figures of authority (policemen, *guardias civiles*, bureaucrats, doctors, teachers, etc.). The urban middle classes who had prudently adopted a more 'proletarian' attire, now reasserted their status through the diligent use of ties and hats. Schoolchildren were trained in the use of the fascist salute and taught to sing the *Falange* anthem, *Cara al Sol* (Face to the Sun). The Catholic Church was restored to its former power and glory. And the press celebrated the diplomatic victories of Hitler and Mussolini over the decadent governments in London and Paris.

The population of Alicante was fully aware of the consequences of the impending defeat and the future that awaited them. Despair and fear were virtually synonymous. Gómez Serrano, who could not be accused of over-identifying with the cause of Negrín, nevertheless wrote on 20 February: 'I have no doubt that they are negotiating a human end to the war: a peaceful transfer of power, without reprisals. Our enemies, bloated with the arrogance of borrowed victories, demand capitulation, pure and simple, but that cannot be.' On the choices that remained, he wrote:

> I cannot come to terms with the need to go into exile. And yet without doubt there will be no choice. Even should the surrender which ends the war guarantee the property and safety of the republicans. Because in the first weeks there will be '*extra-legal justice*' which will seek to get rid of people who are in the way, a '*cleansing*' of this hotbed of '*reds*', while the government makes a song and dance proclaiming its innocence in all such excesses, which it will '*clamp down on*' ... once the work is done.[13]

The *Diputado* also describes the trials and tribulations of arranging for his and his family's departure despite the advantages arising from his position and standing. Passports were issued by the offices of the Civil Governor and required the endorsement of the Military Governor. Gómez Serrano also needed visas from the Mexican consulate before he could apply to the French consulate for transit visas. Finally, he needed the authorisation of the Emigration Inspectorate. Each passport would cost him a total of 172.60 pesetas. Even then, he realised, he would be missing two essentials: foreign currency and a means of travel. In the case of the latter, the Nationalists had controlled the Portuguese border since the first months of the war, and since the fall of Catalonia, the land route to France was also closed to the Republicans. The only possibilities left were by air (for a privileged few) and by sea.

Ángel Pascual Devesa was also weighing up the options and struggling to choose between the anguish of exile and the inherent peril of remaining in a new hostile Spain. He later wrote:

> I considered the matter: the fear of leaving and the fear of staying here. Each alternative had inducements. The victors would want to resolve the animosity that had been building in three years of fighting, and victory would give them the occasion ... No, victory is always generous, victors tend to resolve their anger through magnanimity ... And between brothers! ... But it is sensible to buffer the first encounter, to prevent violence. It would be wise to disappear for a time, even for a short while. And it hurt having to abandon my land when we are on the brink of peace, the calm of a transparent lake asleep in the sun ... Three years of constant anguish, danger, grief, pain; and now with the advent of peace, peace! to leave this beloved place, so much a part of me and I so much a part of it ... No, no! The conflict is over, enough is enough, *post nubile, Febo*.[14]

Chapter 12

One Munich was not enough

Britain and France recognise Franco

On 27 February 1939 the British and French governments concurrently recognised Franco's government. According to an entry in the diaries of Sir Alexander Cadogan, the decision had been taken as early as 15 February. When informed that the government was still seeking concessions from Franco, he wrote, 'Cabinet seem to have agreed in principle to recognition of Franco, but want, if possible, to get some assurances (about reprisals) first. Don't mind this, so long as it doesn't delay recognition.'[1] Although a bitter disappointment to those who supported the Republic, the decision in itself was little more than the anticipated culmination of a policy founded in the spirit of appeasement and formalised in the Non-Intervention Committee set up in London in September 1936. Chamberlain would no doubt have been pleased to read the reports from Burgos of a speech by Franco, in which he declared, 'The hour of truth has come. Today England recognised us. Tomorrow it will be the whole world.'[2] The fascist powers, Germany and Italy, had recognised the rebels in November 1936 and the Vatican followed suit in May 1938. However, the *Caudillo*'s prophesy was not entirely accurate. Mexico and the USSR did not restore full diplomatic relations with Spain until 1977, after his demise.

Recognition was not a mistake. It was too late to be a mistake. It made absolute sense for the government in London to seek friendly relations with the regime it had done so much to install. If Chamberlain was willing to do business with Hitler and Mussolini, it made no sense not to do the same with Franco. The French governments of Blum and Daladier, on the other hand, were more aware of the damage done to western European security but lacked the confidence to assert an independent foreign policy. Believing that British support was crucial for the defence of France, they allowed themselves to be intimidated by threats from London of a unilateral strategy.

Nevertheless, as Churchill pointed out in an article published days before the decision was announced, recognition should have come at a price. Using (not for the last time) the expression 'blood, sweat and tears' to refer to the suffering of the Spanish people, he argued that the French and British 'would certainly be entitled at this juncture to use the lever of Recognition to procure merciful treatment for the beaten side'.³ The government policy led to fierce debates in the House of Commons on the last two days of February. In his statement to the House, Chamberlain argued that as General Franco was now 'in control of the greater part of Spanish territory', as there could be 'no doubt of the ultimate issue of the struggle', and as the Republican authorities were 'scattered', it was no longer possible to regard Negrín's government as the 'Sovereign Government of Spain'.

He further expressed his satisfaction that Franco had offered public guarantees of his own resolve to maintain Spanish independence and to ensure proceedings were only taken in the case of 'those against whom criminal charges are laid'.⁴ That any leader would proclaim their determination to uphold the independence of their nation and that Franco reserved the right under the Law of Political Responsibility to undertake legal action against anyone he deemed unfavourable to his own cause were inconvenient truths that Chamberlain, trained in the art of guileful self-delusion, found easy to overlook. An exasperated member of the opposition breached protocol and demanded he 'be impeached as a traitor to Britain'. When asked if he had received assurances that foreign troops would be withdrawn, the Prime Minister replied, 'Certain assurances have been received, but the recognition is unconditional.'

Before the session was closed, the government was asked to make a statement on the Nationalist air attack against the British ship SS *Stanbrook* on 21 January. The Undersecretary of State, R.A. Butler, confirmed that the vessel had come under attack when in international waters, seven miles off the Barcelona coast. Nationalist aircraft had dropped a total of twenty-four bombs, none of which had hit their target. In response to an official protest to the Burgos authorities, Butler acknowledged that, 'We have had no satisfaction.'

The first effect of recognition was the resignation of President Manuel Azaña. In fact, the Anglo-French submission to Franco was a convenient pretext. By refusing to return to Spain since he crossed the Pyrenees at the beginning of the month, Azaña had already abdicated his responsibilities. On 25 February, aware of the impending announcements from Paris and London, he had abandoned the French capital and settled into a rented house at Collonges-sous-Salève close to the Swiss border. From here, two days later, without notifying Negrín, he sent formal notice of his resignation to Martínez Barrio, President of the Cortes.

In the letter, he argued that he no longer enjoyed the judicial authority required to execute his functions and that the disappearance of the State apparatus made it impossible for him to continue.[5] Zugazagoitia was shown a photograph of Azaña, taken by a member of the press corps at the conference he had called to announce his decision. The now former President of the Republic was wearing the huge, optimistic smile of a man relieved of all his tasks and obligations.[6]

On the other hand, under the terms of Article 74 of the 1931 Constitution, it now fell to the President of the Cortes to assume the functions of an interim presidency pending the election of a new head of state. This was a poisoned chalice that Martínez Barrio, also now residing in France, was understandably reluctant to accept unless he could impose conditions. The 'conservative' Republican (a founding member of *Unión Republicana* – Republican Union) had been Prime Minister under the Second Republic and, curiously, had already served as interim President once before (April–May 1936). For a few hours during the coup d'état (18–19 July 1936), he had also acted again as Prime Minister. In a vain attempt to stall the military insurrection, he had called General Mola, the initial rebel leader, in Pamplona. According to his own account, he appealed to Mola's love of Spain and his sense of duty, to beg him to stand down and 'avoid the horrors of civil war'. Mola responded: 'The government you have been called upon to form will fail; if you manage to form a government, it will not last long; and, rather than a solution, it will only have served to make the situation worse.'[7] It is possible these words still haunted him. In any case, although the absence of the President was used by the British to justify the recognition of Franco, and by Negrín's opponents to highlight the fragility of his authority and hold on power, the resolution of the constitutional crisis was soon overtaken by events in Madrid.

The resignation of the President represented an enormous, if symbolic, blow to Negrín. Throughout the Second Republic, as Prime Minister, in opposition, and finally as President, Azaña had been the most eminent and prestigious leader of the left and the Republican movement. Despite their disagreements and personal animosity, his departure increased the Prime Minister's own vulnerability. In a sense, Azaña had made his farewell speech to the nation as early as July 1938, when he told an audience at the town hall in Barcelona:

> When the torch passes to other hands, to other men, to other generations, let them remember, if ever they feel their blood boil and the Spanish temper is once more infuriated with intolerance, hatred, and destruction, let them think of the dead, and listen to their lesson.[8]

On 28 February 1939, Clement Attlee, Leader of the Opposition, introduced a motion[9] in the Commons that denounced the decision to grant unconditional recognition to Spanish insurgent forces dependent upon foreign intervention as a deliberate affront to the legitimate government of a friendly power. The Prime Minister had little problem defending the outcome of his policy. Franco's victory precluded any alternative. Chamberlain's analysis of the military and political situation could hardly be questioned. He also argued in terms of expediency. Given the geopolitical importance of Spain in 1939, it made little sense to alienate Franco. He might have been speaking on behalf of the Churchill of 1940–41 when he asked, 'Might we not, by establishing friendly relations with him, secure that British interests shall not be jeopardised by anything which happens hereafter.' However, he diligently ignored the flaws of the foundation of appeasement/non-intervention upon which the policy was based and the desperate needs of the vanquished. The reality was that Chamberlain was in no position to make demands of the rebels. As Sir Archibald Sinclair, leader of the Liberal Party, told the House, 'The only possible excuse [...] for not imposing conditions is because the Government's policy has rendered them powerless to impose them, except [...] by going to war.'

On the issue of reprisals, the Prime Minister based his defence on a telegram received from the Burgos authorities on 22 February and which he proceeded to read aloud to the House:

Nationalist Spain has won the war, and it is therefore incumbent on the vanquished to surrender unconditionally. The patriotism, chivalry and generosity of the Caudillo, of which he has given so many examples in the liberated regions, and likewise the spirit of equity and justice that inspires all the National Government's actions, constitute a firm guarantee for all Spaniards who are not criminals.[10]

He also resorted to the standard response of those on the right who, in public, cynically implied that the Republicans were perpetrators of the worst violations of the basic rights of prisoners and the civilian population:

Bitter feelings were naturally aroused in the minds of those who heard terrible stories of what was done to those who were dear to them when they were in the power of those who were then their enemies. It would not be reasonable to ask General Franco to grant beforehand a complete amnesty which would include the men who had been guilty of such horrible crimes.

The violence of uncontrollable and disloyal Republican supporters, particularly at the outbreak of the war, could thus be used to downplay, if not justify, the crimes committed in the name of the insurgency and sanctioned by the authorities. Worse, it was now applied by Chamberlain to pre-empt protests against future breaches of promises that no reprisals would be taken against those Republicans innocent of crimes once the war was over. At the end of January, in private correspondence with a contact in the Foreign Office, the eminent Hispanist Gerald Brenan expressed the fear of many who had supported the Republic. Taking for granted that Franco would approve neither a mass evacuation nor a general amnesty on the grounds that such actions would entail the exoneration of those 'guilty of crimes', Brenan concluded, 'I imagine you know what that means. All who have taken up arms against him or assisted others to do so are technically guilty of a crime which may be punished by death.'[11]

Chamberlain was not mistaken in his denunciations of acts of violence perpetrated by Republican sympathisers. There are indeed copious documented accounts of atrocities carried out against members of the church, fifth columnists, and victims identified as class enemies.[12] The events in Catalonia and Aragón in the first nine months of the conflict are indicative of the level of violence the Anarchist movement was prepared to employ against its adversaries. To highlight the role of the Communist Party in the early repression, Francoist sympathisers point to the massacre of 2,000 Nationalist prisoners at Paracuellos (1936) and the chilling brutality of those who administered the *checas*, and those who ordered the *paseos* and *sacas*. Nor should we forget the purge of anti-Stalinist heretics by Soviet agents within the International Brigades and the Spanish Communist movement itself, and in particular the murder of Andreu Nin and the eradication of the POUM.

Nevertheless, not only is there an obvious quantitative difference between the repression on either side, there is also the fundamental issue that while the violence in the Republican zone was the result of the legal vacuum caused by the outbreak of war, the use of terror in the Nationalist zone was a cornerstone of the insurgents' strategy. At the outset of war, General Mola had famously informed a meeting of political leaders in the region of Navarre where he was based: 'It is necessary to spread terror. We have to create the impression of mastery, eliminating without scruples or hesitation all those who do not think as we do.'[13]

When the writer and intellectual Miguel de Unamuno made his famous protest at a meeting in Salamanca of military and civilian supporters of the rebellion (October 1936), and warned that, '*Venceréis, pero no convenceréis*' (You will win but you will not convince)[14], he misjudged the war aims of the insurgents. They had no need to persuade. They sought instead to control the country through the elimination of as many of the enemy as possible and the constant threat of violence. General Queipo de Llano, who seized control of Sevilla at the very beginning of the struggle, became famous for the harangues that he broadcast over the Nationalist radio and did not shy from encouraging the use of targeted rape as a means of repression. On 23 July 1936 he commended the spirit of Franco's African Army:

> Our brave *Legionarios* and *Regulares*˙ have shown the red cowards what it means to be a man. And incidentally the wives of the reds too. These Communist and anarchist women, after all, have made themselves fair game by their doctrine of free love. And now they have at least made the acquaintance of real men, not wimpish militiamen. Kicking their legs about and squealing won't save them.[15]

The levels of sexual violence against women on both sides is undocumented and there has been little research. Nevertheless, the complicity of officers and leaders, and even the incitement to use rape, was a feature of the Nationalist war strategy. In her psychological biography of Franco, the writer and historian Gabrielle Ashford Hodges wrote:

> like the Nazis in Germany, Nationalist Spain thus provided many perfectly ordinary people with a legal outlet for fundamentally criminal behavior. Franco facilitated a thrilling release for previously repressed impulses, either by suspending an individual sense of morality – supposedly for the "good" of the wider group – or, for those without an ethical code, removing the anxieties related to being caught. Murder, torture, rape and looting became acceptable because they were carried out on behalf of an idealized higher "authority".[16]

As the African Army advanced rapidly north towards Madrid, it left a trail of extreme cruelty and earned itself the title of '*columna de la muerte*' (column of death). Often opposed only by untrained militia, the column occupied town after town through Andalusia, Extremadura and Castilla, raping, looting and executing all those suspected of left-wing tendencies. Following the battle for Badajoz on 14 August 1936, the Nationalist troops were given leave to run amok through the town. When asked by journalists how many of the

---

˙ Soldiers of the Foreign Legion and the colonial army of mercenaries recruited from the indigenous population in Morocco.

local population (militia and civilians) had died, the commanding officer, Lieutenant-Colonel Juan Yagüe, responded that '2,000 was perhaps an excessive estimate of the number murdered.'[17] Spanish historian Francisco Espinosa Maestre has used what municipal records still exist to establish a number of at least 3,800 dead in the period of repression that followed the fall of the city. He describes the scene in Badajoz in the aftermath of the battle as apocalyptic: 'the cemetery was full of dead bodies either burned or piled up waiting to be burned.' He further denounces the repression as 'genocide and war-crime', and suggests that Yagüe would have faced charges before the War Crime Commission 'within the judicial context of post-war Europe, if the Allies had defeated fascism in Spain'.[18]

The officer class of the Nationalist army, their careers shaped in the fighting in North Africa, saw the Spanish peasants and urban working class in much the same way as they had viewed the indigenous population in North Africa, and treated them with the same level of brutality. In the words of historian Mary Vincent, 'The Army of Africa imported colonial war, "pacifying" newly conquered territories in ways long familiar to colonized peoples but new to the European mainland.'[19] Yagüe later acknowledged the extent of the slaughter to a *New York Herald Tribune* correspondent: 'Of course we shot them. What do you expect? Was I supposed to take 4,000 reds with me as my column advanced, racing against time? Was I expected to turn them loose in my rear and let them make Badajoz red again?'[20]

Having failed to take the capital in the autumn of 1936, Franco ordered an air offensive against the civilian population in areas loyal to the Republic. The people of Madrid were the first in Europe to experience this new dimension of total war. The attacks on Durango and Guernica soon followed (April 1937). Meanwhile, following the fall of Málaga in February 1937, the Canadian doctor Norman Bethune* had witnessed the bombing and strafing of refugees by the *Luftwaffe* as they fled eastwards in what he described as 'the crime of the road Málaga-Almería'. On their arrival in the port of Almería, Bethune wrote:

> the refugees were now gathered in the town within the space of a few blocks, where mass murder required a minimum number of bombs. Now Franco sated his thirst for revenge. The port did not matter. A port cannot think, nor defy Fascism, nor bleed. Only people have a brain, a heart, courage.[21]

---

* Bethune set up a mobile blood transfusion service that made a huge contribution in the treatment of troops wounded at the front.

The dichotomy in the nature of the violence in the two zones is admirably summarised in the words of Jesús de Galíndez, a Basque Nationalist, Republican and Catholic, who is quoted by Burnett Bolloten. Having explained (not justified, he insists) the bloodshed in Republican territory as the result of the judicial breakdown caused by the military uprising, the desertion of the forces of order to the Nationalists, and the indiscriminate arming of many sectors of society who could not be trusted with a weapon, he too laments the fact that 'the malefactors who exist in every city, in every nation, came to the surface, and found an easy field for their work.' However, he concludes:

> What cannot be explained, and even less justified, are the crimes, much greater in number and sadism, that were committed precisely by the army, by the police force, by those educated young gentlemen who lacked for nothing and who boasted of their Catholicism.'[22]

It is clear that the most savage atrocities occurred in the aftermath of battle, under the cloak of extended military operations. However, although the wrath of the Nationalists might be mitigated by pre-emptive surrender and the avoidance of battle, few people in Alicante doubted what lay in store. Indeed, Paul Preston argues that the more systematic and ruthless repression occurred in those areas where resistance to the insurgency was least effective.[23] Republican municipal officers, members of trade unions and left-wing parties, masons, unreliable intellectuals, and outspoken critics of the church and military were aware that however far the front still remained geographically, in terms of days and weeks, the enemy was now dangerously close to Alicante. In the month of February alone, the town was bombed eight times.[24]

On 28 February, following the debate in the House of Commons on the recognition of the Franco regime, Undersecretary of State at the Foreign Office, Sir Alexander Cadogan, made the following enigmatic reference to Chamberlain in his diary: 'Went at 6 to House to see P.M. He had "got away with it".'[25] In an earlier entry, on 16 February, Cadogan had written, 'Pray heaven, with any luck, "Spain" will be over soon.'[26] In Alicante on 28 February, Eliseo Gómez Serrano wrote in his own diary, 'What can we do against a whole world that rises against us?'[27] On 2 March the French government announced the appointment of Maréchal Philippe Pétain, the hero of Verdun, as the ambassador to Franco's newly recognised regime.

Chapter 13

The quickest way of ending a war is to lose it

Differing views on how to end the war

Enter Colonel Segismundo Casado López, Chief of the Army of the Centre. A career military officer, freemason and convinced Republican, he served in Africa in the 1920s, and after the fall of the monarchy, was posted to the presidential household guard. By the outbreak of the Civil War, he had reached the rank of major and subsequently returned to regular army duties. He saw action in the defence of Madrid, and at the battles of Jarama and Brunete, and was promoted to colonel. Following the fall of Catalonia, his authority in the capital was greatly enhanced by the absence of his superior, General Rojo, who had chosen to remain in France. On 23 February 1939, either by coincidence or prepped by forces within the PSOE, the Socialist daily newspaper *Avance* carried a hagiographic article featuring his achievements and qualities. It stressed he was not the member of any political party and described him as energetic, stern, disciplined and objective; an officer who enjoyed the absolute confidence of those who served under him, and whose presence in its ranks honoured the heroic Popular Army. His loyalty, the journalist was careful to clarify, was to the Republic.[1]

It is also true that Casado suffered a debilitating chronic stomach condition that caused him significant pain. Nonetheless, a cursory study of his memoirs reveals a man of great personal vanity, with no ability to acknowledge mistakes.[2] According to del Vayo, he had a 'frenzied desire to play the rôle of leading figure', which, together with his political naivety – or in del Vayo's words, his 'lack of balance and critical sense' – proved to be a dangerous combination.[3]

It is not clear at which stage Casado and his supporters resolved to take power. Viñas suggests that by November 1938, following the retreat from the Ebro and the British and French capitulation at Munich, the colonel was already demonstrating an unhealthy interest in a hypothetical post-Negrín government.[4] Casado does not specify a date or occasion in either his original memoirs published in English in London in 1939 or the Spanish edition published in 1968. Nevertheless, he appears to indicate that the fall of Catalonia was the defining moment in a process of increasing disenchantment with Negrín. It offered the definitive proof that the war was lost, and that further resistance was both futile and dangerous.

In addition, he appears to have been encouraged by the declaration of martial law (24 January 1939), which further extended his power and influence in Madrid. He describes his satisfaction at 'taking charge of public order which, in the circumstances could scarcely have been better in the whole zone under my jurisdiction'. He also describes the 'affection and confidence' in which he was held by the population, inspired by 'an austere and hard-working regime, in which there was no vanity or show'.[5]

Casado's conviction that surrender was the only viable military option, and that consequently Negrín was a liability, was compounded by his increasingly public anti-Communism and his perception that the Prime Minister was a Soviet puppet. In his English memoirs, he describes the government at this stage as practically a 'dictatorship', its war policy as 'un-Spanish' and its leader as a man serving 'interests foreign to his country'.[6] He magnanimously acknowledged that the PCE was not wholly to blame for the military debacle and expressed his belief that many officers attached to the party had died heroically. He also commended the Communists for prioritising the morale of their troops and improving their conditions, although he did apply the caveat: 'generally at the expense of others'.[7] His first open conflict with the party leadership came immediately after the declaration of a state of war, when he used his new powers to instruct the military censorship board to forbid the publication by the PCE's official journal, *Mundo Obrero*, of an offensive article attacking the previous Prime Minister, Largo Caballero. When the editors refused to comply with the order, Casado ordered the indefinite closure of the newspaper.

According to the version of Vicente Uribe, the Minister of Agriculture, who intervened on behalf of the PCE, the matter was resolved in a telephone conversation and the ban on *Mundo Obrero* was lifted.[8] Casado, on the other hand, described a subsequent meeting at his headquarters where Uribe warned him that 'his Party's war policy must be accepted, and that if they could not impose their policy any other way, they were prepared to introduce a reign of terror to support it.' The only reference to this incident in the later edition of the memoirs is the allusion to a threat to defy Casado's authority.[9] By the first week of February, Casado had undertaken a series of meetings to gauge the support he might enjoy if he put himself at the head of an operation to deliver a single blow against the government, the Communist Party and the policy of resistance.

He was justifiably confident that he could count on the backing of many members of the higher ranks of the armed forces, but also recognised the contribution that disaffected Republican politicians could make in providing a gloss of legitimacy to an essentially military junta. Casado thus welcomed the overtures from Julián Besteiro Fernández, an eminent member of the parliamentary party of the PSOE. A university professor (of Philosophy and Logic), he was sentenced to life imprisonment in 1917 for his involvement in the general strike of that year. Released under a subsequent amnesty, he won election first to the Madrid town council and then to the Cortes. He became President of his party and the Socialist trade union, *Unión General de los Trabajadores* (UGT – General Union of Workers). However, within the Socialist movement he came into conflict with those who supported direct action and who resisted his move away from radical politics towards a reformist approach. He resigned his posts in the PSOE and UGT in 1931 and was subsequently elected President of the new constituent Cortes.

When members of the far-right wing CEDA* were invited to join the national government in 1934, this new shift in power triggered a revolutionary uprising led by the miners in Asturias. Besteiro, who abhorred violence, earned the resentment of a significant section of his party by openly opposing the revolt. Nevertheless, in the 1936 elections he won more votes than any other candidate on the *Frente Popular* list for Madrid. When war broke out, he refused to leave the capital but made no secret of his dislike of the Communists and his conviction that efforts could, and should, be made to negotiate a peace settlement with the insurgents.

In 1937 he was invited by Azaña to represent him at the coronation of George VI in London, where he held talks with the Foreign Secretary, Sir Anthony Eden, on 11 May to discuss the possibility of British mediation in the war. Neither Eden nor the Republican government in Valencia appeared to take his 'mission' seriously. The vague promises made by Eden included no new proposals and were dismissed by the Spanish Ambassador, Pablo de Azcárate, as '*buenas palabras*' (polite words).[10] By the winter of 1938 Besteiro had come to the conclusion that the gravity of the situation justified extreme measures and was recruited into Casado's incipient conspiracy.

---

* *Confederación Española de Derechas Autónomas* (literally: Spanish Confederation of the Autonomous Right). The party had won the 1933 elections in terms of the popular vote and seats.

Of Casado's contacts in the Anarcho-syndicalist movement, the most crucial were with Cipriano Mera and Melchor Rodriguez. Mera was a veteran of the CNT struggle, who was in prison at the time of the military coup of July 1936. Once released, he took part in the siege of the Montaña Barracks, at which the local population had stifled the revolt in the capital. He participated in the organisation of a column that played an important part in the defence of Madrid, and when the unit was integrated in the Popular Army as the 14th Division, he was appointed commander.[11] He was later promoted to the rank of lieutenant-colonel and the command of the IV Army Corps. Casado described him rather incongruously as 'the best-disciplined officer I had in my service', and remarked on his 'great merits of love of discipline and loyalty to Spain'.[12]

Melchor Rodríguez, on the other hand, had sought to establish a career as a *torero* until he was badly gored and forced to retire. He was an active member of the syndicalist movement, who also spent time in prison under both the monarchy and the Republic. However, he was opposed to the use of violence. During the Civil War he took charge of the Madrid prison service and was eventually entrusted with enough power to put an end to the attacks by militia lynch mobs on the inmates. After his personal intervention to protect right-wingers in the Alcalá de Henares Prison, his actions were recognised by several ambassadors and Don Juan de Borbón, son of Alfonso XIII and next in line to the vacant throne. Among those who owed him their lives were the legendary goalkeeper Ricardo Zamora (who played for both Real Madrid and Barcelona) and Ramon Serrano Suñer, Franco's brother-in-law and future chief of the *Falange*, both of whom were held in the Modelo Prison. His courage in defending the rights and lives of enemy sympathisers earned him the title '*el Ángel Rojo*' (the Red Angel).[13] It also earned him the hostility of the Communist Party, which eventually forced his dismissal.

At this stage of the war, the antagonism felt by the Anarchists towards the Communist Party was both manifest and justified. Nevertheless, the question remains: why did either man have any more confidence in Casado? In a feature run by the *Manchester Guardian* after the coup, a wisely anonymous correspondent blithely and intriguingly suggested the Anarchists 'had a marked tendency to consider Socialism and Communism as worse enemies than a Franco dictatorship under which they could still keep their principle of individualist and terrorist action'.[14]

For obvious reasons, his connections with the fifth column, the final piece of the Casado jigsaw, is the most obscure and the most difficult to document. In the Spanish-language version of his memoirs, Casado reports that his first contact with the enemy occurred on 5 February, when Lieutenant-Colonel

José Centaño appeared at his headquarters (codename: *Posición Jaca*), revealed that he was a Nationalist agent working for Franco's *Servicio de Información y Policía Militar* (SIPM – Information Service and Military Police) and offered his services as liaison.[15] His version is supported by the work of the two historians, Ángel Bahamonde and Javier Cervera Gil, who insist that this was the first occasion Casado was directly approached by a Francoist agent proposing negotiations with Burgos.[16] However, they also report that the Nationalist secret services had received intelligence from fifth columnists of the activities of Casado and Besteiro as early as 26 January.[17] It is also true that unlike other zones, the army command in the Centre-South was largely dominated by professional career officers rather than men who had risen from the militia. Of more ambiguous loyalty to the Republic, and distrustful of Communist influence in political as well as military matters, a section of these men felt duty-bound to act as a vector of fifth column-penetration.[18]

It seems plausible that at this stage Casado was led to believe that Franco was more inclined to negotiate a '*paz honorosa*' (honourable peace) with a military government than a civilian one. Furthermore, it seems probable that seeds were planted in Casado's mind that the *Generalísimo* would look kindly on the person or persons who were able to overthrow Negrín and eliminate the Communist grip on power. It also seems possible that the suggestion was made that Republican officers who assisted the Nationalist cause in the final weeks of the war might then be incorporated into Franco's army (at a lower rank). Unfortunately, it is also quite possible that Casado understood these insinuations as promises.[19]

To what extent British intelligence was involved in the conspiracy is a moot question. There can be no doubt that the leadership of the Conservative Party would have preferred Casado over the ideologically untrustworthy Negrín – the abominable treatment of the Prime Minister throughout his exile in Britain during the Second World War is evidence enough. However, given that Chamberlain's recognition of Franco was simply a question of time, it is difficult to believe that even those at the head of the secret services in 1939 would have invested any substantial time, energy or money in an increasingly peripheral matter. Nevertheless, the conversation that Stevenson had with Sir George Mounsey on 9 February makes it clear that officials of the Foreign Office both in Spain and London were apprised that plans were afoot to overthrow the Negrín government.[20] Both Casado and Besteiro also held meetings with Denys Cowan, the liaison officer of the Chetwode commission, in the second fortnight of February. As Viñas has indicated, his role as go-between with both the Republican and Nationalist authorities meant that Cowan was one of the few people able to travel relatively freely between the two zones and to share intelligence with both sides. On the fall of Barcelona, he had been transferred to Madrid on the orders of an undisclosed authority.[21]

On 28 February, Abbington Goodden, the British Consul in Valencia, dispatched a telegram to the Foreign Office confirming that Casado and Besteiro were forming the nucleus of a new Republican government and that 'Negrín has presumably not been consulted in this matter so that the proposed change is in the nature of a coup d'état.'[22] As Britain had now recognised the Franco regime, this development in the internal politics of the Republic was significant only in the sense that it might hasten the end of the war. Goodden acknowledges J.H. Milanes, the Acting Consul in Madrid, as the source of the intelligence, and Paul Preston notes that the information was passed on to Sir Robert Hodgson, the Chargé d'Affaires in Burgos, Stevenson, and the embassy in Paris.[23] In July 1936 the British authorities had failed to advise the democratically elected government in Madrid that a former RAF pilot had been secretly commissioned to fly General Franco from the Canary Islands to mainland Africa to take command of the colonial army in anticipation of an uprising on the mainland.[24] In February 1939, the Foreign Office now once more chose to ignore their obligations to a friendly power and neglected to provide Prime Minister Negrín with intelligence of a new conspiracy to overthrow the last, legitimate government of the Republic. On the other hand, it is clear that by this stage it was too late for intervention from the British intelligence services or diplomatic corps to have any substantial impact on the events unfolding in the Centre-South Zone.

Chapter 14

El olvido es peor que los recuerdos

Negrín moves his government to Elda-Petrer (Alicante)

On 6 November 1936, as Franco and Mola's armies descended upon the capital, Prime Minister Largo Caballero had decided to abandon Madrid and move his government to Valencia. In the absence of the civilian authorities, General José Miaja was appointed Chief of the *Junta de Defensa de Madrid* (Madrid Defence Committee) and Lieutenant-Colonel Vicente Rojo was designated Chief of the General Staff of the defence forces. The two men became the visible heroes of the siege. On the front, the battle was won by the militia and the International Brigades with the help of Soviet weapons. In February 1939 the circumstances were different. Madrid was not in imminent danger, but Negrín was – not from the Nationalists but from the conspiracy of officers within his own armed forces who were plotting to overthrow him.

It was, in the words of Julián Zugazagoitia, '*un secreto a voces*' (an open secret)[1]. At the summit at Los Llanos, the military high command had openly questioned the policy of resistance, and shortly afterwards Negrín was explicitly warned by Edmundo Domínguez (Commissar Inspector of the Army of the Centre) of Casado's contacts with disaffected Socialists, members of the Anarchist movement, the fifth column and British diplomats.[2] There is no doubt that had Negrín opted to establish a base in Madrid, he and his team of ministers and advisers would have been at constant risk of abduction or worse. Instead, as the Nationalists made preparations for the final offensive against the Republic, the Prime Minister elected to move south-eastwards, beyond the reach of both Franco and Casado, to what Hugh Thomas somewhat ungenerously described as 'the small undistinguished manufacturing town of Elda'.[3]

What is known in the twenty-first century as the conurbation of Elda-Petrer (Elda-Petrel in *castellano*) lies in the valley of the Vinalopó river, just under 400km from Madrid, and about 30km from Alicante and the coast. Today, urban sprawl means the two municipalities are divided by the width of a street. In 1939 the demarcation was more pronounced, but the proximity of the two towns allowed outsiders to consider it a single urban entity. In general terms, the residents of Elda speak *castellano* and those of Petrer speak *valenciano*.

The history of the two municipalities during the war was fairly typical of many smaller provincial towns in the Republican zone. At the outset, self-appointed vigilante groups, led primarily by members of the CNT-FAI, meted out their own brand of revolutionary justice, which included the assassination of a group of *guardias civiles* and a number of 'class enemies'. The Church of Santa Ana was burnt down, commercial premises were looted, and several factories were first expropriated and 'socialised', and then merged in a workers' cooperative. The industrial base was later extended to include weapons factories (especially *Fábrica 11* in Petrer). Although the local authorities took the precaution of constructing air raid shelters, the towns were ignored by the enemy bomber commands, which on the eastern 'front' concentrated their efforts on the coastal regions. The municipal agencies also made provision for hospitals to care for the wounded and refugee centres for those fleeing Madrid. The population suffered the same food shortages and related illnesses as the other areas of the non-occupied zone, and as elsewhere the towns gave up their young men to fight for the Republic.

So, having made the fairly self-explanatory decision not to linger in Madrid, the question still remains: why Elda-Petrer? By this stage, the Communist minister Vicente Uribe was disillusioned with the Prime Minister; no longer the dynamic, intrepid and decisive leader, but instead a man overwhelmed by circumstances and unable or unwilling to take difficult decisions. In his memoirs, Uribe wrote, 'The particularity of this place [Elda] was that it offered no facilities for a government which intended to do any work. No offices, no buildings, no nothing.' He concluded: 'But the really important feature was that nearby there were two aerodromes, with aircraft ready to take off at any time.'[4] Uribe was not the only one to insinuate that Negrín had chosen Elda as a safe hideout pending escape, but the suggestion makes little sense. If his intention was to hide from Franco, the Prime Minister would have followed the example of Azaña, Rojo and Martínez Barrio and remained in France after the retreat over the Pyrenees. If he were hiding from Casado, he would not have invited/ordered him and Matallana to attend a meeting at his headquarters on 2 March. Indeed, at this stage he could not be sure that Casado would not use his contacts with the fifth column to advise Franco's intelligence services of the Prime Minister's location.

On the other hand, a less sceptical analysis suggests that there were, in fact, good reasons for choosing Elda. In the 'non-invaded' territory that remained to the Republic, the town was more central than Madrid, Valencia or Almeria. It was also much farther from the front and the gathering Nationalist armies and had not suffered a single air raid. It was well linked, with road connections to Alicante, Madrid, Valencia, Murcia and Cartagena, and its railway station was on the main Madrid–Alicante line. As Uribe pointed out, it also provided facilities for air transport – the main aerodrome at Monóvar (Monòver) was less than 10km away.

The volume of traffic through the town would also prove to be useful in camouflaging the movements of ministers and military leaders. Furthermore, Elda had demonstrated its loyalty to the Republic, both in elections and at the onset of war, and there was no active presence of fifth columnists. Finally, and crucially, given the catastrophic military situation and the general consensus that Franco saw no need to make genuine concessions on reprisals, it appeared that Negrín's priorities had indeed been reduced to a single concern – the evacuation of as many Republicans as possible. Elda was ideally situated to coordinate a disciplined naval extraction of vulnerable refugees from the ports of Alicante, Cartagena and Gandia.

Curiously, there does not appear to be any substantiated record of when Negrín actually arrived in Elda. The evidence would suggest it was either late on 25 February, after a meeting with Casado in Madrid, or the next day. In his account of the relocation of the government, Alicante historian José Ramón Valero Escandell reproduces a copy of the minutes of the plenary session of the local council on 27 February. In his statement to the assembly, the Mayor, Manuel Alberola Castelló, reported that two days before, the municipal authorities had been ordered to vacate the premises of the *Escuela Castelar* to make way for the staff of the Ministry of the Army.[5]

The Undersecretary at the ministry, Lieutenant-Colonel Antonio Cordón García, in fact played a key role in the transfer of the government headquarters. A member of the Communist Party since 1936, and a veteran of the fighting in Aragón, in 1937 he participated in the suppression of the anarchist/libertarian *Consejo de Aragón*. He was also heavily involved in coordinating weapons purchases from the USSR. On his return to the Centre-South Zone, Negrín gave him the unenviable commission of restructuring an army that was on the verge of disintegration. He was now entrusted with the specific task of setting up a political/administrative structure in Elda-Petrer. According to his memoirs, he left Madrid on 25 February, spent the night in Albacete and arrived in Elda the next day. He subsequently drove on to Murcia to hold talks with Lieutenant-Colonel Emilio Bueno Núñez del Prado, who informed him that contingency arrangements had been made to evacuate government ministers and Communist Party leaders should the need arise. On 27 February Cordón and Hidalgo de Cisneros set out to find Negrín and finally tracked him down to a rest home in San Juan where the Prime Minister had retired

Stamp issued by Alicante Republican authorities. (*Author*)

Eliseo Gómez Serrano. Parliamentary ID card. (*Courtesy Archivo de la Democracia. Universidad de Alicante*)

Dr. Juan Negrín (centre foreground) with Azaña (third from right) and Republican generals. (*Public Domain*)

The prison where José Antonio was held, hours before its demolition in 1990. (*Author*)

José Antonio Primo de Rivera. (*Public Domain*)

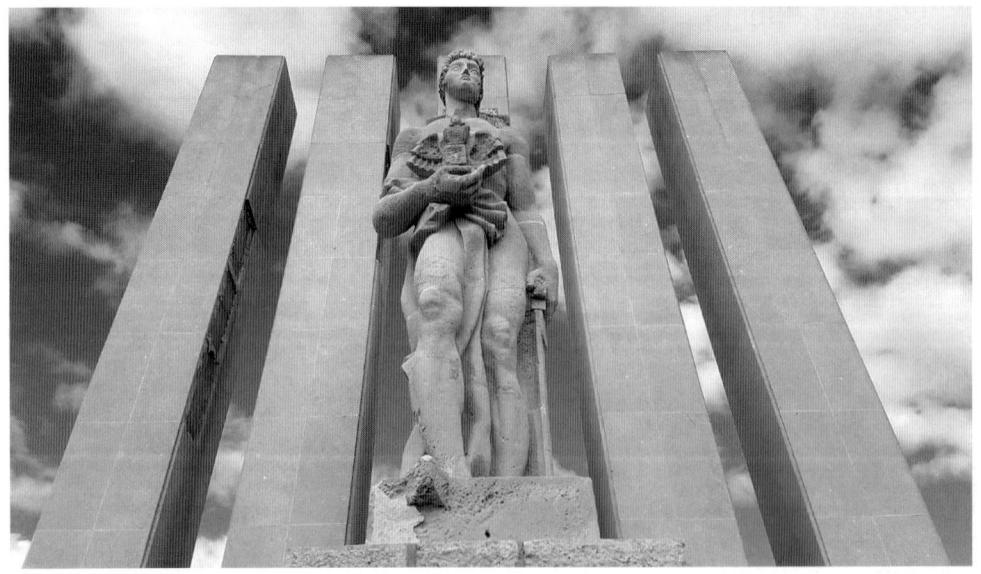
Monument to the *falangistas* of the Vega Baja. (*Author*)

Former Gobierno Civil/Civil Governor's Office. (*Author*)

Cuevas de Canelobre. (*Courtesy Management of Coves del Canelobre*)

Savoia S.M.81 bomber. (*Public Domain*)

Bomb Shelter. Plaza Séneca. (*Author*)

Bomb Shelter. Plaza Balmis. (*Author*)

Aerial photograph of raid on Alicante. (*Ufficio Storico della Aeronautica Militare*)

Air raid on Alicante. (*ABC newspaper*)

Marketplace today. (*Author*)

Market clock and siren. (*Author*)

Palmira. Victim of raid on Marketplace Private archives of the family of Mary Elmes. (*Courtesy of Caroline Danjou*)

Republican propaganda poster. (*Public Domain*)

Casa de Socorro (left). Market is just visible at the end. The Gobierno Militar and Cine Ideal are on the right. (*Author*)

Bathing huts at Postiguet Beach destroyed in air raids. (*Archivo Histórico Municipal de Alicante*)

Wreck of ship sunk by Italian air raid in Alicante port. (*Archivo Histórico Municipal de Alicante*)

Propaganda poster. Image of Negrín. 'To resist one day is a battle won.' (*World History Archive/agefotostock*)

El Poblet. *Posición Yuste*. (*Author*)

One of the houses at *Posición Dakar*. (*Author*)

Air raid shelter at El Fondó aerodrome. (*Author*)

Colonel Casado's radio broadcast on night of his coup. (*Public Domain*)

General Miaja. (*Public Domain*)

Bust of Archibald Dickson on port. (*Author*)

SS *Stanbrook*. (*Public Domain*)

Casado arrives in England. (*Public Domain*)

General Gambara. (*Public Domain*)

Italian troops marching on Alicante. (*Archivo Histórico Municipal de Alicante*)

Italian troops take control of the port. (*Archivo Histórico Municipal de Alicante*)

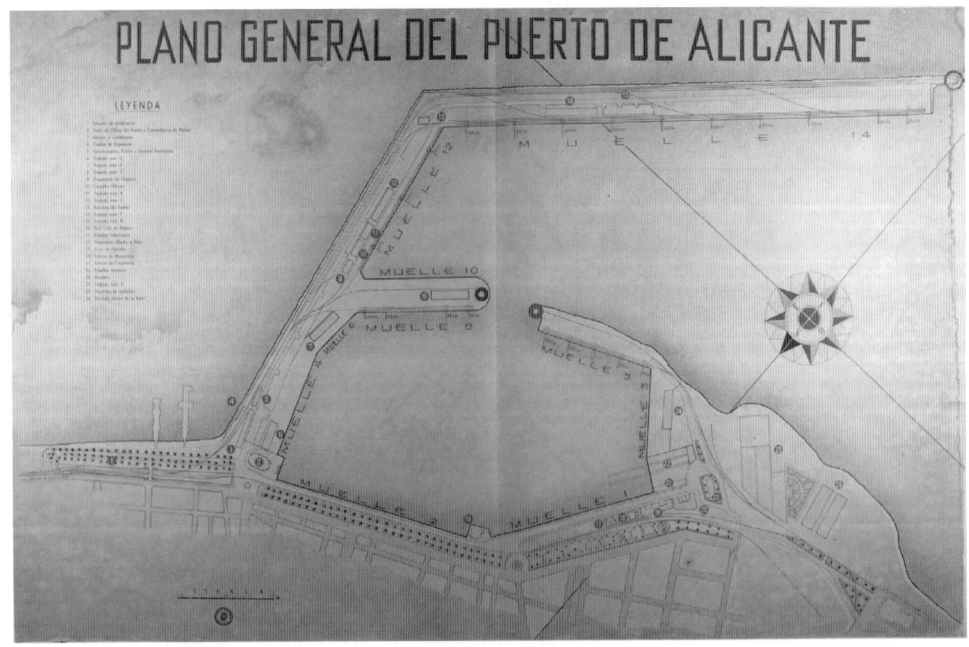

Plan of port. (*Archivo Histórico Municipal de Alicante*)

Italian troops in San Juan. (*Archivo Municipal de San Juan*)

Victory parade. (*Archivo Histórico Municipal de Alicante*)

Generals Gambara and Saliquet at Victory Parade. (*Archivo Histórico Municipal de Alicante*)

Albatera monument. (*Author*)

Lieutenant Faustino Bernabeu Castellón. (*Courtesy of Mari Bernabeu*)

Red prisoner graffito. (*Author*)

Franco meets Mussolini at Bordighera (1941). (*Public Domain*)

for a short respite. He was certainly back in Elda-Petrer on 1 March where he received Cordón in his new office.

The Prime Minister's headquarters had been established in El Poblet, an elegant mansion set in 25 hectares (approximately 250,000m^2 or 62 acres) of land dominated by pine and olive trees. The main house had been constructed at the turn of the century by Vicente Amat Furió, a magistrate of the Supreme Court in Madrid, who was detained in the summer of 1937 and then evacuated on board the British hospital ship HMS *Maine*.[6] At the outbreak of the Civil War, the estate was the property of Plácido Gras Boix, an Alicante lawyer and landowner, who paid special attention to the gardens, made substantial investments in irrigation, and created an 'oasis' in the middle of the often scorched landscape that dominates much of the province. In the municipal area of Petrer, but at some distance from the town centres of both Petrer and Elda, the house was largely hidden by trees, and had a principal gate that gave directly onto the main Madrid–Alicante Road* and over which there was a sign, '*Villa Poblet*'. The property was codenamed '*Posición Yuste*', a reference to King Carlos I (also Holy Roman Emperor Carlos V) who abdicated the Spanish throne in 1556 and retired to the monastery of Yuste in Extremadura. The estate had been confiscated at the onset of the war, and over the next two and a half years had served as a school camp, an air traffic control centre and a *hospital de sangre* – literally blood hospital, a rearguard military hospital.[7]

It seems plausible that the decision to set up the government headquarters on the property was taken by the Republican military intelligence – SIM, *Servicio de Investigación Militar*. There were no defensive installations. Security depended partly on secrecy – no contact was made with the local authorities and relations with local commerce were kept to a minimum. Nevertheless, there is evidence that the estate was protected by a unit of the legendary *XIV Cuerpo de Ejército Guerrillero* (XIV Guerrilla Army Corps), an elite force of Communist fighters set up to operate behind enemy lines.[8] The corps was famous for the raid on the Charchuna Fort at Motril (Granada) in May 1938, in which they were able to rescue 300 prisoners and smuggle them across the frontline to Republican territory. According to Paul Preston, at El Poblet they were armed with machine guns and deployed in trees around the property and in the house itself.[9] Negrín himself estimated that the force was made up of eighty men.[10]

The Prime Minister was accompanied by a skeleton government that included his closest associate, Julio Álvarez del Vayo (Minister of Foreign

---

* The new Madrid–Alicante highway was built slightly to the east, and El Poblet is now only accessible by track.

Affairs and a member of the PSOE), Ramón González Peña (Justice, PSOE), Vicente Uribe (Agriculture, PCE), Segundo Blanco (Health and Education, CNT) and José Moix Regàs (Labour, PSUC). If we accept the definition of capital city as 'the seat of government', Elda-Petrer now became the fourth capital of the Republic in two and a half years, after Madrid (July–November 1936), Valencia (November 1936–October 1937) and Barcelona (October 1937–February 1939). There are, no doubt, some who would argue that during the retreat in January–February 1939, the government also momentarily exercised its authority from Figueras, close to the French border. The last 'full' session of the Cortes in the town's castle (1 February) was attended by fifty-five deputies and presided by Martínez Barrio.

While Negrín gathered his cabinet in El Poblet, the leading figures of the Communist Party, both civilian and military, who had been in the process of assembling in Murcia, now relocated to Elda. Under the guidance of the Agriculture Minister, Uribe, who had arrived first in Negrin's entourage, they found accommodation in a row of houses, known as *'Posición Dakar'*, on the southern outskirts of the town. Over the following days Uribe was joined by: Dolores Ibárruri (*La Pasionaria*) and her assistant Irene Falcón; Jesús Monzón, the Civil Governor in Alicante (1937–38); and writer María Teresa León and her husband, the poet Rafael Alberti. Present on behalf of Stalin were Stoyán Miniéevich Mínev (alias 'Stepanov'), Bulgarian delegate of the Third International (*Comintern*), and Palmiro Togliatti (alias 'Ercoli'), Italian envoy of the *Comintern*. Representing the military were Colonel Enrique Líster, Colonel Juan Modesto and Ignacio Hidalgo de Cisneros.

The most famous of these was of course *Pasionaria*, the woman who helped inspire the resistance of the people of Madrid in 1936. Her undoubted charisma tends to overshadow the contributions of two other women: Margarita Nelken (a Socialist member of Congress who joined the Communist Party in November 1936)[11] and Federica Montseny (anarchist Minister of Health in the Largo Caballero government – and the first female cabinet minister in western Europe). Nevertheless, it would be wrong to underestimate the significance of any one of the three. By the time Negrín opted to move to Elda-Petrer, José Díaz, Secretary-General of the PCE, was gravely ill and undergoing treatment in the USSR. *Pasionaria* was thus seen as the figurehead of the party, although she would not officially take over Díaz's post until his death in 1942.

Jesús Monzón had served as Civil Governor of Cuenca after his term at Alicante and was still a relatively minor player considering the company in which he now found himself. Maria Teresa León was a writer who after the outbreak of war became secretary of the *Alianza de Intelectuales Antifascistas*

(Alliance of Anti-Fascist Writers) and founded the journal *El Mono Azul* (The Blue Overall). She helped in the transfer to Valencia of many of the great works of art in the Prado Museum, which were threatened by the indiscriminate bombing of Madrid by the Nationalist air forces.[12] Her husband, Rafael Alberti, was also active in the *Alianza*, alongside Miguel Hernández (poet from Orihuela, Alicante), Luis Buñuel (film director) and the Spanish–Mexican author Max Aub.

Stepanov was described by Hugh Thomas as one of the men who 'strutted across the stage of Spanish revolutionary history as if they were gods. Disdainful of Spaniards, breathing mystery and power, but actually cynical, fearful of Stalin and bureaucratic.' The British historian also claimed that Stepanov 'established a virtual tyranny over the central committee of the party'.[13] He was instrumental in the party's campaign to bring down the Largo Caballero government and in the suppression of the POUM and other anti-Stalinist heretics.

Togliatti was a founder member of the Italian Communist Party and was appointed Secretary-General after the arrest of Antonio Gramsci by Mussolini's police. In the first edition of the *Spanish Civil War*, Thomas claims that from mid-1937 the PCE 'was guided not by [Secretary-General] José Díaz or *Pasionaria*, but by the far more skilful political tactician, Palmiro Togliatti'. A man who, Thomas also describes as an 'able and ruthless leader'.[14] María Teresa León later wrote that it was impossible to refuse any of his demands: 'He was a comrade, an Italian to whom it was virtually impossible to say no because he always persuaded you with his gift of irresistibility.'[15] He, too, carries responsibility for the brutal repression of the anti-Stalinist left in 1937 and thereafter, especially in Catalonia.

Lister, a *gallego** and long-term member of the PCE, had undergone military training in the USSR during the early 1930s. He played an important part in the founding and preparation of the 5th Regiment and was active in the defence of Madrid, at Belchite and Teruel, on the Ebro, and in Catalonia. He, too, too had participated in the suppression of the *Consejo de Aragón*. Modesto had served in the various battles around Madrid in the first winter/spring of the war, and rose to become Commander of 5th Army Corps. He participated in the fighting at Belchite, Brunete and Teruel, and was made chief of the Army of the Ebro.

Hidalgo de Cisneros was an aristocrat, aviator and fervent Communist who became Chief of the Republican Air Force. He was also at the centre of one of the great legends of the Civil War. In the aftermath of the Battle of Guadalajara

---

* Native of Galicia.

(1937), it was reported that a box containing the mutilated remains of a Soviet pilot, who had apparently become disorientated and landed in hostile territory, were dropped by parachute onto the airfield at Barajas. The macabre payload came with a note in Italian warning of the fate of those who resisted the Nationalist cause. The story suggests that Hidalgo de Cisneros then proposed to lead a retaliatory raid against the Italian mainland. The plan would have involved dispatching a squadron of Tupolev SB-2 bombers *(Katiuskas)* to Menorca, within range of the Italian coast, and from there launching an attack on Rome. Apart from logistical problems (the base at Menorca was hardly equipped to deal with such an undertaking), the ramifications of an air raid on the Italian capital (and possible collateral damage to the Vatican) make it unlikely that the government in Valencia would have seriously entertained the idea.

If the operation did ever reach the planning stage, Hugh Thomas concluded, 'the Republican Cabinet restrained the imperious'.[16] In her own memoirs, Hidalgo's wife, Constancia de la Mora, recalls a different, more extensive plan to retaliate against 'those who murdered our schoolchildren and starved our people', by attacking 'the industrial triangle of Turin, Milan, Genoa [which] was only 480 miles distant from our airdrome at Gerona'. She claims this plan was scuppered by British intervention and the timely decision of the government in London to send a commission to Spain to investigate reports of the bombing of civilians 'from both sides', which would have delegitimised a unilateral response by the Republic.[17]

Of Negrín's decision to move the operational base of his government from Madrid, the poet Alberti later recalled: 'That romantic, heroic Government of resistance had chosen the then small Alicante town of Elda as its provisional headquarters, to resume the struggle.'[18] A more grounded Irene Falcón described the emotions of those Communists who gathered there: 'It was defeat, a horrible, ghastly defeat. For almost three years we had fought with enthusiasm and faith [...] Then, as the end approached, the situation was tragic.'[19] The party members were lodged in a series of relatively new and modest chalets, constructed by local residents as summer homes. It appears that neither the proprietors nor the neighbours were aware of exactly who the new 'tenants' were. It was generally assumed the houses had been commandeered to be used as offices for ministry staff transferred from Madrid. One owner later recalled her pleasant surprise when she recovered her property and found that those who had occupied her home had left it as they had found it.[20]

Chapter 15

His last ounce of courage

The battle for Cartagena and the Republican Navy

No sooner had Negrín established the centre of his government in Levante than the news came that the British and French had recognised the Franco regime, and that Manuel Azaña had resigned as President of the Republic. Not only did the double blow undermine Negrín's legal authority, but it also exposed the growing sense of futility behind the policy of further resistance. Defeat and Franco's refusal to negotiate on the question of reprisals left Negrín a single option: evacuation of as many of those in peril as possible. For this, in addition to time, he needed effective, disciplined military support. A mass extraction of vulnerable Republican supporters would require two fundamentals: a disciplined rearguard action to defend a Mediterranean redoubt, and the deployment of the navy fleet based in Cartagena to provide a defensive shield for the operation. It was unlikely that French and British captains would risk intervention if they were left at the mercy of Franco's own warships.

At this stage decisive action was paramount. Unfortunately, although Negrín remained committed to the cause, the perception was now growing among his associates, allies and adversaries alike that he had lost confidence and was failing to offer the leadership that was required in the new circumstances. Uribe described the difference between the Negrín of 1938 and the Negrín of February as an abyss. He listened to the proposals of the Communists like 'someone listening to the rain', and 'throughout his time in the Republican zone [after the fall of Catalonia] he did not take a single measure that indicated a will to continue the struggle.'[1]

To varying degrees of irritation, members of the government, military and Communist Party were complaining that it was becoming increasingly difficult even to find him. After Cordón had discovered Negrín was not at El Poblet on 27 February as arranged and had then driven around the region in his pursuit, he travelled to Valencia the next day to meet with military leaders who had been told to expect the Prime Minister. When Negrín failed to appear, Miaja in particular was indignant and claimed, 'not even Jesus Christ could ever find him'.[2] When Jesús Hernández arrived in Elda on 4 March, he went looking for the Prime Minister, but nobody knew where he was. He then asked for Uribe, the Minister of Agriculture, only to be told that he was out looking for Negrín.[3]

Indeed, at some point the Prime Minister absented himself from Petrer to make a lightning visit to Madrid. Carmen Negrín, his granddaughter, recalls conversations with her grandfather, his life-partner Feliciana López de Dom Pablo, and his driver in which they describe his trip to the capital. He wanted to see the situation in Madrid with his own eyes, but when he realised he was being followed by men he supposed to be Casado's agents, he slipped his tail by entering a bar. His adversaries spread the rumour that he had spent his time in Madrid in the company of women of ill-repute.[4] Instead, his driver explained, he stood for some time gazing over the ruins of the *Ciudad Universitaria*, the vast campus complex he had played such a large part in building, and which had been largely destroyed in the fighting of the winter of 1936: 'It was like a goodbye to past happy days.'[5]

However erratic his approach to his work schedule and diary arrangements, Negrín persisted in his determination to execute the evacuation plan. Unlike Azaña, he refused to abdicate his responsibilities towards those who had resisted the forces of Franco, Hitler and Mussolini for so long. His behaviour and attitude seem to reflect a man coming to terms with 'history', seeking to do the best he could for those in danger, and exercising his authority to ensure the highest possible level of 'damage limitation'.

He convened a *Consejo de Ministros* (Council of Ministers – Cabinet Meeting) for 28 February, at which the ministers discussed the fall-out from the decisions in Paris and London. On 1 March he met Cordón in his office at El Poblet to discuss a series of promotions within the armed forces. When they went outside into the gardens, Negrín began to outline his plans to reorganise the army. When Cordón reacted with incredulity – 'I thought he was pulling my leg' – the Prime Minister explained that he felt it important that the army and country should perceive that the government was functioning as normal.[6] Cordón would eventually conclude that Negrín had returned to Spain 'not as a determined head of the government firmly resolved to take the reins of power to lead and channel resistance, but as a decent man who wanted to ease his conscience and accept whatever sacrifice, even though he was aware of its possible futility.'[7]

At the beginning of March[8] Negrín then held a critical meeting with Casado, Miaja, Matallana and Buiza, at which he informed them of his intention to address the nation by radio on 6 March and to set out and defend his strategy. The four men were now deeply involved in a conspiracy to overthrow the government. Negrín was fully aware of Casado's covert activities in Madrid. Moreover, Buiza's impatience and forthright objections to further resistance did not encourage confidence in his loyalty and left little doubt that he could not be trusted to follow instructions. The attitudes of Miaja and Matallana appeared to be more ambiguous, but Negrín specifically warned Cordón to be wary not only of Casado but also of the two generals.[9] His decision to enter into discussions with those who were coming to see themselves ever more openly as his enemies, instead of taking decisive measures against them, was an obvious sign of weakness: not of the man, but rather of his position. Writing only months later, Casado scathingly described the new governmental headquarters:

> How is it possible that Dr Negrín and his advisers could expect to carry on government by any sound and honourable means, without men, without archives, without any of the things which are necessary if government is to be effective? Did Dr Negrín imagine that the executive power could function in his little hotel in Yuste with two typists for the work and five hundred (sic) soldiers as an escort? The irony could not be greater.[10]

The next day, the Congressional Standing Committee* met in Paris to discuss Azaña's resignation and agreed to accept Martínez Barrio as the interim President of the Republic. However, no doubt to the relief of the President of the Cortes, they imposed a condition: 'providing, he served exclusively to carry out the humanitarian duty of settling with the least possible damage and sacrifice, the situation of the Spanish people.'[11] Negrín was informed of the decision, which was discussed in cabinet, and responded by radiogram that he was in full agreement. Martínez Barrio never received the reply, or other subsequent communications. Negrín later claimed in his statement to the Standing Committee (Paris, 31/03/1939) that the message had been intercepted – presumably either in Valencia, in the offices of Miaja, or in Madrid, at Casado's HQ.[12] As a result, Martínez Barrio was never appointed President, and the Republic remained without a head of state. The political disintegration of the Republic was almost complete.

Even more significantly, the conspirators, if they were indeed the ones who had sabotaged the communications between Negrín and Paris, had preempted the election of a President whose only mission would be to bring the war to an end. They now needed to act before Negrín could make a radio address that would undermine their own programme. In short, they needed to

---

* *Diputación Permanente de las Cortes*: a committee exercising functions of parliament when not in session.

demonstrate that only they were prepared to end the fighting. Part two of the plan consisted of persuading the authorities, both civilian and military, that the uninvaded territory was facing the imminent risk of a Communist takeover.

Meanwhile, Negrín had made another critical move and approved adjustments in the military hierarchies. He had already promoted Casado to the rank of general (25 February), a measure that was correctly interpreted by Casado as part of a plan to remove him from operational command of the central army. The new appointments were published in the *Diario Oficial del Ministro de Defensa** on 3 March, but at the time the mystery that surrounded them allowed Casado and acolytes to make new claims of Communist conspiracy. Among the changes, Modesto was promoted to the rank of general and Lister was made a full colonel. At the Ministry of Defence, Cordón was given the post of General Secretary (previously held by Zugazagoitia, who had remained in France) and Monzón was appointed to head the General Secretariat. Matallana was assigned to the post of Chief of Central Staff of the Army of the Centre, and thus lost operational command. Lieutenant-Colonel Etelvino Vega was given a potentially vital role as Military Governor of Alicante in place of Lieutenant-Colonel Antonio Rubert, who was dismissed for 'incompetence and doubtful loyalty'.[13] Crucially (given Buiza's growing tendency towards insubordination), Colonel Francisco Galán Rodríguez was named chief of the naval base at Cartagena. The appointment of two Communists to take control of the two ports that were crucial to any evacuation plan indicated not only Negrín's determination to implement an organised seaborne withdrawal, but also his utter dependency on the party.

Indeed, the promotion of so many members of the Communist Party made perfect sense within the context of his isolation. The lack of confidence of the high command was as manifest as the disaffection of the Besteiro, Largo Caballero and Prieto factions in the PSOE. By this stage, in the words of Hugh Thomas, Negrín 'was a politician without a party and a war leader without an army'.[14] Nevertheless, this new development simply confirmed the fears of many, and provided further ammunition to the cause of the anti-Communists. Rumours, half-truths and outright lies abounded – the most damaging that Negrín planned to appoint Modesto to replace Casado as Chief of the Army of the Centre.[15] In his diary entry for 4 March, Eliseo Gómez Serrano, who was still under the impression that Martínez Barrio would be appointed President and was impatiently and optimistically awaiting his arrival, repeated an unfounded report that Lister had already taken over from Casado, and wrote, 'What are Negrín and his army of Muscovites up to? Is this the preliminary of

---

* Official bulletin (gazette) of the Ministry of Defence.

a coup d'état or just an act to force Martínez Barrio to abstain from political changes?'[16] The next day he retracted the previous entry that Lister had taken over command of the central army. He continued: 'The foreign radio stations have nothing interesting to say about Spain. Is there nothing going on here?' He, himself, appeared unaware of what was happening a mere 90km away in Cartagena.

On 3 March Negrín received intelligence from the Governor of Murcia and the chief of the naval base that members of the armed forces both on land and afloat were actively preparing a mutiny. The next day, the newly appointed Colonel Galán travelled eastwards from Madrid, via El Poblet and Murcia, to take command. He was to be supported by a unit of the 206th Mixed Brigade (10th Division) from Valencia. The troops arrived after the colonel, but having been given instructions by Negrín to avoid the use of force, it appears that he had in any case decided that his appearance in the base at the head of a large number of troops might be interpreted as provocative. He therefore ordered the unit to camp outside the town. Buiza, meanwhile, held talks on board the flagship *Miguel de Cervantes* with a group of officers in an attempt to coordinate a response to this new development designed to pre-empt his own plans to rebel.

Their decision became more complex when they received intelligence that they were not only confronting the pro-Negrín forces. What followed was one of the more bizarre and tragic events of the entire war. When the outgoing commander transferred his powers to Galán, the new chief was arrested by Capitan Fernando Oliva, a pro-Casado officer, who took control of the base. This new rebellion was supported by the marines and artillery, which, critically, controlled the coastal batteries. Nevertheless, the insurrection had been born in 'an atmosphere of confusion and relative discoordination among those behind it'.[17] Apparently the anti-Negrín conspirators had failed to factor into their plans the reaction of the local population and officers sympathetic to Franco. At this stage, the fifth column took advantage of the chaos to launch their own uprising. The bicolour (red and yellow) monarchist flag, which Franco had claimed as his own, appeared in windows throughout the town. Supporters of Franco's crusade (both military and civilian) took to the streets, released right-wing detainees, occupied the radio station and telephone exchange, and appealed to the Nationalist army and navy for assistance. At the same time, Nationalist-leaning officers assumed control of various units of the coastal defence systems (including the *La Parajola* battery) and took Galán and pro-Casado officers into their own custody. Amid the growing turmoil, Buiza responded by threatening to shell the base unless the prisoners were released. Among his own officers, he found a general consensus that the fleet should put to sea, but disagreement on whether the ships should sail to another Republican port (presumably Valencia or Alicante), to a Nationalist base (Málaga or the Balearic Islands), or to a neutral country.

Meanwhile, on the understanding that the defensive batteries were now in the hands of the fifth column, the usually circumspect *Generalísimo* took possibly his most hasty and ill-considered decision of the war. He ordered the deployment of approximately thirty vessels and 20,000 troops and ancillary staff from bases in Castellón and Málaga to Cartagena. The men were to be transferred to the new 'front' on transport ships, but the operation lacked coordination, and no naval escort was made available for the relatively defenceless merchant vessels.

On 5 March there ensued a three-way battle between forces loyal to Galán/Negrín, the anti-Negrín and anti-Communist supporters of the Casado faction, and the fifth column. In his account of the uprising, military historian Michael Alpert reports that to add to the chaos, at 1130 on the morning of 5 March, Italian bombers launched a raid on the Republican ships and succeeded in hitting three destroyers: the *Barcaíztegui*, the *Alcalá Galiano* and the *Lazaga*.[18] According to Galán's report, such was the confusion that at one stage the pro-Franco forces in control of the coastal artillery actually opened fire on Nationalist aircraft, believing them to be part of the Republican air force.[19] They then contacted Buiza and threatened to sink the Republican fleet unless it abandoned the base within fifteen minutes.

Buiza was not unaware of the irony that as long as he remained in the harbour, he depended on the 206th Regiment, acting under orders from Negrín, to protect him from the common enemy. At midday he took the critically significant decision to order the fleet to set sail for North Africa with approximately 4,300 people on board: crews, family and an assortment of civilian refugees. One of the last to embark was Galán. The convoy consisted of three cruisers (*Miguel de Cervantes, Libertad* and *Méndez Núñez*); eight destroyers (*Escaño, Ulloa, Lepanto, Jorge Juan, Gravina, Almirante Miranda, Almirante Valdés* and *Almirante Antequera*); and a number of smaller craft, 'escorted' by a submarine, (*C4*).[20]

At this stage, Jesús Hernández arrived in Elda, and in the absence of Negrín and other members of the government, and in his new capacity as Inspector Commissar of the armed forces, he ordered reinforcements to Cartagena. Having rendezvoused with other pro-Negrín troops of their same 10th Division, the 206th entered the city, disarmed the fifth columnists, took control of most of the sixteen coastal batteries and restored order.[21] When two Nationalist transport ships (*Mar Negro* and *Mar Cantábrico*) were sighted approaching the harbour, the *La Parajola* coastal battery on the western side of the bay opened fire and the ships immediately withdrew. According to Alpert, the *La Parajola* artillery was then itself targeted by another battery, still in the hands of the *franquistas*, on the other side of the harbour.[22] The remaining contingent of Nationalist ships were nevertheless ordered to withdraw to a distance of 13 miles from the coast and then instructed to abandon the mission and return to port.

The last two vessels to arrive were the unescorted troop ships, the *Castillo de Peñafiel* and the *Castillo de Olite*. When it came under fire, the former immediately took evasive action and retired. Unfortunately, the officers on board the latter had received no intelligence, and according to a report to the Foreign Office by Alan Hillgarth, the Consul in Palma, the ship had no wireless.[23] The only plausible explanation of what followed is that, in the absence of other shipping, those in command of the vessel assumed the other transport ships had safely docked within the port and had already commenced the disembarkation of the Nationalist troops. As the ship approached the harbour, it came under attack from the only piece of the four 152mm (six-inch) guns (built in Spain under licence from Vickers Armstrong) of the *La Parajola* battery still operational. The second shell struck the ammunition store, which then triggered a series of explosions. Of the 2,112 men on board, 1,476 were killed – the highest number of victims of the sinking of a single ship in Spanish naval history. Of the survivors, 342 were wounded and 294 taken prisoner by the Republican troops on the shore.[24] Given the circumstances and organisational defects of the operation, Franco's dictatorship subsequently resorted to its default response of imposing a veil of silence.

In the meantime, the convoy of Republican ships had been ordered by French authorities to change course and to sail not for Algeria (Buiza's original plan), but Bizerte (French Tunisia), the northernmost city of the African continent. By ignoring demands that he return to Cartagena, Buiza had performed a great service to Franco's cause. The Nationalists had failed to seize the port of Cartagena but had gained a fleet. Not only had the withdrawal deprived the Republic of its navy, but Buiza had maintained it intact and operational. When the ships docked at Bizerte, they came under the control of the French authorities, representatives of a country that had recognised the Franco regime just a week before. The Republic therefore lacked any legal claim to them. Skeleton crews were left aboard for maintenance purposes, while the main body of men serving on the ships, including Buiza, were taken ashore and interned in detention camps. Three weeks later, the ships were handed over to Rear Admiral Salvador Moreno, the representative of Franco's navy. Approximately half of those who had travelled to Bizerte aboard the ships opted to return to Spain and to throw themselves on Franco's mercy.

The 'battle' of Cartagena was the last major episode in the fighting between Nationalists and Republicans of the war, and strangely it was one of the few military successes of the Republic. Nevertheless, the victory was pyrrhic. The Republic had lost its navy, and with it the potential to implement an orderly evacuation plan. On 5 March the Prime Minister received the visit of two friends: Francisco Vega Díaz, chief of the medical corps in the Army of Andalucía, and an ex-student of Negrín; and José Puche, former Director General of the health service of the Republican Army. According to Puche, they had been invited to provide what he described as 'loyal information', in other words intelligence that was not coloured by political bias or tailored to the interests of the Prime Minister. Negrín was anxious to know about conditions in the Army of Andalucía, the morale of the population, the reliability of military chiefs, the health services, the transportation motor pool, the performance of the political commissars, food supplies, and the facilities at airports and seaports. It appeared to Puche that Negrín was anxious to assess the capacity of each sector to resist any longer and to determine whether there remained a will to continue the struggle.

At the same time, Puche sensed that Negrín was disillusioned and appalled by the notion of further conflict, even within a wider war against fascism. He appeared to have assimilated the general view that further resistance was futile and was aware that he had been deserted by the civilian and military authorities of the uninvaded territory. Although it was incumbent upon him as Prime Minister to avoid a dishonourable and unconditional defeat, he seemed reconciled to the reality that his time was up.[25]

Part Three

The End

Chapter 16

Usted haga como yo, no se meta en política

The second coup d'état

The Cartagena mutiny was to have been an integral part of the military plot to depose Negrín and his government. Despite the disastrous loss of the navy, the initial failure of the rebellion did not derail the conspiracy. There are obvious difficulties in judging the mood of the Republican zone, but there can be little doubt that Negrín was increasingly isolated, that both the armed forces and the civilian population were desperate for a swift end to the fighting, and that anti-Communism had become a powerful weapon. Two and a half years earlier, the leaders of the military insurrection – Mola, Sanjurjo, Queipo de Llano and Franco – defended the coup as a pre-emptive strike designed to prevent a Communist takeover and the formation of a dictatorship of the proletariat. That the evidence they produced to support this thesis was largely based on the fiery rhetoric of a Socialist leader (Largo Caballero of the PSOE) and a series of four forged documents reminiscent of the Zinoviev letter mattered little to those who were anxious to overthrow the Republic and to restore the military, religious, economic, political and social hierarchies under which their privileges were guaranteed.[1]

By March 1939 Franco's anti-Communist crusade had taken control of two-thirds of Spain, but military victory was insufficient. Franco was intent on eradicating the disease. He had even sponsored the research of Professor Antonio Vallejo Nágera, head of the Psychiatric Services of the Nationalist Army, into the existence of a 'red gene' and the defects/deficiencies (physical and psychological) that made people vulnerable to Marxist proselytising. Vallejo was able to carry out tests on a sizeable cohort: Spaniards and foreigners taken prisoner by Franco's armies and detained in concentration camps. At San Pedro de Cardeña he was assisted in his work by Gestapo operatives who collected anthropometric data and interrogated the prisoners. His findings suggested an association between a particular biopsychic personality and a predisposition towards Marxism. He also found a link between 'Marxist fanaticism' and 'mental weakness' and detected the presence of psychopaths among the Marxist horde.[2]

According to Enrique Moradiellos, Franco had 'fantastic, obsessive ideas [...] on the hidden and divisive power of freemasonry and the existence of a universal Judaeo-masonic-Bolshevik conspiracy against Spain and the Catholic faith'.[3] Paul Preston suggests this may have been in part because he had been rejected twice when he submitted applications to join masonic lodges (in 1924 and 1932).[4] After the war he would introduce the *Ley de represión de la masonería y el comunismo* (01/03/1940 – Law for the Repression of Masonry and Communism) designed to eliminate 'secret societies of all types and *clandestine** international forces'.[5]

In March 1939, with equally insubstantial and unsubstantiated evidence, Casado used the same tactics the Nationalists had applied in July 1936. In the first version of his memoirs, the only proof of a Communist plot he offered was the constant repetition of his allegation that there was one. He even went so far as to suggest the Prime Minister himself had supported the conspiracy against his own government: 'Dr Negrín knew perfectly well that he was unpopular and on that account encouraged and precipitated the abortive Communist *coup d'état*.'[6] On the other hand, it is also true that many of the actions of the PCE and the Soviet advisers during the war had confirmed the fears of those who opposed both communism as an ideology and the party as a mechanism of social and political repression.

Casado was fully aware that by overthrowing the Negrín government he would not only seize power but would also establish his anti-Communist credentials, which he ingenuously believed would impress Franco. Nor did Negrín do anything publicly to mitigate the growing perception that he was in thrall to the Communist Party. At the height of the Cartagena crisis, Hernández met him unexpectedly at El Poblet at 3am on 5 March. According to the former Minister of Education and Health, 'He looked dishevelled. He hadn't shaved, he had his hat down round his ears, and his trousers tucked into his socks, like a cyclist. He looked weary.' Hernández claims he took advantage of the encounter to question the wisdom of his last appointments of various leading Communists to positions of power. Negrín apparently replied, 'They were an answer to the demands of your comrades. I have tried to make them happy, knowing it would all be pointless anyway ... even prejudicial.'[7] Hernández also suggests that he later confronted *Pasionaria*, whose response was as empty as it was grandiloquent: 'The appointments that we advised Negrín to make were in line with our policy of cleansing the army of traitors and waverers, to bring to heel the capitulators and intriguers, and to replace

---

* The italics are the author's.

them with men of faith, tested under fire in a hundred battles, willing to give their lives in the cause of the people.'[8]

Casado's claim that Negrín was 'trying to precipitate events in order to put the Communist Party in power'[9] was simply self-serving, but the Prime Minister's actions, the rumours emanating from sources within both the Republican camp and the fifth column, and the lack of official communications almost certainly persuaded many in the political class that a Communist coup was indeed imminent. The British Consul in Valencia, Goodden, was satisfied that Casado's assertions were at least plausible. On 6 March he telegraphed the Foreign Office with a report that, 'a Communist plot to seize Valencia was discovered late yesterday afternoon and […] several hundred Communists were arrested during the night.' He also informed London that Casado was 'forming a military Government which would no longer recognise the authority of Dr Negrín and that they were ready to come to terms with Spanish Government'. He finished his brief with an enigmatic reference to events on the east coast: 'I understand that yesterday's abortive revolt at Cartagena was of a communist nature.'[10]

On 5 March Negrín convened another *Consejo de Ministros* for 1700 hours at *Posición Yuste*, the second since his arrival, to discuss developments in Cartagena and the content of the address that he was due to deliver to the nation the next day. In the build-up to the cabinet meeting, Vega Díaz described the havoc inside the mansion. There was a group of twenty people running around like in a madhouse. He heard del Vayo shouting down one phone trying to confirm that a tank unit had been ordered to Cartagena. On another phone, an indignant Negrín was unsuccessfully trying to contact Casado. According to Vega Díaz, in the middle of the mayhem Negrín managed remarkably to remain in control.[11]

Miaja was not at El Poblet when the cabinet meeting began. Strangely, General Matallana, the new Chief of General Staff and accomplice in the conspiracy, did obey orders to travel to Elda in case the government should need to consult him. At some point during the meeting, Negrín found Matallana and asked him to contact Miaja and request his presence. A disgruntled Miaja declined, giving reasons of ill-health and suggesting that he would make the trip from Valencia the next day. Cordón also reports a telephone call from Hernández warning his cabinet colleagues that something was afoot in Valencia that required an immediate response. When Cordón asked the Prime Minister for instructions, Negrín said, 'Do whatever you think best. I swear I just wish they would all rebel and get it over with once and for all.'[12]

Meanwhile in Madrid, Casado had convened his own meeting of the men who would accompany him in the new *Consejo Nacional de Defensa* (CND –

National Council of Defence[13]) and announced that the *coup d'état* had been scheduled for that evening. All the members of the new junta were present except General Miaja, who remained in his office in Valencia and therefore was not present at either the Madrid or the Elda-Petrer meetings. Casado put forward the name of Julián Besteiro as President of the Council, but the Socialist politician declined the honour on the grounds that under martial law, and in view of the resignation of the President of the Republic, the 'lawful thing' was for the presidency to be occupied by a military officer. Casado was thus nominated President, though within hours he relinquished the post in favour of the absent Miaja. Those in attendance then approved the text of the council's manifesto.

The assembly was later joined by Domínguez Aragonés, Vice-President of the UGT and Inspector Commissar of the Army of the Centre, who swiftly understood that his own opposition to the coup made him little more than a hostage. Nevertheless, he resisted Casado's attempts to claim UGT involvement in the council. In his own account of the evening, written only weeks later, he gave an intriguing insight into the manner and behaviour of those who were about to seize power.[14] Casado, despite the pain from his gastric ulcer, remained overexcited, friendly, even jovial. Besteiro was infantile and yet drained.[15] Carrillo, like San Andres, appeared distracted and said little. Val, Marín and Prada seemed calm and self-confident, unable to hide their delight. Mera was taciturn, even sullen. As they waited, they exchanged stories about Negrín: that he enjoyed *tortillas* (omlettes) made with a dozen eggs; that he could eat as much as four men with healthy appetites; that every night he slept with three women; that every day he demanded his assistants procure new women; and that he mistreated his ministers. Besteiro apparently had the final word: 'He shows no respect for the dignity of his office.'[16]

In Elda-Petrer, the cabinet adjourned their own session at 2300 and sat down for dinner with the military representatives. Over the next ninety minutes, two major events took place, but the order in which they occurred varies according to the different versions of the protagonists and witnesses on both sides and is in any case wholly irrelevant to the outcome. What is clear is that there was a telephone conversation and a radio broadcast. According to Antonio Cordón, at approximately midnight Matallana received a call from Casado. Still holding the phone, he turned to those at the table and told them, 'He says he has risen in revolt.' When Negrín took the telephone, the following conversation ensued:

'Explain General, what is this they are telling me?'
'I have risen in revolt.'

'Against whom?'
'Against you.'
'Then you are relieved of your post.'
'As I expected.'

Negrín then took his place at the table and put his head in his hands. Casado told Cordón that he refused to negotiate with an 'illegal' government and renounced the rank of general as he did not recognise the legitimacy of the government that had promoted him. On the same principle he rejected the notion of an official transfer of power from the Negrín government to his own, which would have upheld the democratic integrity of the new regime.[17]

In his memoirs, Cordón makes no suggestion that the government had heard Casado's broadcast. On the other hand, writing in 1940, Álvarez del Vayo recalled that while they were having dinner, the ministers were advised that Casado was delivering a live radio address, and that in response it was Negrín who telephoned Casado.[18]

Casado's version is understandably longer. He had first taken the precaution of ordering troops to occupy key points in Madrid, including the Ministry of the Interior, the offices of the intelligence services, military headquarters, the Bank of Spain and the Ministry of Communications. The announcement that the National Council had taken power was broadcast at midnight, at a time when audiences were accustomed to listen in for the latest news bulletins. After the emotional announcement by Besteiro, Miguel San Andres (Minister of Justice) read the manifesto, which began:

> Spanish Workers, People of Anti-Fascist Spain –
> The moment has come in which we must proclaim to the four winds the truth of the situation in which we find ourselves. As revolutionaries, as proletarians, as Spaniards, and as anti-Fascists, we cannot continue passively to accept any longer the improvidence, the lack of foresight and organization, and the absurd lethargy shown by the government of Dr Negrín. These critical times through which we are passing, and the climax which is approaching, impel us to end the silence and uncertainty which have increased our mistrust in the handful of men who still claim the title of government, but in whom nobody believes and nobody trusts.[19]

Mera and Casado then each made personal statements. Casado based his own on an appeal to the very principles that had guided Negrín over the last few weeks. He warned the Nationalists: 'We shall not cease fighting till you assure us of the independence of Spain. The Spanish people will not lay down their arms whilst it has no guarantee of peace without crime.' He insisted the Republic would fight to the end, 'to avoid that our country shall be merged (sic) in a sea of blood of hatred and persecution', and warned the Nationalists, 'If you continue to make war, you will find our heroic fighting morale implacable, sharpened like the steel of our bayonets.' Both the tone and content of his address represented a radical change from his reports to Negrín that, given the military situation, lack of arms and overwhelming superiority of the enemy, further resistance was futile.[20] It is also interesting that the members of the council avoided references to the Communist Party.

According to Casado's account, after the broadcast it was he who received a call from Negrín, who told him that what he had done was 'madness'.[21] His version nevertheless coincides in two key aspects with that of Cordón: the refusal to accept his promotion, and his refusal to send representation to Elda-Petrer or receive representation in Madrid to perform an official transfer of power from the government to the new council.

From *Posición Yuste*, Cordón contacted military headquarters in Valencia and spoke to General Menéndez, acting as group chief in the absence of Matallana. It was clear from the evasive answers that he received that the general's staff were complicit in the '*pronunciamiento*"*. He then contacted General Antonio Escobar, Chief of the Army of Extremadura, who reported that all was quiet on his front. Cordón received a similar reply from General Domingo Moriones Larraga, the army chief in Andalucía. It appears that by this stage both Casado and Menéndez were under the impression that Matallana had been arrested. In his own account, Casado claims he authorised Menéndez to contact Negrín and warn him, 'that if before three hours General Matallana is not at his Headquarters, I shall shoot every member of the Government.'[22] In the Spanish version of his memoirs, he amended this slightly to read, 'If General Matallana, who they are holding as a hostage, is not back at his post within the next three hours, I shall use the swift and very violent means at my disposal to liberate him.'[23]

When Menéndez phoned Cordón, he clarified the terms of the threat. Unless Matallana was released quickly, the rebels would not only shoot the representatives of the government they had taken prisoner in Madrid, but they would also execute everyone at El Poblet. Neither Casado nor Menéndez was in any mood to understand the discordant detail that Matallana was not being held against his own will. The risks involved in appearing to defy the authority of the council would certainly explain why Cordón and Negrín now

---

* Insurrection. This is the Spanish word used traditionally to refer to a coup d'état (especially in the nineteenth century).

took the decision to expedite the return of the obviously insurgent general to Valencia. He had in any case been free to leave before. Matallana had tears in his eyes as he took his farewell from all those present at El Poblet. At the last moment, Negrín said, 'tell your colleagues that their behaviour has been dishonourable.'[24] López Fernández, the 'furiously anti-communist'[25] secretary of General Miaja, later made the implausible and unsubstantiated claim that his release had been obtained in exchange for forty Russian advisors whom Casado had taken as hostages.[26]

Those leaders in Elda-Petrer had at least been made aware of the peril they now faced and the imminency of the danger was highlighted by developments in Alicante (capital). Cordón was informed that Colonel Ricardo Burillo was issuing instructions that were understood to include an order to arrest Negrín and his ministers. Burillo was a career soldier who, like many at the outset of war, joined the Communist Party in the belief that it offered the most disciplined and effective response to the Nationalist war machine. He fought in the defence of Madrid and took part in the repression of the POUM. He was stripped of command of the Army of Extremadura and later expelled from the PCE after accusations of negligence during the collapse of the front in the summer of 1938. He served as chief of police in Madrid, and having declared his support for Casado, was then appointed by Miaja to head the forces of public order in Levante.[27] On the arrival of Etelvino Vega as the newly nominated Military Governor of Alicante (4 March), Burillo refused to authorise the transfer of powers from Vega's predecessor, Lieutenant-Colonel Antonio Rubert. Although Cordón ordered Burillo's arrest, Casado's proclamation from Madrid was followed instead by the detention of Vega, who served as governor for a little more than twenty-four hours.[28]

At this stage, in the early hours of Monday, 6 March, it was clear to those at *Posición Yuste* and *Posición Dakar* that not only had they lost power, but they also needed to arrange a swift escape strategy: not from the enemies of the Republic, but from their enemies within the Republic. A civil war that had started with *a coup d'état* would now close with another one. In the words of Hernández, 'The volcano had erupted. The lava was going to swallow us all in the most appalling shame and confusion.'[29]

Chapter 17

El destino infortunado de España, derrotada y maltrecha

The flight of the government

As the events of 5–6 March unfolded, the Prime Minister's friend Francisco Vega Díaz later wrote that on his last day in Spain, 'Juan Negrín was pale, gaunt, his eyelids half swollen, soaked in sweat, unshaven [...] he looked utterly dejected and ill.'[1] Carmen Negrín quotes a letter in which Negrín told Feliciana López de Dom Pablo that he had not eaten or slept properly in five days and was on the verge of exhaustion.[2] The prime exponent, if not architect, of the policy of all-out resistance against the combined forces of Franco, Hitler and Mussolini, Negrín declined to offer any armed resistance to the new insurgents. Unlike Casado, he could not contemplate using violence against fellow Republicans who had shared the sacrifices and hardships of the previous thirty months. Even when he dispatched Galán to Cartagena, he had taken the precaution of warning him to avoid any military engagement with the forces supporting Buiza.

For a few hours, and if once more we accept the 'seat of government' definition, Spain had three capitals: Burgos, the headquarters of the Franco regime recognised by Britain and France; Elda-Petrer, the provisional base of the legitimate government of the Republic, still recognised by the USA, USSR and Mexico; and Madrid, the historical capital now the control centre of the insurgent Casado faction. From Elda, Negrín realistically had nowhere else to go. Two-thirds of Spain was occupied by Franco, and Madrid and Valencia were now controlled by Casado. Anthony Beevor reports that when Negrín was informed of the arrest of Etelvino Vega by Casado's agents in Alicante, a mere 30km from *Posición Yuste*, he said to del Vayo, '*Ich, auf alle Fälle, werde gehen*' (In any event, I'm going). Other accounts suggest Negrín was not responding to the specific detention of Vega (which may indeed have occurred later) but rather to a generalised deterioration in the government's position in Alicante.[3]

In a letter to Prieto, three and a half months later, Negrín claimed he had returned to the Centre-South Zone in February:

to raise spirits, to readjust the services to the new circumstances [and] to unify the elements of effective resistance. The measures we took [...] would have enabled us to continue fighting until now. To continue fighting because there was no alternative, if we couldn't win, [we had] to save whatever could be saved, or at the very least, to save our dignity.[4]

In his own memoirs published in 1940, Alvarez del Vayo echoed Negrín's analysis:

Resistance for a further six months was no idle dream. It only needed the strengthening of public moral, the reorganization of services, and the removal from posts of authority of certain unreliable and defeatist elements, to say nothing of accomplices of the enemy. Both Madrid and Valencia could have held out, but even if those two cities had fallen, a line defending part of the province of Albacete, the province of Murcia, part of Almeria, the province of Alicante and the south of Valencia could still have been maintained [...] There was in any case no other solution, save that of abandoning the struggle and leaving the rebels to ravage the central zone with fire and sword.[5]

However, Negrín's German aside to del Vayo was the ultimate acknowledgement that his mission to protect the greatest possible number of Republicans by forcing Franco to make concessions, and by mounting a huge operation to evacuate those most in danger, had failed. Aware that he was a prize that Casado would not wish to lose, he saw no option but to flee Spain for the second time in a month, in the knowledge that this time there would be no return. Given that Franco controlled the land borders (France, Andorra, Portugal and Gibraltar), Casado was tightening his grip on the Mediterranean shore from Valencia to Cartagena, and in any case the Nationalist navy was now blockading the same coast, there remained only one escape route.

Air Chief Ignacio Hidalgo de los Cisneros and Colonel Carlos Núñez Mazas (Undersecretary at the Air Ministry) had made provision for this contingency, and a small fleet of Douglas DC-2s and de Havilland DH.89 Dragon Rapides was placed on standby to ferry Negrín, his team and the PCE leaders from the nearby aerodrome at El Fondó, near Monóvar to exile and safety. At 1000, Negrín left *Posición Yuste* for the last time, in the company of del Vayo, the man who had accompanied him through each of the crises of the last months, and the man Casado dismissed as Negrín's 'black shadow' or the 'evil genius of Spain'.[6] While the others of his ministerial team, with government files and their personal luggage, drove directly to the airfield, Negrín decided to make a detour to take his leave of the Communist representatives who had stood with him to the end.

In his account of the government's last days in the Vinalopó, Valero Escandell reports an interview with a post office employee, in which he was told that during the 3km drive to *Posición Dakar*, Negrín stopped at the telegraph office where he dispatched an order to the air base at Rabasa that an aircraft be made ready to take off in thirty minutes.[7] If the post office worker's report is accurate, Negrín's motives remain unclear. By now Alicante was hostile territory and, in any case, the Prime Minister did not modify his plans first to confer with the leadership of the PCE and then to escape via Monóvar. One possible explanation is that Negrín wished to facilitate the rescue of an ally trapped in the town, but if that is the case, their identity remains a mystery.

It was Negrín's first visit to *Posición Dakar* and he had no notion of its whereabouts. Once the ad hoc assembly had gathered, members of the politburo tried to dissuade Negrín from leaving. Given his insistence that he could do no more, it was decided to evacuate *Pasionaria* immediately. Eventually the Prime Minister did agree to send a final communication to Casado urging a negotiated resolution to the new conflict that would avoid bloodshed between the two Republican factions. Negrín subsequently drafted a document, a copy of which del Vayo was careful to preserve. The Prime Minister described the council's actions and statements as 'unjustifiable' and complained of the 'impatience of those who are unaware of the real situation'. He expressed disappointment that the junta had not waited to hear his address to the nation, which was scheduled for that evening, and asserted that, 'if we wish for a settlement with our adversaries, we must first avoid all bloody conflict between those who have been brothers in arms.'

Finally, he repeated his plea that 'the transfer of authority should take place in a normal and constitutional manner.' 'Only in this way,' he concluded, 'can the cause for which we have fought remain unsullied.'[8] The offer to arrange a peaceful transfer of power was both generous and significant. Not only would it contribute to the legitimacy of the new regime, but it would also facilitate its international relations (specifically with the USA and Mexico) and presumably grant some level of control over Republican assets abroad.

It appears that in Madrid, Besteiro and Miaja were strongly opposed to any deal or indeed contact and insisted that Negrín was stalling.[9] An interesting theory given that Casado's forces were closing in on Elda and that the longer Negrín waited for a reply, the greater the danger he, his government and the leaders of the PCE faced, and the more nervous those anxious to carry out the evacuation became. The Spanish-born Mexican writer Edmundo Domínguez

Aragonés described the refusal to accept the proposal as 'an act of arrogance and foolish and sterile pride'.[10]

Del Vayo later recalled his own thoughts on these last moments in Spain:

> I stood on the terrace gazing out over the Levant countryside, clear and lovely on that early spring morning – a countryside made for men to live in contentedly and at peace. Every tree, every stone, every movement of light and shade, held for me a meaning unknown in other and happier days. With a cold feeling in my heart, I watched the little children playing in the meadows below. Would their youth be enriched by the gift of freedom, or were they doomed to grow up in a régime foreign to the spirit of the country, from which all true liberty and happiness had been banished?[11]

By 1430 it was clear that no response from Madrid would be forthcoming. There are two versions of what then triggered Negrín's decision to abandon *Posición Dakar* and set off for the aerodrome. The first suggests he was informed that the rebels had occupied the military command headquarters in Alicante, and the second was the arrival of an adjutant with news that Casado's troops had taken Albacete.[12] When they finally arrived at El Fondó thirty minutes later, del Vayo was made aware of the indignation of his colleagues who had not eaten and had been waiting in the blazing sun for five hours.

By this stage the first two flights carrying *Pasionaria* and other communist leaders had already arrived in Oran (French Algeria). They had taken off at approximately 1300 and arrived in North Africa an hour later. The first *Dragon Rapide* had been carrying Antonio Cordón, Colonel Núñez Maza, Rafael Alberti and María Teresa León. *The Manchester Guardian* confused the passenger manifest and 'poetically' described Alberti as the Undersecretary for Air.[13] Those arriving on the second aeroplane included *Pasionaria*, Falcón, Monzón and the French deputy and observer Jean Catelas. There is a suggestion in Cordón's memoirs that *Pasionaria* was irked that he had left while her own aircraft was still on the ground.[14] In her own version, *Pasionaria* describes how she embraced each of the members of Líster's guerrilla unit, deployed to defend the aerodrome from Casado's forces, before boarding the aeroplane. Her last vision of Spain for almost exactly thirty-eight years was of these same men, 'With their weapons aloft, in salute, in a promise, in hope.'[15]

León was equally lyrical: 'When we landed in Oran, our airplane had just enough fuel not to crash into the ground. We had left behind the blues of Spain, the white splashes of Levante villages, and yet, we took so much with us in that tiny, red dragon.'[16] In another version, she and Alberti professed that when their daughter was born in 1941, they christened her Aitana, as their lasting memory of the flight into exile was the vision of the huge mountain range that lies to the north of Alicante.[17]

Once they had been disarmed, the newly arrived party was treated kindly by the local police authorities and *Pasionaria* was even asked to sign autographs. They were accommodated in a hotel until they could board a ship for mainland France. The pilots and mechanics of the two aircraft were treated less sympathetically. According to Silvio Zurueña, the pilot on the first airplane, the prolonged exile of the four men began when they were detained by six *gendarmes* and led away for internment in the daunting castle at Mers el Kebir. Their passengers apparently abandoned them to their fate. Zurueña completes his account with: '*Así paga el Diablo a quien le sirve*,' (literally: 'Thus the Devil pays those who serve him').[18]

Negrín and his government team left Spain for Toulouse on board a Douglas DC-2 of the LAPE (*Líneas Aéreas Postales Españolas* – Spanish Postal Airline), which took off at approximately 1500. In a conversation with Carmen Negrín, the Prime Minister's driver later described how Negrín had offered to find him a seat on the aeroplane. Before he boarded the aircraft, he said, 'If you feel safe enough, stay, but if not come with us.' The driver chose to stay.[19]

Del Vayo later wrote, 'It was the first long daytime flight over rebel territory that the Douglas had made. But our grief at leaving Spain blinded us to all other anxieties.'[20] Negrín would never return. From Toulouse, he travelled to Paris, and once established in the capital, he set about alleviating the suffering of the vast numbers of Spanish refugees still trapped in concentration camps. Through the SERE, he embarked on a course of evacuating as many Republicans as possible to the Americas. He also worked to ensure supplies continued to reach the Centre-South Zone and to hire shipping for the evacuation of Republicans from the east coast. Ultimately, although Casado's coup spared him the indignity of the final surrender to the Nationalists, for the rest of his life he had to endure attacks not only from Franco and Casado but also from people within his own party, led in particular by Indalecio Prieto.

A fourth airplane left much later the same day carrying a number of leading Communists, including Hidalgo de Cisneros, Uribe,[21] Modesto and Líster. The aviation chief later recalled seeing the headlights of military vehicles approaching the aerodrome as they took off. He assumed the lorries were carrying troops loyal to Casado.[22]

At a final meeting of the politburo held at the airfield, it had been decided that three of the leading members of the Communist movement – Palmiro Togliatti, Pedro Checa and Fernando Claudín – should remain behind to coordinate resistance to Casado and to initiate the reorganisation of the party. They were all arrested (apparently as they were leaving the El Fondó on their way to Murcia[23]) and transferred to prison in Alicante. However, amid the chaos in the aftermath of the coup, and the conflicting loyalties of the Republican authorities, they were released by a friend of Claudín's who worked in military intelligence. They eventually abandoned Spain on 23 March (with Jesús Hernández) from the airfield at Totana (Murcia) and followed *Pasionaria*'s route to North Africa, then France, and finally the USSR. They were followed from the same aerodrome by officers of the 206th, who had played a key role in suppressing the Casado insurgency in the southern area of the Levante. After the departure of the last PCE hierarchs, they commandeered three aircraft and escaped to Algeria.[24]

Towards the end of March Alvarez del Vayo was invited by the Parliamentary Committee of the Friends of Republican Spain to London to address a cross-party group of some 100 MPs at the House of Commons. He recalled the statement made by Sir Henry Croft, a spokesperson for 'The Friends of National Spain', in March 1938, and his description of Franco as 'a gallant Christian gentleman'.[25] Del Vayo felt that many in London still hid behind this self-delusion, and still believed that 'self-interest' would prevail, and that Franco would prove 'magnanimous' in victory. In response, he besought them, 'from a humanitarian standpoint, to stir the British government to quick and energetic action to dissuade Franco from carrying out reprisals'. He was, however, realistic enough to understand that the Foreign Office 'was not disposed to jeopardize its relations with the "new Spain"– which the British policy of non-intervention had helped put into power'.[26]

Nevertheless, del Vayo did detect a small change in attitudes. In a separate account of his meeting in Westminster, he wrote that just as in France, he sensed that some on the right were coming round to an understanding of the 'tremendous mistake which had been made in allowing Germany and Italy to convert Spain into one of their zones of influence, and the repercussions that their Spanish victory would have on the whole of European politics, especially in the Mediterranean'. In response to a question from a Conservative MP, 'Don't you think, Señor del Vayo, that Madrid and the rest of Republican Spain could still be saved if France and England sent out sufficient forces immediately?', he was forced to reply, 'I'm afraid that it is now just a little too late.'[27]

Chapter 18

Written in the blood of a Spanish soldier

The civil war within the civil war

In Alicante the coup took Gómez Serrano completely by surprise. In his diary he wrote tellingly: 'Yesterday evening we were on the verge of a communist dictatorship. At midnight, out of the blue, Unión Radio Madrid broadcast the news that a National Defence Council had been set up [...] to achieve an honourable peace settlement.'[1] Meanwhile in Madrid, although Casado renounced his position as President of the National Defence Council within hours of taking power, he nevertheless retained his post as Councillor for National Defence and remained the driving force behind the movement. Of the other members of the nine-man council, the most eminent were the two Socialists, Julián Besteiro (Councillor of State)[*] and Wenceslao Carrillo (Councillor of Public Order).

The latter was a lifelong activist in the UGT, Socialist Youth of Spain (*Juventudes Socialistas de España* – JSE) and the PSOE. He was elected to the Madrid City Council in 1931 and subsequently to the Cortes as member for Córdoba. He was elected again in 1936 having lost his seat in the 1934 elections. During the Civil War he served as Undersecretary at the Interior Ministry and then Director-General of Security under Largo Caballero. He was the father of Santiago Carrillo, an ambitious member of the PCE, who had played a key role in the creation of the JSU and was understandably dismayed at his father's involvement in the coup, not only because of the impact on the PCE and the Republic, but also because of the ramifications for his own career. In an open letter released in May 1939, he broke off all contacts with his father and used the full range of Stalinist rhetoric to denounce the council and its members as 'counter-revolutionary', 'traitors', 'prefascist', 'pro-fascist', 'Trotskyist' and 'enemies of the people'. Writing much later (in the 1990s), he exposed his greatest fear: 'And what would my comrades of the JSU and the party think of me?'[2] His worst nightmare was realised when his father ordered the detention of Communists throughout Republican territory.

---

[*] For a description of Besteiro's career and ideas, see chapter 13.

Santiago Carrillo would eventually become Secretary General of the PCE on *Pasionaria*'s retirement in 1960.

Casado's coup triggered what observers delighted in describing as a civil war within the Civil War. It was, in fact, the second time that Republican loyalist factions had indulged in open warfare with each other. The first fratricidal battle had occurred in Barcelona in May 1937, between those in favour of immediate social revolution (anarchists, POUM) and those who wished to restore the constitutional order and focus on military priorities (Socialists, Communists and Republicans). As Vincent synthesised, the revolutionary decentralisation of power 'led to competing demands for resources as the war effort demanded efficiency, direction, and centralized command. The problems of the collectives faced in forging a new, spontaneous, local social order while simultaneously providing resources with which to fight a modern war proved to be entirely insurmountable.'[3]

Casado's anti-Communism and resolve to negotiate an immediate peace settlement with Franco now led to a desperate battle for control of Madrid. If he had expected the Communists to submit quietly and gracefully, he had miscalculated: if only because, of the four corps of the Army of the Centre, three were commanded by Communist officers (Colonel Luis Barceló Jover, Colonel Bueno and Colonel Antonio Ortega). On the other hand, the absence of Secretary General Díaz (undergoing treatment in Moscow), the exfiltration of the main members of the politburo, and the detention of Checa and Claudín meant the military chiefs in Madrid lacked the coordination and leadership to which they were accustomed.

Having heard the radio broadcast of the new junta, the Communist faithful established their HQ in the Villa Eloísa in Ciudad Lineal, in the northeastern section of Madrid, and prepared to implement the contingency plans that they had been preparing since they had received intelligence of Casado's conspiracy. At dawn on 6 March Major Guillermo Ascanio of the Army II Corps launched an attack on the *Nuevos Ministerios* and ordered an advance along the Paseo de la Castellana.*

That night, troops of the II Corps took *Posición Jaca*, the headquarters of the Army of the Centre, close to the airport at Barajas. Unwilling to await further orders, a detachment of troops then inexplicably murdered three members of Casado's staff: Colonels Otero Ferrer, Pérez Gazzolo and Fernández Urbano. However, they failed to capture Casado himself, who by this stage had taken

---

* New Ministries. An administrative-government complex in the northern section of Madrid. Today the area is considered central. The Castellana is a major highway running north-south to the traditional centre of the capital.

refuge with other officers in the basement of the Ministry of Finance in the Calle Alcalá, where he set up his command centre.

After establishing radio contact with Madrid area commanders, Casado came to the conclusion that the II and III Corps remained loyal to Negrín and the Communist Party. In his conversation with Colonel Ortega of the III Corps, he warned, 'I have the support of everyone who cares for Spain, and remember that anyone who tries to oppose the will of the people will be shot.'[4] Nevertheless, to the dismay of Casado, Lieutenant Colonel Luis Barceló Jover, commander of the I Corps, was finally persuaded by Ascanio to join the resistance to the coup. According to Jesús Hernández's account, Casado then telephoned the command post of the 7th Division in the Casa de Campo and ordered the chief field officer to dispatch heavy artillery and a machine-gun battalion to defend the junta's own position. Apparently, the officer replied, 'Come and get them yourself, traitor.'[5] On 8 March the 42nd Mixed Brigade withdrew from the Casa de Campo front and advanced towards the centre of the capital, taking the Palacio Real (Royal Palace) and the arsenal in the Teatro Real (Royal Theatre). They then linked up with Ascanio's troops and by nightfall Communist troops controlled most of the centre, including the Retiro Park, and were in position to move against Casado's HQ.

However, the victories of the forces loyal to the Communist Party were achieved without the foundations that were essential if they were to consolidate their successes. In the other parts of the Republican zone, the transition of power from Negrín's government to the Defence Council, both in the armed forces and among the civilian population, had been far less problematic and the pockets of armed resistance were gradually crushed. The fact that the pro-Casado forces controlled the telephone system exacerbated the isolation of the Communist military officers and hampered coordination. When news did eventually reach the Communist troops in Madrid, it was that the government they were defending had left Spain, that the politburo had all but disappeared, and that their cause lacked leadership and direction. According to Hugh Thomas, the only contact they had with the PCE outside Madrid was through intermittent calls from Togliatti who was in hiding in Alicante.[6] Thus, 'abandoned' by the party command, aware that even should they defeat Casado they would rapidly come under attack from the overwhelmingly superior forces of Franco's armies, officers and troops in the capital grew increasingly dispirited.

Furthermore, Bahamonde and Cervera also argue that Casado was able to count on the passive support of Franco, who, acting on intelligence from the fifth column and his SIPM, concluded that his own cause would be best served if Casado was given time to disarm the Communists. The two historians describe a relatively low-profile Nationalist offensive at the Casa de Campo, designed to draw troops of the 42nd Mixed Brigade away from the battle in the centre of Madrid, and how the Nationalists refrained from shelling the highly vulnerable bridge at Arganda to allow the safe passage of pro-council reinforcements.[7] In an entry that revealed either guilelessness or cynicism, the Alicante diarist Gómez Serrano expressed his surprise that Franco did not take advantage of the crisis to occupy Madrid, and concluded that presumably he sought to win the war with the minimum effort and by way of peace negotiations. The next day (10 March) he went even further: 'It is inexplicable that the enemy has not made the most of the opportunity to attack sectors of Madrid. What fine allies they have finally found in the communists!'[8]

The decisive blow came from IV Corps, under the command of anarchist Colonel Cipriano Mera, a fervent anti-Communist who had pledged his support to Casado before the coup. He withdrew his men from the Guadalajara front and took Alacalá de Henares and Torrejón on 9 March. They subsequently advanced on Madrid, entered the city through Ciudad Lineal and fought their way to the Ministry of Finance. In his memoirs, Casado made an interesting use of the first-person singular when he wrote, 'On the 10th the situation changed, since the arrival of strong reinforcements and the heroic behaviour of the Assault Guards and the 4th Army Corps put me in a position rapidly to overcome the rising.'[9] The next day, a further offensive by the IV Corps drove the Communists from their strongholds in the west and north of the city.

Hugh Thomas reports that from Alicante Togliatti then sent orders to the military leaders to cease hostilities and to negotiate with the council,[10] and Casado agreed to use Colonel Ortega, who had been captured and relieved of his command of III Corps, as a go-between. A settlement was agreed whereby the Communist troops would return to their positions of 5 March, there would be an immediate exchange of prisoners and the council would guarantee that there would no reprisals. The number of casualties varies enormously according to the source: Anthony Beevor suggests as many as 2,000 soldiers lost their lives in the fighting, although more recent studies have lowered the figure substantially.[11]

Echoing the back-to-front logic of General Franco, Casado labelled those who had remained loyal to the constitutionally formed government as the 'rebel forces' and described the fighting in Madrid as the 'military revolt of the Communist Party'. Nevertheless, the six conditions set by the Council for a ceasefire (12 March 1939) included an explicit reference to Communist prisoners: 'The National Council of Defence will set at liberty all arrested members of the Communist Party who have committed no crime.'[12]

Unfortunately Casado later reneged on the promise and many of those loyal to the party and the Republic were kept in detention – with tragic results.

The council also ordered the execution of Lieutenant-Colonel Luis Barceló Jover and his political commissar, José Conesa, whom Casado claimed were most to blame for the fighting. Casado refused to be swayed by pleas for clemency from other council members. The fact that Barceló had refused to commit his troops to the battle until pressure was brought to bear by other officers was ignored. Casado later wrote of him, 'I have an idea that this officer was not at heart a Communist. Probably, his excessive ambition drew him into the activities of the Communist Party.'[13] The most plausible explanation for the executions appears to be that they were ordered as a reprisal for the murder of the three colonels on 6 March – before Barceló had joined the battle.

Some mopping-up operations against isolated pockets of resistance in Extremadura and Valencia were still required, but with the battle for Madrid won, Casado was able to focus his attention on his main plan: to negotiate a peace settlement with Franco.

It appears that throughout the Republican zone the coup and the victory in the capital were greeted overwhelmingly with relief by a population ever more anxious to see an end to the war. In December 1939, describing his own involvement in Spain, George Orwell claimed the feeling was not new. Referring to his experiences in 1937, he wrote: 'Looking back on casual contacts with peasants, shopkeepers, street-hawkers, even militiamen, I now suspect that great numbers of these people had no feelings about the war whatever, except a wish that it were over.'[14] Of the situation in Alicante, Pacual Devesa later wrote:

> We had been at war for more than two years, it was too much. The people were overwhelmed in body and soul. The test was proving too hard. We had paid enough for our faults, the sins of the country did not deserve such a long and bitter purgatory [...] Grief and calamities strained every hour and darkened every spirit. The losses on the fronts, and the stabbings in the back, the misery, the prisons, the air raids ... We couldn't cope any more, enough was enough. The end could no longer be postponed.[15]

Writing of the situation in March 1939, Paul Preston concluded, 'The Casado action received unexpectedly wide support because it tapped into deep seams of war weariness. Hunger and demoralization were rife in the central zone where anarchist and Socialist hostility to the Communists and their policy of resistance to the end just reflected a desire for the war to be over.'[16]

In Alicante, on 6 March, Gómez Serrano observed:

The news [of the coup], repeated this morning on the Valencia radio station, has caused a shock wave in Alicante. People are aware that it is an anti-communist movement (the communists have no place in the National Defence Council), fed up with this ambitious and unscrupulous party, they felt a sense of relief at the disappearance of the disturbing perspectives of Saturday.[17]

He goes on to describe the detention of the new governor, Etelvino Vega, who he portrays as part of the Communist conspiracy to overthrow the government. The operation, he asserts, was carried out without difficulty by a unit of assault guards, who surrounded the governor's headquarters, disarmed the sentries and arrested Vega in his own office. The assault guards also occupied the premises of the Communist Party and took over the offices of the Communist newspaper *Nuestra Bandera* (Our Flag).

Having described the situation in Alicante, Gómez Serrano commented on the fighting in Madrid, provoked, he writes, by the 'senseless Communist attempted coup'. The next day, he made an intriguing report of an incident that he assumed was an attempt to seize control of Alicante on behalf of the Communists. He describes the arrival in Alicante of ex-minister Jesús Hernández, three Communist officers – Enrique Líster, Juan Modesto and Valentín González (also known as *El Campesino* – the peasant) – and a force of 100 heavily armed men. According to Gómez Serrano, the intervention of local party chiefs thwarted their plans and the 'rebels' were disarmed. The leaders then abandoned the town, leaving behind parts of their uniforms and dozens of 'magnificent' submachine guns and long-range artillery pieces, and boarded an aeroplane for France.[18] In his own memoirs, Hernández makes no mention of the event and affirms he was still in Spain at the end of March.[19] On the other hand, it is not impossible that while in Valencia he might have embarked on a covert mission with men from the pro-Communist XXII Corps to liberate Pedro Checa from the custody of the new Casado authorities. Nonetheless, there is no doubt that Líster and Modesto were passengers on the fourth aeroplane that left Monóvar at the last moment on the night of 6 March. If the incident did indeed take place, the real identities of those involved remains as much a mystery as Gómez Serrano's source. It may well be a symptom or an example of the anti-Communist paranoia that the Defence Council had propagated.

On the same day, Gómez Serrano reported that two eminent members of the Communist community in Alicante – Ricardo Millá, a former Mayor, and José González Prieto, editor of the Communist newspaper, *Nuestra Bandera* – had been arrested. He also observed that the newspaper had appeared on the newsstands without the hammer and sickle emblem and without the subheading 'Organ of the Communist Party'. He further detected a sense of demoralisation, even panic, among his former Communist allies, and could not resist the comment, 'What a difference 48 hours can make!'

On 7 March delegates of the Committee of the Popular Front in Alicante published their own manifesto, acclaiming the Defence Council as the legitimate and genuine representation of Republican Spain. They also voted to exclude the Communist members from the committee and called on all *alicantinos* to stay loyal to their liberal, republican tradition, to defend the new 'supreme authority', to maintain discipline and to respond with 'blind obedience' to all orders. The document concluded: '*Alicantinos*, let us collaborate in the national republican enterprise of our supreme Council. For Spain. For the Republic. For freedom.'[20] On 9 March the anarchist chairman of the town council (Mayor), Ángel Company Sevilla, described the Defence Council as 'the maximum expression of our Popular Front'.[21] The members of the local council then agreed to expel all Communist councillors and to transmit their support for the Defence Council to the authorities in Madrid.

Similar motions were passed by the municipal governments of Novelda (7 March), Alcoy, Orihuela (9 March), Denia (10 March) and Elda (13 March). In various towns, through either political conviction or an instinct for self-preservation, various Communist councillors resigned from the party.[22] On 9 March, the Socialist newspaper *Avance* reported the decision of the local branch of the Communist Party of Jijona (Xixona) to proclaim its allegiance to the Defence Council, 'presided by the illustrious General José Miaja', which it recognised as the 'authentic voice of the will of the people'. The local party also announced its intention to put all its weapons at the service of the new government. Furthermore, the members unanimously passed a motion condemning 'the anti-Spanish attitude of certain elements which have infiltrated our party'.[23] In Villena on 10 March, members of the Communist Party voted to resign from the party and dissolve the local branch. Five days later, the premises of the *Juventudes Socialistas Unificadas* in Alicante were sacked, and a bust of Lenin and a portrait of Santiago Carrillo destroyed.[24] The executive committee opted to close the provincial delegation, at least provisionally.[25]

On 11 March, almost as a foresight of what lay ahead for the town of Alicante, Gómez Serrano makes a passing reference in his diaries to Gastone Gambara, the general whom Mussolini had appointed Chief of General Staff of the *Corpo di Truppe Voluntari*. A veteran of the First World War and the Ethiopian conflict (in command of a division of *Camicie Nere* – Black Shirts), he had been severely wounded at the Battle of the Ebro. Now back in Spain, he had been received by Franco and presumably informed of the *Generalísimo*'s plans for the final offensive against the Republic.

The next day Gómez Serrano went to the docks in Alicante to watch the evacuation of several hundred Republicans[26] aboard the tramp steamer SS *Ronwyn*. The fare had been fixed at 50 pesetas (approximately €50 in today's prices). Gómez Serrano expressed surprise at the obvious joy of those who were escaping, his own desire to remain with his family, and his relative optimism. The government, he believed, had been taken over by honest men and the formation of the Defence Council would at least reduce the speed at which Spain was rushing towards a precipice. He concluded, 'We can now see the possibility of an honourable peace.'[27]

From his own vantage point in France, the former Chief of General Staff, General Vicente Rojo, observed, 'The fate of the Spanish people passed from the hands of a Government that was more or less in disarray, to those of men, who while they may have been driven by a noble calling, were to follow it along the most reprehensible path.'[28]

Chapter 19

El abrazo de Vergara

Peace negotiations with the Nationalists

A hundred years earlier, in the summer of 1839, the first Carlist civil war was ended by a peace settlement between those forces loyal to Queen Isabel, and the Carlists who had sought to depose her in favour of the pretender, her uncle, Carlos. The two enemy generals then met and reconciled with a fraternal embrace at Vergara (Basque Country). The Carlist commander, General Maroto, later gave his own disproportionately enthusiastic account of the event:

> peace was sealed in a spirit of utmost joy and harmony ... Soldiers, who had neither been humiliated nor defeated, set down their fearsome arms for the sake of the fatherland; as a tribute to peace, they forgot all bitterness and expressed the heroic action in a brotherly embrace ... so typical of the Spanish approach to life![1]

It appeared that there were now influential members of the military hierarchy of the Republic who had chosen to believe that if Negrín's civilian government could be removed, a comparable miracle was possible with Franco. They had also persuaded themselves that the *Generalísimo* might be more willing to deal with soldiers rather than the politicians of the Second Republic. Even more so once those soldiers had demonstrated tangible proof of their anti-Communism. Thus, they chose to ignore the reality that, through his actions and words, Franco had amply demonstrated his intransigence and his ruthless pursuit of his war aims and ambitions, which included neither reconciliation nor compromise.

Regardless of the outcome of Casado's coup and his victory over the Communists, there can be little doubt that he made a genuine effort to negotiate with the Nationalists and genuinely believed in his mission, his 'first duty'. According to his own account[2], he had told Negrín at their last meeting (1 March) that he believed 'the only solution was direct discussion between the two armies'.[3] However, the title of Chapter VI of his memoirs, 'Peace Negotiations', is misleading; there were no peace negotiations.

During the fighting in Madrid, the National Defence Council (CND) had approved a three-point plan that included guarantees of national independence, the expatriation of those who chose, and a commitment not to carry out reprisals. Matallana and Casado were nominated as chief negotiators. The plan, it was assumed, was foolproof. Franco would clearly be intent on defending Spain's independence and the two generals were the most suitable interlocutors. As if he was totally unaware of events in the Nationalist territories, Casado also thought that the *Caudillo* would support the evacuation of Republicans 'since the reconstruction of Spain could never be undertaken in an atmosphere of hatred and bloodshed'.[4] Acknowledging the 'insatiable thirst for vengeance' of many Nationalists, and that the worst criminal instincts are often hidden 'behind the sword, the wig and the cassock', he argued that the departure of those guilty of political crimes and crimes of bloodshed would 'open the way to conciliation and perhaps political and social harmony'.[5]

In the first version of his memoirs, Casado claims that on 12 March he was approached by two agents of the SIPM – the (in)aptly named Lieutenant-Colonel José Centaño de la Paz,* and a man whose name he could not recall† – who presented themselves as Franco's envoys and conduit for negotiations. In the later edition of his memoirs, Casado admits that Centaño, who was, it seems, a member of his staff, had first declared his role as agent of Franco to him at a meeting on 5 February.[6] On 20 February Centaño presented Casado with a document from Franco demanding surrender, offering guarantees for those not guilty of crimes, and warning that further resistance would be punished.[7]

On 13 March, following a debate in the council, Casado delivered his peace plan to Centaño, who undertook to communicate the details to the authorities in Burgos. According to Casado, the two Nationalist agents presented him with a 'cunningly drawn up' document that became known as '*The Generalissimo's Concessions*', which was no more than the document of 20 February.[8] According to the text, Nationalist Spain would be 'generous' to those who had not committed crimes, and 'benevolent' towards senior officers and officers who, in the last stages of the war, served the interests of Spain. Safe conduct would be offered to those innocent of crime who surrendered to the Nationalist army. It did not require legal expertise to understand that the validity of the guarantees depended on Franco's definition of 'crime'.

Franco, the eternal prevaricator, or as Gabrielle Ashford Hodges described him, 'the Sphinx without a secret',[9] having urged extreme haste, now took almost a week to respond to Casado's initiative. In the meantime, the CND

---

* de la Paz: of the Peace.
† He is probably referring to the SIPM agent, Manuel Guítian.

turned its attention to the question of evacuation. In the words of Casado: 'I worked out in the greatest secrecy, a plan for evacuating the civil population, with the idea of gaining time and avoiding any repetition of the wild exodus from Catalonia. The method, organisation and execution of this important service was kept secret.'[10] So secret, in fact, that the details were never disclosed. In his later memoirs, Casado does outline the chain of command he and Matallana drew up for the operation and acknowledges that the scheme was overtaken by events.[11] More to the point, the only effective plans made by Casado and his team were for their own escape.

While the CND awaited a reply from Burgos, there were two major international events. On 15 March, in defiance of the Munich accords, Nazi Germany occupied Prague, and the European war that Negrín had foreseen came a step closer. The night before, Gómez Serrano had described the collapse of Czechoslovakia with British and French acquiescence. He issued a particular (if private) warning to France that her day of San Martín was coming.[*] Two days later, the Nationalist government agreed a non-aggression treaty with Portugal. The Iberian Pact was signed by the Portuguese Prime Minister, António de Oliveira Salazar, and the Spanish Ambassador in Lisbon, Nicolás Franco, the *Caudillo*'s brother.

The CND finally received a response from Franco on 19 March, a response that dashed any hopes of 'peace with honour' or that the *Caudillo* would treat them any more favourably than he would have Negrín. More surprising than Franco's answer was the idea that any member of the council had expected otherwise. The *Generalísimo*'s agents reiterated that Franco would accept nothing short of unconditional surrender. Unwilling to negotiate terms, he was only prepared to dictate the conditions under which the capitulation would take place. Moreover, he refused to grant Casado the privilege of representing the CND at talks. Such a gesture would appear to recognise parity between the enemy armies. Instead, he instructed Casado to nominate two lower-grade officers as interlocuters.

In the meantime, Casado ordered that servicemen should no longer wear the red star symbol that had been introduced by Largo Caballero during his time as Prime Minister and Minister of Defence (September 1936–May 1937). On 21 March Gómez Serrano noted in his diary that the star had indeed been removed from the uniforms of the troops on parade at the military headquarters in Alicante. On the same day, he reported the appearance of Wenceslao Carrillo of the CND in Alicante. According to Vicente Ramos,

---

[*] San Martín is the traditional day for the slaughter of a pig. The complete proverb is: *A cada cerdo le llega su San Martín* – San Martín comes to every pig.

the Minister of the Interior was making a routine tour of the Levante to ensure all Communist officials had been removed from positions of authority. Carrillo apparently expressed his satisfaction that his 'inspection' had proved unnecessary – Communist influence had been swiftly and effectively stifled.[12]

Domínguez Aragonés was also in the Levante region in his capacity as Vice-President of the UGT and was seeking to make arrangements to evacuate a thousand union officials. He believed Carrillo had finally acknowledged the need to rescue the most vulnerable Republicans and accepted that Franco's word on reprisals was worthless. However, the council was doing nothing to extricate those in danger. Gómez Serrano reported that Carrillo had also confirmed that the CND was involved both in official negotiations with the government in Burgos and contacts with the fifth column. However, the minister added that, 'whatever guarantees Franco might give, he would not be caught in Spain.' Gómez concluded that the time had come to pack.[13] And yet he did not.

On 23 March Lieutenant-Colonel Antonio Garíjo and Commander Leopoldo Ortega flew to Burgos with Casado's final proposals, which included a not unreasonable request that the two sides should agree a twenty-five-day schedule for the surrender of Republican territory by zones, which would enable a staggered programme of evacuation. After brief talks, the representatives of the Burgos government, Colonels Luis Gonzalo and José Ungría, withdrew to consult with a higher authority. When they returned, they insisted the new Nationalist regime would not negotiate terms and would accept only unconditional surrender. Garíjo and Ortega were presented with a document entitled 'Rules for the Surrender of the Enemy Army and the Occupation of its Territory'.[14] Crucially, the Republic was ordered to deliver its air force to Nationalist aerodromes by 1800 on 25 March – a huge undertaking, given the shortage of time, logistic problems and the unpredictable response of some pilots – and to arrange for the surrender of all other forces on 27 March. Significantly for the people of Alicante, Clause 7 referred to Republican seaports:

> The Madrid authorities should make certain of obedience from the forces which are garrisoning coastal towns, so that if they are under their absolute control the rapid occupation of Almeria, Cartagena, Alicante and Valencia may be proceeded with, to help the return of normality to national life. In this case, the authorities mentioned should give strict orders that on the appearance of our ships a tug shall go out with technicians and hostages to be handed over to the Nationalist authorities who come to take over the towns.[15]

Gonzalo and Ungría informed the Republican emissaries that the Nationalists would not agree to the drafting of a document setting out the conditions and mutual guarantees given. In response, the CND, sent a radiogram in which they declared that more time was required to arrange for the surrender of the air force, demanded a written confirmation of the '*Generalissimo's* concessions' and requested a second conference. Franco consented to another meeting on 25 March at which, according to Casado, the Nationalist representatives agreed that a written record of the guarantees and concessions be drafted and signed by both sides. However, at six o'clock, they announced the deadline on the ultimatum to surrender the air force had passed, and the Republic's failure to comply meant that negotiations were to be terminated. Despite unfavourable climatic conditions, Garíjo and Ortega were ordered to abandon Burgos immediately.

In Madrid, the CND sent another dispatch offering to surrender the air force the next day, but it was too late. Franco had already launched an offensive in the south, where the troops under the command of General Juan Yagüe (the 'butcher of Badajoz') advanced across the Sierra Morena and captured Pozoblanco. In one day, the Nationalists took 30,000 prisoners and occupied 2,000km².[16] In his memoirs, Casado declared, 'We realised that the enemy had no intention of proceeding in good faith.'[17]

The next day, a fresh attack was launched from Toledo and the Nationalist radio broadcast a message to the enemy troops outlining the concessions that had been made at Burgos and advising them to cease resistance. Republican troops began to lay down their arms and surrender, or deserted to the Nationalist side, or simply voted with their feet and returned to their families. As the fronts disintegrated, officers were powerless to prevent fraternisation and men who had been fighting for nearly three years embraced and celebrated. On the evening of 27 March Casado instructed the members of the CND to make their way to Valencia. Too late in the case of the President, Miaja; he had already left. Julián Besteiro, the eminent Socialist, elected to remain in Madrid, still clinging to the belief that, as he had committed no crime, he would be treated fairly by the victors. Before he left, Casado appointed Melchor Rodríguez (the anarchist 'Red Angel') as Mayor of Madrid, and it was he who surrendered the capital to Franco's army and the fifth column. At 1300 on 28 March, at the Clinical Hospital of the University City, Colonel Adolfo Prada, the commanding officer of the Army of the Centre, surrendered to his Nationalist counterparts.

Casado was unable to fulfil his self-appointed mission to negotiate an honourable peace settlement. However, far worse than this failure was the fact that he prevented Negrín from carrying out his own plans. Throughout the month of February, Negrín still had cards to play. The enemy was aware that so long as the Prime Minister retained power with the support of the PCE, the Republic would continue to resist, and Franco was aware that he could not count on the patience of Hitler and Mussolini for an indefinite period. Both dictators had more ambitious plans for their military resources elsewhere. Negrín still had a navy and a disciplined fighting force, guaranteed by officers loyal to the PCE and the courage and resilience of members of the party. The Republic had constantly shown its effectiveness in defence, particularly at Madrid and during the Levante offensive (April–July 1938), and Franco was no doubt aware of the difficulties of overcoming an organised rearguard action and a well-defended Mediterranean redoubt. The legitimate government of the Republic also held considerable assets in foreign banks and institutions and arms (stockpiled in France) that Negrín was prepared to use as a bargaining chip. As a final resource, he was even prepared to offer himself as an 'expiatory victim' in return for leniency towards the mass of defeated Republicans.[18]

In Casado's defence, Orwell, who shared the colonel's distrust of the PCE, wrote in his review of the colonel's memoirs:

Colonel Casado's name will always be among those that are remembered in connection with the Spanish Civil War. He it was who overthrew the Negrín government and negotiated the surrender of Madrid – and, considering the actual military situation and the suffering of the Spanish people, it is difficult not to feel he was right.[19]

If we ignore the overgenerous claim that Casado had negotiated the surrender of the capital, the fact remains that he seriously diminished the position of the Republic. By mid-March, not only had Casado disposed of Negrín, but through his actions he had seriously undermined the military capacity of the loyalists and thus lessened the possibility of effectively negotiating with the enemy. Franco was fully aware that members of the CND were prepared to make peace at virtually any cost. Julián Besteiro, included in the council to provide a form of political legitimacy, had made no secret of his anti-Communism, his opposition to Negrín's government and his desire for an immediate ceasefire. His contacts with the fifth column[20] ensured that Franco knew that the CND's public commitment to resistance if the Nationalists failed to negotiate lacked substance.

Moreover, once Casado's planned rebellion had triggered the Cartagena rising, Admiral Buiza's hasty and unauthorised decision to sail the fleet to North Africa had deprived the Republic of its navy. The Republic was left vulnerable to seaborne attacks, merchant shipping was left defenceless and hopes of an organised evacuation wrecked. In the fighting that followed the coup, Casado had achieved his greatest victory: the defeat of the Communists. However, in so doing, he had also dismantled the military authority of the PCE and diminished the Republican army.

On a personal level, Casado appeared to believe that his peers in the Nationalist army would react favourably to both his own status as a career soldier and the council's sense of chivalry. Neither meant anything to Franco. Casado also assumed that his anti-Communism and his triumph in Madrid would stand him in good stead with the *Caudillo*. As the CND abandoned the capital, they chose not to release all the Communists held in detention since the first fortnight of the month. Men and women who had fought valiantly in defence of the Republic were not simply abandoned to their fate; they were delivered to the Nationalists. In the words of Paul Preston: 'It is clear he [Casado] was happy to pay for Franco's mercy in Communist blood.'[21] Again, Casado was wrong. As Hitler would swiftly discover, Franco's concept of gratitude was unidirectional. He only repaid his own debts or rewarded those who helped him when he had no choice or when there was further advantage to be gained.

In short, before the coup of 5 March, Negrín was in a much stronger position to force concessions from Franco, and/or evacuate the maximum number of vulnerable Republicans than Casado ever was afterwards. It is easy to ignore the reality that the villain was Franco, that negotiations failed because the *Caudillo* had no interest in negotiating. However, Gómez Serrano summed up the contradictory attitudes of those who supported Casado: 'The CND and all of us have been despicably tricked. What more could have been expected of the enemy that confronts us. After all, fascists.'[22] How were they cheated, when they were aware of the nature of their adversaries and aware of their war aims? Unfortunately, the colonel's disloyalty and ingenuousness proved decisive.

On 27 March, with final victory imminent, Franco announced Spain's adhesion to the Anti-Comintern Pact. The country now overtly closed ranks with Nazi Germany, Fascist Italy and the Imperial Japanese war machine. Intentionally or not, through their embargo on arms sales to the Republic, the governments of France and Britain had contributed as much to Franco's victory as Hitler and Mussolini. The French now found themselves with hostile, fascist dictatorships on three of their land borders. The British found their position in the Mediterranean threatened not only by Italy but also by Spain. However, those in the most imminent danger from Franco's wrath were the vast numbers of Spanish Republicans trapped in their own homeland. The Centre-South Zone, the last Republican territory, was on the verge of reunification with a country under military occupation by its own army, and under a dictatorship seemingly intent on denying all rights to those who had proved their disloyalty to Spain by defending the Republic. The promulgation of the *Ley de Responsabilidades Políticas* meant that those most active in the defence of democracy were aware that they were facing a *muerte civil* (*civiliter mortuus* – civil death). Since 1937, the *Sección Político-Social* (Political-Social Section) of the *Delegación Nacional de Servicios Documentales* (National Records Services), based in Salamanca, had been gathering intelligence on the enemy. During and after the war, the commission compiled approximately three million separate entries on suspected hostiles, and its work would prove invaluable in the repression of members of left-wing parties, union activists, masons and other miscellaneous undesirables.[23]

Of Franco's attitude towards his allies and his adversaries, the British Consul in Palma Alan Hillgarth wrote:

He does not like but fears the German, he hates the Italian, he hates the French even more and he does not like but would tolerate the British if he were quite certain that we were strong enough to win a war with Germany. Really he loathes all foreigners and is so supremely individual that he loathes most of his fellow countrymen as well.[24]

Chapter 20

Una gota de pura valentía vale más que un océano cobarde

Evacuation

Local historian Vicente Ramos described the atmosphere in Alicante during the second fortnight of March 1939 as, 'Indecision, anxiety, almost total paralysis of economic life, the prelude to chaos.'[1] At 1200 on Friday, 25 March, enemy aircraft bombed Alicante for (probably) the seventy-first[2] and, according to many records, the last time. Most of the bombs fell in the sea and the coastal road out of town. There were no casualties, but the air raid added to the tension, particularly among the refugees now swarming into the town.

By 29 March the town had been virtually taken by the fifth column. There was no resistance. At 1830 Gómez Serrano observed lorries packed with *falangistas* making their way up the Paseo de Soto, chanting, '*¡Franco, Franco, Franco! ¡Arriba España!*' Groups of people on street corners raised their arms in the fascist salute. Gómez later observed that the Republican flag (red, yellow and purple tricolour) had been lowered and the old/new monarchist flag (red, yellow, red) had been raised at the offices of the Civil Governor. Later, the street lighting 'in all its splendour' was turned on for the first time in more than two years. The next day, *falangistas* wearing red and black armbands were guarding public buildings and had captured places of strategic importance including: the anti-aircraft defence posts, the Rabasa air base, the studios of Radio Alicante, the main post office, and the water and electricity company. They had also occupied the newspaper offices of *Nuestra Bandera* and were preparing to use the presses to issue their own daily, *¡Arriba España!* Finally, they had taken the telephone exchange, and calls to Alicante were greeted with the message: 'In the service of Spain, and at the orders of the *Caudillo*.'[3]

As an added precaution, the fifth column/*Falange* had set up roadblocks on the main roads into Alicante from Madrid, Murcia, Valencia, Villafranqueza, San Vicente and Albufereta where they disarmed all those wishing to enter the town. In the circumstances, the local *Falange* leader, José Mallol, felt it incumbent upon himself to take over the responsibilities of Civil Governor. In a radio address on 30 March he called on the population to embrace the values of the new regime and promised to direct all his efforts towards restoring peace and public order, and ensuring the welfare of the population. As a synthesis of Franco's objectives, he declaimed: Peace, Love, Work, Justice, Forgiveness. He did at least get one right. He closed his address with *¡Viva Franco! ¡Viva Alicante! ¡Arriba España!*'.[4]

The evacuation process had started some time before Casado's coup. According to the records compiled in the *Archivo de la Democracia* (Democracy Archives) of the University of Alicante[5], the first reported extraction of refugees after the fall of Catalonia was effected with the help of the crew of a fishing boat. On 7 February the *San Rafael* left Águilas, on the coast of Murcia, for North Africa, with five passengers aboard. Of the sixty-four voyages in February and March recorded in the *Archivo*, between seventeen and eighteen departed from ports in the province of Alicante (nine from Alicante; three from Santa Pola; two or three from Villajoyosa; and one each from Benidorm, Javea and Torrevieja).

Distance and Nationalist control of the Catalan coast meant that Algeria was a more obvious option than France. The most common destination was Oran, at a distance of slightly less than 300km from Alicante (whereas Marseille was approximately 750km). Oran had other appeals. The politician Carlos Esplá, one of the leaders of *Izquierda Republicana* in Alicante, apparently likened the North African town to 'a district of Alicante where the people spoke a mixture of French, Valencian and Spanish'.[6] The first recorded evacuation from the port of Alicante was carried out by the British freighter the SS *African Trader*, which left with sixty-seven passengers (mostly women and children connected in some way to the PSOE) on 22 February. After a severe storm, the ship finally reached the coast of Africa two days later. The ship made a second crossing from Alicante to Oran between 19 March and 21 March with 853–859 refugees[7]. In the meantime, hundreds of desperate Republicans had been rescued by motorboats, yachts, patrol boats, trawlers, mine-sweepers and coastguard launches. On 7 March the SS *Stanhope* docked in Alicante with a cargo of flour and left two days later with approximately sixty refugees. The SS *Marionga* arrived in Alicante in the last week of February carrying a supply of coal. She too left Alicante on 9 March with 120 passengers bound for Marseille.[8] On 12 March SS *Ronwyn* set sail for Ténès (Algeria) with 646 evacuees.[9]

The single most important rescue operation was carried out by the crew of the SS *Stanbrook* under the orders of Archibald Dickson, whose courage and sense of decency shamed the politicians at the Foreign Office and Admiralty in London.[10] The *Stanbrook* first made news in 1937 when the Admiralty chose to recognise the 'legitimacy' of the Nationalist blockade of the Basque Country, an attempt to starve the population into surrender by denying access to the Basque ports by foreign merchant shipping. In the words of Constancia de la Mora, when 'Britannia decided not to rule the waves.'[11] According to Michael Alpert, the attitude of the Admiralty reflected its dislike of the merchant skippers (considered 'profiteers') and its preference for the insurgents over the Republicans, 'whose original sin had been the mutiny and the murders of officers in 1936'.[12]

Despite instructions to the contrary, under Dickson's predecessor, the *Stanbrook* took part in the successful running of the blockade. Much to the chagrin of First Lord of the Admiralty, Sir Samuel Hoare, Royal Navy vessels stationed in the area had no option but to afford protection to those British ships operating out of St Jean de Luz that ignored the warnings of the government in London and defied the threats of the Nationalists. Following the lead of William Roberts, Captain of SS *Seven Seas Spray*, which had picked up a cargo of 3,600 tons of foodstuffs from the port at Alicante, a number of ships, including the *Stanbrook*, managed to reach Bilbao and deliver supplies to the desperate population.[13] In May the SS *Habana* evacuated approximately 4,000 Basque children from the same city and took them to the relative safety of a temporary exile in Britain.[14]

Born in Cardiff in 1892, Dickson joined the Merchant Navy at the age of 15, before serving in the First World War as a temporary lieutenant in the Royal Navy.[15] In the final weeks of the Civil War, according to the account that he gave in a letter to the *Sunday Dispatch*,[16] the new skipper of the *Stanbrook* was given orders to leave Marseille on 17 March 1939 and to sail in ballast to Alicante to collect a consignment that included oranges, tobacco and saffron. Dickson, who had been Master of the *Stanbrook* for twelve months, described the ship as a small, 1,383-ton cargo vessel, 230ft long, with a beam of 34ft, and with accommodation for her twenty-four-man crew. He reported a relatively quiet voyage, except for an incident with a 'Franco destroyer' that ordered him not to enter the harbour at Alicante. Dickson was able to use the weather conditions to evade the Nationalist vessel and docked, regardless of the danger, at 1800 on 19 March. After a week waiting in vain for his cargo in the port, he made a fruitless trip to Madrid, where he was told his shipment had, in fact, now been dispatched and was *en route* to the coast by lorry.

On 27 March the trucks did indeed deliver the cargo to the quay. However, at the same time, the crew reported that a crowd of 1,000 desperate Republicans had also gathered on the dockside hoping to find escape from the nightmare of Franco's victory. In his diary entry for 28 March (the date 27 March has been deleted), Gómez Serrano reports his visit to the port to observe the proceedings: 'This evening the boat that arrived a few days ago is due to leave. How many people will it take? There are thousands and thousands in the port.'[17] Port officials asked Dickson to carry the refugees to Oran and vowed that they all had valid passports and that the French authorities would do nothing to prevent them disembarking. Dickson had been given instructions only to take refugees on board if they were in real need, but when he saw the condition of many of those waiting, and on the understanding that they would soon be landed in Oran, he agreed to let them embark. He reported:

> Amongst the refugees were all classes of people, some of them appearing very poor indeed and looking half starved and ill clad and attired in a variety of clothes ranging from boiler suits to old and ragged pieces of uniform and even blankets and other odd pices (sic) of clothing. There were also some people both women and men who appeared very well to do and whom I assumed to be the wives and relatives of officials.[18]

By 2100, amid relative calm, the refugees began boarding the ships while customs officers checked their passports. However, after processing the documents of about 800 would-be passengers, the officials appeared to lose control of the situation at the gangway: 'it became choked with a struggling mass of people, which included some of the guards and Customs Officials who at this time decided to join the throng of refugees; and threw down their arms and equipment and joined in the stampede to get aboard.' In the circumstances, the crew had little choice but to allow all those waiting on the quayside to follow. By 2230, with the last on board, Dickson described the scene rather bizarrely as, 'like one of the Thames holiday steamers on a Bank Holiday only many times worse.' He insisted that in his thirty-three years at sea he had never seen anything like it and hoped he never would again. According to one witness who arrived at the last moment:

> The ship was full up to the main mast. There were people everywhere; in the holds, on the bridge, on the areas above the galley and the engine-rooms: the plimsoll line was no longer visible, and they were beginning to pull anchor. Thousands of desperate people were still arriving, shouting and weeping ... The *carabineros* closed the entrance to the port and to get on the *Stanbrook*, we had to climb one of the ship's ropes.[19]

Abandoning the cargo on the quayside, the captain then ordered his crew to set sail for North Africa. Alicia González Beltrán (passenger 2278) has stated that it was Dickson himself who threw ropes into the water to help the last two refugees to board the ship.[20] He estimated that he was carrying 1,835 passengers – in fact, there were 2,638 refugees on board the ship, including 147 children, of whom fifteen were under one year of age.[21] The most eminent was Rafael Millá (passenger 1204), the former Communist Mayor of Alicante.

Dickson offers a graphic description of an air raid on the town and port as the *Stanbrook* left the harbour, in which he reports 'the flash of the explosions' and 'the shock of the exploding shells'. This account is supported by various sources including Vicente Ramos, who in his monograph on the history of the *Teatro Principal* (Main Theatre) describes how one bomb crashed through the roof, failed to explode, and came to rest on the stage.[22] Others suggest there is no record of an air raid on the night of 27–28 March. For some local historians, the last officially registered attack was on 25 March,[23] and in his diaries, Gómez Serrano, who was very thorough in his observations of aerial attacks, makes no mention of any incident. The third option is the most plausible: that the Italians launched an attack on ships believed to be entering or leaving the harbour. Indeed, Paul Preston suggests: 'The ship [*Stanbrook*] was attacked by Francoist aircraft but miraculously, without lights. Captain Dickson manged to manoeuvre through the rebel gauntlet.'[24] One of the youngest of the evacuees, Helia González (passenger 2277), who was 6 years old at the time, later recalled seeing the 'fans of spray' as the shells hit the water.[25] She also remembered how her mother, Isabel Beltrán (2276), was holding her younger sister Alicia (2278) in her arms and had shifted her from one shoulder to the other, moments before a blast caused another passenger to lose his grip on the funnel and to land boot first exactly where Alicia had been resting her head.[26]

Hunger and cold were thus compounded by fear of enemy aircraft and ships. Some passengers huddled around the funnel for warmth. Others threw any identity documents into the water in case they were intercepted by a Nationalist vessel. Some younger women began singing to raise their spirits and were joined by members of the crew. The captain took a small group of women on a tour of the ship, and they then volunteered to help in the galley.[27] Despite the difficulties, the ship made the twenty-two-hour crossing safely and arrived off the North African coast on 29 March. The greatest peril was caused whenever a rumour spread that another vessel had been seen off the port or starboard side, triggering a rush to one side of the boat or the other, which in turn caused the *Stanbrook* to list dangerously.

The French officials in Oran were neither prepared nor predisposed to help the evacuees. The ship was not allowed to dock in the harbour until the next day, when some 140 passengers were allowed to disembark. Although the authorities did expedite the process of bringing ashore the remaining women and children, many of the men were forced to continue on board for four weeks without proper sanitation (a single head) and without the basic conditions of personal health and hygiene. In its files, the Foreign Office holds a copy of a telegram received on 6 April by the International Commission from their agent in Oran: 'Conditions on Stanbrook for 2,300 men appalling. Impossible to move on deck. No possibility making latrines owing lack of space for workmen. No washing facilities. Grave danger disease breaking out. Authorities absolutely prohibit landing.'[28]

Exiles who had arrived earlier made efforts to provide food, medicines, soap, clothes and tobacco, and some of the local population took advantage of the situation to approach the ship and offer food in return for personal items of value. The fear of a typhus outbreak eventually persuaded the colonial authorities to authorise the disembarkation of all the passengers. Once the evacuees had been vaccinated and allowed to shower, they were transferred to internment camps. The fate of those who had been unable to escape proved even worse.

The *Stanbrook* was not the last refugee ship to leave Alicante. Hours after Dickson had set sail for Oran, on the early morning of 29 March, the SS *Maritime* (of the Mid-Atlantic Shipping Co.) put out to sea with thirty-two passengers and set a course for Marseille. The 5,801-ton merchant steam ship was substantially larger than the *Stanbrook* and equipped to take at least as many refugees in considerably greater comfort. And yet, rather than save some of the thousands of refugees who had converged on the port, its captain chose to allow only high-ranking civil and military authorities and their families on board. Among those fortunate enough to be given passage were the former Mayor of Alicante, Lorenzo Carbonell, the former Military Governor of Alicante, Lieutenant Colonel Antonio Rubert, who had taken the precaution of changing into civilian dress, and the Civil Governor, Manuel Rodríguez Martínez, who did at least order the release of all the Communists held in custody in Alicante before he left.[29]

The rescue of those who did escape Alicante by sea was largely the work of the *Comisión de Evacuación de la Federación Provincial Socialista* (Evacuation Commission of the Socialist Provincial Federation).[30] The abandonment of thousands of people in the port was little short of a dereliction of duty and caused outrage among the Socialists who had been instrumental in persuading the *Maritime* to dock in Alicante. Luis Deltell, of the Evacuation Commission, who witnessed the departure of the ship, later wrote:

At that moment, there remained neither friends, nor comrades, not even a modicum of humanity. There were men sentenced to death and men who had been saved; the ship had a displacement of three thousand tons (three times more than the *Stanbrook*) and only twenty (sic) people were able to embark. Some day we will settle accounts![31]

Nevertheless, according to the minutes of a meeting of the Socialist Provincial Federation held in July 1939 in Oran, the passengers were powerless to overrule the Ship's Master who had chosen to ignore the plight of the refugees. He allegedly claimed that 'he would not allow any more Spanish assassins on his ship'.[32] A few hours later, members of the Evacuation Commission who had failed to board the *Maritime* left Torrevieja for North Africa on board a small fishing boat.

At the same meeting in Oran, the federation claimed responsibility for the evacuation of 5,146 refugees to North Africa. The breakdown by ship was given as:

*Rotroin**	13/03/39	680 passengers
African Trader	21/03/39	1,250 passengers
Stanbrook	30/03/39	3,016 passengers
Smaller vessels		200 passengers

Regardless of the many discrepancies in figures among the different sources, the actions of the local Socialist Federation were clearly more effective than those of the central government. The minutes[33] also claim that of the total of people saved, 1,420 belonged to the PSOE and 3,736 to other parties and organisations. In the case of the *Stanbrook*, the minutes indicate the following breakdown:

Socialists	572
Communists	196
CNT	304
Republicans	590
Foreign supporters	184
No know political affiliation	470

The figures suggest that there was no coordinated boycott of members of the Communist Party, as has been reported in other cases.[34] However, it is

---

* I believe this was the SS *Ronwyn*.

impossible to rule out the actions of individuals who may well have refused travel documents and passage to party members or simply given preferential treatment to members of other groups of the now extinct Popular Front.

The most fortunate were those who were able to secure passage on one of the innumerable flights that ferried senior military officers and political officials to North Africa. On 29 March General Miaja, President of the Council of National Defence, left Spain for North Africa from the military aerodrome at Rabasa in Alicante. He was accompanied by his aides-de-camp and members of his family. Miaja was one of the most truly ambiguous and mysterious figures of the Civil War. A man possibly of accidental loyalty to the Republic, in the sense that he was stationed in Madrid at the onset of fighting, he was believed by people on both sides of the conflict to have been a member of the *Unión Militar Española* (Spanish Military Union – UME), the clandestine group of right-wing army officers who supported the overthrow of the Republic.[35] He later joined the Communist Party, though Hugh Thomas suggests that, in fact, he had membership cards of all the political parties in Madrid, even the JSU (the Unified Socialist/Communist Youth Movement).[36]

He was involved in some of the most crucial actions and was appointed to positions of huge responsibility and authority, and yet his impact on the war lacked any substance. On the night of 18–19 July 1936 he was appointed Minister of War in Martínez Barrio's government, which survived only a few hours. During the defence of the capital he was made President of the *Junta de Defensa de Madrid* (Madrid Defence Committee) and feted as a hero by many sections of the population, even though his involvement was more symbolic than practical. As Commander of the Army of the Centre, he participated in the battles of Jarama and Guadalajara, although his own contribution to the military successes of the Republican army was questioned.[37] In 1938 he was named Commander of the Central Army Group, but in January 1939 he sabotaged General Rojo's plans for diversionary offensives to relieve the pressure in Catalonia.

At the meeting of members of the high command with Negrín at Los Llanos in February 1939, he was the only member of the military to offer any support to the Prime Minister's doctrine of continued resistance. When Casado declared his rebellion against Negrín, he insisted that Miaja, the highest-ranking officer of the conspiracy, be made President of the CND, and yet Miaja was the one member of the new council not present in Madrid that night. The US journalist Herbert L. Matthews (of the *New York Times*) said of him: 'The picture of the loyal, dogged, courageous defender of the Republic – a picture built up from the last days of the siege of Madrid – was a myth. He was weak, unintelligent, unprincipled.'[38] In Helen Graham's introduction to the Civil War, Miaja does not even warrant a reference in the index.[39]

Chapter 21

Wo bleibt Gambara?

The tragedy of the port

On 27 March the Nationalists launched the final offensive, and finding no resistance, were able to advance rapidly on all fronts. The Foreign Office in London took special care to preserve a copy of the translation of Franco's final message to the Republican army, which appeared in the *Manchester Guardian* newspaper:

> The Nationalist Government repeats all its previous offers of a generous pardon for all who have not committed crimes. Neither military service with the Republicans nor the fact of belonging to anti-Nationalist political parties will be regarded as reasons of criminal proceedings. Legal tribunes alone will deal with crimes committed during the Republican occupation. Surrender to the Fatherland is honourable, but it would be criminal lunacy to shed further blood for a lost cause and for a few interested individuals.[1]

On 28 March the Republicans surrendered Madrid. Many of the men who laid down their arms travelled across the city by Metro (the underground train system) to Vallecas in the east, where they sought transport to the Mediterranean coast. Casado and the other members of the CND also fled the capital, with the exception of Besteiro, who, trusting in the goodwill of Franco, remained and was immediately arrested. Melchor Rodríguez, appointed Mayor of Madrid by Casado, officially handed control of the city to the new military authorities.

On 29 March the Nationalists occupied the cities of Albacete, Ciudad Real, Cuenca, Jaen and Sagunto; and the Republican air force submitted to Franco's demands and surrendered. The next day, the French colonial authorities officially transferred control of the Republican fleet at Bizerta to Rear Admiral Salvador, the representative of the new Francoist regime (recognised by France since 27 February).[2] Meanwhile, thousands of Republicans were gathering on the Mediterranean coast where, word had spread, ships would be waiting to take them to exile and safety. Those who had assembled in Valencia were redirected to Alicante. At the same time, the Republican authorities in the town ordered the release of all prisoners who had been incarcerated for their support of the Nationalist cause.

One of the most eminent post-Civil War Spanish historians, Manuel Tuñón de Lara, was 23 years old when the war finished.[3] Having travelled overnight on a tank transporter, he reached Alicante at dawn on 29 March to find a town in chaos, its palm trees ripped apart by the bombs, the docks in ruins and many of its buildings derelict. It was now, for the briefest of moments, that Alicante witnessed the collision of diametrically opposed ideologies and visions of Spain. The triumphant fifth column emerged from anonymity and cars raced around the centre proudly bearing red and yellow monarchist flags while vanquished Republican soldiers wound their way down to the port area. And as the town held its breath, the two sides were forced to co-exist. The *falangistas* and their new supporters were heavily outnumbered and lacked sufficient weaponry to engage battle-hardened troops. The Republicans were committed to a single mission, to escape before the Nationalist armies occupied the town. The fighting was over, the only excuse for further violence was self-defence, and so long as nobody attacked them, the Republicans had nothing to gain by resorting to arms. There was certainly isolated gunfire and sporadic outbursts of aggression, but they were minor incidents considering the town was temporarily shared by men and women of two enemy camps who had endured more than two and a half years of savage war.

As the battle cry among the Republicans became *¡Al puerto!* (To the port), the town continued to fill with a multitude of humanity, including officers and soldiers of the Popular Army, officials of the Republican state (Civil Governors, Mayors, town councillors), and representatives of the parties and trade unions. The refugees withdrew to the docks where, according to Tuñón de Lara, they swiftly improvised a stronghold protected by sandbags, military vehicles and patrols. The historian also recalls that the Republicans were not a demoralised, shapeless mass, but a community with a social fabric; there were emotional reunions, old relationships were renewed and new friendships were forged.[4]

On 20 March Sixto Agudo (alias '*Blanco*'), a major in the 28th Mixed Brigade, had been convened to a meeting with Jesús Hernández and Vicente Uribe. When he and his staff arrived in Valencia, they found the two men had left with Fernando Claudín. A week later, he was persuaded to transfer to Alicante and travelled south in a requisitioned ambulance. He described what he found as 'surreal':

the streets and avenues of the town were packed with a multitude that had a single obsession, ¡Al Puerto! Republican warriors, members of town councils and Popular Front committees, separated from their units and their villages, in total confusion, were searching for the port of their salvation, the sea ... but what was missing were the boats.[5]

Carmen Caamaño (PCE) had acted as secretary to Jesús Monzón, the Civil Governor of Alicante (1937–1938), and relocated with him when he was made Civil Governor of Cuenca. When he was transferred to Madrid, she was appointed governor in his place. In March 1939, in the final stages of pregnancy, she travelled to Alicante and gave birth in a friend's house in San Juan, before making her way to the port with her newborn son. She later told Ronald Fraser that she had arranged passage on a British freighter, but when the captain saw the mass of people preparing to board his ship with her, he pulled up the gangplank and ordered his crew to set sail. She concluded, 'Defeated, we were now being betrayed. I don't believe I could bear to relive such anguish. Seeing those boats arrive and then turn away. Too many emotions for one person to bear.'[6] Nevertheless, on the port, she was then reunited with her husband, the artist Ricardo Fuente, who told her, 'Now the three of us can die together.'[7]

As night fell on 29 March, the refugees on the port lit bonfires. The next day, as if to compound their misery, it began to rain. Tuñón del Lara watched the comings and goings of Etelvino Vega, of Rafael Henche de la Plata (the Mayor of Madrid before the Casado coup), of Rodríguez Vega (Secretary-General of the UGT), and a succession of politicians, soldiers and academics. He was also aware of the activities of those among them who were seeking a solution to the crisis.

On 27 March the International Delegation for Spanish Evacuation and Relief* had arrived in Valencia on board the French-owned freighter the *Lezardrieux*. The delegation of six Frenchmen (three parliamentary deputies, a civil servant, a journalist and a doctor), three Britons (including Sir George Young), one American and one Finn immediately recognised their mission had been reduced to arranging for a mass evacuation. According to the account of Laurin Zilliacus (the Finnish representative), the next day 367 Republicans – 'selected by unanimous agreement between all Republican parties in Valencia,

---

* On behalf of the officially named: *Comité international de coordination et d'information pour l'aide à l'Espagne républicaine* (International Committee of Coordination and Information for Aid to Republican Spain). Supported in Britain by the National Joint Committee for Spanish Relief.

who drew up the lists in the presence of our delegates' – were taken aboard the *Lezardrieux* and transferred to Oran.[8]

In the meantime, Colonel Casado had left Madrid from the Algete aerodrome and was flown to the Manises airport in Valencia on a thirty-seater Douglas aircraft, which had been presented to the Republican air force by sympathisers in the USA.[9] Soon after his arrival, he held talks with members of what he called the *Comité Internacional de Coordinación* (International Coordination Committee). Although he does not name the French representatives, whom Martínez Leal identifies as Albert Forcinal (the chairman of the delegation), André Ulmann (journalist) and Charles Tillon (Communist deputy), he reports that the Communist members (presumably the latter two) pleaded with him to free all Communists still held in custody.[10] They were ill-informed, Casado claimed, as all had already been freed. This was a blatant untruth; there were still significant numbers of party-members incarcerated in the Centre-South Zone, especially Madrid, Guadalajara and Jaén.[11]

When asked how much more time there was to evacuate the refugees in Alicante, Casado declined to expose the reality: that the fronts had collapsed, that any strategy of a planned withdrawal was entirely theoretical and that the question of timing lay in the hands of the Nationalists. At this point in the Spanish version of his memoirs, Casado offers a curious insight into his shifting attitudes by using Franco's title, the *Generalísimo*.[12] Zilliacus later offered perhaps the most discerning of all descriptions of the Colonel: 'a wishful thinker with grandiose sentiments and exalted ideas about himself.'[13] The Presidential Undersecretary, José Sánchez Riquena, meanwhile, told a press conference in Valencia that the CND was still anxiously working on the evacuation plan, and declared:

> Rest assured this will be carried out in the widest possible sense [...] All those who should and wish to leave, will leave, and when all have done so, then the members of the National Defence Council will also depart from Spain. Only then, and not a minute earlier than they should.'[14]

In fact, the existence of an evacuation plan was an illusion. According to the British Consul in Valencia, Abbington Goodden, on 25 March, he had held talks with Antonio Pérez García, the Minister of Labour in the CND, the man who had been given responsibility for coordinating the operation. In his report to London, the consul described Pérez as 'completely dazzled and incapable of coming to any decision'. He gave a vague indication that lists of people to be evacuated were being drafted but could only offer a number between 10,000 and 40,000. He had made no arrangements to charter ships and no arrangements with the French authorities to facilitate the arrival of vast numbers of refugees. Goodden concluded: 'The Council appears to be incapable of formulating any plan.' However, he also makes the point that they had 'little money abroad, no ships for evacuation, no diplomatic mission to plead their cause and inadequate means of communication with foreign countries'.[15] Casado's refusal to negotiate a transfer of power with Negrín, and the desertion of the navy, had proved crucial. However, the council's failure to prioritise the processing of passports and other travel documents, and to arrange transport for Republicans in the central zone to the east coast, also indicated a lack of political will or competence.

After their meeting with Casado, while the Colonel was making arrangements for his own evacuation, the three Frenchmen of the International Delegation abandoned Valencia. Forcinal travelled to Gandia, and Tillon and Ullman made their way to Alicante to prepare for the arrival of two French ships, the *Winnipeg* and the *Ploubazlanec* (both belonging to the *Compagnie France Navigation*), with a combined capacity to extract more than 6,000 refugees. However, the delegation was still unable to persuade either the French or the British navy to offer the protection demanded by the ship's owners and captain. In Alicante Colonel Burillo and Tillon set up a local ad hoc *Junta de Evacuación* (Evacuation Committee) with the participation of soldiers and left-wing party officials to deal with practical arrangements for an orderly embarkation should the occasion occur. By this stage there were between 12,000 and 15,000 men, women and children[16] in the port, desperately waiting for the arrival of the ships that had been promised.

The next day at 1330, Casado was invited by local Nationalist agents to make an address on Radio Valencia, in which he made an appeal to the population to remain calm in order to avoid fighting and bloodshed. Displaying his usual hubris and disdain for uncomfortable truths, he told listeners:

> The good faith of the victors is beyond doubt. We have secured a decent and honourable peace in the best possible conditions and without bloodshed. I can assure you that nothing has happened in the Loyalist zone that was not part of our plans when we took power in Republican Spain on 5 March. According to the promises made by Franco, all those who are innocent of blood crimes will remain free. General Franco has promised me that he will not oppose the evacuation. He has not put his signature to a guarantee, because that would have been a humiliation that no victor could be compelled to accept, but you can trust his word. He has kept all the promises that he has made me. ¡*Viva España!*[17]

It is uncertain what Casado meant by 'promises' and so it is difficult to refute this last claim. However, it does appear clear that he was not convinced by the guarantees made to him of clemency for all those officers who expedited the end of the Republic. On the other hand, it is not unreasonable to suppose that the one commitment that Franco was prepared to uphold was that Casado himself and the members of the Defence Council would be allowed safe passage out of Spain. According to his own account, having taken note of the hostile atmosphere in Valencia, Casado judged it opportune to head for Gandia in the expectation of rescue by the Royal Navy. He and his party thus acquired the necessary vehicles (possibly a Chrysler, a Packard and a Rolls Royce[18]) and drove south. Each town they passed had been taken by the Nationalists.[19]

They arrived at their destination at 1600 (29 March) and Casado held new talks with Forcinal of the International Delegation, who updated him on their attempts to send ships to Alicante and reported on plans to embark the 150 people waiting at Gandia on the HMS *Galatea*. In February the British Consul in Valencia had received specific instructions from the Foreign Office:

> In the event of collapse of Republican Government, you are authorised to provide facilities for evacuation of members and officials of Government and their families if they apply to you for such facilities, if accommodation in H.M.Ships is available after evacuation of British subjects and if you are satisfied that they are in imminent and immediate peril of their lives.[20]

Goodden was now apparently on board the *Galatea*, discussing the necessary arrangements with the captain. It also appears that the consul vetoed the plans of the senior naval officer in the area, Rear-Admiral John Cronyn Tovey (commander of destroyer flotillas in the Mediterranean), to escort the *Winnipeg* and the *Ploubazlanec* into Alicante harbour, and insisted that HMS *Sussex* remain at Gandia with HMS *Galatea* and HMS *Nubian*, a move that would facilitate the extraction of Casado. According to historian Peter Anderson, the decision was largely motivated by reports from Allan Hillgarth (the vice-consul in Mallorca) that relations with the new Franco regime would be damaged if the Rear-Admiral's proposal were implemented, and confirmation from the consul in Alicante that there were no British subjects in the port and thus no irrefutable diplomatic justification for the mission.[21]

The report of the International Delegation, prepared by Sir George Young and published after the events, included the following paragraph:

> The Delegation wish to put on record that the Admiral and Naval Officers risked exceeding their instructions in order to give every co-

operation to the Delegation and to show every courtesy to the members of the Republican Government, whereas the British Consul and Consular Authorities went to the opposite extreme.[22]

While Casado also gives a detailed description of his arguments with British officials over the terms under which they would agree to evacuate his party,[23] he is, moreover, highly critical of his treatment by the Royal Navy. It is not impossible that he wished to distance himself publicly from British officialdom in general rather than risk suggestions of collusion between the CND and British intelligence.

In his memoirs, he claims that he spoke by phone with Colonel Burillo, who had installed himself at the command headquarters of the port authorities in Alicante and was told it was impossible to reach Alicante by road. He then allowed himself to be persuaded by members of the Defence Council and International Delegation to remain in Gandia. At 1900 (29 March) he was informed by the British Consul that the embarkation of all those on the port had been authorised and he subsequently boarded the *Galatea*. The remaining refugees began embarking at 0600 the next morning. The operation was delayed as the damage to the port made it impossible for the warships to dock normally and it was necessary to ferry the evacuees out to the ships.[24]

Having spent an uncomfortable night on deck, and given his chronic stomach condition, Casado was sent to the ship's infirmary and then transferred to the navy hospital ship HMS *Maine*. He reached Marseille on 3 April, travelled north by train, crossed the Channel and was in London by 2000 the next day.[25] In neither language version of his memoirs does Casado give a satisfactory explanation of why the vast majority of the refugees were directed to Alicante when he and his acolytes departed from another port 70km to the north, and therefore considerably closer to Valencia where many of the Republicans had assembled. He does suggest that Alicante was 'farthest from the fronts',[26] but the port at Gandia was under British control and the presence of British warships largely neutralised the danger of intervention by Franco's navy, which is precisely the factor that discouraged other ships from entering the harbour in Alicante. Casado's own decision to use Gandia therefore made perfect sense. On the other hand, one can only speculate about the motives behind massing the refugees on the dockside in Alicante while their leaders, the members of the CND, escaped through Gandia.

According to the extensive account of the events in Valencia and Gandia offered by Bahamonde and Cervera, Goodden was made extremely uncomfortable by the presence of the International Delegation, in particular the British representatives, and in particular a man of such social prestige as

Sir George Young. It seems clear that their demands for mass evacuation of refugees contravened the policy of the government, as defined by Halifax and the diplomatic corps, of a much more discriminating extraction plan sanctioned by Franco.[27]

In his statement to the House of Lords on 9 March, the Secretary of State for Foreign Affairs (Viscount Halifax) had made it clear that he did not share 'the fear on the Republican side that resort might be had to indiscriminate reprisals by General Franco'. Quoting the Prime Minister's speech in the Commons at the end of February, he maintained that Franco had issued adequate assurance that there would be no 'general proscription of Republican supporters that the then Spanish Government believed themselves to have reason to fear'. Finally, he contended that 'it would be quite impossible and quite improper for any foreign Government outside Spain to claim to be in a position to judge the blameworthiness or otherwise of any individuals, or, as he put it, to lecture the Spanish Government upon how they should carry on the task of government resting upon their shoulders.'

Addressing the question of evacuation, Halifax adeptly applied the well-honed cynicism of the Foreign Office of the 1930s and insisted that if Franco's assurances were genuine, then the evacuation of thousands of Republican sympathisers was obviously unnecessary. He concluded that mass evacuation of people, 'the culpability of whom in regard to crimes which might be alleged against them we have no means of judging, is not a proposal that we could in the present circumstances accept'. He further dismissed the idea as administratively unfeasible. His only concession was to uphold the traditional protocol that the commanders of British ships should undertake to rescue political leaders and others whose lives were in danger. In his statement, he also declared that the government had reached the conclusion that no action should be taken without the prior consent of the Spanish authorities, which suggests that Franco had indeed approved the arrangements to evacuate Casado from Gandia.[28]

Fearful that an influx of significant numbers of refugees in Gandia might jeopardise their plans for a discreet and limited withdrawal of Casado's entourage, the authorities had proposed that new arrivals be redirected south to Alicante where French merchant ships would soon commence the evacuation of those in the port. It is not clear if this initiative came from Casado, Goodden, or Mr Edwin Apfel, the Manager of the Alcoy and Gandía Railway and Harbour Company Ltd, whose duties included management of the port facilities.[29] The outcome was the same. Specifically, those in control in Gandia knew that a major operation in Alicante was contingent on the support of the British navy and were also aware that this was no longer a plausible option.

In Alicante the refugees waited in vain. To facilitate an orderly, eventual boarding of any vessels that might arrive, they had been separated into groups according to ideological affinity: Communists, Socialists, Anarchists, Republicans and members of the armed forces. Although there were sightings of ships off the coast, the frequent rumours that they were soon to enter the harbour proved false. Without protection from warships, the risk of challenging the Nationalist blockade was too high. On 30 March, Gómez Serrano wrote:

> I've been to the port. A huge, motley crowd of thousands of soldiers of the disbanded republican army gave a tragic impression. Men, women, children standing for hours awaiting the arrival of a hypothetical boat which will save them from what they imagine to be the thirst for revenge for yesterday's enemy.[30]

The same day, at question time in Westminster, the equally sceptical Conservative MP for the Isle of Wight, Captain Peter Macdonald, asked the Under-Secretary of State for Foreign Affairs, 'What reason is there to believe that the lives of these people are in danger?'[31] The question appears to have been rhetorical.

With the town largely under the control of the *Falange* and other assorted fifth columnists, the coast patrolled by the Nationalists, and the Republicans encamped on the docks, there remained one last element to complete the picture: agents of those foreign powers that had played such a huge part in Franco's victory. On 29 March Italian troops of the Littorio Division of the CTV, under the command of General Gastone Gambara, had been ordered to advance on the town. They met no resistance as they passed through Almansa, Villena and Elda. At approximately 1800 on 30 March they reached the outskirts of Alicante. Gómez Serrano notes in his diary that the clocks had been changed. Until this point the time in the Republican zone had been one hour ahead of the Nationalist zone, but turning the clocks back proved to be more than a mere metaphor.

From the main Madrid road the Italians marched along the avenida de Orihuela, Maisonnave, Paseo de Soto, Alfonso el Sabio, and down the avenida Zorrilla* towards the town hall and the port. They gradually replaced the civilians who were holding strategic locations in the town and took up positions around the port area. In his diary, Gómez Serrano was strangely impressed by the quality and elegance of their uniforms.[32] It is generally agreed that the Italian troops were not overzealous in their duties and turned a blind

---

* Today: Avenida de la Constitución.

eye to many Republicans who chose to escape their custody. It appears that after talks between Gambara, Charles Tillon and Burillo, and the consuls of France, Argentina and Cuba, the Italians agreed to respect a neutral zone, from which Republicans would be permitted to embark on any boats that braved the Nationalist blockade and entered the harbour. It also appears that Franco had not authorised the pact and had no intention of facilitating mass evacuation.[33] General Andrés Saliquet, the Commander of Franco's Army of the Centre, had issued instructions to Gambara to use force to subdue the remnants of the Republican army (*Réduzcanlos por la fuerza de las armas*),[34] and the Italian general deserves some credit for avoiding a bloodbath by ignoring these orders and by negotiating the peaceful surrender of the Republicans within the confines of the port. More fervent Spanish officers would doubtless have shown less diplomacy and less concern for the sanctity of life.

In the meantime, other towns of the province had also fallen to the enemy. The Nationalists took control of Elche on 26 March and Franco's troops entered Denia on 28 March, hours after the last air raid. In Alcoy the mayor transferred power to the chief of the *Falange* on 29 March; members of the Italian CTV occupied the city three days later. On 31 March, Italian troops, who had previously occupied Castalla, arrived in Onil singing the '*Giovinezza*'*. González de Pablo's friend at the aircraft plant, 'Sr Vicente', had long since returned to Elda, telling his young associate, 'It's over.' The French girl, Gillet, had travelled down to Alicante in the company of a member of the air force, in search of a French boat. Bicolour flags were raised and the owner of the bar in the main square invited everyone to a glass of Moscatel†. The premises of the SAF-15 were eventually occupied by troops from the Nationalist air force. The workers, including González de Pablo, were 'politely' invited to leave the town.[35]

The last Republican Military Governor of the province was Lieutenant-Colonel José Muñoz Vizcaino of the *Carabineros*, who was left no choice but to accept the post on 28 March when his predecessor escaped Alicante aboard the SS *Maritime*. He was stationed in San Juan and had occupied the Finca Pedro José where he had excavated a bomb shelter for his neighbours (which eventually proved unnecessary) and organised a distribution point for whatever food supplies he was able to requisition for the ever more desperate population. On his 'appointment' to military command, he met with José Mallol Alberola and other members of the *Falange* to negotiate the peaceful surrender of Alicante to the rebels. His actions undoubtedly helped to avoid

---

* The official hymn of the *Partito Nazionale Fascista* – National Fascist Party.
† A white wine from the Marina Alta area in the north of the province.

bloodshed between the defeated Republicans based in Alicante and the advancing Nationalists.

However, the misery of those in the port continued until, at midday on 31 March, two ships were clearly visible approaching the harbour entrance. Any last hope was dispelled when it became clear they were flying the red and yellow standard of the Nationalists. The ships were minelayers, the *Vulcano* and the *Júpiter*, which had set out from Castellón carrying men of the 121 and 122 battalions of the Galician Corps serving with Franco's Army of the Levante. The writer Eduardo de Guzmán, one of those trapped on the port, described his own sense of relief that all hope of rescue had now gone as 'waking from a Dantesque nightmare'. Using the present tense, he recalled his emotions at that moment:

> It is, in other words, the death of hope for us all. But surprised and bewildered, I am aware of an unexpected phenomenon: that the loss of hope, the farewell to all types of personal dreams, the certainty of an imminent and tragic outcome does not increase the fears, anguish, and anxiety of recent days. The effect is diametrically opposed. Suddenly, I feel an extraordinary sense of calm, a strange respite which is in stark contrast with the tormented turmoil I have felt since, many hours ago, we were confined in the port.[36]

The International Delegation estimated that had the British and French governments provided the necessary resources, 60,000 Republicans could have been rescued. They further calculated that, 'but for the instructions issued by those governments, [the total] would have been about 6,500.' Instead, they reported that in the course of their stay: 'The total number that were evacuated [...] was no more than 650.'[37] Commentators rightly bemoan the attitudes of the British and French governments in refusing to deliver the protection required to carry out a successful extraction of the refugees in Alicante. The actions of Archibald Dickson and his crew are indeed an indictment of the perfidious response of the government in London. However, at the same time, there is a tendency to overlook the defection of the Republic's own fleet. Casado's conspiracy triggered Buiza's rash decision to sail the ships at Cartagena to neutral territory under the control of the French, who had already recognised Franco's regime. Their actions deprived the Republicans of the vessels and protective shield upon which Negrín's own plans for mass evacuation had logically depended.

Casado closes his memoirs with a chapter entitled, 'I accuse', which, as one would expect, finds no space for self-criticism. Of the evacuation crisis, he writes: 'The whole responsibility of what happened in Alicante rests on the shoulders of the pseudo-Government of Negrín and the French Government. I have more than sufficient proof of this, which leaves no room for doubt.'[38] His claim to have evidence to demonstrate his contention is somewhat undermined by his failure to provide it. Equally revealing is his exclusion from responsibility of the government in London. Again, one can only speculate as to his motives.

Vicente Rojo, the former Chief of General Staff, later wrote, 'The fate of the Spanish people [had] passed from the hands of a government more or less overwhelmed by circumstances to a group of men, perhaps driven to act by a noble cause, who pursued it in the most reprehensible manner.'[39]

In his diary, Gómez Serrano noted that in the town many men were now wearing bicolour or *Falange* badges in their lapels – not only those whom he would have suspected of pro-Franco sympathies, but also many who had supported the Republic. In a final reflection on the nature of the Civil War, and civil wars in general, he wrote, 'the two sides are not separated by trenches, but intermingle in every village and even in many families.' The tragedy of the war, he insisted, was that brother fought brother and, between them, they destroyed their mutual homeland. Therefore, he concluded, 'The victor in a certain sense also proves to be the defeated, and his joy is tempered by the pain of the damage caused.'[40] He was wrong; Franco felt no remorse. In his last moments on the port in Alicante, Guzmán overheard the warning words of a fellow Republican: 'Soon we will envy the dead.'[41]

Chapter 22

And the almond tree shall flourish

Campo de los Almendros

On 1 April 1939, from his headquarters in Burgos, General Franco issued his final war bulletin: 'Today, the Nationalist troops, having captured and disarmed the Red army, have achieved their final military objective. The war has ended.'[1] It soon became apparent to those who had trusted in Franco's clemency that the attainment of military objectives did not imply peace. Nor did it preclude the use of violence in pursuit of the *Generalísimo*'s political and social objectives. He was congratulated on his victory by Hitler and Mussolini, and Pope Pius XII dispatched a telegram to express his own satisfaction:

> Lifting up our hearts to the Lord, with Your Excellency, we offer our sincere gratitude for the anxiously awaited victory of Catholic Spain. We pray that this dear country, now peace has been achieved, will undertake with new vigour its ancient and Christian traditions, which made it so great. With these sentiments we send Your Excellency and all the noble Spanish people our apostolic blessing.

In his last entry in his diary for 1 April, Gómez Serrano describes Alicante as a town full of Italian soldiers, but also notes the reappearance of priests in traditional cassocks and *guardias civiles* in uniform. The new authorities distributed a free kilo of potatoes per person and promised the arrival over the next few days of abundant supplies of sugar, meat, condensed milk, chickpeas, beans, lentils, peas and cod. A decree was also published ordering the return of properties, both urban and rural, to their previous owners. Gómez heard people ask why Franco had not come earlier. He also records the news that the USA had recognised Franco's government and closes the diary with a final reference to the Non-Intervention Committee in London, which had made such a significant contribution to the defeat of the Republic. He asks if it will now be closed down, or whether it will be allowed to remain in place so that its chairman, Lord Plymouth, might continue to receive his generous expenses.[2] In fact, it was not dissolved until 20 April, three weeks after Franco's triumph.

On 4 April the victors held an impressive parade through the streets of Alicante presided by generals Gambara and Saliquet and representatives of the local *Falange*.[3] Less than 2km away, approximately 20,000 men had been interned in a makeshift concentration camp, while another 2,500 women and children were being held in the town centre.

The arrival of the Nationalist troops in the port had heralded the end of the Civil War and several of the Republicans now trapped in the port opted to take their own life. According to Ronald Fraser, 'Suicides spread like an epidemic.'[4] Tuñón de Lara believed there were more than forty.[5] However, the modern consensus suggests that in fact there were relatively few. Basing his research on the records of the municipal cemetery, Ors Montenegro suggests there may have been only eight such incidents.[6] Similar research available in the *Archivo de la Democracia* at the University of Alicante suggests there may have been another nine.[7] The most notorious case was that narrated by two witnesses, Carmen Arrojo and Julio Pérez Roda, who watched a man sit down in front of his daughter, put a cigar in his mouth, light it and then cut his throat from ear to ear. The man's name was Francisco Oliver, and another witness apparently remarked, 'Well, that gentleman who has just killed himself was the Mayor of Azira.'[8] Tuñón de Lara was close to another refugee who shot himself in the head. As grey matter splattered over those close to him, one man who was enjoying a bowl of lentils, threw it to the ground in disgust and complained, 'Why couldn't the bastard go kill himself somewhere else?'[9] Another survivor, the Socialist activist Angelita Rodríguez, later recalled those around her trying to rouse a man who had apparently fallen asleep on the dockside. When they removed his blanket, they discovered he had slashed his wrists.[10]

Sixto Agudo had been unofficially appointed military commander of the Communist forces on the docks. He claimed there was a real danger that the 'psychosis of suicide' might spread, and that therefore members of his party took the precaution of hiding the bodies of those who had taken their own life.[11] Nonetheless, and regardless of the bleak future that awaited them, the vast majority of the Republicans on the port refused to submit to the ultimate despair. In the words of Agudo, 'they did not think of themselves as vanquished, despite the military defeat.'[12] Fraser quotes the words of the anarchist militia leader, Saturnino Carod: 'I will not deny my enemies the pleasure of shooting me. If I am to die, it will be at their hands. As long as I'm alive, I'll do everything in my power to escape. Our duty is to continue fighting.'[13]

At 1800 on 31 March, the newly arrived Nationalist troops began the transfer of Republicans from the port area. The operation was suspended at 2200, leaving some 2,000 people to spend a last night of 'freedom' next to the sea. Eduardo de Guzmán was one of those left to meditate on their next destination.[14] The following morning, they were marched along the Postiguet beach, past the balneary facilities wrecked by the Italian air force, until the road forked left. Above was the looming presence of the Santa Barbara castle and ahead Guzmán could see the entrance to the railway tunnel that ran under the Sierra Grossa and which reminded him of a mousehole. At this point, as if to confirm the efficacy of Franco's propaganda services, a group of onlookers cried out, 'Here come the Russians.' When Guzmán turned to see if there were indeed any Russians, the man marching next to him clarified, 'We're the Russians.' The author guessed that of those who had spent the last night on the port, perhaps between twenty and thirty had not been born in Spain, but he was quite certain none of them were Russian.

The procession continued north up the Valencia road to an area of ground known to the people of Alicante as *La Goteta*, set between the main road and the *Sierra Grossa*. The last detachment of Republicans now joined their comrades from the port and substantial numbers of other prisoners taken in the last days of the conflict. With the aid of a limited supply of barbed wire and a series of machine-gun posts, the Spanish and Italian troops had improvised a concentration camp lacking in any shelter from the elements and even the most basic of hygiene facilities. Women and children were separated from the multitude, driven to the centre of town in trucks, and interned in one of the main cinemas (*Cine Ideal*) and the central theatre (*Teatro Principal*).[15] The small number of women who refused to abandon their partners and hid among the men exposed themselves to other dangers. In her memoirs, Angelita Rodríguez, one of those captured on the port, recalled how an anarchist comrade from her hometown of Ciudad Real was raped by guards when she relieved herself at the edge of the camp.[16]

Other groups, such as military officers, were led away to spillover camps in the *Plaza de Toros** (between 10,000 and 12,000), the castles of Santa Barbara (approximately 4,000) and San Fernando, and the main town prison, the *Reformatorio*.[17] The chaos of the last weeks of the Civil War makes it impossible to establish precise figures for the prisoners taken. The number held at La Goteta is no exception. Although some estimates range up to 45,000, given the area of the camp, it is generally assumed by historians today that the number is closer to 20,000.[18]

Perhaps the last word on the matter belongs to Guzmán, who argues that while those in the camp believed the number to exceed 40,000, the quantitative aspect was in fact far less significant than the qualitative aspect. The camp was filled with those who had resisted until the very end in the face of the

---

* Bull ring.

combined malevolence of Franco, Hitler and Mussolini. Although many scientists, intellectuals, artists, doctors, engineers, politicians and military officers had gone into exile, and in spite of the organisational failings and lack of resources, the people of the ten 'uninvaded' provinces that remained had defended their freedom and maintained vital services. Not only those officers of the 'skeleton state' that still existed, but also the unions, those who had taken control of workshops and factories, and those working in the agricultural collectives. Not only those fighting in the trenches, but also those who safeguarded communications and transport. And those doctors and surgeons who, in the face of extreme shortages, ensured treatment and care in the hospitals and medical centres. And those who were able to keep the schools open and even managed to prevent the universities from closing completely. Guzmán insisted that within a radius of one kilometre from where he stood with his companions there were thousands of brave souls who had not deserted their posts: engineers, architects, lawyers, academics, industrial workers and farm workers who:

> with no hope of reward, knowing their names would neither appear in any history book nor be remembered by future generations–forgotten, unknown, even by their own children–had written anonymous pages of incomparable self-denial and sacrifice.[19]

For the first three days the detainees, many of whom had barely eaten in the days leading up to their internment, received no food. The only sustenance available were the half-ripe almonds on the trees dotted around the camp and water from a natural well. When they had eaten all the fruit, the prisoners ate the leaves, and then some began to gnaw on the bark. To those who underwent this new phase of suffering and indignities, the concentration camp would forever be known as the *Campo de los Almendros* (Field of Almond Trees). It is also the title of Max Aub's novel, written in 1968 as part of the series *El laberinto mágico* (The Magic Labyrinth), which did so much to disseminate the story of the end of the Civil War in Alicante.

In the centre of town the women and children fared a little better. In a report she later drafted for the Communist Party, one of the detainees, Pilar Medrano, wrote that there were approximately 1,500 women and 1,000 children.[20] The first morning, Italian troops distributed packets of biscuits and every twenty-four hours the women were given a small tin of lentils and an equally small tin of sardines to be shared between two. The guards also provided milk for the young children. Angelita Rodríguez later recalled that in the *Cine Ideal* infants were passed from one woman to another to persuade the Italians that there were more children in the cinema than there actually were. In this way, they were able to supplement the milk supplies.[21] It appears that, as in other circumstances, many Italians lacked the crusading zeal and relentlessness of those they had been sent to support. According to Rodríguez, they delivered messages for the women and men who had been separated, and even offered to arrange visits.[22]

In the *Campo de los Almendros*, just as they had waited on the port listening to reports that boats were on their way and watching the vessels that appeared on the horizon, now the internees heard the constant rumours that trucks bearing rations were expected at any moment. They kept vigil in the hope that one of the military vehicles passing along the main road would in fact prove to be a lorry carrying food. On the second day, they observed people walking down the same road carrying palm fronds. It was, they realised, Palm Sunday, the first day of *Semana Santa* (Holy Week or Easter).

In *valenciano*, Alicante is known to its population as '*la millor terreta del món*' (the best land in the world*) and *alicantinos* claim that their town does not have weather, it has climate: a benign winter followed by a glorious spring, hot and humid summer and an agreeably warm autumn. There is one exception to this rule, April, which is notoriously unpredictable and often produces heavy rain and cold spells, which regularly take visitors by surprise. Rather than enjoying the respite of pleasant evenings, the prisoners had to endure downpours that intensified their despair and discomfort. The showers soaked their clothes, their blankets and the ground where they lay down to sleep. Guzmán also recalls the fires that they built in a wretched effort to dry their clothes and keep warm, and in defiance of the orders that were broadcast over an improvised public address system. And if hunger, cold and fear were insufficient, by this stage every detainee was also suffering the torment of lice.

The nights were further disturbed by the sound of sporadic gunfire as individual prisoners chose to make a desperate bid to escape. It is impossible to know how many men were able to flee the camp, but such was the situation in Spain that unless they could make it to the border with France or join up with a guerrilla group in the mountains, their chances of survival were not that much better outside the camp. No one could be sure of what lay ahead: a firing squad, prison or forced labour. Few would avoid punishment. None would return to the life they had led before. To add to the sense of helplessness, the camp received regular visits from *Falange* gangs searching for men with whom

---

* The more accurate translation is probably: 'the best *soil* in the world'. But this lacks the panache required by the tourist trade.

they had a particular score to settle. Again, it is impossible to know how many men were dragged away and dispatched by the roadside.

On the fourth day, food supplies eventually arrived and were distributed among the prisoners: a tin of sardines between two (62.5g each) and a bread roll between five (62.5g each). Many complained that the effect was simply to increase the sensation of hunger. Two days later, they received more rations: a tin of lentils (200–250g) between four and a bread roll between five. Guzmán later wrote that it took longer to open the can than it did to eat the food. The prisoners gave up their last possessions, usually their watch, to obtain extra rations from the guards. One of Franco's slogans during the war was '*Ni un hogar sin lumbre, ni un español sin pan*' ('No home without heat, no Spaniard without bread'). These privileges were not, however, necessarily to be extended to the vanquished.

Chapter 23

En el yermo de la historia

The Albatera concentration camp

In the introduction to Volume 10 of his *Historia de España* (History of Spain), Manuel Tuñón wrote, 'millions of Spaniards locked the windows of their houses when the victors occupied the towns, they wept silently.' Only the victors were allowed to mourn their dead and lament their losses in public. Of the defeated, he wrote:

> For that immense mass of Spaniards, "peace" and "victory" meant prisons, concentration camps, summary courts martial, the firing squad. The children of "the reds" were not allowed to study, the wives of "the reds" had their heads shaved […] In the euphoria of victory, the conquerors also deprived themselves of the best intellectuals, technicians, skilled labour … obsessed as they were with the idea of punishment and revenge.[1]

In his work *Holocaust in Spain*, Paul Preston calculates that in the Civil War 200,000 men and women were murdered or executed without due judicial process behind the lines and another 200,000 died on the fronts. He suggests 20,000 Republicans were executed in the aftermath of the fighting.[2] The last figure is relatively conservative; Anthony Beevor suggests the number was probably closer to 50,000.[3] As late as July 1939, Count Ciano reported a daily toll of 250 executions in Madrid and 150 in Barcelona alone.[4] When *Reichsführer* Heinrich Himmler visited Spain in October 1940, before the infamous Franco–Hitler summit at Le Hendaye, he was reported to be shocked at the numbers of Republican prisoners and the rate of executions. He expressed his surprise that the vanquished had not been more usefully integrated into the labour force of the new Spain.[5] Tuñón de Lara believes that the total of post-war executions was probably closer to 40,000. In response to the claims by Franco sympathisers that these figures are exaggerated, he argues that the uncertainties surrounding the extent of the repression are due to the Francoist regime's official silence, lack of records and failure to provide due judicial process in the court hearings.[6] Indeed, the dearth of official records was not an administrative oversight, but the deliberate policy of a regime intent not only on implementing ideological cleansing but also on destroying evidence of its crimes and preventing the eventual declassification of compromising documents.

Anthony Beevor also reports that at the beginning of 1940 there were 270,719 Republicans held in what he described as the 'Franquist Gulag'.[7] There are no figures for those who died of disease and starvation in Franco's prisons, concentration camps and forced labour units. It is difficult to estimate the number in exile. It is true that more than half a million fled to France and North Africa, but there are no official numbers for those who returned to Spain. Beevor suggests a total of approximately 150,000.[8] Of those who did not, thousands suffered incarceration at the hands of the Nazi and Vichy authorities. Beevor also records the abduction of 12,043 children from Republican parents in a single year (1943), and the transfer of custody to the *Auxilio Social**, to orphanages and religious bodies. Some of these children were then given in adoption to families of proved loyalty to the Franco dictatorship.[9] Finally, the new authorities applied the terms of Franco's infamous Law of Political Responsibilities to purge teachers and other professionals and to punish Republican sympathisers (and their widows) by imposing fines and appropriating assets.

However, when analysing the post-Civil War repression, the figures are both unreliable and misleading. As Paul Preston concludes: 'The statistical vision of the Spanish holocaust is not only flawed, incomplete and unlikely ever to be complete. It also fails to capture the intense horror that lies behind the numbers.'[10]

In April 1939 the town of Alicante had become a vast prison complex. The last Republican bastion, a bottleneck that had been sealed before the refugees could escape. What happened to those taken prisoner in the very place that their leaders had claimed would provide salvation is a simple reflection of Franco's vision of the new Spain. The mass transfer of detainees from the *Campo de los Almendros* to a camp at the small town of Albatera commenced on Good Friday (7 April). The men were marched across town to the rail depot in the south of the town (*Estación de Murcia* also known as *Estación de Benelúa*). As they passed the port area, they observed young soldiers swimming in the harbour. They learned from the guards that rumours had spread throughout the town that the Republicans had thrown jewels, gold, foreign coins, even works of art into the water rather than let them fall into the hands

---

* *Social Aid*. A charitable welfare organisation set up during the Civil War; to provide care to those in need in the Nationalist zone.

of the Nationalists. Mallol Alberola claimed that much of the treasure had been plundered from churches.[11] It appears that the divers found a significant number of suitcases and weapons, but no precious stones or indeed anything of value.[12]

Once at the station, the men were herded into a holding area without food or water, and then loaded onto cattle trucks and freight cars, one hundred to a wagon,[13] for the relatively short journey to Albatera. By now the weather had changed and their distress was compounded by the heat. Guzmán later recalled, 'clear skies, not a single cloud, with dazzling luminosity, but we hardly noticed. The beauty was trumped by the physical discomfort, the incessant jolting of the train and the effort required to avoid falling out.'[14] During a fifteen-minute halt at Elche, local women offered the prisoners oranges and water cooled in *botijos**. As the train continued southwards, Guzmán observed women and children at the side of the track, greeting them with the clenched fist salute.

Behind them, those men transferred to Albatera left behind significant numbers of Republican prisoners still held in the Santa Barbara castle and the *Plaza de Toros*. One of the women detained on the port, Carmen Caamaño, later suggested that at this stage some twenty-four of the women held in the *Cine Ideal* were transferred to a detention centre, ominously named *Casa de Ejercicios Espirituales* (House of Spiritual Exercises), a Jesuit retreat opposite the Reformatory in Benalúa.[15] According to the research of the journalist Carlos Hernández de Miguel, in 1939 (christened by the Francoists '*El Año de la Victoria*' – the year of the victory), the new authorities operated a total of ten concentration camps in the province of Alicante.[†] Including the town itself, which he qualifies as a giant detention facility, he also lists the *Campo de los Almendros*, and other centres in Albatera, Alcoy, Denia, Elche, Elda, Monóvar, Orihuela and Villena.[16]

Of these, the most notorious was the camp at Albatera. The men transferred from Alicante were swiftly disabused of any hopes they may have harboured that new surroundings might bring an improvement in their conditions. The camp had originally been opened in October 1937 to hold enemies of the Republic. The leading *falangista* José Mallol Alberola was one of the first prisoners to arrive and described the location as 'a wasteland, with huge variations in temperature, humid and cold by night, asphyxiating heat by day, with mosquitoes like aeroplanes'.[17] It was designed to hold 2,000 inmates, although the number of internees never exceeded 1,039; until April 1939,

---

* Earthenware water jugs.
† According to the same author, there were a total of 296 camps throughout Spain.

when it received between 12,000 and 20,000 prisoners.[18] The first to enter the camp immediately occupied the few *barracones* (huts) that had been constructed, but rapidly vacated them when they found the buildings infested with every type of parasite.

So crowded was the facility that at night the men were unable to lie flat on the ground or turn over in their sleep without disturbing all the other men around them. The camp was rectangular in shape, approximately 700m by 200m, with two continuous barbed wire fences, and watchtowers in each corner, manned by troops of Company 3 of the 6th Battalion of the San Quintin Regiment (Valladolid)* armed with submachine guns.[19] The prisoners were warned that any approach to the interior fence would be interpreted as an attempt to escape, the punishment for which was death. Guzmán reports an incident of one prisoner who had somehow come into possession of an orange. As he tried to peel it, it fell to the ground and rolled against the barbed wire. In desperation, he went forward to retrieve it and was detained by a guard. He was sentenced to death the next day. He was so weak that when taken to face the firing squad, he fell to his knees. His executioners fired twice but failed to kill him. The officer in charge then approached to apply the *coup de grâce* but it took him three shots before the prisoner was finally dispatched. Guzmán concluded that there was little point in not trying to escape, as they would shoot you anyway under any pretext.[20] On the other hand, many prisoners were also aware that in their hometowns and villages they would be marked men. In the words of Hugh Thomas, 'The summer of 1939 was a fiesta for the informer, for the vengeful and for the bloodthirsty.'[21] Therefore, many in the camp came to the sad conclusion that they were safer behind the barbed wire.

Nevertheless, the conditions were no better than those of the Nazi labour/extermination camps, and rations were no more generous than in Alicante. According to Guzmán, during the first fortnight of their incarceration at Albatera, prisoners received the following supplies:

Tuesday, 11/04/39: a quarter of a tin of lentils and a fifth of a bread roll each.

Wednesday-Friday, 12–14/04/39: for 3 days the inmates were given nothing.

Saturday, 15/04/1939: a tin of sardines between three and a roll between five.

Sunday-Thursday, 16–20/04/1939: nothing

Friday, 21/04/1939: 66g of sardines and 60g of bread

---

* Later replaced by colonial troops (Group 2 – Melilla).

In the period between 11 April and 27 April the inmates had four meals, which represented a total intake of 266g of sardines, 250g of bread and approximately 100g of lentils.[22]

Even worse was the lack of water. In the *Campo de los Almendros* the Republicans had at least had access to a natural well. At Albatera there were no supplies at all, and with rising temperatures and little shade, the situation of the inmates swiftly became critical. Either through incompetence or malice, the camp officers failed to arrange for the delivery of water from Orihuela. Eventually, when water tankers did arrive at the camp, the quantities were so inadequate that fights broke out between the desperate prisoners. One comrade told Guzmán, 'I am beginning to glimpse hope that they won't starve us to death. Before that, we'll die of thirst.'[23]

Many prisoners also suffered the extra misery of doing without cigarettes, especially as tobacco would have alleviated their hunger. The hard ground, shortage of space, occasional showers and insect infestations meant no detainee was able to sleep properly. The absence of medical or hygiene facilities in such crowded conditions made the inmates increasingly vulnerable to disease. After some days, the men were allowed to dig latrines, but the heat and the lack of water for washing exacerbated their discomfort. Malnutrition led to extreme constipation and stomach cramps. There were inevitable cases of scabies, dysentery, typhus, pneumonia and tuberculosis.

During the fifteen months that the facilities were under the control of the Republican authorities, the camp received visits from foreign representatives and officials of the Red Cross. There were five recorded deaths. In the last three weeks of April 1939 there were 138 reported deaths (78 from inanition and 60 from other diseases).[24] If the situation of many was alleviated by packages containing supplies they received from home, it is also true that fear of identifying themselves, or of incriminating their families, meant that many others refused to give the camp officials their real names and addresses, and therefore excluded themselves from such privileges.

Conditions were slightly improved by the release of prisoners under the age of 16 and those over the age of 60, but the men in charge of the huge mass of detainees who remained felt no responsibility for their welfare. Indeed, in camps throughout Spain, the Francoist authorities weaponised the climate. Men were exposed to extreme heat and extreme cold and denied shelter and appropriate clothing. For days the prisoners at Albatera had only their blankets as shelter from the heavy rain showers that continued to torment them. Guzmán recalls one inmate shouting, 'The next time someone tells me about the wonderful weather in Alicante in springtime, I'll break his neck.'[25]

Of his arrival in the camp, one prisoner, Josep Sala, later recalled being told, 'You are prisoners of war and as such you do not even have a right to the air that you breathe.'[26] In fact, the inmates were not treated as prisoners of war, they were felons for whom no suffering, no punishment was excessive. They were starved, beaten and humiliated. The member of one visiting commission told his colleagues: 'There are so many criminals in Spain. The more that die, the fewer we will have to kill.'[27] On the other hand, as the country emerged from the chaos and disruption of war, there was a slight increase in the rations, the water supply was gradually improved, and over time tents were erected to offer at least some protection from the elements.

The worst misery to endure, however, came when the prisoners were made to stand in formation for hours while commissions from the *Falange* and the Church marched up and down, row by row, looking for suspects, who were then removed from the camp and summarily dispatched at the side of the road. Guzmán reports that on Easter Saturday (8 April) the prisoners were forced to stand 'on parade' for nearly four hours, while seven different commissions sought out their prey. Eighteen prisoners were selected to face retribution.[28]

It goes almost without saying that there are no official records of the number of Republicans executed either within the camp or by visiting *Falange*/Church delegations. Efforts were made among the prisoners to protect the most vulnerable from the Francoist thirst for revenge. In his oral history of the Civil War, Ronald Fraser recounts the story of a young Communist brigade commander, Narciso Julián, who, together with two comrades, dug a hole under their tent where they could hide whenever Francoist commissions arrived. After several months his presence in the camp was revealed by one of the inmates, who offered the information while undergoing a beating by guards, and Julián surrendered to the prison officers. The time lapse saved his life; by this stage the extra-judicial summary executions were no longer 'officially' encouraged.[29]

There were also campaigns to encourage Republicans to seek redemption and integration in the new Spain. Unfortunately, they were based on Franco's perception of history. He appeared to have taken note of Unamuno's famous warning to the Nationalists, delivered during his speech in Salamanca in October 1939: '*Venceréis, pero no convenceréis*' (You will win but you will not convince).[30] He apparently reminded those in his inner circle of the need to '*No solo vencer, sino convencer*' (not only win but also convince).[31] However, as Unamuno had predicted, Franco's concept of persuasion was based entirely on the stick. Prisoners were threatened with punishment if they failed to attend the regular church services held in the camp and were obliged to sing the *Falange* anthem *Cara al Sol* (Face to the Sun) three times a day while giving the fascist salute.

On the occasion of a visit to the camp by the Military Governor, Joaquín Carballo Álvarez, the *Hoja Oficial de Alicante* published a report claiming the prisoners had expressed 'hatred towards their leaders who had so grossly misled them, and admiration and even devotion towards our Caudillo Franco.'[32] Given the physical distress and fear the inmates were forced to endure, the first premise cannot be ruled out, but the second is no less cynical than it is implausible. The Albatera camp was eventually closed on 17 October 1939. Some survivors were released to return to their families and face the malevolence of those now in control of their hometowns. Many were relocated to less transitory prisons and labour camps; in particular at Porta Coeli, north of Valencia.

Alicante was spared the mass killings and systematic rape suffered by Republicans in those areas that only fell to the Nationalists after fierce fighting. Nevertheless, the new authorities submitted the population to political and social repression at all levels. High-profile Republican leaders were detained, tried before summary courts-martial, and executed. According to research based on civil registers, the historians Torres Fabra and Ors Montenegro calculate that in the province of Alicante approximately 724 people were executed by firing squad between 1939 and 1945.[33] Perhaps the most shocking case was that of a 16-year-old girl from Dolores, executed for defacing a poster of José Antonio.[34] Another Alicante-based historian, Tébar Rubio-Manzanares, calculated that 729 Republicans were executed during the same period and that between 313 and 678 people were killed 'extrajudicially' between 1939 and 1941. In Alicante town he estimates there were 579 executions.[35] Activists and sympathisers were condemned to years of forced labour. Tébar Rubio-Manzanares concludes that 'the post-war penal code represented the prolongation of the war via other means against the internal enemy.'[36] On the other hand, the new regime used the notion of redemption through work as a means not only to punish those who had defied the values of eternal Spain, but also to provide cheap labour for the restoration of the national infrastructure and in the development of industries controlled by those of proven loyalty to the new Spain. Republican prisoners thus played a key role in the reconstruction of the country in both the public and private sectors,[37] and in the construction of Franco's greatest folly, the *Valle de los Caídos* (Valley of the Fallen), designed as a memorial to his triumph, and his own mausoleum.

Professionals of dubious ideological background were purged, particularly in education. Censorship was rigorously applied, first by the *Falange* and then by the Church. The dictatorship sought to enforce its will in all social areas. Speakers of Catalan, Basque (*euskera*) and Galician (*gallego*) were denied the right to use their language in official and administrative affairs or in the media. In Alicante many *valenciano* speakers discouraged the use of the language among their own children for fear of repercussions should they use it by accident in public. People who failed to observe linguistic protocols were advised to speak *cristiano* (Christian – Castilian Spanish, the 'language of the Empire'). Divorce was outlawed, civil marriages performed during the Republic were ruled invalid. Strict codes of conduct and dress were dictated by the clergy. On 8 April 1939 the Mayor of Alicante issued a proclamation insisting that in the interests of preserving the good name of the town, it was important that the population should refrain from using the foul language that had become customary under the Republic. He also reminded all *alicantinos* that blasphemy was prohibited and that under the existing by-laws, 'the inhabitants of the city are to display the proper composure, in their language and behaviour, on all occasions and in all places, and to refrain from any offence against religion, morals, good manners, decency and culture.'[38]

The dictatorship was built on the foundations of Army, Church and *Falange*. Political activity was controlled by the single party – the *Movimiento Nacional* (National Movement) – and labour was controlled by the 'vertical union', a top-down organisation in which the leaders, following government guidelines, determined workers' conditions. Young people underwent political and social indoctrination during the extended period of national conscription or their service in the *Sección Feminina* (Women's Section) of the *Falange*.

Lacking any understanding of economics, Franco imposed a disastrous policy of autarky, which together with long periods of drought, condemned the mass of the population to years of privation. Food shortages were even more critical than they had been during the war. International isolation and exclusion from the European Recovery Program (Marshall Plan) exacerbated the hardships. After he revisited Spain at the end of the 1940s, the Hispanist Gerald Brenan acknowledged the logic of withholding any economic aid that 'might appear to be bolstering up the Franco regime'. However, he concluded that sanctions punished the wrong people and that nothing was to be gained from 'condemning the Spanish working classes to starvation and misery'.[39] Nor was it reasonable to overlook the fact that the plight of the Spanish people was largely due to the Non-Intervention policy of the western powers. Brenan later recounted a conversation with a monarchist and erstwhile Franco supporter, who told him,

> Things couldn't be worse here than they are. One can't live, one can't eat. Everyone is starving – everyone that is, except the people who are plundering the country. Never, never has Spain been so low before. And there's nothing to be done. So long as *ese hombre*, that man, is at the head of things, there's no hope. You're a foreigner – tell me, why don't the other countries do something to help us?[40]

Part Four

Aftermath

Chapter 24

No ha llegado la paz; ha llegado la victoria

General Franco remained in power until his death on 20 November 1975, the thirty-ninth anniversary of José Antonio's execution in Alicante. In the 1950s, as Europe became immersed in the unfolding drama of the Cold War, his impeccable anti-Communist credentials made him a useful ally for the USA and brought an end to Spain's international isolation. In the following decade, economic reforms and the rapidly expanding tourist trade brought relative prosperity to many. In his final years, Franco made constitutional arrangements for the dictatorship to continue beyond his own death and boasted that he was leaving Spain '*atada y bien atada*' (tied down and well tied down). He was buried in the *Valle de los Caídos* – the only one of those entombed in the vast monument who had not suffered a violent death during the Civil War. His body remained there until 2019, when, under the terms of the *Ley de Memoria Histórica* (Law of Historical Memory – 52/2007), the Socialist Prime Minister ordered his body be exhumed and removed from the mausoleum.

After the fall of Alicante, the remains of the founder of the *Falange*, José Antonio Primo de Rivera, were disinterred and carried on foot by *falangistas* (bearing the coffin on their shoulders) to El Escorial near Madrid. On 16 April 1939, in a diatribe on Radio Alicante, the fascist ideologue Ernesto Giménez Caballero told listeners:

> What curse weighed on your destiny? What have you done Alicante, what have you done? If of all the cities in Spain you were the one with the greatest sin, then of all the cities in Spain, you must be the one that offers the Caudillo the greatest level of service, self-sacrifice and zeal.[1]

In 1959 José Antonio's body was moved again, to lie in the *Valle de los Caídos* together with tens of thousands of other casualties of the Civil War. When Franco was exhumed, the Vice-President of the government justified the decision to leave José Antonio's remains untouched in the basilica by explaining that (like the others buried in the valley) he was a victim of the Civil War. Under the terms of the new law, his body was nevertheless eventually exhumed and transferred to the San Isidro cemetery in Madrid in April 2023.

General Gastone Gambara, commander of the Italian *Corpo di Truppe Volontarie*, which occupied Alicante at the end of March 1939, was later appointed ambassador in Madrid. In the Second World War he served in France, Greece and North Africa – where his qualities as an officer failed to impress Rommel – and finally in the brutal war against the partisans in the Balkans. After the war, and despite evidence of his responsibility for atrocities in Yugoslavia, Italy refused to extradite him to face charges of war crimes.

Doctor Juan Negrín, the Prime Minister of the Republic, escaped first to France and then to Britain when the Nazis occupied Paris. In London he sought to play a role as head of a government-in-exile, but was snubbed by the British government. Anxious that Spain might join the Axis powers, the Foreign Office was reluctant to do anything that might offend Franco. Nevertheless, Negrín resisted official suggestions that he relocate to the USA. He was probably the most honourable of all leaders in the Civil War and was the one treated most badly by both sides. His enemies within the PSOE forced his expulsion from the party in 1946 and he was not reinstated (posthumously) until 2008. He died in Paris in 1956 and is buried in the Père Lachaise Cemetery. Three years earlier, he had been invited to attend the coronation of Queen Elizabeth II in London.

Manuel Azaña, the last President of the Republic, remained in exile in France until his death in Montauban in November 1940. At the funeral, the Vichy authorities refused to permit the honours due to a deceased head of state. The local prefect even refused to allow his coffin to be covered with the Republican flag, insisting that the only legal standard was that of the new Francoist regime. The Mexican ambassador subsequently provided a flag of his own country and thus enabled Azaña's family to bury him with a Republican emblem. In 1978 his widow, Dolores Rivas Cherif, in exile in Mexico, was finally granted a pension by the Spanish state.

Julián Zugazagoitia, Minister of the Interior under Negrín, had worked to restore legal procedures and to suppress the revolutionary violence in the Republican zone. He was personally responsible for protecting many enemy sympathisers from reprisals. He escaped to France in February 1939, and the following year published his memoirs of the Civil War.[2] He was arrested by the Gestapo in Paris in July 1940 and handed over to the Spanish authorities. Found guilty of 'rebellion' by a military court, he was executed by firing squad in November 1940.

Francisco Largo Caballero, Socialist Prime Minister (September 1936–May 1937), joined the mass exodus from Catalonia in January 1939 and remained in France, even after the German invasion. The Vichy judicial authorities rejected Franco's demands for extradition, but in 1942 he was detained by the

Germans, and after a long period in the custody of the Gestapo, was eventually transferred to Sachsenhausen, where he spent the last two years of the war. He died in 1946. In 1978, after Franco's death, his body was returned to Madrid and buried in the civil cemetery.

Julio Álvarez del Vayo was Minister of Foreign Affairs twice during the Civil War. He left Monóvar on the same aircraft as Negrín in March 1939 and spent most of his exile in Mexico and the USA, where he became increasingly radical. Before his death, in Geneva in May 1975, he was elected President of the *Frente Revolucionario Antifascista y Patriota* (FRAP – Antifascist and Patriotic Revolutionary Front) and encouraged a renewed armed struggle against Franco's dictatorship. Three members of the group were among the last five people executed by the regime in September 1975.

Lluis Companys, President of the *Generalitat* of Catalonia, was arrested by the Germans in August 1940. He had refused to leave France until he could locate his son, who was undergoing therapy and had been lost in the mass exodus from Paris in the spring. He was escorted to the Spanish border and delivered to the Spanish authorities. While in custody in Madrid, he was brutally tortured, and was then transferred to Barcelona to stand trial on charges of 'military rebellion'. He was sentenced to death and executed by firing squad at the Montjuic castle. Popular legend tells that he went to his death barefooted as he wished to feel the soil of his homeland when he took his last breath.

José Antonio Aguirre, *Lehendekari* (President of the Basque Country), was more fortunate. After undertaking an extraordinary escape route, which led him to Berlin (where he saw Hitler from afar and attended a memorial service for King Alfonso XIII), he reached Sweden and then travelled to South America. He eventually moved to New York for the rest of the war and worked at the University of Columbia. In 1946 he returned to France, where he established the Basque government-in-exile. Changing international circumstances eventually led the French government to clamp down on unwelcome foreign activities on French territory. He died in 1969 and was buried in Saint-Jean-de-Luz.

Constancia de la Mora and her husband, Ignacio Hidalgo de los Cisneros, settled in Mexico City and after the Second World War were eventually reunited with their daughter/step-daughter Luli, who had been sent to the USSR as one of the 2,000 children of Communist parents evacuated during the Civil War. After their divorce, de la Mora broke her ties with the Communist Party, while Hidalgo de los Cisneros relocated to Warsaw and then Bucharest and remained a loyal member of the party until his death in 1966. De la Mora died in a road accident in Guatemala in 1950 while accompanying a touring party (which included Nancy Johnstone).[3]

Segismundo Casado, the leader of the anti-Negrín coup, settled in West London where he was treated with greater benevolence than Negrín. He was offered employment in the BBC (under the pseudonym Juan de Padilla) and given help to publish his memoirs within months of his arrival. Although still married, he entered a new relationship with an Englishwoman, Norah Purcell.[4] He later travelled to Colombia and Venezuela before finally returning to Spain in 1961. He was absolved of charges of 'military rebellion' but denied an army pension. In 1968 he published the second version of his memoirs, in Spanish and with adjustments made to overcome the concerns of Franco's censors. He died in Madrid the same year. At no point, either in his writings or in his correspondence, did he accept any responsibility, or express any regret, for the catastrophic final outcome of the war.

Julián Besteiro, the Socialist leader who joined the Casado conspiracy and believed in Franco's promises that those who had not shed blood or committed crimes in defence of the Republic should not fear reprisals, remained behind in Madrid at the end of March. He was, in the words of Paul Preston, guilty of 'culpable naivety'.[5] He was detained by the new authorities in the capital on 29 March 1939 and put on trial in July on charges of supporting military rebellion. He was given a life sentence that was eventually 'reduced' to thirty years of hard labour – Besteiro was 69 years old at the time of his court-martial. The irony that in 1939 he had indeed supported a military coup against the legitimate government of Spain appears to have been lost on the prosecution. Franco rejected petitions for leniency and an ailing Besteiro was refused medical care. He died in prison in September 1940.

Probably the most enigmatic element in Casado's conspiracy was General Matallana. An old-school, professional member of the officer class, he would undoubtedly have been happier if the outbreak of the Civil War had caught him in the Nationalist zone rather than the zone loyal to the Republic. In the later stages of the war, he was clearly opposed to Negrín and the policy of all-out resistance, but his ambivalence towards the legitimacy of the government predates the defeat on the Ebro and the collapse of the Catalonian front. He was arrested in Valencia on 29 March 1939 and stood trial in August. At the hearing he claimed he had made contact with the fifth column early in the conflict and had provided intelligence on the International Brigades, the quarters occupied by Soviet pilots, and the shipment of supplies through Cartagena. He then described his own attempts to destabilise the Republican war effort by sabotaging diversionary offensives during the Ebro and Catalonia campaigns. Nevertheless, the court found him guilty of military rebellion and imposed a thirty-year prison sentence.⁶ Franco eventually relented, and Matallana was pardoned and released from prison in May 1941. Nevertheless, his treatment by the new regime does appear to undermine his claims that he had colluded with the fifth column and had actively promoted the victory of the Nationalists. Hugh Thomas suggested it was difficult to determine whether Matallana was treacherous or defeatist.⁷ He might have added that the general was both overcautious and incompetent, one of the military legacies of the monarchy that the Republic failed to displace.

Admiral Miguel Buiza, who had effectively handed the fleet over to the Nationalists by sailing the ships under his command to North Africa, expressed his regret at his actions by joining the French Foreign Legion and then the Free French. As a member of the French Africa Corps, he fought against Rommel in the Tunisian campaign. After the war, he participated in the smuggling of Jewish settlers into Palestine, was detained by the British and held in a concentration camp at Haifa. He settled in Oran, and then, after Algerian independence, he transferred to mainland France where he died in 1963.

Having finally been released after fifteen months in seven different Republican jails, Edwin C. Lance, the honorary attaché at the Madrid Embassy, known as the 'Spanish Pimpernel', was one of the last British citizens to be evacuated from Valencia. After the intervention of Skrine Stevenson and Sir George Young,⁸ he was extricated from Spain aboard a British destroyer. He settled in the Channel Isles and died in 1970, according to one newspaper report, in Alicante.⁹

Mr Edwin Apfel, the manager of the Gandía port facilities, had been instrumental in saving the lives of many people on both sides of the Civil War, but did not escape the wrath of the local *Falange*, who were reluctant to overlook his role in assisting Republican evacuees in the last weeks of the conflict. It is not implausible that the actions taken against him were based more on business interests than political issues.¹⁰ Although an expulsion order against him was challenged and overturned through the efforts of the new British Ambassador in Madrid, Apfel was then accused of having engaged in Marxist propaganda during the Civil War. In a letter to the embassy in Madrid, a consular official in Valencia who witnessed the subsequent military trial wrote: 'The President of the Tribunal did not appear to be wholly unbiassed [sic].'¹¹ Hoare's own account of the court proceedings offers a significant insight into judicial procedures in Franco's Spain:

> From start to finish, there was no vestige of any attempt at judicial treatment. No witnesses were produced. Not a single question was put

to Mr. Apfel during the court proceedings. The prosecution relied upon the gossip of an unnamed boy who was said to have declared to some equally unknown person that Mr. Apfel was a communist, and upon a French book of leftist tendencies and a piece of red stuff supposed to be a red flag that were discovered in his flat. His counsel was removed the day before the trial and there was, therefore, no time to instruct a new counsel in the details of the case [...] After a short sitting, the Court adjourned for luncheon and at its afternoon session condemned him to six years and one day's imprisonment.[12]

Apfel eventually served a total of two years in a Francoist prison before diplomatic pressure persuaded the dictatorship to release him.[13]

After the Civil War Mary Elmes, the Irish volunteer aid worker at the hospitals in Murcia and Alicante, continued her humanitarian work in the south of France – in particular rescuing Jewish children from the Vichy authorities. In 1943 she was detained in Toulouse and then transferred to the infamous Gestapo-run Fresnes Prison. She was awarded the *Légion d'honneur*, and after her death in 2002 she was recognised by the state of Israel as 'Righteous Among the Nations'.

Archibald Dickson, the hero of the final days of the Republic, died with all his crew in November 1939 when the *Stanbrook* was sunk in the North Sea by a German U-boat (U-57). In 2009 Dickson's son and daughter were invited to an event organised by the *Comisión Cívica por la Recuperación de la Memoria Histórica** in Alicante to celebrate the seventieth anniversary of the *Stanbrook*'s rescue mission. They had been largely unaware of their father's role and acknowledged that the response of so many relatives of people who had been saved on the *Stanbrook* was deeply moving. Arnold Dickson told the local newspaper:

> I don't think my father was a political creature, but he was a good man. He was the skipper and did what he thought had to be done. It wouldn't have mattered to him that the people belonged to one side or the other. He saw people suffering and took them on board.[14]

Amado Granell was one of the fortunate Republicans to escape Alicante on the *Stanbrook* (Passenger No. 2073). Five years later he was a member of the legendary Spanish Ninth Company (*La Nueve* – Nine) of Leclerc's 2nd Armoured Division that landed in France in the summer of 1944. Much to

---

* Civic Commission for the Recuperation of Historical Memory.

the chagrin of de Gaulle, it was men of *La Nueve*, rather than French troops, who proved to be the first Allied unit to reach the centre of Paris and link up with the Resistance during the battle for the French capital. Granell and his comrades carried the flag of the Spanish Republic and daubed their half-tracks with the names of Civil War leaders and events, including: *La Pasionaria*, Almiral Buiza, Guernica, Madrid, Ebro, Guadalajara and Teruel. Towards the end of his life, Granell moved to Alicante where he opened a small shop of electrical appliances. He was killed in a road accident near Valencia.[15]

As the situation in Alicante at the end of March 1939 deteriorated, Eliseo Gómez Serrano, the diarist and deputy for Alicante (*Izquierda Republicana*), ignored suggestions that he should seek refuge abroad and expressed his conviction that, as he had committed no crimes, he had nothing to fear. He also conveyed his bemusement at the determination of so many people, whom he believed were in no danger, to risk everything by fleeing Spain.[16] He was arrested by the Nationalist authorities on 3 April 1939, detained in the Alicante Reformatory and brought to trial before a court martial accused of participating in the 'rebellion'. The defence based its case on the fact that Gómez Serrano had not committed a single act of violence and that his party had not been involved in any crimes that might have occurred in Alicante. Nonetheless, the court ignored all calls for clemency and the defendant was sentenced to death. He was executed on 5 May 1939, along with other Republicans from Elche and Almoradí. As he left the Reformatory, he turned to a group of female prisoners and said, 'Never forget what you are going through and whatever you witness tonight.'[17] He was the first Republican to face a firing squad in Alicante after the occupation of the town by the Nationalists. Carlos Esplá, the Alicante-born writer and politician[*] who escaped to Mexico, wrote of his colleague, 'He was betrayed by his own integrity, his tendency to believe other people to be as good as he was.'[18]

José Muñoz Vizcaino, the last Military Governor of the Republic in Alicante, having negotiated the peaceful surrender of the troops stationed in Alicante, was arrested by the Nationalists and sentenced to thirty years' imprisonment for supporting the 'rebellion'. After serving time in penitentiaries in Alicante and Madrid, he was finally released in 1947.[19]

His ephemeral predecessor, Colonel Etelvino Vega, who had been incarcerated by the new pro-Casado authorities at the beginning of March, was released too late to make his escape from the Nationalists. Once in Albatera, he was recognised by a Francoist officer as one of the most high-profile Communist

---

[*] A member of *Izquierda Republicana*, he was head of propaganda in the Caballero and first Negrín governments.

militia leaders remaining in the country. He was arrested, tried before a summary court martial and sentenced to death. Before the sentence was carried out, he asked a fellow prisoner, Justo López Megías, to take a handkerchief, his last possession, and to ensure it reached his wife. He was executed by firing squad on 15 November 1939 against the walls of the Alicante cemetery, together with twenty-six other Republicans, and buried in a mass grave. However, his wife fled to the USSR with their son, and López Megías was unable to deliver the handkerchief. After sixty years, the widows of López Megias and Vega made contact after an article appeared in *El País* newspaper describing the efforts of the latter to claim a pension from the Spanish state. The widow of López Megias was thus able finally to complete her husband's mission.[20]

Eduardo Rubio Funes, captain of the Assault Guards in Alicante at the outbreak of war, had played a key role in the suppression of the revolt, in foiling the attempts to liberate José Antonio, and in the victory of the *milicianos* in the battle for Albacete. It also appears that he was in charge of the firing squad that executed the Military Governor, General José García Aldave, and other rebel officers in October 1936.[21] He was later given command of the 71st Mixed Brigade (which incorporated the Alicante Red columns) and fought at Guadalajara. In his article '*Alicante Rojo*', Ilya Ehrenburg described him as an impulsive *andaluz* (Andalusian). He had observed him teaching a group of fighting men, who had previously been textile, metallurgical and agricultural workers, in a seminar on military tactics that lasted from eight o'clock until eleven o'clock at night, in a church illuminated by candles, 800m from the front. Rubio Funes was captured at the end of the war by the Nationalists and incarcerated in the *Reformatorio*. He was condemned to death at his court martial on 3 May 1939 and executed in Alicante on 17 May 1939.

At the end of the war, the great Orihuela poet Miguel Hernández, who had served as political commissar in the Republican army, was able to reach Portugal on foot. However, the Portuguese border police detained him and handed him over to the *Guardia Civil*. He spent several months in jail, during which time he composed perhaps his most famous poem, *Nanas de la cebolla* (Onion lullabies) – in response to a letter from his wife describing the hardships she and their young son were forced to endure. Inexplicably released (perhaps through an administrative oversight[22]), rather than seek refuge abroad, he visited his wife and child in Cox and then travelled to see his parents in Orihuela, where he was rearrested. A death sentence was eventually commuted to thirty years' imprisonment. After several transfers between different penitentiaries, he was finally assigned to the Alicante Reformatory, a prison designed to hold 600 inmates, and where, by the time the poet arrived, the population had risen to 3,600. In 1942, at the age of 31, he succumbed to tuberculosis in the prison infirmary.²³ Franco's new Spain proved hostile territory for poets. Federico Garcia Lorca was murdered in Granada by *falangistas* in 1936, and Antonio Machado died in exile in France in 1939, days after crossing the border ahead of the Nationalist army.

The anarchist journalist, Eduardo de Guzmán, who found himself trapped at the port of Alicante and was then interned at the *Campo de los Almendros* and Albatera, was eventually transferred to penitentiary centres in Madrid. He stood trial with Miguel Hernández and was sentenced to death. Like the poet, he was also shown 'clemency' and the sentence was reduced to imprisonment. He was released in 1948 but was barred from working in journalism. For twenty years he made a living as a translator and by writing *novelas de quiosco* (literally: news-stand novels – pulp fiction). Working under such exotic pen names as Charles G. Brown, Edward Goodman, Anthony Lancaster, Richard Jackson and Eddy Thorny, he wrote up to thirty police and adventure stories a year. In 1974 he published the second part of his Civil War memoirs, *El año de la victoria*, which won the *Premio Internacional de Periodismo* (International Journalism Award).[24]

Saturnino Carod, the anarchist detained in Alicante in March 1939, was held in the *Campo de los Almendros* and at Albatera until he escaped in May 1939. He managed to cross the border into France and eventually joined the unit of Francisco Ponzán,[25] working with the French Resistance. He later returned to Spain, was arrested, and condemned to death in 1949. The sentence was commuted to twenty-five years' imprisonment, and he was released in 1960. He maintained an active role in the struggle against the dictatorship until Franco's death and was detained on two more occasions in the decade of the 1960s.

Narciso Julián, the Communist officer who was discovered in the Albatera camp, was taken to Madrid where he faced a court-martial with sixteen other defendants. The trial lasted eleven minutes. He was sentenced to death and was held for more than a year pending his execution. He later described how each evening a prison officer (sometimes smoking a cigar) would read out to the assembled prisoners the list of those who were to be executed the next morning:

> Often he would read out only the first name, Pedro, and pause for several minutes. Everyone with that Christian name went through agony until he read out the first surname. It might be a common one, several people might share it. Agony again: Until finally, he read out the second surname.[26]

Julián was eventually pardoned but continued to campaign against the dictatorship. Between 1939 and 1970 he spent a total of twenty-five years in prison.

Carmen Caamaño, the ex-governor of Cuenca who gave birth days before the end of the war, and with her new-born son was then able to find her husband on the port among the thousands of Republicans, fled to San Juan with her family when the Italians arrived, but was recognised by fifth columnists and arrested. She spent the next years of her life in and out of prison, and her son was brought up by a family in Alicante. They were not properly reunited until he was 12 years old. Constant police surveillance eventually precluded the clandestine work she had undertaken for the Communists in their attempt to rebuild the party from the base, but she remained active in the defence of women's rights and participated in the *Asociación Española de Mujeres Universitarias* (AEMU – Spanish Association of University Women). Only in the 1960s did Franco's regime allow her to return to her work as a librarian and archivist.

After the Campo de Almendros, Albatera and Portacoeli, Major Sixto Agudo was transferred first to a forced labour camp in Madrid and then to Mallorca where, in 1940, he managed to escape and flee to France, where he was interned in the Gurs concentration camp. Having volunteered for service in a labour division, he joined the XIV Spanish Guerrilla Corps and thus participated in the incipient French Resistance. In 1943 Jesús Monzón, the unofficial leader of the Communists in south-west France, requested he re-enter Spain to assist in the organisation of the clandestine party structures. He was detained in 1944 and spent the next seventeen years in Franco's prisons. In May 1962 he fled once more to France and became a member of the Central Committee of the PCE. After Franco's death he returned to Spain and sat in the new democratic Aragón Assembly as a member for the PCE (and then *Izquierda Unida* – a coalition of left-wing political organisations, including the PCE). In 1988 he was elected Mayor of Alcampell (Huesca).

Lieutenant Faustino Bernabeu Castellón, a native of the small town of Jijona, 25km north of Alicante, was serving on the Toledo front at the end of March 1939 when it became clear that further resistance was futile. He reported to his commanding officers to request orders and discovered they had abandoned their posts. He requisitioned a truck, and with a group of men, reached Alicante as the Italians were entering the town. At the port he was reunited with one of his superiors who had just received the news that the enemy was in control of the town. The young captain put a pistol to his head and shot himself. Bernabeu and a friend abandoned their arms and escaped along the Postiguet beach. As they walked up the main Valencia road, a car pulled up and a Francoist officer, in uniform, asked them where they were going. To their not inconsiderable surprise, he then announced he was on his way to Alcoy and offered to take them as far as Jijona. Bernabeu subsequently enjoyed several days reaccustoming himself to civilian life before a neighbour denounced him to the police. He was duly arrested, transferred first to Alcoy and then Alicante, accused of 'military rebellion', and sentenced to death. He spent months of anguish awaiting his fate in a cell so overcrowded that it was impossible for all the prisoners to lie down at the same time. One of the inmates, a skilled carpenter, alleviated the conditions by allocating the space available and drafting a plan whereby each prisoner took his turn at sitting, standing and lying on the floor.

Bernabeu's sentence was eventually commuted to thirty years' imprisonment, and he was transferred to El Dueso penitentiary in Santoña on the north coast. He then 'volunteered' to serve in a labour battalion, where he remained until he fell ill with typhus. Although the prisoner made a full recovery, a kindly nun prepared a medical report suggesting that he was unfit to return to his unit. Barred from his hometown under the terms of the law of *'destierro'* (internal exile/banishment), he was transferred to Valencia to undertake two years of military service in the new Spanish Army. He only returned to Jijona in 1963 after a spell in North Africa. He was active in union affairs and after Franco's death was elected to the town council. On the night of 23 February 1981, when right-wing rebel forces (Francoist nostalgics) seized control of the Parliament in Madrid, and the military commander of the Valencia region ordered tanks to patrol the city, Bernabeu received the visit of an acquaintance in the *Guardia Civil* who recommended he stay at home. If the situation deteriorated, the agent explained, the local forces could not guarantee his safety. As in 1936, the coup failed.

* * *

The Spanish Civil War concluded in Alicante. But the end to the fighting brought neither peace nor reconciliation. Throughout the dictatorship, a single narrative was permitted: the glorious Catholic crusade that had saved Spain from the 'reds'. Upon Franco's death in 1975, those in power offered concessions on democratic change and individual liberties on condition that no action be taken against those who had administered and exercised power for the previous forty years. A huge majority of the population thus acquiesced to the tacit understanding that the price of democracy was a renunciation of the right to expose the malfeasance of the dictator and the exponents of his regime. As a result, there was no retribution and no public inquiry into the crimes committed by the *franquistas* during the war and between 1939 and 1975. Nor did the state assist in the recovery or identification of the bodies of tens of thousands of Republicans buried in unmarked mass graves across the country. Those who had suffered, and their sons and daughters, were persuaded that the survival of the much-vaunted democratic transition was contingent on the goodwill of the exponents of Francoism, who were willing to relinquish political control to retain social and economic power. The *quid pro quo* for political reform was not so much a pact of amnesia as a contract to ignore, even obscure, the recent history of the country. There was a danger, the new democratic leaders alleged, that an investigation into certain events would open old wounds. They failed to appreciate that many of these old wounds had never healed, and never would heal until the causes were addressed.

After years of official silence, and popular submission, Alicante has gradually come to terms with the events of perhaps the darkest period in its history. There is little left today to remind residents and visitors of the dictatorship. In the offices of the Banco de España customers can still 'enjoy' a stained-glass window showing the *franquista* symbol of the *Águila de San Juan* (the Eagle of Saint John). There is an ugly, reinforced concrete cross still standing in the town centre (*Cruz de los Caídos* – Cross of the Fallen). It was originally designed as a tribute to those who died fighting for the Nationalist cause, but with the restoration of democracy, a Socialist Mayor decided the monument be rededicated to '*Todos los hombres y mujeres que murieron en defensa de sus ideales*' (All the men and women who died in defence of their ideals). The declaration excludes the innocent civilian victims who lost their lives and military personnel conscripted into armies they had no sympathy for. On the outskirts of the town, on the road to the airport, the old *franquista* memorial to the Vega Baja *falangistas* who sought to liberate José Antonio is still visible, but the *Falange* symbols have long since been removed and the monument has fallen into disrepair. Every year a tiny group of *falangistas* meet on 20 November outside the building that was once a prison to remember the execution of their founder. There is an impressive memorial at the site where he was first buried in the Alicante cemetery.

On the other hand, university professors, volunteer workers in private associations and the staff of archives across the province have produced extraordinary research work revealing much that the Francoist regime sought to bury. Today, schoolchildren can visit the reopened and restored air raid shelters. There is a bust of Archibald Dickson on the port, in honour of his rescue mission. There are plaques in the marketplace commemorating the bombing of May 1938, and every year dignitaries and local residents gather to remember the victims. The town council has changed the names of streets and squares associated with the Francoist regime, often in the face of opposition from inconvenienced residents who are unaware of, or indifferent to, the significance of a particular name.

A small monument has been raised at the *Campo de los Almendros* and there is a particularly underwhelming memorial to those who suffered in the Albatera concentration camp, now in the municipal area of San Isidro. Work has been undertaken at the municipal cemetery of Alicante to provide a more dignified alternative to the mass graves improvised in times of war and then ignored by the dictatorship. In the El Fondó primary school there is a model of a *Dragon Rapide* as a monument to the role of the aerodrome in the evacuation of Negrín's government. Where the Alicante Prison used to stand (today the site of the local courts), there is a memorial to Miguel Hernández, located precisely in the space occupied by the prison infirmary where he died.

Today, Alicante is a comfortable, prosperous town, a hub of the tourist industry. In terms of passenger numbers, it has the fifth most important airport in Spain (after Madrid, Barcelona, Palma de Mallorca and Málaga) and the town is a popular port of call for cruise operators. The most significant tourist attraction is the vast medieval castle of Santa Barbara, built on a huge rock formation overlooking the town, and offering spectacular views of the Mediterranean. Hundreds of Republicans were held there at the end of the war in the same appalling conditions as those who suffered in the *Campo de los Almendros* and Albatera. On one of the eastern balconies several of the victims etched graffiti into the stones that still make up the floor. One simply wrote '*prisionero rojo*' (red prisoner). This book is for him.

Dramatis Personae

All Spanish people have two surnames (the first of each parent). Of those who are active in public life, some are known with the two surnames, others under only one. I have respected the protocol of common use.

ÁLVAREZ Del VAYO, Julio: Socialist. Minister of Foreign Affairs (1936–37, 1938–39). Pro-Negrín.

AZAÑA, Manuel: Left Republican. President of the Second Republic (1936–1939).

AZCÁRATE, Pablo (de): Republican Ambassador in London.

BESTEIRO, Julián: leading member of the right-wing of the PSOE. Supporter of Casado.

BUIZA, Miguel: Admiral. Naval chief. Supporter of Casado.

CASADO, Segismundo: Colonel, Commander of the Central Army. Leader of the anti-Negrín faction.

CORDÓN, Antonio: leading Communist officer, Undersecretary at the War Ministry.

DALADIER, Edouard: French Prime Minister

FRANCO, Francisco: *Generalísimo* and *Caudillo*. Chief of the Nationalist army, head of state (dictator) 1936–1975.

GÓMEZ SERRANO, Eliseo: Deputy for Alicante for *Izquierda Republicana*, author of diaries of huge historiographical value.

HERNÁNDEZ, Jesús: Communist. Member of Politburo. Minister of Health and Education and subsequently Political Commissar for the Centre-South Zone.

IBURRARI, Dolores / *La Pasionaria*: Legendary Communist leader.

LARGO CABALLERO, Francisco: leading member of the left-wing of the PSOE. President of the Government (Prime Minister) 1936–1937.

MARTÍNEZ BARRIO, Diego: member of *Unión Republicana*. President of the *Cortes* (Speaker) – Former Prime Minister.

MATALLANA, Manuel: Republican General. Supporter of Casado.

MIAJA, José: Republican general. Commander-in-Chief. Supporter of Casado.

MOLA, Emilio: General, '*el director*': Architect of the military rebellion. Chief of the army in the north. Killed in air crash 1937.

de la MORA, Constancia: Aristocratic supporter of Republic and PCE. Active in humanitarian work.

NEGRÍN, Juan: President of the government (Prime Minister) of the Republic (1937–1939). Member of the PSOE.

PRIMO DE RIVERA, José Antonio: Leader (Co-founder) of Falange Española – the Spanish Fascist party. Executed November 1936.

ROJO, Vicente (Lt. General): Republican general. Chief of General Staff.

URIBE, Vicente: Minister of Agriculture (September 1936–March 1939) under Largo Caballero and Negrín. Leading member of the Communist Party.

ZUGAZAGOITIA, Julián: Socialist journalist. Minister of the Interior under Negrín.

Glossary

ALICANTE ROJO – the militia battalions recruited in Alicante province that were integrated in the 71st Mixed Brigade and fought at the Battle of Guadalajara.

ALICANTINO – native of Alicante. Also feminine: *alicantina* and plural: *alicantinos* or *alicantinas*.

AÑO DE LA VICTORIA – the *franquistas* referred to 1939 as the 'Year of the Victory'. The slogan appeared on official documents.

AVIAZIONE LEGIONARIO – Italian Air Force expeditionary unit in Spain.

BOE (*Boletín Oficial del Estado*) – Official State Gazette.

CALLE - street, as in calle Alcalá: Alcalá Street.

CARABINEROS – elite frontier and coastal police.

CARLISTAS – traditionalist (anti-liberal), ultra-Catholic followers of the dynastic line of Prince Carlos, pretender who claimed his right to the throne under Salic Law when his niece was proclaimed Queen Isabel in 1833.

CASTELLANO – Castilian. The name in Spanish by which the Spanish language is known by most Spaniards. To distinguish it from other official languages: Basque, Galician, Catalan, Aranese.

CAUDILLO – title bestowed on Franco, similar to '*Führer*' or '*Duce*'.

CAUSA GENERAL – inquiry ordered by the Francoist authorities after the Civil War to investigate the repression in those areas held by the Republic.

CEDA – *Confederación Española de Derechas Autónomas* (Spanish Confederation of the Autonomous Right). Coalition of right-wing parties.

CHECAS – headquarters of self-appointed autonomous militia police forces whose aim was to expose and eliminate pro-Franco elements in Republican territory.

COMISARIO POLÍTICO – political commissar, supervising ideological and organisational reliability of a unit.

COMITÉ PROVINCIAL del FRENTE POPULAR – Popular Committee of the Popular Front. Committee set up by representatives of the Popular Front to fill the administrative vacuum caused by the war.

CNT-FAI – *Confederación Nacional de Trabajo* (National Confederation of Labour) – *Federación Anarquista Ibérica* (Iberian Anarchist Federation) – Anarchist movement.

CONDOR LEGION – autonomous military legion/unit deployed by Hitler in support of Franco in Spanish Civil War.

CONSEJO NACIONAL DE DEFENSA – CND – National Council of Defence, Casado's government after coup of 05/03/1939.

CONSEJO DE MINISTROS – the Cabinet, or a cabinet meeting.

CORPO TRUPPE VOLONTARIE – Mussolini's 'volunteer' corps fighting for Franco.

CORTES – the historical name for the Spanish Parliament.

DIPUTACIÓN – the institution and headquarters of the provincial council (the equivalent of the county council).

DIPUTACIÓN PERMANENTE DE LAS CORTES – Standing Committee of the Cortes, a committee exercising functions of Parliament when not in session.

DIPUTADO/A – member of Cortes/Parliament.

ESTADO DE GUERRA – state of war (martial law).

EUSKADI – the Basque Country.

FALANGE – Fascist 'Party' founded by José Antonio Primo de Rivera.

FALANGE ESPAÑOLA TRADICIONALISTA Y DE LAS JUNTAS DE OFENSIVA NACIONAL SINDICALISTA (FET de las JONS) – Franco's single party, the result of an enforced union between the Falange and the monarchists (Carlists).

FRANQUISTA – Francoist. Adjective with lower case 'f' (*franquista*) to denote anything related to Franco.

FRENTE POPULAR – Popular Front. Electoral alliance of left-wing and Republican parties that won the 1936 general election.

FUERO DE LOS ESPAÑOLES – one of Franco's 'Fundamental Laws' that established the rights, liberties and duties of the Spanish people (1945).

FARE – *Fuerzas Aéreas de la República Española*. Air Force of the Spanish Republic.

GALLEGO – native of Galicia in north-west Spain. Also feminine: *gallega* and plural: *gallegos* or *gallegas*.

GENERALÍSIMO – Franco's military title as 'supreme commander'.

GENERALITAT – autonomous government of Catalonia.

GOLPE DE ESTADO (often simply GOLPE) – *Coup d'état*.

GUARDIA CIVIL – police force with military organisation and discipline.

GUARDIA DE ASALTO – Security and Assault Corps. Special force set up by, and loyal to, the Republic.

ILICITANO – native of Elche. Also feminine: *ilicitana* and plural *ilicitanos* and *ilicitinas*.

JUVENTUDES SOCIALISTAS UNIFICADAS – (JSU) Unified Socialist Youth. Merger of Socialist and Communist youth movements.

INTERNATIONAL BRIGADES – foreign volunteers who fought for the Republic during the Spanish Civil War.

IZQUIÉRDA REPUBLICANA – (IR), Republican left.

LEGIÓN – the Spanish Foreign Legion.

LEHENDAKARI – President of the Basque government.

LEVANTE – a name often used unofficially to refer to the eastern Spanish seaboard and inland areas. It usually denotes the region of the modern-day autonomous communities of Valencia and Murcia.

LUFTWAFFE – German Air Force.

MADRILEÑO – native of Madrid. Also feminine: *madrileña* and plural *madrileños* and *madrileñas*.

MIXED BRIGADE – unit of the Republican Army (regiment/brigade). In design a pocket division that combined infantry and artillery, etc.

MOVIMIENTO NACIONAL – commonly used name for Franco's single party (see FET y de las JONS), later shortened to *Movimiento*.

NATIONALISTS – the forces that supported the military uprising of July 1936 and the cause of General Franco. In fact, the insurgents called themselves '*Nacionales*' (Nationals), but the Nationalist label is accepted by most modern historians.

NKVD – *Naródnyy komissariát vnútrennikh dyél* – People's Commissariat for Internal Affairs. Soviet secret police.

NON-INTERVENTION – Franco–British policy designed on paper to avoid internationalisation of Spanish war by preventing both sides from purchasing arms on international markets. Gave the legitimate, democratic government of the Republic and the military insurgents the same political and legal status. Although Germany, Italy and the USSR endorsed the agreement and participated in the Non-Intervention Committee (London), the terms were ignored by Hitler, Mussolini and Stalin.

PCE – PARTIDO COMUNISTA ESPAÑOL – Spanish Communist Party.

PNV – PARTIDO NACIONALISTA VASCO – Basque Nationalist Party.

POUM – PARTIDO OBRERO DE UNIFICACIÓN MARXISTA – Workers' Party of Marxist Unification, anti-Stalinist left-wing party.

PS – PARTIDO SINDICALISTA – party set up to add political support to the anarchist/syndicalist movement.

PSOE – PARTIDO SOCIALISTA OBRERO ESPAÑOL – Socialist Party. Literally: Spanish Workers' Socialist Party

PSUC – PARTIT SOCIALISTA UNIFICAT DE CATALUNYA – Catalan Communist Party. Literally: Unified Socialist Party of Catalonia.

PASEO – the 'walk' or 'stroll' or 'drive'. The abduction of enemy individuals and their subsequent unlawful execution.

POSICIÓN DAKAR – HQ of PCE leaders in Elda (March 1939).

POSICIÓN JACA – command centre of Republican Army of the Centre in Madrid.

POSICIÓN YUSTE – HQ of Negrin's Republican government in Elda-Petrer (February–March 1939).

PUCHERAZO – electoral fraud, election rigging.

REFORMATORIO – Reformatory Centre. Main prison in Alicante.

REGULARES – 'indigenous' colonial troops recruited in Morocco that fought in Franco's Army.

RIF WAR (1921–1926) – conflict between Spanish colonial forces and the Berber tribes of the Rif mountain zone (Morocco) under Abd el-Krim.

ROJOS – Reds. Term used pejoratively by Franco's supporters to refer not only to Socialists and Communists, but also to all those loyal to the Republic.

SACA – the removal of prisoners from prison and their execution.

SECCIÓN FEMININA – The Women's Section of the Falange. Organisation in which women performed 'social service' and learnt the skills and duties required of patriotic wives.

SECOND REPUBLIC (1931–1939) – proclaimed when an increasingly unpopular King Alfonso XIII abandoned Spain.

SERE – two versions: *Servicio de Evacuación de Refugiados Españoles* or *Servicio de Emigración de los Republicanos Españoles*. Spanish Republican Evacuation or Emigration Service.

SIM – *Servicio de Investigación Militar* – Republican Military Investigation Service.

SIPM – *Servicio de Información y Policia Militar* – Military Intelligence and Police Service. The Nationalist/Francoist military intelligence agency.

UGT – UNIÓN GENERAL DE TRABAJADORES – (UGT – General Union of Workers), Socialist trade union.

VALENCIANO – Valencian, the language of the Valencia area. Identified by many as Catalan.

VALLE DE LOS CAÍDOS – literally Valley of the Fallen. Monument (with basilica) near El Escorial, in the Cuelgamuros Valley (Madrid). Although in theory a memorial to all those who fell in the Civil War, it was little more than an excuse to construct a giant mausoleum for Franco.

VEGA BAJA – the southern part of the province of Alicante, includes Orihuela, Albatera, Callosa, Torrevieja and Guardamar. The area where irrigation depends on waters from the River Segura.

WEHRMACHT – German armed forces.

ZARZUELA – traditional Spanish light opera.

Chronological Table

1931
14 April — Alfonso XIII abandons Spain. Proclamation of the Second Republic

1933
3 December — Right-wing alliance wins general election

1936
16 February — *Frente Popular* wins general election
10 May — Manuel Azaña appointed President of the Republic
17–18 July — Military coup. Outbreak of Spanish Civil War
09 September — Non-Intervention Committee meets for first time, in London
05 November — First air raid in Alicante
06 November — Government flees Madrid. Relocates to Valencia Siege of Madrid begins
20 November — Execution in Alicante of José Antonio, leader of the *Falange*

1937
05–24 February — Battle of Jarama
07 February — Málaga falls to Nationalists
08–18 March — Battle of Guadalajara
03–07 May — Internecine street fighting in Barcelona
17 May — Fall of Largo Caballero
New Negrín government
19 June — Bilbao falls
29 October — Republican government relocates to Barcelona
14 December — Republican army launches Teruel offensive

1938
22 February — Nationalists retake Teruel
25 May — Italian air force bombs Alicante market

13 June	France closes border
24 July	Republican army crosses the Ebro
30 September	Munich pact
16 November	Battle of Ebro ends in defeat for the Republic

1939

26 January	Fall of Barcelona
	Mass exodus of Republican refugees into France
27 February	Britain and France recognise Franco regime
	President Azaña resigns
	Negrín moves government to Elda-Petrer
04–06 March	Cartagena mutiny
	Republican navy sails to North Africa
05 March	Colonel Casado leads coup d'état
06 March	Negrín, government and PCE leaders leave Spain
06–13 March	Fighting between Casado's forces and the Communists
28 March	Madrid surrenders to Nationalists
	Stanbrook sails from Alicante
30 March	Italian troops occupy Alicante
01 April	Franco proclaims end of Civil War

1975

20 November	Death of Franco

1977

15 June	First democratic elections in Spain since 1936

1978

06 December	Democratic constitution ratified by referendum

1981

23 February	Coup d'état of army officers loyal to the principles of *franquismo* against the new democracy.

2019

24 October	Franco's remains exhumed and removed from Valle de los Caidos

Presidents of Government/Prime Ministers of the Republic during the Civil War

President of Government	Party/Affiliation	From	To
Santiago Casares Quiroga	IR	13/05/1936	18/07/1936
Diego Martínez Barrio	UR	18/07/1936	19/07/1936
José Giral Pereira	IR	19/07/1936	04/09/1936
Francisco Largo Caballero	PSOE	04/09/1936	17/05/1937
Juan Negrín	PSOE	17/05/1937	05/03/1939
José Miaja (President of the CND)	CND	05/03/1939	28/03/1939

CND Consejo Nacional de Defensa
IR   Izquierda Republicana
PSOE Partido Socialista Obrero Español
UR Unión Republicana

Alicante Officials
Mayors of Alicante during the Second Republic 1931–1939

Mayor/President of Town Council	Party / Affiliation	From	To
Lorenzo Carbonell Santacruz	PRRS	1931	1934
Alfonso Martín Santaolalla	PRR	1934	1936
José Pascual de Bonanza Pardo	Independent	1936	1936
Lorenzo Carbonell Santacruz	IR	1936	1936
Rafael Millá Santos	PCE/UGT	1936	1937
Santiago Martín Hernández	PSOE/UGT	1937	1938
Ángel Company Sevilla	FAI	1938	1939
Ramón Hernández Fuster	PS	1939	1939

Civil Governors during the Civil War 1936–1939

Governor	Party / Affiliation	From	To
Francisco Valdés Casas	IR	22/02/1936	13/07/1937
Nemesio Pozuelo Expósito	PSOE/UGT	July 1937	Did not take up the post

Governor	Party / Affiliation	From	To
Jesús Monzón Reparaz	PCE	18/07/1937	28/05/1938
Ricardo Mella Serrano	PSOE	28/05/1938	17/03/1939
Manuel Rodríguez Martínez	PSOE/CND	17/03/1939	28/03/1939
José Mallol Alberola	MN	28/03/1939	

Military Governors during the final weeks of the Civil War 1936–1939

Governor	Party / Affiliation	From	To
Lt-Col Manuel Hérnández Arteaga	–	–	04 March 1939
Lt-Col Etelvino Vega	PCE	04 March 1939	06 March 1939
Col Ricardo Burillo Stholle	CND	06 March 1939	–
Major José Muñoz Vizcaino	CND	28 March 1939	28 March 1939
José Mallol Alberola	MN	28 March 1939	30 March 1939

CND   Consejo Nacional de Defensa
IR   Izquierda Republicana
MN   Movimiento Nacional
PCE   Partido Comunista de España
PRR   Partido Republicano Radical
PRRS   Partido Republicano Radical Socialista
PS   Partido Sindicalista
PSOE   Partido Socialista Obrero Español

José Mallol Alberola seized control of these posts but was not appointed officially. Colonel Ricardo Burillo Stholle's appointment was not official.

The information in these tables is accurate to the best of my knowledge. However, in the case of the Military Governors, there appear to be no official records and names and dates vary according to the source. The official history of Alicante proclaims: 'In terms of the political activity in Alicante, the short space of time between 24 March and 30 March has become a dark mystery.' (*Crónica de la muy ilustre ciudad de Alicante* – Ayuntamiento de Alicante)

Sources include:
Archivo Histórico Provincial de Alicante/Archivo de la Democracia (Universidad de Alicante)
Diccionario biográfico de políticos valencianos 1810–2003 (editors: Paniagua and Piqueras)
Hoja Oficial de Alicante, El Luchador, Nuestra Bandera, Avance
https://alicantepedia.com/bases-de-daros/gobierno-gobernadores-civiles-y-subdelegados
Ramos, Vicente: *La Guerra Civil en la provincia de Alicante. Tomo 3º* (Alicante: Biblioteca Alicantina, 1974)

Epigraphs and chapters

It began in the second fortnight …

Ángel Pascual Devesa, in *Reflexiones y recuerdos*.
Pascual Devesa was a physician, mason, poet and one of the leading inspirations of the local fiestas: the *Hogueras de San Juan* (*Fogueres de Sant Joan* – The Bonfires of Saint John)

Chapter 1   A strong and threatening tide of history
Wyndham Lewis: 'Spain is an overflow of sombreness … a strong and threatening tide of history meets you at the frontier.'
in *The Wild Body: A Soldier of Humour*

Chapter 2   *Akra Leuka*
In Greek: Ἄκρα Λευκή. The name given to a military base believed to have been located in the area now occupied by the town of Alicante. It was probably founded in 231 BCE by Hamilcar Barca, a Carthaginian general and father of Hannibal. The name means 'white promontory'. It may or may not be near the site of the Iber-Roman site of Lucentum.

Chapter 3   *José Antonio ¡presente!*
The slogan of the Falange after the death of their leader José Antonio. Literally: 'José Antonio present'; as in a roll call, meaning his spirit and example lived on.

Chapter 4   Your children will be next
Republican propaganda poster.

Chapter 5   *Malditos, malditos, malditos los causantes de tanto dolor …*
Eliseo Gómez Serrano: 'Cursed be those who cause so much pain'.

Chapter 6   Bullets hurt, corpses stink
George Orwell's summary of war in *Looking back on the Spanish War*.

Chapter 7   An ocean of darkness and death, but an infinite ocean of light and love

George Fox, founder of the Quakers (Religious Society of Friends): 'I saw also that there was an ocean of darkness and death, but an infinite ocean of light and love, which flowed over the ocean of darkness.'

Chapter 8   *Cerca del agua perdida del mar*

Miguel Hernández, the most famous Alicante poet, born and raised in Orihuela: 'Next to the lost water of the sea', from the poem *Cerca del agua te quiero llevar.*

Chapter 9   Stay out of the range of the artillery fire

According to NKVD operative Walter Krivitsky, this was Stalin's motto.

Chapter 10   The end may justify the means as long as there is something that justifies the end

Leon Trotsky.

Chapter 11   Red Sunset

A graphically significant headline used by Churchill in an article on the Civil War published in 1938. '*Rojo*' (red) was used pejoratively by the Nationalists as a label originally for socialists and communists and then as a blanket name for all supporters of the Republic. The name was embraced by many on the Left. The image is also used in the lyrics of Joan Manuel Serrat's iconic song *Mediterráneo* in which he says/sings: '*a tus atardeceres rojos se acostumbraron mis ojos*'.

My eyes became used to your red sunsets. On occasion, Franco's intelligence services referred to the Levante coast as '*la Costa Roja*' (the Red Coast).

Chapter 12   One Munich was not enough

Foreign Minister Julio Álvaro del Vayo's comment comparing France and Britain's approach to Czechoslovakia and Republican Spain.

Chapter 13   The quickest way of ending a war is to lose it

George Orwell in *Second Thoughts on* James Burnham.

Chapter 14   *El olvido es peor que los recuerdos*

Elia Barceló, academic and writer from Elda: 'Forgetting is worse than memories.'

In her novel about recollection and forgetting: *Las largas sombras.*

Chapter 15   His last ounce of courage
'One man scorned and covered with scars still strove with his last ounce of courage to reach the unreachable stars; and the world will be better for this.' Miguel de Cervantes, *Don Quijote de la Mancha*.

Chapter 16   *Usted haga como yo, no se meta en política*
Franciso Franco: 'Do as I do, don't get involved in politics.'

Chapter 17   *El destino infortunado de España, derrotada y maltrecha*
José Martínez Ruiz, known to all *Alicantinos* as '*Azorín*', is one of the province's most famous writers. He was born in Monóvar in 1873. His mother was from Petrer. The quote 'the unfortunate fate of Spain, defeated and battered' was a reference to the work of the '*Generación del 98*'.

Chapter 18   Written in the blood of a Spanish soldier
Segismundo Casado: Of his memoirs, published in London in 1939. He did not in fact shed blood, but then he also claimed his narrative was 'illuminated with the light of truth.'

Chapter 19   *El abrazo de Vergara*
The hug/embrace of Vergara. The treaty/gesture of reconciliation between the two armies at the end of the First Carlist War, 1839.

Chapter 20   *Una gota de pura valentía vale más que un océano cobarde*
Miguel Hernández: 'A drop of pure courage is worth more than an ocean of cowardice.' From the poem[7] *Nuestra juventud no muere* in the collection *Viento del pueblo* (1936–1937).

Chapter 21   *Wo bleibt Gambara?*
General Rommel, 1941, in the North African desert, during Operation Crusader: 'Where is Gambara?' demanding to know where the Italian reinforcements were.

Chapter 22   And the almond tree shall flourish
Eccliastics: 12.1 (St. James).

Chapter 23   *En el yermo de la historia*
Miguel Unamuno: 'In the wilderness of history', from the poem *Me destierro a la memoria*.

Chapter 24 *No ha llegado la paz. Ha llegado la victoria.*
'This is not peace. It's victory.' (Literally: Peace has not arrived. Victory has arrived). Spoken by the father in the final scene of the film *Las bicicletas son para el verano* (Bicycles are for the Summer), based on the play written by Fernando Fernán Gómez, and directed by Jaime Chávarri.

Acknowledgements

Everything possible has been done to locate the ownership of materials used in this book. I regret any omissions or mistakes.

I should like to express my gratitude to the following people who have helped in the preparation of this book:

Carmen Negrin, of the *Fundación Negrín*, who kindly shared information and stories about her grandfather, the last Prime Minister of the Spanish Republic.

All the staff at the Alicante Municipal Archive for their help and support.

Alicia Cerdá of the Archives and Library of Monóvar, for her help with the plan of the aerodrome.

José Ramón Valero Escandell of the University of Alicante, who took the time to show me round Elda and Monóvar and generously shared photos, information and insight, and the map of Elda-Petrer.

Gaspar Belmonte of the municipal archives of San Juan de Alicante, who provided me with vast quantities of fascinating information about the Civil War in the village.

Mary and Natalia for sharing with me the story of their father/grandfather Faustino Bernabeu. His story, and theirs, is the story of so many Republican families.

Linda Palfreeman for her help on the work of Sir George Young and his role in the final evacuation. And for so generously sharing documents with me.

Paco Moreno and Mercedes Guijarro Anton of the University of Alicante and the University Archives, who gave me invaluable guidance at the beginning of my research. And Catalina Iliescu for always being there to offer help and support.

John Sanderson and Juan Antonio Ríos Carratalá, for their help in researching the dramas of the *Stanbrook* and the marketplace. Alicia González Beltrán for her wonderful stories of the voyage of the *Stanbrook* and her exile in North Africa.

Peter Anderson of the University of Leeds, who gave me insights into the events at Gandia and with great generosity shared his research into the Apfel case.

Juanjo Morant, the manager of the Cuevas de Canelobre, for answering all my questions, providing photographs, and offering insights of life in Busot during the Civil War.

Caroline Danjou for allowing me to use the photograph of her mother, Mary Elmes, with the young patient Palmira.

The staff at Pen & Sword for their kindness and assistance.

My family for their unfailing hospitality on my trips to Britain.

My son, David, for his help in all things technical and for challenging the many ideas I always took for granted.

Notes

Chapter 1: A threatening tide of history
1. Archivo Municipal de Alicante. (Digital records, available at: https://www.alicante.es/es/documentos/actas-municipales-del-primer-pleno-del-ayuntamiento-republicano-16-abril-1931.) Retrieved 22/01/23. The quote appears in the minutes of the inaugural session of the new council 16/04/1931.
2. *Latifundismo* can only be understood as the ownership and control of large rural estates by a tiny number of wealthy landlords. The quote is from *Spain 1808–1975* (OUP, 1982) p.603.
3. See *In Place of Spendour* (London, 2021) p.151.
4. In *The Spanish Civil War* (OUP, 2005) p.8.
5. Vincent: *Spain 1833–2002* (OUP, 2007) p.135.
6. For a detailed study of the response of the Right to the Republic and its machinery of propaganda, see Preston: *Arquitectos del Terror* (Barcelona: Penguin, 2021).
7. In the introduction to Luis Bolín: *Spain. The Vital Years* (London: Cassell, 1967).
8. See, for example Cyril Connolly, *A Spanish Diary* in *New Statesman & Nation* 20/02/37. The ideological and strategic dichotomy caused damaging divisions on the Left and led to the events of Barcelona 1937, so graphically, if not necessarily accurately, described by Orwell in *Homage to Catalonia*. Orwell's experiences are also reflected in Ken Loach's film *Land and Freedom*. Violent resentments resurfaced in the final days of the war.
9. For example, Vincent reports more than 6,500 clergy and members of religious orders were killed. In *Spain. 1833–2002* (OUP, 2007) p.139.
10. The complete council was:
    Presidente:
    General de División Miguel Cabanellas Ferrer
    Members:
    General Andrés Saliquet Zumeta
    General Miguel Ponte y Manso de Zúñiga
    General Emilio Mola Vidal
    General Fidel Dávila Arrondo
    Coronel Federico Montaner Canet
    Coronel Mayor Fernando Moreno Calderón
    The membership of the Junta was extended in August, to include:
    General Francisco Franco Bahamonde
    General Gonzalo Queipo de Llano y Sierra.
11. See *In Place of Spendour* (London, 2021) p.212
12. For a detailed analysis, see Howson, *Arms for Spain* (London, 1998). And specifically for his conclusion: p250. Or his article *Lies and swindles in the Spanish Civil War* in *The Independent* 09/12/1998. Preston suggests that the USSR did provide some state-of-the-art weapons but also 'obsolete artillery and small arms', in *The Spanish Civil War* (London, 2006) p.191.

13. Quoted in *The Nuremberg Trials*, Heydecker and Leeb, p.157 (London, 1962).
14. *A New International History of the Spanish Civil War* (London: Macmillan, 1994) p.171. The figures are based on a report from the Soviet Academy of Sciences, *International Solidarity with the Spanish Republic 1939–1939*, pp. 329–30. For a breakdown of Soviet supplies, based on Soviet/Russian archives and western publications, see Howson, *Arms for Spain* (London, 1998) pp.141–2. In his *Summary of Material Supplied by the USSR* (p.302) he calculates:
    Aircraft: 657
    Tanks: 331
    Armoured Cars: 60
    Machine guns: 17,780
15. In *Step by Step* (London, 1949) p.319.
16. *Daily Herald*, 10/08/1936.
17. *The Editor's Cockpit*, quoted in *Spanish Front, Writers on the Civil War* (OUP, 1986) p.76.
18. Moradiellos: *Historía mínima de la Guerra Civil española* (Madrid, 2016) p.255.
19. Published in *The Manchester Guardian*, 27/11/1937.
20. Vicente Rojo. In his report of 20/09/1938: Archivo Histórico Nacional – Archivo General Rojo. Caja 2/4.
21. *The Spanish Holocaust* (London, 2013) p. xx of the Introduction.
22. The research is available in *La economía de la guerra civil* (eds: Martín Aceña and Martínez Ruiz) (Madrid, 2006). Also *Las consecuencias demográficas de la Guerra Civil* at http://www.usc.es/estaticos/congresos/histec05/a2_ortega_silvestre.pdf. (accessed 09/12/2021). There is a summary of their findings at *¿Cuántas víctimas se cobró la Guerra Civil? ¿Dónde hubo más?*, in *El País*, 11/02/2019.
23. *Historia mínima de la Guerra Civil Española* (Madrid, 2016) pp.275–6.

Chapter 2: *Akra Leuké*

1. Writer and academic Juan A. Ríos Carratalá, of the University of Alicante, puts the population at 73,071 at the beginning of the decade. He also reports that 39% of the male population were illiterate, and 44% of women. Finally, he affirms that two thirds of the young people of school age did not attend an educational centre. See his article: *La actividad cultural en Alicante durante la II República*, available from the Cervantes Virtual Library at http://www.cervantesvirtual.com. García Andreu reports 21.62% of men were illiterate and 37.54% of women. On the question of schooling, he only states that as 26.8% of young people of between 10 and 15 years of age were illiterate, this would suggest that more than a quarter of that age group at least were not attending school. On the other hand, he does not refer to primary schools. See: *Alicante en las elecciones Republicanas (1931–1936)*, (Alicante, 1985) p.21.
2. See García Andreu: *Alicante en las elecciones Republicanas* (1931–1936), (Alicante, 1985) pp.22–3.
3. From Gordon, John and Cora: *Poor Folk in Spain* (London: Bodley House, 1922) p.177.
4. Results from the *Acta del Escrutinio Oficial* of the *Junta Provincial Electoral/ 16 de febrero de 1936*. Archivo de la Diputación de Alicante.
5. Archivo de la Diputación de Alicante: *Acta del escrutinio de las elecciones para Diputados a Cortes celebradas el 16 de febrero de 1936*. p.5.
6. Archivo de la Diputación de Alicante: *Acta del escrutinio de las elecciones para Diputados a Cortes celebradas el 16 de febrero de 1936*. pp.9–10.
7. This version of events is taken directly from an article, *Detalles de los sucesos de Torrevieja. La versión oficial*, published in *La Vanguardia* 05/03/1936, p.25. The story appears in English in Preston: *The Spanish Holocaust* (London: Harper, 2013) p.123.

8. Much of the account that follows is based on his *Diarios de la guerra civil* (Universidad de Alicante, 2008). This entry is on p.112.
9. See: Gómez Serrano, *Diarios de la guerra civil* (Universidad de Alicante, 2008) p.118.
10. From Ramos, *La Guerra Civil en la provincia de Alicante. Tomo 1º* (Alicante, 1972) pp.96–7.
11. According to records of the Archivo General del Cuartel General de la Armada, cited on the website of the Real Academia de la Historia (dbe.rah.es), Carre Chicarro was incarcerated in Málaga and murdered in reprisal for air raids by the Nationalists.
12. Ramos, *La Guerra Civil en la provincia de Alicante. Tomo 1º* (Alicante, 1972) p.134.
13. Archivo Municipal de Alicante. The deaths are registered in the records of the Alicante Cemetery.
14. In *Diarios de la guerra civil* (Universidad de Alicante, 2008) p.115.
15. In an article published in *Información* 28/11/16, his grandchild claims that at his exhumation, forensic scientists found a bullet hole in the back of his head, which would suggest he had been executed.
16. In *Campo de los almendros* (Mexico, 1968) p.241.
17. *Diarios de la guerra civil* (Universidad de Alicante, 2008) p.120.
18. In *News Chronicle*, 24/10/1936. Reproduced in Gibson: *En busca de José Antonio* (Barcelona, 1980) p.301.
19. This, and much of the narrative that follows, is based on de la Mora's own account, first published in 1940: *In Place of Splendour*. The references here are based on the edition published in 2021 by The Clapton Press, pp.241–257.
20. *In Place of Splendour* (London, 2021) p.241.
21. A list, with map, is available in Paula Pineda Marimón: *Las colonias infantiles en Sant Joan D'Alacant durante la Guerra Civil Española (1936–1939)* pp.2–3. Four are still standing: Finca Abril (events venue), la Pinada (residence for retired rail workers), el Reloj (council property) and la Manzaneta (private property) pp.10–11. For more details, see Carles Salinas Salinas, *La infància refugiada en les colònies col·lectives de l'Alacantí, 1936–1939* p.120.
22. *Ibid.*, p.242, and Paula Pineda Marimón: *Las colonias infantiles en Sant Joan D'Alacant durante la Guerra Civil Española (1936–1939)* p.4.
23. Archivo Municipal San Juan de Alicante: Registro de Salida nº 36 de 18/02/1937.
24. Archivo Municipal San Juan de Alicante: Registro de Salida nº 89 de 28/02/1938.
25. Archivo Municipal San Juan de Alicante: Registro de Salida nº 323 de 16/07/1938.
26. 06/09/1937. From the *Lugares de la memoria de Sant Joan d'Alacant*. Published by the Archivo Municipal San Juan de Alicante. Section 2.
27. *In Place of Splendour* (London, 2021) p.246.
28. From the local pro-republican newspaper, *El Luchador*, 19/19/1936.
29. *In Place of Splendour* (London, 2021) p.245.
30. For example: Berenguer Escoda, Manuel: *Biografía de Juan Gósalbez Casar* (Ayuntamiento de San Juan de Alicante. p.67. Given the lack of consensus, official ratification of the new name was postponed.
31. Reported in *Bandera Roja*, 09/03/37. *Bandera Roja* described itself as the voice of the UGT, PSOE, PCE and JSU (according to the Hemeroteca del Archivo Municipal de Alicante).
32. In *El año de la victoria* (Madrid, 2001) p.133.
33. This summary is based largely on the work of the most eminent of modern Alicante historians, Francisco Moreno. See: *Primeros días de la sublevación militar del 18 de julio en Alicante*, article in *Información*, 19/07/2011. Moreno suggests that more than 1,000 people from Elche joined the new columns.

34. *La Guerra Civil en la provincia de Alicante. Tomo I* (Alicante, 1974) p.116.
35. See: Ramos, *La Guerra Civil en la provincia de Alicante. Tomo I* (Alicante, 1974) pp.113–126 and Moreno, *Primeros días de la sublevación militar del 18 de julio en Alicante*, in *Información*, 19/07/2011. Also Mainar: *La Guerra Civil en la Comunidad Valenciana. Vol. 5, Todos al frente* (Alicante, 2007) pp.101–102.
36. In *Reluctant Warriors* (OUP, 2012) p.27.
37. In *Antifascistas* (London: Lawrence & Wishart/IBMT, 2012) p.46. For more details on the role of the British in the battle, see Baxell: *Unlikely Warriors* (London: Aurum, 2012), chapter 8/*Their Finest Hour?* For a first-hand witness report, see Walter Gregory: *The Shallow Grave* (London: Gollancz, 1986) pp.41–65; and Jason Gurney: *Crusade in Spain* (Readers Union, 1974) pp.99–165. Also, the website of the International Brigades Memorial Trust at http://www.international-brigades.org.uk.
38. The article *Cartas desde el Batallón Rojo* is a short but interesting reflection on the Red Battalion and includes testimonies of some who fought in its ranks: *El País*, 05/01/09. For more details, see Robert Llopis and Luis Botella: *Fer la guerra. Diccionari i testimonis dels combatents de Benissa en la Guerra Civil (1936–1939)* (Instituto Gil Albert). See also: *Historia de las brigadas mixtas* (Engel, 2005) p.99.
39. *Bandera Roja*, 15/04/1937. I have no explanation of the relevance of the reference to 'anaemic English women'. See also another article in *Bandera Roja* of 23/01/37, in which the commanding officer, Domingo Barrera, described the conditions in which the men were fighting.

Chapter 3: *José Antonio ¡presente!*
1. Alonso Mallol, Director General of Security, ordered his detention for contempt, incitement to rebellion, and slander. For a full account, see Angosto, *El Hombre que pudo evitar la Guerra* (Alicante, 2006) p.207.
2. José Antonio was referencing the German philosopher Springer, but the words were his own: "A última hora, siempre ha sido un pelotón de soldados el que ha salvado la civilización." In *En busca de José Antonio* (Barcelona, 1980) p.148, Ian Gibson suggests the missive delivered to Mola was in fact a copy of a manifesto written by José Antonio at the beginning of May.
3. The article/interview is available in Spanish and English in Gibson, *En busca de José Antonio* (Barcelona, 1980) pp.303–308.
4. The ideological tendency of each local newspaper appears as defined by Moreno in *La prensa en la provincia de Alicante durante la Guerra Civil (1936–1939)* (Instituto Juan Gil-Albert, 1994).
5. *El Luchador* 20/07/1936. Available online at the *Biblioteca Virtual de la Prensa Histórica* of the Ministry of Culture.
6. *La Guerra Civil en la provincia de Alicante. Tomo I* (Alicante, 1974) pp.88–92. A slightly different version of events is offered by the *falangista* José Mallol Alberola in *La Estampida* (Crevillente, 2000) pp.24–5, but the salient details he offers are similar. He does not, however, mention any problems with the trucks.
7. *The Battle for Spain* (London, 2006) p.84.
8. For example: Gerardo Muñoz Llorente in *Información* in an article, *Paseos y sacas*, published 28/02/2016. However, this information has been disputed. See for example footnote 21 below.
9. See Ramos: *La Guerra Civil en la provincia de Alicante. Tomo I* (Alicante, 1974) p.139.
10. Archivo Histórico Nacional: CAUSA GENERAL,1397, 1941 / 1949 Exp.1 Pieza cuarta de Alicante. Checas. p.17. These files have now been transferred to the Centro de la Memoria Histórica de Salamanca.

11. Archivo Histórico Nacional: CAUSA GENERAL,1395, 1941 / 1949 Exp.1 Pieza Principal de Alicante. Partido Judicial de Alicante (Alicante) p.157.
12. In *The Spanish Civil War* (OUP, 2005) p.133.
13. Archivo Histórico Nacional: CAUSA GENERAL,1397, 1941 / 1949 Exp.1 Pieza cuarta de Alicante. Checas. p.16.
14. As most victims were abducted in cars, Beevor and Preston prefer: '*taken for a ride*': in *The Battle for Spain* (London, 2006) p.84, and *The Spanish Holocaust* (London, 2013) p.263 respectively. In the novel *Thus Bad Begins* (Penguin, 2017), Javier Marías and his translator Margaret Jull Costa translate '*darle a uno el paseo*' as '*to take someone for a stroll*'. Beevor gives an excellent summary of the nature of the revolutionary violence, pp.83–5. Helen Graham defines *checas* as clandestine, illegal detention centres run by parties, unions and militia committees; see *The Spanish Civil War* (OUP, 2005) p.65.
15. Proclamation of 28/07/1936.
16. In *The Spanish Holocaust* (London, 2013) p.254.
17. Edition of 28/08/1936.
18. Flaquer: *La opinión pública alicantina durante la Guerra Civil* (Madrid, 1992) p.50.
19. Ramos: *Lorenzo Carbonell, Alcalde popular de Alicante* (Alicante, 1987) p.209.
20. See Ramos: *La Guerra Civil en la provincia de Alicante Vol. 1* (Alicante, 1972) p.146. For full names of parties and unions in English and Spanish, see Glossary.
21. For more details on the political institutions, see Ramos *La Guerra Civil en la provincia de Alicante. Tomo I* (Alicante, 1974) pp.145–150 and 168–182.
22. in *Eye Witness* (London: Muller, 1955) p.71.
23. For a full account, see Preston, *The Spanish Holocaust* (London, 2013) pp.341–380.
24. *Eye Witness* (London: Muller, 1955) p.71.
25. See: Ors and Santacreu: *Violencia y represión en la retaguardia* (Prensa Alicantina, 2006) pp.36–37. For Gabarda's research, see *La represión en la retaguardia republicana. País Valenciano 1936–1939* (Valencia: Institució Alfons el Magnànim-Centre Valencià d'Estudis i d'Investigació, 1996).
26. In Preston, *The Spanish Civil War* (London: Harper Perennial 2006) p.125.
27. 26/11/37. Reproduced in *Step by Step* (London, 1949) pp.177–8.
28. Aldeguer, *Alicante 1939* (Alicante, 1999) p.63.
29. In Tébar Rubio-Manzanares: *Derecho penal del enemigo en el primer franquismo* (Universidad de Alicante, 2017) p.177.
30. From Serrano Suñer, Ramón: *Memorias* (Barcelona, 1977) p.170.
31. See Ramos: *La Guerra Civil en la provincia de Alicante. Tomo I* (Alicante, 1974) p.138. And Ors, *La represión de guerra y posguerra en Alicante, 1936–1945:* http://rua.ua.es/dspace/handle/10045/3784 (accessed 09/12/2019). Tébar suggests the events took place over two nights, not one; see: *Derecho penal del enemigo en el primer franquismo* (Universidad de Alicante, 2017) p.182.
32. Reproduced from the website of the *Fundación Nacional Francisco Franco*. The phrase '*Ojalá fuera la mía la última sangre española que se vertiera en discordias civiles*' is the epitaph on the memorial to José Antonio in the Alicante cemetery marking the space where his body was first buried.

Chapter 4: Your children will be next

1. See: *The Spanish Civil War* (London: Penguin, 1977) p.979. In the Readers' Union edition of 1962, Thomas had originally claimed the Italians sent 763 aircraft. Alpert suggests the number of aircraft was 759: *A New International History of the Spanish Civil War* (London: Macmillan, 1994) p.171. In a more recent study, Díez Pomares suggests the total number of aircraft was 764. See *Los bombardeos italianos sobre el País Valenciano*

durante la Guerra Civil española (*Pasado y Memoria. Revista de Historia Contemporánea* 15, 2016. p.184). There is some remarkable footage of the Italian air force in an Italian propaganda film at: https://www.youtube.com/watch?v=uiBE0Q8GPmY&ab_channel=FotosAntiguasdeMallorca (accessed 30/11/2021).
2. *España en llamas. La guerra civil desde el aire* (Madrid, 2003) p.19.
3. For a full account of the strategies developed by the Germans in Spain, see Néstor Cerdá: *The Road to Dunkirk: British Intelligence and the Spanish Civil War* in War in History Journal, Vol.13, No.1 (2006) p.20.
4. Quoted in Beevor: *The Battle for Spain* (London, 2006) p.200.
5. in *Homage to Catalonia* (London, 1938) and *Looking Back on the Spanish Civil War* (London, 1943).
6. *In Stalin's Secret Service* (New York, Harper & Bros. 1939/Hyperion, 1979) p.91.
7. The account that follows is largely based on Gónzalez de Pablo's own testimony that is available at *La Hispano Suiza–Aviación–Guadalajara-Alicante (1936–1939)* at alicantevivo.org/2010/03/la-hispano-suiza-aviacion-guadalajara.html. Retrieved 22/01/23.
8. There were other factors that may have influenced the Nationalist decision not to order air raids on Alicante. See notes 13 and 15 below.
9. From an interview with Juanjo Morant (*Encargado de les Coves del Canelobre*) 21/01/2022.
10. Details from Gómez: *Diarios de la guerra civil* (Universidad de Alicante, 2008) pp.168–9 and Ramos: *La Guerra Civil en la provincia de Alicante. Tomo 3º* (Alicante, 1974) pp.139–140.
11. In *Diarios de la guerra civil* (Universidad de Alicante, 2008) p.167.
12. Account based on: Martínez Mira: *Alicante 1936–39. Tiempos de Guerra* (Alicante, 2005), Gómez: *Diarios de la guerra civil* (Universidad de Alicante, 2008) pp.168–9 and Rubio: https://www.alicantepedia.com/fotografias/bombardeos-sobre-alicante-durante-la-guerra-civil-1936–39. Retrieved 22/01/23.
13. See https://turiguiasalicante.com/refugios/.
14. See Moreno, *Alicante, una provincia de la retaguardia republicana* in *1939 La Guerra terminó en Alicante* (Alicante, 2019) p.7.
15. From intelligence reports cited in Solé i Sabaté: *España en llamas. La guerra civil desde el aire* (Madrid, 2003) pp.267–9.
16. Pérez Oca. *25 de Mayo. La Tragedia Olvidada* (San Vicente, 2006) pp.89–90. The author provides fascinating context, background and oral testimonies, although the way he presents his research through a fictional investigator somewhat undermines the rigorousness of the narrative. I quote the information of the air defences with that caveat.
17. Hansard: https://hansard.parliament.uk/Commons/1932-11-10/debates.
18. See: Cerdan Tato, *Alicante: la masacre de los Savoia* in Canelobre 7/8, *La Guerra en Alicante* (Instituto Juan Gil-Albert) p.74; and Pérez Oca. *25 de Mayo. La Tragedia Olvidada* (San Vicente, 2006) p.65.
19. Cited in Mark Derby, *Petals and Bullets* (Sussex Academic Press, 2015) p.71.
20. In *Air Raid* (London: Routledge, 1938) p.15.
21. See, for example, the story of the Marquess Puebla de Parga, in Fraser, *Blood of Spain* (New York, 1979) pp.195–200. Also: the 'memoirs' of Capt. E.C. Lance as recounted to C.E. Lucas Philips: *The Spanish Pimpernel* (Watford: Companion Book Club, 1960). If one can overlook the fictional approach to the history of the war, the book still contains insights into official and extra-official British attempts to extract British nationals and Franco sympathisers.
22. In Anderson: *British Government Maritime Evacuations in the Spanish Civil War* in War in History Vol.26 (I). 2019. pp.65–85.

23. *Ibid.*, p.75.
24. For an account of his work in Spain, see *Warrior without Weapons* (London, 1951); section two, *Spain*, pp.87–134.
25. From Cairncross: *The Enigma Spy* (London: Century, 1997) p.56. Cairncross describes the high-profile release of Arthur Koestler as his team's most significant achievement.
26. FO 371/21378 W 20121. (The National Archives). The text of the memo is quoted in Anderson, *British Government Maritime Evacuations in the Spanish Civil War, 1936–1939* (*War in History*, 2016) p.76.
27. C.E. Lucas Philips: *The Spanish Pimpernel* (Watford: 1960) pp.101, 125, 166.
28. *The Spanish Pimpernel* (Watford: 1960) p.103.
29. Berenguer Escoda, Manuel: *Biografía de Juan Gósalbez Casar* (Ayuntamiento de San Juan de Alicante) p.68.
30. Alpert: *The Spanish Civil War at Sea* (Yorkshire, 2021) p.186.
31. This account is taken from the work of Santacreu Soler, *Los bombardeos de Alicante*, in *La Guerra Civil en la Comunidad Valenciana* (Alicante, 2007) p.90.

Chapter 5: *Malditos, malditos, malditos los causantes de tanto dolor…*
1. I am particularly grateful to Antonia Carratalá Ferrándiz who survived the attack and her son Juan Antonio Ríos Carratalá for sharing her experiences.
2. Archivo Municipal de Alicante. Inhumaciones Cementerios. II.12.1933–1944 / May 1938.
3. Ramos. *La Guerra Civil en Alicante*. p.250–1. Some historians, like Ramos, believe there were nine planes, others like Pérez Oca (see below) insist there were seven.
4. *Diario Información*, 24/04/2016, *¿Qué fue de Tullio de Prato, el bombardero del 25 de mayo?* Based on research in the Italian military archives.
5. Chant, Chris: *Aircraft of World War II* (Kent: Grange, 2000) p.285.
6. See Díez Pomares, *Los bombardeos italianos sobre el País Valenciano durante la Guerra Civil española* (*Pasado y Memoria. Revista de Historia Contemporánea 15*, 2016) p.186.
7. Author's private conversations and reports of witnesses in Martínez Mira. *Alicante, Tiempos de Guerra* (Alicante, 2005) pp.141–153; Pérez Oca. *25 de Mayo. La Tragedia Olvidada* (San Vicente, 2006) pp.135–154; and Gómez: *Diarios de la guerra civil* (Universidad de Alicante, 2008) pp.530–31. There is also an interesting short, animated documentary film *El Olvido* by Xenia Grey, nominated for a Goya Award in 2019.
8. Pérez Oca. *25 de Mayo. La Tragedia Olvidada* (San Vicente, 2006) p.136.
9. UN Archives R4211/7A/34924/30988.
10. In Hart-Davis: *Man of War. The Secret Life of Captain Alan Hillgarth* (London: Century, 2012) p.160.
11. FO 371/21391 (The National Archives).
12. FO 371/20546 (The National Archives).
13. See: Cerdan Tato: *Alicante: la massacre de los Savoia* in *La Guerra en Alicante* (*Canelobre*, No. 7/8, 1986) p.78.
14. Cited by Butler: *The Extraordinary Story of Mary Elmes* (Dublin, 2017), p.22.
15. The figures are based on the research of Matilde Dobón Giner, Carlos Moreno Ponce and Héctor Pastor Pastor of the *La Memoria Recuperada* Project of the University of Alicante, published at https://memoriarecuperada.ua.es/documentos/las-victimas-del-bombardeo-sobre-el-mercado-y-la-ciudad-de-alicante-sufrido-el-25-de-mayo-de-1938. Retrieved 22/01/23. Their work includes a list of the victims.
16. *Diarios de la guerra civil* (Universidad de Alicante, 2008) p.530.
17. *Reflexiones y recuerdos* (Universitat d'Alacant, 2019) p.251.

18. *Diarios de la guerra civil* (Universidad de Alicante, 2008) p.531.
19. Cited in Cerdan Tato: *Alicante: la massacre de los Savoia* in *La Guerra en Alicante* (*Canelobre*, No. 7/8, 1986) p.80.
20. For example: Anthony Beevor, *The Spanish Civil War*; Preston *The Spanish Civil War*; Raymond Carr *Spain 1808–1975*.
21. *The Spanish Civil War* (Readers Union) p.537.
22. *Life and Death of the Spanish Republic*, p.382.
23. FO 371/22609/W6923 (The National Archives). In fact, the British government urged both sides to cease bombing open towns. Chamberlain consistently refused to condemn the Nationalists in isolation.
24. UN Archives: File R4211/7A/34924/30988 - Protection of Civil Populations against Bombing. Discussions at the 104th Session of the Council, January 1939.
25. UN Archives R4211-7A-34924-30988.
26. See Alpert, *The Spanish Civil War at Sea* (Yorkshire, 2021) p.210 and Solé i Sabaté: *España en llamas. La guerra civil desde el aire* (Madrid, 2003) pp.198–9.
27. From the website *Dénia.com*. As a 'footnote' to an endnote, it is impossible not to include a phrase from the text that demonstrates the dangers of automatic translation. The English version describes 'the constant sound of mermaids that warned of the presence of German and Italian aviation flying over the municipality'. There would be a certain poetic beauty to this, were the subject not so sad. See: Dénia.com https://www.denia.com/en/el-ataque-sobre-la-via-el-bombardeo-a-denia-mas-sanguinario/ (accessed 04/04/2022).
28. UN Archives: File R4211/7A/34924/30988.
29. Hansard: https://api.parliament.uk/historic-hansard/commons/1938/dec/19/spain (accessed 10/01/2022).
30. Archivo Histórico del Ejército del Aire. Sig. A 168/54. Operations report, dated 07/11/1938.
31. Solé i Sabaté: *España en llamas. La guerra civil desde el aire* (Madrid, 2003) p.232. The authors suggest that the casualties included eleven soldiers and seventy-five civilians; a total of eighty-six deaths.
32. For a full account of the aerial bombardments of urban centres by the Republican air force, see: Solé i Sabaté: *España en llamas. La guerra civil desde el aire* (Madrid, 2003). Especially: pp.133–138, and 230–232.
33. FO 371/24128/W4694. (The National Archives). Memo. from Michael Cresswell, dispatched by Sir R. Hodgson on 15/03/1939. I assume Hemming was a member of the Civil Service, but it is not clear if he was in Spain on official business or in some other capacity. Cresswell later played a huge role in Allied rescue missions in the Iberian Peninsula as MI9 agent '*Monday*'.
34. Hansard: https://api.parliament.uk/historic-hansard/commons/1938/jul/20 (accessed 10/01/2022).
35. UN Archives R4211-7A-36750-30988.

Chapter 6: Bullets hurt, corpses stink

1. See Beevor: *The Battle for Spain* (London, 2006) p.376.
2. The expression belongs to Thomas, *The Spanish Civil War* (Penguin, 1977) p.868.
3. *Ibid.*, p.869. For a full account of these campaigns, see Campanario Larguero: *¿Por qué se suspendió el desembarco republicano en Motril en diciembre de 1938? La versión oficial del General Vicente Rojo frente a los documentos*. Revista de Historia Militar # 117, 25/06/2015, pp.91–122.

4. For a full account of the first battle, see: Beevor, *The Spanish Civil War 1936–1939*. (London, 2006). Chapter 24, pp.274–286.
5. In the introduction to his book *The Archaeology of the Spanish Civil War* (Routledge, 2020).
6. There is an interesting article in *El País* 06/01/19: *La otra batalla de Brunete: una matanza inexplicable* on the archaeological research of the CSIC (*Consejo Superior de Investigaciones Científicas*) into the battle.
7. *Así cayó Madrid* (Madrid, 1977) p.109.
8. Beevor says there were sixty-four deputies present: *The Battle for Spain* (London, 2006) p.380.
9. According to Martínez Barrio, Speaker of the Cortes in *Memorias* (Barcelona, 1983) p.391.
10. *Diarios de la guerra civil (1936–1939)*, (Universidad de Alicante, 2008) p.648.
11. From his *Memorias* (Barcelona, 1983) p.390.
12. For the '13 points', see *Aims of the Spanish Republic: the 13 Points of Dr. Negrín's government*. In Archives of the Trades Union Congress: 292/946/17b/2(i).
13. For the full text of the speech, see Moradiellos: *Textos y discursos políticos* (Madrid, 2010) pp.312–26.
14. From *Freedom's Battle* (London, 1940) p.280.
15. From Martínez Barrio, *Memorias* (Barcelona, 1983) p.395.
16. This is a paraphrase of comments made in *Memorias* (Barcelona, 1983) p.391.
17. In *Guerra y Vicisitudes de los Españoles Vol. II* (Paris, 1968) p.228–9.
18. In *Mi embajada en Londres durante la guerra civil española* (Barcelona, 1976) p.121.
19. In *Freedom's Battle* (London, 1940) p.282.
20. Archivo Histórico Nacional: Archivo Marcelino Pascual. Caja 1. Carpeta 13.
21. The undated, pencil-written note is in the same Caja 1. Carpeta 13 of the Archivo Marcelino Pascual (Archivo Histórico Nacional).
22. Archivo Histórico Nacional: Archivo General Rojo. Caja 5. Carpeta 8.
23. *Ibid.*, p.282.
24. In *¡Alerta los pueblos!* (Barcelona, 1974) p.167.
25. In *Juan Negrín* (Sussex Academic Press, 2010) p.282.
26. For more details, see: Thomas: *The Spanish Civil War* (London, 1962) p.561, Preston: *The Spanish Civil War* (London, 2006) p.291, and Anthony Beevor: *The Battle for Spain* (London, 2006) p.358.
27. *In Place of Splendour* (London, 2021) p.333. Her determination to support the Republic and the Republican government led her to make a sweeping denunciation of the POUM as fascist agents (p.289), and her reports of Nationalist armies at times seemed to suggest they were composed only of Italian or German troops (see for example her description of the Battle of the Ebro, pp.331–2).
28. This appears in the Spanish-language version: *Así cayó Madrid* (Madrid, 1977) p.113. In the first edition/version of these memoirs, published in English under the title *The Last Days of Madrid* (London, 1939), Casado reproduces what appears to be a fictitious conversation with Negrín, in which he tells the Prime Minister: 'Our war industries were reduced by seventy per cent by the fall of Catalonia.' p.109.
29. For a full account of the fate of the Republican army in France, see Whitehead, *Spanish Republicans and the Second World War* (Yorkshire, 2021). Chapters 4 and 5.
30. In *¡Alerta los pueblos!* (Barcelona, 1974) pp.166–7.
31. Archivo Histórico Nacional –Archivo General Rojo. Caja 5. Carpeta 8.
32. In *Guerra y Vicisitudes de los Españoles Vol. II* (Paris, 1968) p.231 and a footnote on p.232.
33. *General Miaja, Defensor de Madrid* (Madrid, 1975) p.280.

34. For a thorough analysis, see: Preston, *George Orwell and The Spanish Civil War*. The Len Crome Lecture, 2013. Available at the website of the International Brigade Memorial Trust.
35. In *Looking back on the Spanish War* in *The Penguin Essays of George Orwell* (Penguin, 1984) p.223.
36. *Reluctant Warriors* (Oxford, 2012) pp.157–8.
37. This is taken from a review of James Matthews' ground-breaking book *Reluctant Warriors* (Oxford, 2012) by Antonio Muñoz Molina, which appeared in *El País* 25/10/2012 and is available in English at https://english.elpais.com/elpais/2012/10/25/inenglish/1351163552_542343.html. Retrieved 23/01/23.
38. For detailed analysis of the role of chaplains and political commissars, see Matthews, *Reluctant Warriors* (Oxford, 2012), chapters 4 and 5.
39. *Reluctant Warriors* (Oxford, 2012) pp.102–03.
40. These figures are taken from Preston: *The Last Days of the Spanish Republic* (London, 2017) p.49.
41. *Guerra y Vicisitudes de los Españoles Vol. II* (Paris, 1968) p.242. Preston refers to his proposal in *The Last Days of the Spanish Republic* (London, 2016) p.60.
42. The English translation is from the *Official Journal of the League of Nations*, 18th Assembly, September 1937. Special Supplement No. 169. The speech is available in the original Spanish in Moradiellos: *Textos y discursos politicos* (Madrid, 2010) pp.85–96.
43. In Galeazzo Ciano's diaries: *Il diario del conte Ciano* (L'Universale, 2020) p.65.
44. '*Fa le operazioni da magnifico comandante di battaglione. Il suo obbietivo è sempre il terreno. Mai il nemico.*' In *Il diario del conte Ciano* (L'Universale, 2020) p.29. There is a translation into English of the full reference in Moradiellos, *Franco. Anatomy of a Dictator* (London, 2018) p.45.
45. Moradiellos, *História mínima de la Guerra Civil española* (Madrid, 2016) p.255.
46. *Looking Back on the Spanish War* in *The Penguin Essays of George Orwell* (Penguin 1984).

Chapter 7: An ocean of darkness and death, but an infinite ocean of light and love

1. For a detailed account of the process of socialisation/municipalisation in Alicante, see: Quilis Táuriz, Fernando: *Las municipalizaciones durante la Guerra Civil en la ciudad de Alicante: 1936–1939* in *Anales de la Universidad de Alicante. Historia Contemporánea. 1984–1985*, 3-4: 349–365. (Universidad de Alicante. Departamento de Historia Contemporánea, 1985).
2. *Spanish Civil War* (North Carolina, 2015) p.236.
3. See Moreno: *Alicante, una provincia de la retaguardia republicana* in *1939. La guerra terminó en Alicante* (Comisión Cívica para la Recuperación de la Memoria Histórica) p.2.
4. Published in *Bandera Roja* 22/12/36. Hemeroteca/Newspaper Archives of the Archivo Municipal de Alicante.
5. *Bandera Roja* 19/01/37.
6. For a full description of attempts to improve supplies, see *La opinión pública alicantina durante la Guerra Civil* (Madrid, 1994) pp.153–60.
7. Modern Records Centre, Warwick University. WRO/16, National Joint Committee for Spanish Relief, MSS.308/3/NJ/1-36. From a letter from M.M.Miller to W. Roberts, 11/08/1937. Miller includes a report that one doctor was taking libel action against Young, after the baronet had called him a 'drug-fiend'.
8. Much of the narrative that follows is based on Butler, *The Extraordinary Story of Mary Elmes* (Dublin, 2017); Derby, *Petals and Bullets. Dorothy Morris. New Zealand Nurse*

in the Spanish Civil War (Sussex, 2015); and *Firing a Shot for Freedom. The Memoirs of Frida Stewart* (London, 2020).
9. Butler, *The Extraordinary Story of Mary Elmes* (Dublin, 2017) p.15.
10. *Firing a Shot for Freedom. The Memoirs of Frida Stewart* (London, 2020) p.114.
11. *Ibid.*, p.110. Chalmers was former Secretary of the London Zoological Society. For his own account of his experiences in Spain, see: My House in Málaga (London: Clapton Press, 1938).
12. See the website of the *BCA'37 UK - The Association for the UK Basque Children* at https://www.basquechildren.org/, for more information.
13. Derby, *Petals and Bullets* (Sussex Academic Press, 2015) p.59.
14. García Ferrandis, Xavier / Martínez-Vidal, Àlvar (2019), "*La ayuda humanitaria de los British Quakers durante la Guerra Civil española (1936–1939): el caso del Hospital Infantil de Polop de la Marina (Alicante)*", Asclepio, 71(1): p.253.
15. Butler, *The Extraordinary Story of Mary Elmes* (Dublin, 2017) p.18.
16. García Ferrandis, Xavier / Martínez-Vidal, Àlvar (2019), "*La ayuda humanitaria de los British Quakers durante la Guerra Civil española (1936–1939): el caso del Hospital Infantil de Polop de la Marina (Alicante)*", Asclepio, 71(1): p.253. https://doi.org/10.3989/asclepio.2019.05. p.7.
17. Cited in Mark Derby, *Petals and Bullets* (Sussex Academic Press, 2015) p.73.
18. For a full account of the history of the Polop Hospital, see the article cited above in endnote #13 by García Ferrandis and Martínez-Vidal.
19. From a letter cited in Butler, *The Extraordinary Story of Mary Elmes* (Dublin, 2017) p.19.
20. Cited in Mark Derby, *Petals and Bullets* (Sussex Academic Press, 2015) p.83.
21. *Ibid.*, p.83.
22. *Ibid.*, p.129.
23. See *Diarios de la guerra civil* (Universidad de Alicante, 2008) p.619.
24. *Diarios de la guerra civil* (Universidad de Alicante, 2008) p.629.
25. There are more recipes in Gutiérrez Rueda: *El hambre en el Madrid de la Guerra Civil 1936–1939* (Madrid, 2015) pp.114–5.
26. From Preston: *The Last days of the Spanish Republic* (London, 2017) p.40.
27. Figure quoted in Gutiérrez Rueda: *El hambre en el Madrid de la Guerra Civil 1936–1939* (Madrid, 2015) p.129.
28. *Blood of Spain* (New York, 1979) p.488.
29. From Gutiérrez Rueda: *El hambre en el Madrid de la Guerra Civil 1936–1939* (Madrid, 2015) p.136.
30. *Blood of Spain* (New York, 1979) p.487.
31. In *Guerra y Vicisitudes de los Españoles Vol. II* (Paris, 1968) p.229. He offers a slightly different version on p.241: 'Let us hope we can carry out part two as successfully.'.
32. *General Miaja, Defensor de Madrid* (Madrid, 1975) pp.265–7. Preston describes López as '*fiercely anti-Communist*'. He also reports that the meeting took place in Perpignan (*The Last Days of the Spanish Republic* [London, 2016] pp.62–3).
33. Mark Derby, the biographer of nurse and aid-worker Dorothy Morris, suggests the service was still operating in the last week of February and that Morris had an Air France booking on a flight out of Alicante at the end of the month that was cancelled after the Paris government recognised Franco. *Petals and Bullets* (Sussex Academic Press, 2015) p.94.
34. *Freedom's Battle* (London, 1940) p.274.

Chapter 8: *Cerca del agua perdida del mar*
1. References from *The Last Optimist* (London, 1950) pp.289–90.
2. *Diario de Sesiones de la Diputación Permanente de las Cortes* 31/03/1939. Reproduced in *Juan Negrín. Textos y discursos políticos* (Madrid, 2010) p.351.

3. In *Freedom's Battle* (London, 1940) p.275.
4. See Moradiellos: *Juan Negrín. Textos y discursos políticos* (Madrid, 2010) p.351. If one accepts López Fernández as a reliable source, then after their meeting at Toulouse, Negrín would have had more than a 'premonition' (see endnote 32, chapter 7).
5. FO 371/24127/W2424. (The National Archives). A Foreign Office Minute, dated 10/02/1939.
6. *Oxford Dictionary of Popes* (OUP, 2009) pp.321–323 and 323–325, and Beevor, *The Battle for Spain* (London, 2006) pp.224, 235, 241
7. FO 371/24128/4650. (The National Archives). The translation is by R.M.Hodgson in a letter to Halifax (11/03/39), from the newly accredited British Embassy in Burgos.
8. Vicente Uribe in *Memorias de un ministro comunista de la República* (Spain: Renacimiento, 2019) p.187.
9. *Freedom's Battle* (London, 1940) p.276, or from the original Spanish quoted in *Juan Negrín. Textos y discursos políticos* (Madrid, 2010) p.329: 'Against people with that attitude, the rebels don't need motorised divisions. To break through the front, they just need a few bicycles.'.
10. *Juan Negrín. Textos y discursos políticos* (Madrid, 2010) p.327.
11. Reproduced in *Juan Negrín. Textos y discursos políticos* (Madrid, 2010) p.331.
12. For a fuller account, see *Bombardeig de Xàtiva 1939* (ed. Germán Ramírez Aledón) (Xàtiva, 2016) and Mainar Cabanes: *El bombardeo de Xàtiva* in *La Guerra Civil en la Comunidad Valenciana Vol. 15* (Alicante, 2007) pp.115–123. For more on the 49th, see Engel: *Historia de las Brigadas Mixtas* (Madrid, 2005) pp.76–77.
13. For a full account of the surrender of Menorca, see Alpert, *The Spanish Civil War at Sea* (Yorkshire, 2021) pp.226–8 and Bahamonde and Cervera Gil: *Así terminó la Guerra de España* (Madrid, 2000) pp.215–219. Thomas claims 600 Republicans were saved, *The Spanish Civil War* (Penguin, 1977) pp.884–6.
14. https://hansard.parliament.uk/Commons/1939-02-13/debates. Retrieved 22/01/23.
15. FO 371/24146/W3051. (The National Archives) Dated 16/02/1939.
16. FO 371/24146/W2951. (The National Archives) Dated 15/02/1939. The text cited is a Foreign Office translation.
17. BOE., 13-II-1939.
18. In *Memorias* (Barcelona, 1977) p.245.
19. Sandoval, José and Manuel Azcárate: *Spain 1936–1939* (London: Lawrence & Wishart, 1963) p.134.
20. *Freedom's Battle* (London, 1940) pp.277–78.
21. *Diario de Sesiones de la Diputación Permanente de las Cortes* 31/03/1939. Reproduced in *Juan Negrín. Textos y discursos políticos* (Madrid, 2010) pp.351–2.
22. It should be said that Alicante historian Vicente Ramos also claims the summit was held in the final days of the month: *La Guerra Civil en la provincia de Alicante Vol. III* (Alicante, 1973) p.136.
23. For an analysis of morale at the front see Matthews, *Reluctant Warriors* (OUP, 2012) pp.159–173: with particular reference to: pay, rations, health (including control of parasites), communications, protection from the elements, weapons and training.
24. For more details, see Preston: *The Last Days of the Republic* (London, 2017) pp.110–11. For a full account in Spanish, see Viñas: *El desplome de la República* (Barcelona, 2010) pp.196–.
25. *The Last Days of Madrid* (London, 1939) p.125.
26. In his statement to the *Diputación Permanente de la Cortes* 31/03/1939. Reproduced in *Juan Negrín. Textos y discursos políticos* (Madrid, 2010) pp.351–52.
27. *Diarios de la guerra civil* (Universidad de Alicante, 2008) p.667.

Chapter 9: Stay out of the range of the artillery fire

1. *Freedom's Battle* (London, 1940) pp.276.
2. In his statement to the *Diputación Permanente de las Cortes* in Paris 31/03/1939. Reproduced in *Juan Negrín. Textos y discursos políticos* (Madrid, 2010) p.352.
3. For a summary of their operations, see Preston: *The Spanish Holocaust* (London, 2013) pp.423–24. For a more complete analysis of the work of the British and French missions, see: Rousselot, *The Chetwode and Vincent missions during the Spanish Civil War: Examples of humanitarian inflation and rivalry?* (*Relations internationals*, Volume 176, Issue 4, 2018).
4. In *Warrior without Weapons* (London, 1951) p.103 and p.107. Junod offers a full account of his activities for the Red Cross in Spain in section two of his book – especially the chapters: *Camaradas and Caballeros* (pp.87–110) and *The Exchange of Lives* (pp.111–126).
5. FO 371/22609/W6768. (The National Archives). The letter from Leche to Halifax is dated 17/05/1938.
6. *Warrior without Weapons* (London, 1951) p.98.
7. https://api.parliament.uk/historic-hansard/commons/1938/dec/20/spain#S5CV0342P0_19381220_HOC_584. Retrieved 22/01/23.
8. Azcárate, *Mi embajada en Londres durante la Guerra Civil española* (Barcelona, 1976) p.252, and https://api.parliament.uk/historic-hansard/commons/1938/dec/20/spain#S5CV0342P0_19381220_HOC_584.
9. FO 371/22661/W15124 (The National Archives).
10. *In Place of Splendour* (London, 2021) p.337.
11. From Edwards, *The British Government and the Spanish Civil War* (London: 1979) p.204.
12. FO 371/24147/W2014. (The National Archives). Telegram from Stevenson is dated 03/02/1939.
13. FO 371/24147/W2105. (The National Archives). Telegram dated 06/02/1939.
14. FO 371/24147/W2766. (The National Archives). Memorandum on conversation between Cadogan and Azcárate.
15. *The Manchester Guardian*, 16 April 1938.
16. See Howson *Arms for Spain* (London, 1991) Chap.17. In particular p.121. For a full account of the gold, see Bolloten: *Spanish Civil War* (North Carolina, 2015) chapter 14: *Spanish Gold Shipped to Moscow* pp.145–158.
17. See *Fundación Andreu Nin* at http://www.fundanin.org/. A short and highly plausible account of the murder of Nin is available in Beevor, *The Struggle for Spain* (London, 2006) pp.272–3. For a full account of the repression of the POUM, see Bolloten *Spanish Civil War* (North Carolina, 2015) chapter 48, pp.498–515.
18. For a full account, see Steven Koch: *The Breaking Point. Hemingway, Dos Passos and the Murder of José Robles* (New York: Counter point, 2005).
19. *In Stalin's Secret Service* (New York, Harper & Bros. 1939/Hyperion, 1979) p.115. For examples of Soviet covert operations in Spain, pp.102–106.

Chapter 10: The end may justify the means as long as there is something that justifies the end

1. See Viñas, *El Desplome de la República* (Barcelona, 2010) p.178.
2. *The Gathering Storm*, (London: Cassell & Co., 1948) p.167.
3. *Diarios de la guerra civil* (Universidad de Alicante, 2008) p.602.
4. In *The Spanish Civil War* (North Carolina, 2015) p.87.
5. In a speech to the Central Committee in Valencia, March 1937, reproduced in Díaz, *Tres Años de Lucha* (Paris: Ebro, 1970) p.390.

6. *El Desplome de la República* (Barcelona, 2010) p.145.
7. In *Spain. 1833–2002* (OUP, 2007) p.147.
8. From his speech to the Cortes in Valencia, 01/12/1936. Reproduced in *Tres Años de Lucha* (Paris, 1970) p.270.
9. In *Step by Step* (London, 1949) p.178.
10. The figures are based on Preston, *The Last days of the Spanish Republic* (London, 2017) p.28, and Viñas, *El Desplome de la República* (Barcelona, 2010) p.147.
11. In *Yo, Ministro de Stalin en España* (Madrid, 1954) p.159. For Hernández's full account of the Nin case, *ibid.*, pp.158–181. For a full account of Negrín and the Nin case, see Jackson, *Juan Negrín* (Sussex Academic Press, 2010) chap.4.
12. *Ibid.*, p.157.
13. *The Spanish Civil War* (London, 2006) p.258. For a detailed account of Negrín's appointment, see Beevor, *The Battle for Spain* (London, 2006) p.271–2.
14. *Yo, Ministro de Stalin en España* (Madrid, 1954) p.129.
15. From *In Stalin's Secret Service* (New York, 1939) p.101.
16. Quoted by Jackson in *Juan Negrín* (Sussex Academic Press, 2010) p.57, from the *Archivo Fundación Juan Negrín* (carpeta 31p. nos. 14/267). Apart from Negrín, the other three men mentioned who shared responsibility were respectively: the Prime Minister, Minister of the Air Force and Navy and President of the Republic respectively. Bolloten disputes the argument that the Cabinet was fully aware of the policy: *Spanish Civil War* (North Carolina, 2015), p.150.
17. *The Spanish Labyrinth* (CUP, 1971) p.329.
18. FO 371/22631/W14601. (The National Archives) In a letter from Stevenson to Foreign Secretary, Lord Halifax (31/10/1939).
19. In a letter to Prieto (23/06/1939). Reproduced in Moradiellos *Juan Negrín. Textos y discursos políticos* (Madrid, 2010) p.395. He added the caveat: 'if my memory serves me well'.
20. In the same letter to Prieto (23/06/1939). Indalecio Prieto never forgave Negrín for dismissing him as Minister of Defence (April, 1938). For many years after the Civil War, he sought to undermine Negrín's work with Republican refugees, and his position in the government-in-exile and the PSOE. He was particularly critical of the Prime Minister's relations with the PCE.

Chapter 11: Red sunset

1. In *Diarios de la guerra civil* (Universidad de Alicante, 2008) p.654 and p.665.
2. See: Ramos: *El Teatro Principal en la historia de Alicante* (Alicante, 1965) p.511.
3. Based on cinema listings in the local press: *Nuestra Bandera* and *Avance*, February, March 1939.
4. For a detailed analysis, see: Francisco Joaquín Cerdá Bañón's doctoral thesis, *Historia del cine en Alicante durante la Guerra Civil Española (1936–1939)* (Universidad de Murcia, 2016). Figures for 1938–39 appear on p.374.
5. *Nuestra Bandera* 12/01/1939, 18/01/1939 and 19/01/1939.
6. Described by Gómez Serrano in *Diarios de la guerra civil* (Universidad de Alicante, 2008) p.635. Restrictions from *Nuestra Bandera* 10/01/1939 p.2. Official orders from Civil Governor in *Avance* 10/01/1939.
7. Figures from José Miguel Santacreu Soler and Albert Girona Albuixech: *La agonía de la retaguardia* in *La Guerra Civil en la Comunidad Valenciana Vol. 15*, p.48.
8. *Diarios de la guerra civil* (Universidad de Alicante, 2008) p.672.
9. See Santacreu and Girona, *La Guerra Civil en la Comunidad Valenciana, Vol.15.*, pp.45–49.

10. FO 371 /22361. (The National Archives). The files include an example of the bags used, which was sent to London by the Acting Consul in Madrid (J.H.Milanes). In Spanish, the message reads: *"No nos importa lo que penséis, nos basta saber que sufrís y sois españoles. Todo es mentira en las propagandas rojas, este es el pan de cada día en la España de Franco: El que guardamos en nuestros graneros para compartirlo el día de la liberación, con los hermanos cautivos"*.
11. Cited by José Ramón Valero Escandell in *El territorio de la Derrota* (Alicante, 2004) pp.38–39.
12. Compare: Flaquer's table (based on press reports) in *La opinion pública alicantina durante la Guerra Civil* (Madrid, 1994) pp.64–6 and Pérez, *25 de Mayo* (San Vicente [Alicante], 2006) pp.195–7.
13. *Diarios de la guerra civil* (Universidad de Alicante, 2008) pp.671–72.
14. *Reflexiones y recuerdos* (Universitat d'Alacant, 2019) p.263. The Latin expression *post nubile, phoebus* can be translated as *after the clouds (or after the storm), the sunshine*.

Chapter 12: One Munich was not enough

1. Dilks (ed.): *The Diaries of Sir Alexander Cadogan* (London: Cassell, 1971) p.149.
2. In *The Manchester Guardian*, 28/02/1939.
3. In *Step by Step* (London, 1949) pp.318–19.
4. https://api.parliament.uk/historic-hansard/commons/1939/feb/27/recognition-of-general-francos-government#S5CV0344P0_19390227_HOC_49. Retrieved 22/01/23.
5. Martínez Barrio: *Memorias* (Barcelona, 1983) p.408.
6. *Guerra y Vicisitudes de los Españoles Vol. II* (Paris, 1968) p.236.
7. *Memorias* (Barcelona, 1983) p.364.
8. The translation is from Thomas, *The Spanish Civil War*, (Penguin, 1977) pp.956–7. There is an audio of the speech (Barcelona Town Hall, 18/07/1938) at https://www.youtube.com/watch?v=5eYT_CTG2bI&ab_channel=DefensadeMadrid. This excerpt is taken from the last four minutes of the speech. Retrieved 22/01/23.
9. https://api.parliament.uk/historic-hansard/commons/1939/feb/28/spain#S5CV0344P0_19390228_HOC_331. Retrieved 22/01/23.
10. The response was based on a telegram (No.88) from Sir R. Hodgson, the British Agent in Burgos, FO371/24128.
11. FO 371/24147/1817. (The National Archives). Brenan is primarily recognised as the author of *The Spanish Labyrinth* (CUP., 1943), *The Face of Spain* (London: Turnstile Press, 1950) and *South from Granada*. (London: Hamish Hamilton, 1957).
12. The *Causa General*, the report of the inquiry ordered by Franco in 1940 into crimes committed by Republicans is available at the website of the Archivo Histórico Nacional via the government portal: PARES http://pares.mcu.es/.
13. The translation is taken from Preston, *The Spanish Holocaust* (London, 2012) p.179.
14. This is the version popularised by Thomas in *The Spanish Civil War* (Penguin, 1977) p.503, based on *Unamuno's Last Lecture* by Luis Portillo published in the *Horizon* Journal (December 1941). As Portillo was not present at the event, some historians question the accuracy of the wording of Unamuno's intervention. See, for example: Severiano Delgado, *Arqueología de un mito: el acto del 12 de octubre de 1936 en el paraninfo de la Universidad de Salamanca* (Madrid: Sílex, 2019) The full quote in Portillo's article is: *You will win, but you will not convince. You will win, because you possess more than enough brute force, but you will not convince, because to convince means to persuade. And in order to persuade you would need what you lack - reason and right in the struggle. I consider it futile to exhort you to think of Spain. I have finished.'*.

15. See Ian Gibson, *Queipo de Llano. Sevilla, Verano de 1936* (Barcelona: Grijalbo, 1986) p.84. The translation is taken from Preston, *The Spanish Holocaust* (London, 2012) p.149.
16. In *Franco. A Concise Biography* (London: Wiedenfeld and Nicholson 2000) p.129.
17. *The Manchester Guardian*, 17 August 1936.
18. *La Columna de la Muerte*, (Barcelona, 2003) p.257. After extensive research, Espinosa provides a breakdown of the figures for the repression both in the city and province of Badajoz, pp.228–250.
19. *Spain 1833–2002* (Oxford, 2007) p.151. See also Preston: *Arquitectos del Terror* (Barcelona, 2021) p.248.
20. In John T. Whitaker: *We cannot escape history* (New York: Macmillan 1943) p.113.
21. Quoted in Spanish at http://www.caum.es/CARPETAS/cuadernos/cuadernospdf/libro3/malaga.pdf. Retrieved 20/11/2014.
22. In *The Spanish Civil War* (University of North Carolina, 2015) p.53.
23. In *Arquitectos del Terror* (Barcelona, 2021) pp.252–4.
24. On 4, 6, 10, 12,13, 18, 19 and 21 February. See Flaquer: *La opinión pública alicantina durante la Guerra Civil* (Madrid, 1994) p.177.
25. See Dilks (ed.): *The Diaries of Sir Alexander Cadogan* (London: Cassell, 1971) p.154.
26. *The Diaries of Sir Alexander Cadogan* (London: Cassell, 1971) p.149.
27. *Diarios de la guerra civil* (Universidad de Alicante, 2008) p.675.

Chapter 13: The quickest way of ending a war is to lose it

1. *Avance. Crónica de Madrid* 23/02/39. Roberto Castilla, *Un jefe militar: Colonel D.Segismundo Casado.*
2. *The Last Days of Madrid* (London, 1939).
3. In *Freedom's Battle* (London, 1940) p.290.
4. Viñas and Fernando Hernández Sánchez: *El Desplome de la República* (Barcelona, 2010) pp.89–90.
5. *The Last Days of Madrid* (London, 1939) p.101.
6. *The Last Days of Madrid* (London, 1939) pp.100–101.
7. *The Last Days of Madrid* (London, 1939) p.96.
8. *Memorias de un ministro comunista de la República* (Spain: Renacimiento, 2019) p.188.
9. For his full account, see *The Last Days of Madrid* (London, 1939) pp.103–105. The same incident, minus the second conversation, appears in the Spanish edition, *Así cayó Madrid* (Madrid, 1977) p.117.
10. Azcárate discusses Besteiro's visit in *Mi embajada en Londres durante la guerra civil española* (Barcelona, 1976) pp.65–6.
11. Biography at the website of the *Real Academia de la Historia*: https://dbe.rah.es/biografias/12654/cipriano-mera-sanz.
12. *The Last Days of Madrid* (London, 1939) p.188.
13. The details are from the biography that appears on the website of the *Real Academia de la Historia*: at: https://dbe.rah.es/biografias/119485/melchor-rodriguez-garcia (Retrieved 20/01/23).
14. 09/03/1939 under the headline: *Casado, the man behind the events in Madrid. Future of the 'Contradictory Alliance' he leads.*
15. *Así cayó Madrid* (Madrid, 1977) p.189.
16. *Así terminó la Guerra de España.* (Madrid, 2000) p.314, footnote 76.
17. They cite a report addressed to Colonel Jiménez Ortoneda in *Así terminó la Guerra de España.* (Madrid, 2000) p.265.
18. *El golpe del coronel casado, el final de la Republica.* Radio Nacional de España. 27/09/2019.

19. For more details on Casado's contacts with the fifth column and 'promises' made, see: Bahamonde, *Así terminó la guerra de España* (Madrid, 200) pp.264–9; Cordón, *Trayectoria* (Sevilla, 2008) p.694; or Preston, *The Last Days of the Spanish Republic* (London, 2017) pp.30–2 and p.150.
20. FO 371/24127/2424 (The National Archives). See chapter 8.
21. *British Intelligence and the Spanish Civil War* at https://www.academia.edu/6538032/British_Intelligence_and_the_Spanish_Civil_War.
22. FO 371/ 24128/W3576 (The National Archives).
23. *The Last Days of the Spanish Republic* (London, 2017) p.140.
24. see Whitehead, *Franco. History to the Defeated* (London, 2018). Chapter 1.

Chapter 14: *El olvido es peor que los recuerdos*
1. In *Guerra y Vicisitudes de los Españoles Vol. II* (Paris, 1968) p.250.
2. Domínguez Aragonés in *Los vencedores de Negrín* (Mexico, 1976) pp.96–9.
3. *The Spanish Civil War* (London: Penguin, 1977), p.892.
4. In *Memorias de un ministro comunista de la República* (Sevilla, 2019) p.192.
5. *El territorio de la derrota* (Alicante, 2004) pp.90–93.
6. Details taken from Mira Perceval Verdú and Rico Navarro: *Vicente Amat Furió (1857–1943) su contribución a la historia de Petrer* (Festa, 2012).
7. The details about El Poblet are based on the report of the *Comissió Llegat Històric*, published by the *Consell Valencia de Cultura* 26/05/2014.
8. For details of the XIV Cuerpo, see Secundino Serrano, *Maquis. Historia de la guerrilla antifranquista* (Madrid, 2004) pp.41–45.
9. See *The Last Days of the Spanish Republic* (London, 2017) p.155.
10. In Moradiellos: *Juan Negrín. Textos y discursos políticos* (Madrid, 2010) p.359. Del Vayo suggests there were about 100, in *Freedom's Battle* (London, 1940) p.296.
11. For more on Nelken, see Preston, *Doves of War* (London: Harper Collins 2003).
12. For her own account, see *Memoria de la melancolía* (Sevilla, 2020) pp.255–81.
13. In *The Spanish Civil War* (London: Penguin, 1977), p.341.
14. These references appear in the 1961 edition, reproduced in the Readers Union edition (London, 1962) p.217. They do not appear in the revised edition (Penguin, 1977).
15. In *Memoria de la melancolía* (Sevilla, 2020) p.159.
16. In *The Spanish Civil War* (London, 1962), p.442, footnote 2. The anecdote does not appear in the revised edition (Penguin, 1977).
17. *In Place of Splendour* (London, 2021) p.336.
18. In *El País*, (*La arboleda perdida*) 06/01/1985. *Comienzo por el final*.
19. In an interview given to José Ramón Valero Escandell in 1986, reproduced in *1939 La Guerra terminó en Alicante* of the Comisión Cívica de Alicante para la Recuperación de la Memoria Histórica (Alicante: Compas, 2019) p.19.
20. Interview in the local Alicante newspaper *Información*, 06/06/2016: https://www.informacion.es/cultura/2016/06/06/ultimo-refugio-comunista-6144962.html. Retrieved 22/01/23.

Chapter 15: His last ounce of courage
1. In *Memorias de un ministro comunista de la República* (Sevilla, 2019) p.196.
2. *Trayectoria* (Paris, 1971) p.476. The reference to Jesus Christ appears in the later edition (ed. Viñas): (Sevilla, 2008) p.701.
3. *Yo, Ministro de Stalin en España* (Madrid, 1954) p.253.
4. A similar story recounted by Casado can be found in Jackson: *Juan Negrín* (Sussex Academic Press, 2010) p.267.
5. From a conversation with Carmen Negrín 29/03/22.

6. *Trayectoria* (Paris, 1971) p.476.
7. *Ibid.*, p.470.
8. Cordón says the meeting took place on 02/03/1939 (*Trayectoria* [Sevilla, 2008] p.706), Casado claims it was the day before (*The Last Days of Madrid* [London, 1939] p.128) and Miaja's secretary suggests it was the day after and that Casado was not present (*General Miaja* [Madrid, 1975] p.280).
9. *Trayectoria* (Sevilla, 2008) p.703. In the Paris, 1971 edition, he does not mention Matallana, p.477.
10. *The Last Days of Madrid* (London, 1939) p.128.
11. Martínez Barrio: *Memorias* (Barcelona, 1983) p.415.
12. Moradiellos: *Juan Negrín. Textos y discursos políticos* (Madrid, 2010) pp.360–61.
13. According to Uribe's version in his Report to the Communist Party, dated 01/05/1939. In Archivo Histórico del PCE: Dirigentes/Uribe Galdeano, Vicente/Escritos/Informes/Caja 33/Carpeta 1-2.
14. *The Spanish Civil War* (Penguin, 1977) p.905.
15. Casado himself assumed he was to be replaced by Modesto, *The Last Days of Madrid* (London, 1939) p.126.
16. *Diarios de la guerra civil* (Universidad de Alicante, 2008) p.677.
17. *Así terminó la Guerra de España.* (Madrid, 2000) p.430.
18. *The Spanish Civil War at Sea* (Yorkshire, 2021) p.231. In this edition, Alpert does not give the names of the ships.
19. Archivo Histórico del Partido Comunista. Tesis, Manuscritos y Memorias. 35/9.
20. Most of these details are taken from Alpert, *The Spanish Civil War at Sea* (Yorkshire, 2021) p.231.
21. According to his own account in *Yo, Ministro de Stalin en España* (Madrid, 1954) p.253.
22. *The Spanish Civil War at Sea* (Yorkshire, 2021) p.232.
23. FO 371/24128/W4305 (The National Archives). Telegram No.57, dated 12 March 1939.
24. Archivo Municipal de Cartagena: *Cartagena Histórica* Núm. 2. January 2003 pp.5–14. There is also a video available at https://www.regmurcia.com (last accessed 30/07/2022) containing footage and interviews with men from both sides involved in the Nationalist naval operation. Hillgarth's report (FO 371/24128/W4305) that the ships had been sunk by Republican aircraft was wrong.
25. This is based on Vega Fernández's own account: *El último día de Negrín en España*. In *Claves*, 22/05/1992. An extract is available at https://www.lainsignia.org/2009/febrero/dial_002.htm (accessed 30/11/2019). Preston describes the account as 'entirely credible' in *The Last Days of the Spanish Republic* (London, 2017) endnote 38, Chapter 9, p.347. His own description appears on pp.203–204.

Chapter 16: *Usted haga como yo, no se meta en política*
1. For a fascinating study of the four documents, etc., see Herbert R. Southworth: *Conspiracy and the Spanish Civil War* (London: Routledge/Cañada Branch, 2002), Part 1, pp.1–128.
2. This account of Vallejos' research is based on an article by the journalist Rodolfo Serrano in *El País*, 07/01/1996: *En busca del 'gen rojo'*. See also: Preston, *The Spanish Holocaust* (London, 2013) pp.514–15.
3. *Franco. Anatomy of a Dictator* (London, 2018) p.29.
4. In *Arquitectos del Terror* (Barcelona, 2021) p.24 and p.26. Preston gives an extraordinarily detailed account of those (including Mauricio Carlavilla, Juan Tusquets and José Mª Pemán) who propagated the Jewish-masonic-Bolshevik anti-Spain conspiracy theory, so admired by Franco and those of his ilk.

5. Archivo de la Democracia of the University of Alicante: Francisco Moreno Sáez, *La represión franquista en la provincia de Alicante*.
6. *The Last Days of Madrid* (London, 1939) p.184.
7. *Yo, Ministro de Stalin en España* (Madrid, 1954) p.255–6.
8. *Yo, Ministro de Stalin en España* (Madrid, 1954) p.257.
9. *The Last Days of Madrid* (London, 1939) p.130.
10. FO 371/24128/W3926 (The National Archives). Wireless telegram no. 70, 06/03/1939.
11. *El último día de Negrín en España. Claves*, 22/05/1992. https://www.lainsignia.org/2009/febrero/dial_002.htm.
    Also: Preston, *The Last Days of the Spanish Republic* (London, 2017) pp.205–06.
12. From Cordón's memoirs: *Trayectoria* (ed. Viñas): (Sevilla, 2008) p.713.
13. The English translation is the one chosen by Casado: *The Last Days of Madrid* (London, 1939) p.138. The following description of events in Madrid is based on these memoirs; pp.138–155. *The Manchester Guardian* variously used the translations 'Council of National Defence' and 'National Defence Council'. The full council was:
    President: José Miaja (Army)
    Foreign Affairs/Vice-President: Julián Besteiro (PSOE)
    Defence: Segismundo Casado (Army)
    Interior: Wenceslao Carrillo (PSOE)
    Finance: Manuel González Marín (CNT)
    Labour: Antonio Pérez (UGT)
    Justice: Miguel San Andrés (IR)
    Education/Health: José del Río (UR)
    Communications/Public Works: Eduardo Val (CNT).
14. The descriptions are taken from *Los vencedores de Negrín* (Mexico, 1976) p.154.
15. The word in Spanish in this edition is 'desvahído', which I believe is a spelling or typing mistake. I have assumed the word is 'desvaído', meaning: *faded, washed-out, diminished*.
16. Domínguez Aragonés, *Los vencedores de Negrín* (Mexico, 1976) p.153. Besteiro apparently said, '*Qué olvido de la dignidad del cargo*', literally: 'What forgetfulness of the dignity of his office.'.
17. *Trayectoria* (Sevilla, 2008) p.715. In the Paris edition (1971), Cordón only gives Negrín's side of the dialogue, i.e. the words that the others could hear in Elda: '*Explain General, what is this they are telling me?*' and after a pause: '*Very well. You are relieved of your post.*' p.484.
18. *Freedom's Battle* (London, 1940) pp.293–4.
19. The English text is taken from Casado: *The Last Days of Madrid* (London, 1939) pp.140–1.
20. All the text/translations are taken directly from *The Last Days of Madrid* (London, 1939) p.148.
21. This chronological order is supported by Domínguez Aragonés, who attended the broadcast. *Los vencedores de Negrín* (Mexico, 1976) pp.170–172.
22. *The Last Days of Madrid* (London, 1939) p.154.
23. *Así cayó Madrid* (Madrid, 1977) p.151.
24. Cordón: *Trayectoria* (ed. Viñas): (Sevilla, 2008) p.722.
25. According to Viñas, *El desplome de la República* (Barcelona, 2010) p.114 (footnote).
26. In *El General Miaja*, (Madrid, 1975) pp.289–90.
27. For more details on Burillo's career, see Bolloten *Spanish Civil War* (North Carolina, 2015) p.686 and endnote 13, pp.924–5.
28. Gooden, the Consul in Valencia, informed the Foreign Office: 'A refusal of Military Governor Alicante to resign in similar circumstances did not, apparently produce any disorders there.' (FO/371/24128). Cordón: *Trayectoria* (ed. Viñas): (Sevilla,

2008) p.721. In the Paris edition: *Trayectoria* (1971), Cordón reported that Burillo had ordered the arrest of members of the PCE p.485–6. A more detailed account is available in Viñas: *El Desplome de la República* (Barcelona, 2010) p.338.
29. *Yo, Ministro de Stalin en España* (Madrid, 1954) p.260.

Chapter 17: *El destino infortunado de España, derrotada y maltrecha*
1. *El último día de Negrín en España. Claves*, 22/05/1992. https://www.lainsignia.org/2009/febrero/dial_002.htm. Retrieved 20/01/23 Also: Preston, *The Last Days of the Spanish Republic* (London, 2017) p.230. As Preston points out (endnote 38, p.347), Vega (writing fifty years after the events) describes events of 5 and 6 March 1939 as if they had occurred on a single day.
2. From a conversation with Carmen Negrín 29/03/22.
3. Beevor explains that he used German to ensure those around him would not understand: *The Battle for Spain*. (London, 2006) p.393. Valero Escandell reports that Negrín received the news of the arrest later when he was at the *Posición Yuste* on his way to the aerodrome: *El territorio de la derrota* (Alicante, 2004) p.164. This is also supported by del Vayo *Freedom's Battle* (London, 1940) p.301. However, it seems reasonable to believe that developments in Alicante (including or not the detention of Vega) were sufficient to convince Negrín that there existed a real and imminent danger to the welfare of those at El Poblet.
4. Letter of 23/06/1939. Reproduced in Moradiellos *Juan Negrín. Textos y discursos políticos* (Madrid, 2010) p.398.
5. *Freedom's Battle* (London, 1940) p.288. I have excluded the final phrase of the paragraph that reads: '[leaving the rebels] to murder the defenceless population with impunity.'.
6. *The Last Days of Madrid* (London, 1939) p.128.
7. *El territorio de la derrota* (Alicante, 2004) pp.162–3.
8. In *Freedom's Battle* (London, 1940) pp.298–9.
9. See Preston, *The Last Days of the Spanish Republic* (London, 2017) p.232.
10. *Los vencedores de Negrín* (Mexico, 1976) p.172. His reflection is made in the form of a rhetorical question: ¿Fue un acto de soberbia y de orgullo necio y estéril?.
11. *Freedom's Battle* (London, 1940) p.300.
12. The first version is del Vayo's. It seems plausible that he is referring to the arrest of Vega: *Freedom's Battle* (London, 1940) p.301. The second is from Preston, *The Last Days of the Spanish Republic* (London, 2017) p.234.
13. *Manchester Guardian* 07/03/1939. Available also in *The Guardian Book of the Spanish Civil War* (Hants.: Wildwood House, 1987) p.314.
14. *Trayectoria* (Sevilla, 2008) p.727.
15. Dolores Ibárruri: *El único camino* (Madrid: Castalia, 1992) p.614. In fact, thirty-eight years and a week; she returned to Madrid on 13 May 1977, after the death of Franco and the legalisation of the PCE by Adolfo Suárez.
16. In *Memoria de la melancolía* (Sevilla, 2020) p.286.
17. When Irene Montero and Pablo Iglesias (both ministers in the government of Pedro Sánchez) chose to call their own daughter Aitana, Iglesias wrote: 'Leaving Alicante for exile [...], Maria Teresa León y Rafael Alberti said goodbye to their country while observing for the last time the Sierra de Aitana covered in red flowers. That vision inspired first the name of the daughter of the two poets, and later the name of many more daughters, like ours. For us, the name Aitana pays homage to the Spanish exile.' *Facebook* 02/08/2019.
18. http://www.adar.es/wp-content/uploads/2014/12/Alas_gloriosas_31.pdf p.9. Retrieved 20/01/23. A similar account appears in Luis Martínez Mira: *Alicante 1936–1939* (Ayuntamiento de Alicante, 2005) pp.169–70.

19. From a conversation with Carmen Negrín 29/03/22.
20. *Freedom's Battle* (London, 1940) p.301.
21. There is some confusion about whether Uribe left with La *Pasionaria*, or in the last aircraft. I am inclined to believe the version of de la Mora. She writes that her husband (Ignacio de Hidalgo), 'left on the last plane, together with the Minister of Agriculture, Vicente Uribe, who had stayed with him to make sure all the others were flown to safety'. See *In Place of Splendour* (London, 2021) p.377.
22. See Preston, *The Last Days of the Spanish Republic* (London, 2017) p.235.
23. According to Santiago Carrillo: *Memorias* (Barcelona: Planeta, 2012) p.370.
24. See Engel. *Historia de las brigadas mixtas* (Madrid, 2005) p.208.
25. Cited by Herbert Southworth in *Guernica! Guernica! A Study of Journalism, Diplomacy, Propaganda, and History* (University of California Press, 2021) Notes to Book II, Chapter 1, Endnote 15, p.434. Also Thomas: *The Spanish Civil War* (Penguin, 1977) p.897. This at least is my assumption, although it is true that del Vayo referred to him as the 'Christian General' in *The Last Optimist* (London, 1950) p.307.
26. In *The Last Optimist* (London, 1950) p.307.
27. In *Freedom's Battle* (London, 1940) p.303.

Chapter 18: Written in the blood of a Spanish soldier

1. *Diarios de la guerra civil* (Universidad de Alicante, 2008) p.678.
2. *Memorias* (Barcelona: Planeta, 2012) p.368. For more detail on Santiago Carrillo's reaction, see Preston: *The Last Stalinist* (London: Collins, 2015) chapter 3. For the full text of the open letter, see for example: https://agendacomunistavalencia.blogspot.com/2018/09/carta-de-santiago-carrillo-su-padre.html.
3. In *Spain. 1833–2002* (OUP, 2007) p.145.
4. *The Last Days of Madrid* (London, 1939) p.168.
5. *Yo, Ministro de Stalin en España* (Madrid, 1954) p.281–2.
6. *The Spanish Civil War* (Penguin, 1977) p.909.
7. *Así terminó la Guerra de España*. (Madrid, 2000) p.399. Bahamonde and Cervera produce what is probably the most graphic and comprehensive account of the struggle in Madrid: pp.363–404.
8. *Diarios de la guerra civil* (Universidad de Alicante, 2008) p.682–3.
9. *The Last Days of Madrid* (London, 1939) p.173.
10. *The Spanish Civil War* (Penguin, 1977) p.909. Preston reports the order came from Togliatti and Checa: *The Last Days of the Spanish Republic* (London, 2016) p.246.
11. Beevor: *The Battle for Spain* (London, 2006) p.394. The figure of 20,000 that appears in Bahamonde and Cervera, *Así terminó la Guerra de España*. (Madrid, 2000) p.402 may be a misprint. Preston discusses the findings of different researchers in *The Last Days of the Spanish Republic* (London, 2017) p.250, and suggests the number may have been as low as 233–243.
12. This translation is taken from Casado: *The Last Days of Madrid* (London, 1939) p.176–7.
13. *The Last Days of Madrid* (London, 1939) p.187.
14. In *Review of Hotel in Flight by Nancy Johnstone* (The Adelphi, December, 1939), reproduced in *Orwell in Spain* (Penguin, 2020) p.331.
15. *Reflexiones y recuerdos* (Universitat d'Alacant, 2019) p.257–8.
16. *The Spanish Civil War* (London, 2006) p.297.
17. *Diarios de la guerra civil* (Universidad de Alicante, 2008) p.679. 'The disturbing perspectives' to which he refers are presumably the rumours of a Communist takeover.
18. *Diarios de la guerra civil* (Universidad de Alicante, 2008) p.680.

19. See, for example, *Yo, Ministro de Stalin en España* (Madrid, 1954) p.297. Hernández writes that he left Spain with Togliatti, Checa and other PCE leaders on 28 March. Ramos gives the 25th as the day Hernández left Spain with Checa, Togliatti et al: *La Guerra Civil en la provincia de Alicante. Tomo 3º* (Alicante, 1974) p.149.
20. Cited in Ramos: *La Guerra Civil en la provincia de Alicante Vol. III* (Alicante, 1973) pp.151–2.
21. *Ibid.*, p.154.
22. Details on reaction of provincial authorities is based on Ramos: *La Guerra Civil en la provincia de Alicante Vol. III* (Alicante, 1973) pp.155–6.
23. *Avance*, 09/03/1939. Available in the Hemeroteca/Newspaper Archives of the Archivo Municipal de Alicante.
24. Preston: *The Last Days of the Spanish Republic* (London, 2017) p.248.
25. This account is taken from Ramos: *La Guerra Civil en la provincia de Alicante Vol. III* (Alicante, 1973) pp.156–7.
26. According to records in the Archivo de la Democracia de la Universidad de Alicante, the total was 646. The number was reproduced in the report of the *Comisión Cívica de Alicante para la Recuperación de la Memoria Histórica: 1939 La guerra terminó en Alicante* p.35. A passenger manifest is available at: https://alicantepedia.com/fotografias/ronwyn-pasajeros-y-tripulantes. Retrieved 22/01/23.
27. *Diarios de la guerra civil* (Universidad de Alicante, 2008) p.684.
28. *¡Alerta los pueblos!* (Barcelona, 1974) p.172.

Chapter 19: *El abrazo de Vergara*
1. Cited for example in José Calvo Poyato: *Momentos Estelares de la historia de España* (Barcelona: Penguin, 2018) p.191.
2. Much of the following account is based on Casado's memoirs, written in English weeks after his departure from Spain, and published in London: *The Last Days of Madrid* (London, 1939), Chapters VI (Peace Negotiations) and VII (The Army does not Surrender) pp.193–269.
3. *The Last Days of Madrid* (London, 1939) p.196.
4. *Ibid.*, p.201.
5. *Ibid.*, pp.205–6.
6. *Ibid.*, p.207 and *Así cayó Madrid* (Madrid, 1977), p.189. For fuller accounts of Centaño's approaches to Casado, see Bahamonde and Cervera: *Así terminó la Guerra de España* (Madrid, 2000) pp.249, 257, 259 and 314 5, and p.314 5. And Preston: *The Last Days of the Spanish Republic* (London, 2017) pp.123, 150, 178 and 274. Also: Chapter 13 of this book.
7. See Preston: *The Last Days of the Spanish Republic* (London, 2017) pp.124–5.
8. The full text in Spanish, *Así cayó Madrid* (Madrid, 1977), pp.202–03 and in English: pp.211–2.
9. In *Franco. A Precise Biography* (London: Wiedenfeld & Nicolson, 2000) p.257. The original is the title of a short story by Oscar Wilde.
10. *The Last Days of Madrid* (London, 1939), p.215.
11. *Así cayó Madrid* (Madrid, 1977), pp.205–06.
12. *La Guerra Civil en la provincia de Alicante Vol. III* (Alicante, 1973) p.158.
13. *Diarios de la guerra civil* (Universidad de Alicante, 2008) p.692.
14. The full text is available in Spanish, in *Así cayó Madrid* (Madrid, 1977), pp.219–24, and in English: *The Last Days of Madrid* (London, 1939) pp.226–31. I have modified the translation of the title of the document in English.
15. Cited by Casado in English in *The Last Days of Madrid* (London, 1939) pp.230.
16. In Thomas, *The Spanish Civil War* (Penguin, 1977) p.912.

17. *The Last Days of Madrid* (London, 1939) pp.236.
18. See for example: Preston, *The Last Days of the Spanish Republic* (London, 2016) p.60.
19. *Review of The Last Days of Madrid by S. Casado. Time and Tide*, 20/01/40. Reproduced in *Orwell in Spain* (Penguin, 2020) p.333.
20. For his contacts with Antonio Luna García, see Preston, *The Last Days of the Spanish Republic* (London, 2017) p.30 and pp.44–5.
21. *The Last Days of the Spanish Republic* (London, 2017) p.50.
22. *Diarios de la guerra civil* (Universidad de Alicante, 2008) p.695.
23. See website of Ministry of Culture at: http://censoarchivos.mcu.es/CensoGuia/fondoDetailSession.htm?archivoId=1&id=1040739&eventDescendiente=descendienteDetail.
24. FO 371/24147/W10266. (The National Archives). Hillgarth's report is dated 18/06/1939.

Chapter 20: *Una gota de pura valentía vale más que un océano cobarde*

1. *La Guerra Civil en la provincia de Alicante Vol. III* (Alicante, 1973) p.159.
2. The exact number of air raids is still a question of debate. Flaquer provides a table (based on research of the press) that lists a total of seventy-two attacks, showing as main targets: the town, the port, the CAMPSA installations, railway stations and the Rabasa airbase: *La opinion pública alicantina durante la Guerra Civil* (Madrid, 1994) pp.64–6. On the other hand, Pérez lists 71 raids, 481 deaths, 790 wounded, and 705 buildings damaged or destroyed, *25 de Mayo* (San Vicente [Alicante], 2006) pp.195–7.
3. Aldeguer Jover and Santo Matas: *Alicante, 1939* (San Vicente [Alicante], 1999) p.103.
4. Aldeguer Jover and Santo Matas: *Alicante, 1939* (San Vicente [Alicante], 1999) pp.106–07. Ramos: *La Guerra Civil en la provincia de Alicante. Tomo 1º* (Alicante, 1972) pp.193–194.
5. The data from the Archives is available online in an extraordinary document at: https://archivodemocracia.ua.es/es/exilio-republicano-africa/. Section 3. Retrieved 20/01/23.
6. Cited by Pedro L. Agosto, *El hombre que pudo evitar la Guerra* (Alicante: Instituto Juan Gil-Albert, 2006) p.245.
7. A passenger manifest is available at: https://alicantepedia.com/fotografias/african-trader-pasajeros-y-tripulaci%C3%B3n-2%C2%BA-viaje. Retrieved 20/01/23.
8. Manifest: https://alicantepedia.com/fotografias/marionga-pasajeros-y-tripulaci%C3%B3n. Retrieved 20/01/23.
9. Manifest: https://alicantepedia.com/fotografias/ronwyn-pasajeros-y-tripulantes. Retrieved 20/01/23.
10. The story of Dickson and the *Stanbrook* is also told in Whitehead, *Franco. History to the Defeated* (London, 2018) in which a failure in editing led to a mistake in the captain's name, for which the author offers public and profuse apologies.
11. *In Place of Splendour* (London, 2021) p.287. The Nationalists had neither been recognised by Britain, nor granted belligerent rights.
12. See *The Spanish Civil War at Sea* (Yorkshire, 2021) p.210.
13. For more details, see Alpert: *The Spanish Civil War at Sea* (Yorkshire, 2021) pp.159–162. Among the British ships that shadowed the British ships was the *Hood*. The role of Vice-Admiral Blake appears to have been decisive in persuading the authorities in London that the Spanish blockade was not in a position to offer a genuine threat in the face of British naval power.
14. For more on the Basque children, see the website of the *BCA'37 UK - The Association for the UK Basque Children:* https://www.basquechildren.org/.

15. From the Roath Virtual War Memorial: https://roathlocalhistorysociety.org/local-history/war-memorials/roath-virtual-war-memorial/roath-virtual-war-memorial-d/. The site provides information and photographs of Dickson and the *Stanbrook*. (Retrieved 20/01/23).
16. The letter is dated 2–3/04/39 and was sent from Oran. A copy of the original dispatch is available online at: https://web.archive.org/web/20140802131238/http://www.elpais.com/elpaismedia/diario/media/200904/01/espana/20090401elpepinac_2_Pes_PDF.pdf. Retrieved 20/01/23.
17. *Diarios de la guerra civil* (Universidad de Alicante, 2008) p.695.
18. Letter to the *Sunday Dispatch*. See endnote #16. Retrieved 07/02/23.
19. Cruz Merino (passenger number: 125). Cited by Juan Martínez Leal in *Alicante en la hora final de la Républic. La tragedia del puerto* in *1939 La Guerra terminó en Alicante* (Comisión Cívica de Alicante para la Recuperación de la Memoria Histórica (Alicante, 2019) p.27.
20. In an interview with the author on 10/11/22.
21. A full list of the passengers is available in Santacreu: *Una presó amb vistes al mar* (University of Alicante, 2008) pp.269–389. The number of children is based on the records of the French customs authorities, which are cited by Juan Martínez Leal in *Alicante en la hora final de la Républic. La tragedia del puerto* in: *1939 La Guerra terminó en Alicante* (Comisión Cívica de Alicante para la Recuperación de la Memoria Histórica (Alicante, 2019) p.30.
22. For example: Valero Escandell: *Stanbrook, el barco de una derrota*. In *El País*, 18/02/14; Graham Davies: *Outwitting Franco* (KDP, 2020) p.98. Martínez Leal in *Alicante en la hora final de la Guerra Civil - De puerta del exilio a prisión* published in *Información* 28/03/19, refers to Dickson's reports and those of other witnesses, but also reiterates that the last officially recorded air raid was on 25/03/39. For Ramos' account, see *El Teatro Principal en la historia de Alicante* (Alicante, 1965) p.511.
23. For example, in his article *The Italian Bombings over Valencia during the Spanish Civil War: A Photographic Study*, (Cañada Blanch Centre – LSE, published in *Pasado y Memoria. Revista de Historia Contemporánea 15*, 2016) p.183, Gaspar Díez Pomares asserts the last air raid in the Valencia region took place on 28/03/1939 in Gandia. See also Flaquer, *La opinion pública alicantina durante la Guerra Civil* (Madrid, 1994) pp.64–6. Or Pérez, *25 de Mayo* (San Vicente [Alicante], 2006) pp.195. In his novel *Pasajero 2058* (San Vicente [Alicante], ND), based on the testimonies of *alicantinos* who witnessed the events, Francisco Escudero Galante makes no reference to an air raid.
24. *The Last Days of the Spanish Republic* (London, 2017) p.295.
25. In *Último barco al exilio*. Published in *El País* 23/03/14.
26. González Beltran, Helia and Alicia, Desde la otra orilla (Elche, 2006) p.20.
27. Recollections of Carmen Bernabéu Castelló (passenger 2132) reported by her niece Mari Bernabeu and her grand-niece Natalia Ferrer in an interview 26/04/22.
28. FO 371/24154/W5943 (The National Archives). Telegram signed by Robert Wheeler.
29. See: Cerdán Tato, *La lucha por la democracia en Alicante* (Madrid, 1978) p.61.
30. See Introduction to Moreno, F., Vargas, B. (2007): *Dramas de refugiados*, (Centro Francisco Tomás y Valiente de la UNED Alzira-Valencia, Instituto de Historia Social, Valencia, 2007). And Martínez Leal. *Los barcos del exilio*. University of Alicante Archivo de la Democracia at: https://archivodemocracia.ua.es/es/exilio-republicano-africa/3-los-barcos-del-exilio.html (Retrieved 20/01/23).
31. Letter from Deltell to Rodolfo Llopis (09/04/1939) in: Moreno, F., Vargas, B.: *Dramas de refugiados* (Centro Francisco Tomás y Valiente de la UNED Alzira-Valencia, Instituto de Historia Social, Valencia, 2007) p.44.

32. Moreno, F., Vargas, B.: *Dramas de refugiados* (Centro Francisco Tomás y Valiente de la UNED Alzira-Valencia, Instituto de Historia Social, Valencia, 2007) p.222.
33. The minutes are reproduced in Annex 8 of Moreno, F., Vargas, B.: *Dramas de refugiados* (Centro Francisco Tomás y Valiente de la UNED Alzira-Valencia, Instituto de Historia Social, Valencia, 2007). Curiously the minutes also refer to a separate group of 184 women (presumably not affiliated to a specific ideological group) and 372 children.
34. For example: Domínguez Aragonés, *Los vencedores de Negrín* (Mexico, 1976) p.227.
35. See Bolloten: *Spanish Civil War* (North Carolina, 2015) p.291. The rumours suggest that General Rojo had also been a member of the UME.
36. *Spanish Civil War* (Penguin, 1977) p.532.
37. For a sample of opinions on his competence and role, see Bolloten: *Spanish Civil War* (North Carolina, 2015) p.292–7. Bolloten argues that Miaja was little more than a figurehead, his prestige and popularity constructed by the propaganda machine of the PCE in the belief that the population needed a hero.
38. Quoted by Bolloten in *Spanish Civil War* (North Carolina, 2015) p.294.
39. *The Spanish Civil War. A Very Short Introduction* (OUP, 2005). On the other hand, Graham describes General Rojo as a talented officer, 'an imaginative and innovative strategist', whose 'commitment to the Republic was firm and unambiguous'. p.91.

Chapter 21: *Wo bleibt Gambara?*
1. In FO 371/24128/W5195. (The National Archives). The article appeared in the newspaper on 27/03/1939. An unnamed civil servant took the trouble to cut out the text and file it with Foreign Office papers.
2. For more details, see Alpert, *The Spanish Civil War at Sea* (Yorkshire, 2021) p.234.
3. Much of the following narrative is taken from his account *Puerto de Alicante 29 de Marzo – 1 de Abril de 1939*, published in the journal *Canelobre* No.7–8, of the Instituto Juan Gil-Albert (Alicante, 1986).
4. His account of the defences arranged to protect those on the port [*Puerto de Alicante 29 de Marzo – 1 de Abril de 1939* in *Canelobre* No.7–8, p.153] is disputed by Mallol Alberola in *La Estampida* (Callosa, 2000) pp.140–3. The *falangista* leader denies the existence of any defensive arrangements. On the other hand, it is supported by Cerdán Tato in *La lucha por la democracia en Alicante* (Madrid, 1978) p.7 and Sixto Agudo in *Notas sobre el final de la guerra civil* (Archivo Histórico del Partido Comunista – Tesis, Manuscriptos y Memorias. Carpeta 32/2).
5. *Notas sobre el final de la guerra civil* (Archivo Histórico del Partido Comunista – Tesis, Manuscriptos y Memorias. Carpeta 32/2.
6. *Blood of Spain* (Penguin,1981) p.503.
7. Archivo de la Democracia of the University of Alicante. From an interview with Martínez Leal and Ors Montenegro published in: *Las cárceles de la posguerra en la provincia de Alicante. Un estudio de la represión franquista (1939–1945)* (Alicante 1994).
8. From a letter published in *The New Statesman and Nation*, 23/12/39. Courtesy of Linda Palfreeman. In the magazine, his surname is given as *Filliacus*, which presumably is a printing mistake.
9. Casado: *Así cayó Madrid* (Madrid, 1977) p.255.
10. See Martínez Leal: *Alicante en la hora final de la Guerra Civil - De puerta del exilio a prisión* published in *Información* 28/03/19 and Casado: *Así cayó Madrid* (Madrid, 1977) p.259.
11. See Preston, *The Spanish Holocaust* (London, 2013) pp.477–8.
12. *Así cayó Madrid* (Madrid, 1977) p.258. It is true that the memoirs were first published in Madrid in 1968 under terms imposed by the censors of Franco's dictatorship. However, the use of '*Generalísimo*' was not common among Republicans.

13. Laurin Zilliacus, in a letter published in *The New Statesman and Nation*, 23/12/39. Courtesy of Linda Palfreeman. See note 3 above for confusion over surname.
14. Published in *Avance* 29/03/39. Sánchez Requena himself remained committed to his promise. He did not leave Spain and was detained by the new authorities in Alicante.
15. FO 371/24154/W5088 (The National Archives). Telegram no.68, 26/03/1939.
16. In the absence of any records, the number is of course an estimate. One Republican captured by the Italians, Olegario Uviedo Murciano, claimed there were 40,000–50,000: *Yo caí en el Puerto de Alicante (Valencia, 1983)* p.72. However, these numbers are not corroborated by others on the port. Tuñón de Lara says no fewer than 15,000: *Puerto de Alicante 29 de Marzo – 1 de Abril de 1939* in *Canelobre* No.7–8, p.153. The writer Eduardo de Guzmán reported 'more than 20,000': *El año de la Victoria* (Madrid, 2001) p.32. The Communist leader Sixto Agudo says there were at least 20,000: *Notas sobre el final de la guerra civil* (Archivo Histórico del Partido Comunista – Tesis, Manuscritos y Memorias. Carpeta 32/2). Among the historians, Fraser believed there were 15,000. *Blood of Spain* (New York, 1979) p.502. Preston suggests 12,000: *The Last Days of the Spanish Republic* (London, 2017) p.296. Bahamonde and Cervera settle for between 12,000 and 15,000: *Así terminó la Guerra de España*. (Madrid, 2000) p.494.
17. The text is based on Max Aub's Spanish-language version in *El Campo de los Almendros* (Mexico, 1968) p.201. There is an English version in Preston: *The Last Days of the Spanish Republic* (London, 2017) p.290.
18. According to Aub: *El Campo de los Almendros* (Mexico, 1968) p.201–02. I have allowed myself this licence because, although this work is defined as a '*novela-reportaje*' (novel/report) and the dialogues, upon which the narrative is largely based, are entirely fictitious, I believe Aub remained faithful to the background facts. His six-volume series *El laberinto mágico* plays a huge part in our understanding of the Civil War. In his introduction to *Field of Honour* (London: Verso, 2009), the historian Ronald Fraser cautioned 'against reading the novel as *history*' but also wrote, 'Aub took great pains to ensure the accuracy of his historical detail.'.
19. Casado's account of his last days in Spain: *The Last Days of Madrid* (London, 1939) p.264–9 and *Así cayó Madrid* (Madrid, 1977) p.263–6.
20. FO 371/24154/W5155 (28/02/1939) (The National Archives).
21. *British Government Maritime Evacuations in the Spanish Civil War, 1936–1939* in *War in History*, 2019, Vol.26 (1) pp.83–84. Based on FO 371/24154/W6012, FO 371/24154/W5263 and FO 371/24154/W6705 (The National Archives).
22. The report is in the private archives of Sir George Young's family. Courtesy of Linda Palfreeman. It is also reproduced in Palfreeman: *Aristocrats, Adventurers and Ambulances* (Sussex Academic Press, 2014) pp.197–203 (Appendix to Part Two).
23. *The Last Days of Madrid* (London, 1939) pp.266–8.
24. This account is taken from Eladi Mainar Cabanes and Robert Llopis i Sendra: *La dimensión internacional de la salida del Consejo Nacional de Defensa, marzo de 1939* in *El pasado que no pasa: la Guerra Civil española a los ochenta años de su finalización* (Universidad de Castilla-La Mancha, 2020) pp.435–444.
25. Details of the journey are from the website of the *Real Academia de la Historia* at: https://dbe.rah.es/biografias/11094/segismundo-casado-lopez.
26. *The Last Days of Madrid* (London, 1939) p.256.
27. *Así terminó la Guerra de España*. (Madrid, 2000) pp.470–71.
28. *Hansard*. 0 March 1939 vol 112 cc78–136. Available at https://api.parliament.uk/historic-hansard/lords/1939/mar/09/spain.
29. For a more detailed account, see Bahamonde and Cervera, *Así terminó la Guerra de España*. (Madrid, 2000) pp.482–83. In *Blood of Spain* (Penguin, 1981), Fraser claims that Apfel, in particular, was 'assiduous in this task'. p.505.

30. *Diarios de la guerra civil* (Universidad de Alicante, 2008) p.697.
31. https://hansard.parliament.uk/Commons/1939-03-29/debates/1ad5d40f-f932-43d1-9ae9-bf3b265ec1cb/Spain?highlight=spain#contribution-0a9bd539-50fa-49e3-8b61-61e7dcdbfb97 (Retrieved 24/01/23).
32. *Ibid.*, p.697.
33. See for example: *1939 La Guerra terminó en Alicante* of the Comisión Cívica de Alicante para la Recuperación de la Memoria Histórica (Alicante, 2019).
34. Martínez Leal, *La tragedia del puerto* in *Canelobre* No.7–8, of the Instituto Juan Gil-Albert (Alicante, 1986) p.164.
35. *La Hispano Suiza-Aviación – Guadalajara-Alicante (1936–1939)* at alicantevivo.org/2010/03/la-hispano-suiza-aviacion-guadalajara.html.
36. *El año de la Victoria* (Madrid, 2001) p.34.
37. The copy of the report is in the private archives of Sir George Young's family. Courtesy of Linda Palfreeman. Also, Palfreeman: *Aristocrats, Adventurers and Ambulances* (Sussex Academic Press, 2014) pp.197–203.
38. *The Last Days of Madrid* (London, 1939) p.287.
39. *¡Alerta los pueblos!* (Barcelona, 1974) p.172.
40. *Diarios de la guerra civil* (Universidad de Alicante, 2008) p.697.
41. *El año de la Victoria* (Madrid, 2001) p.29.

Chapter 22: And the almond tree shall flourish
1. Of the many translations of this bulletin, this one seems to me the most elegant: Bolloten, *Spanish Civil War* (North Carolina, 2015) p.793.
2. *Diarios de la guerra civil* (Universidad de Alicante, 2008) p.698.
3. There is footage of the event on the website of the *Archivo de la Democracia* of the University of Alicante, at: https://archivodemocracia.ua.es/es/exilio-republicano-africa/2-el-final-de-la-guerra-civil.html.
4. *Blood of Spain* (New York, 1979) p.503.
5. *Puerto de Alicante 29 de Marzo – 1 de Abril de 1939* in *Canelobre* No.7–8, p.153.
6. Archivo Municipal de Alicante. Inhumaciones Cementerios. II.12.1933–1944. *La Represión Franquista* in *1939 La Guerra terminó en Alicante* of the Comisión Cívica de Alicante para la Recuperación de la Memoria Histórica (Alicante: Compas, 2019) p.51. The *falangista* leader Mallol Alberola suggests there were only four cases. See: *La Estampida* (Callosa, 2000) p.135.
7. Comisión Cívica para la Recuperación de la Memoria Histórica de Alicante: https://archivodemocracia.ua.es/es/exilio-republicano-africa/2-el-final-de-la-guerra-civil.html. Retrieved 24/01/23. Their conclusion is that there were at least the eight cases on the port reported by Ors, and possibly nine more. A total of 16. This number was supported by Gambara. On the other hand, Cerdán Tato quotes a report from General Saliquet to Franco on 01/04/1939, in which he claims sixty-eight people took their own life. See: *La lucha por la democracia en Alicante* (Madrid, 1978) p.6.
8. Accounts from *El último pedazo de la II República* in *El País* 01/04/09 and *Levante-EMV*, 02/04/09 respectively. The story is also reproduced in Martínez Leal, *Alicante en la hora final de la República* in *1939 La Guerra terminó en Alicante* of the Comisión Cívica de Alicante para la Recuperación de la Memoria Histórica (Alicante, 2019) p.44. Cerdán Tato reports that in fact the victim was not the Mayor of Azira, but rather an FAI infantryman; see: *La lucha por la democracia en Alicante* (Madrid, 1978) p.5.
9. *Puerto de Alicante 29 de Marzo – 1 de Abril de 1939* in *Canelobre* No.7–8, p.153.
10. From Marcos González: *La dama roja. Las memorias de Angelita Rodríguez* (San Vicente, Alicante, 2004) p.58.

11. In *Notas sobre el final de la guerra civil* (Archivo Histórico del Partido Comunista – Tesis, Manuscriptos y Memorias. Carpeta 32/2).
12. *Ibid.*
13. In the *Blood of Spain* (New York: Pantheon, 1979) p.506.
14. The narrative that follows is based on his experiences: *El año de la Victoria* (Madrid, 2001) pp.35–47.
15. There are still gaps in the history of the detention of the women and children detained on the port. Several observers simply refer to their internment in two cinemas (for example Martínez Leal in *La Guerra terminó en Alicante* [Canelobre 6/7] p.165). At this stage the *Teatro Principal* was used exclusively for the projections of films. Preston refers to a single cinema (presumably the *Ideal*) in *The Last Days of the Spanish Republic* (London, 2016) p.296. In *Alicante, 1939* (San Vicente, 1999) Aldeguer and Santo Matas refer to two cinemas (*Ideal* and *Central*). In his highly detailed monograph *El Teatro Principal en la historia de Alicante*, local historian Ramos makes no reference to its use as an internment facility.
16. In *La dama roja. Memorías de Angelita Rodríguez* (Alicante, 2004) p.65.
17. These figures are based on Cerdán Tato, *La lucha por la democracia en Alicante* (Madrid, 1978) pp.17 and 21, and Ricard Camil Torres Fabra and Miguel Ors Montenegro, published in *Muerte y éxodo de los vencidos*, in: *La Guerra Civil en la Comunidad Valenciana* (Prensa Alicante, 2007) Vol.16, p.58. Gabarda provides a list of the registered deaths in the castle and reformatory: *Els afusellaments al País Valencià (1938–1956) (Generalitat Valenciana, 1993)* pp.417–18 and pp.418–20 respectively.
18. Guzmán estimated between 40,000 and 45,000: *El año de la Victoria* (Madrid, 2001) p.89. Preston quotes 45,000: *The Spanish Holocaust* (London: Harper, 2013) p.480. Journalist Carlos Hernández de Miguel refers to 'more than 30,000', over a ten-day period: *Los campos de concentración de Franco* (Barcelona, 2021) p.29. Gabarda cites a figure of 25,000–30,000 in *Els afusellaments al País Valencià (1938–1956)* (Generalitat Valenciana, 1993) p.40. In the absence of definitive numbers, I am inclined to accept the consensus of Alicante historians, which suggests that there were approximately 19,000 men in the camp.
19. *El año de la Victoria* (Madrid, 2001) pp.90–91.
20. Archivo Histórico del PCE. Tesis, Manuscritos y Memorias. Sig. 70/3.
21. In *La dama roja. Memorías de Angelita Rodríguez* (Alicante, 2004) pp.65–6. Reproduced in a special supplement of *Información*, 28/03/2009. p.49.
22. In *La dama roja. Memorías de Angelita Rodríguez* (Alicante, 2004) p.67.

Chapter 23: *En el yermo de la historia*

1. *España bajo la dictadura franquista* Volume X of *Historia de España* – ed. Manuel Tuñón de Lara. (Barcelona: Labor, 1981) pp.13–14.
2. In the Prologue, (London, 2013) p.xi.
3. *The Battle for Spain* (London, 2006) p.405.
4. For example, see Edouard de Blaye: *Franco and the Politics of Spain* (Pelican, 1976) p.131. Or Thomas: *The Spanish Civil War* (Penguin, 1977) p.924.
5. See for example, Preston: *Franco. Caudillo de España* (Barcelona, 1994) p.489.
6. *España bajo la dictadura franquista* Volume X of *Historia de España* (Barcelona: Labor, 1981) p.18. Footnote 1.
7. *The Battle for Spain* (London, 2006), (London, 2006) p.405. The expression 'Franquist Gulag' is in fact part of the chapter title. The adjective 'Francoist' is more common.
8. *Ibid.*, p.405.
9. *Ibid.*, p.407.

10. From the *Prologue*, xi–xx. (London, 2013).
11. *La estampida* (Crevillente, 2000) p.136.
12. In Guzmán, *El año de la Victoria* (Madrid, 2001) pp.183–4.
13. Much of the narrative that follows is based on the personal experiences of Isidro Benet, as told to Isabel Mª Abellán and published as *Isidro* (Murcia, 2016). And Guzmán, *El año de la Victoria* (Madrid, 2001).
14. *El año de la Victoria* (Madrid, 2001) p.191.
15. There is remarkably little information on the fate of the women and children after their internment in the town centre. Carmen Caamaño's recollections are included in an interview with Martínez Leal and Ors Montenegro in: *Las cárceles de la posguerra en la provincia de Alicante. Un estudio de la represión franquista (1939–1945)* (Alicante 1994) in the Archivo de la Democracia of the University of Alicante and Archivo de Fuentes Orales Instituto de Cultura Juan Gil Albert.
16. In *Los campos de concentración de Franco* (Barcelona, 2021) pp.29–30.
17. *La estampida* (Crevillente, 2000) p.49.
18. These data are taken from Hernández, *Los campos de concentración de Franco* (Barcelona, 2021) p.341. Again, the failure of the new regime to keep records makes it impossible to offer more than approximate figures. The lowest estimate was 6,800, given by officials of the Nationalist army on the occasion of a visit from the Military Governor and reported in the *Hoja Oficial de Alicante*, 28/04/39.
19. From the website of the San Isidro Town Council: https://sanisidro.es/turismo/para-visitar/campo-de-concentracion-de-albatera/. The land on which the camp was 'constructed' is now part of the San Isidro municipal area. The measurements are based on a plan of the camp reproduced in *Canelobre*, 31–32, *Alicante en los años cuarenta* (*Canelobre*: Spring–Summer 1995), p.39. An annex had also been added to the main camp.
20. *El año de la Victoria* (Madrid, 2001) pp.351–2.
21. *The Spanish Civil War*, (Penguin, 1977) p.923. Citing the words of Rafael Abella.
22. *Ibid.*, p.255.
23. *Ibid.*, p.208. For a graphic personal account of the conditions inside the camp, see Olegario Uviedo Murciano in *Yo caí en el Puerto de Alicante* (Valencia, 1983) pp.82–92.
24. Data from Hernández: *Los campos de concentración de Franco* (Barcelona, 2021) pp.79 and 341.
25. *El año de la Victoria* (Madrid, 2001) p.253.
26. From a compelling documentary produced by *la Sexta* TV channel with the participation of: the journalist, Carlos Hernández de Miguel; the professor and writer, María Isabel Abellán; the son of Isidro Benet; and the archaeologist, Felipe Mejías (University of Alicante), entitled *Campos de concentración de Franco: los últimos supervivientes* at: https://www.atresplayer.com/lasexta/programas/lasexta-columna/temporada-11/campos-de-concentracion-de-franco-los-ultimos-supervivientes_614335226584a85ef4703f91/.
27. According to Guzmán in *El año de la Victoria* (Madrid, 2001) p.259.
28. *El año de la Victoria* (Madrid, 2001) p.217.
29. *Blood of Spain* (New York: Pantheon, 1979) pp.507–08.
30. Thomas, *The Spanish Civil War*, (Penguin, 1977) p.503.
31. See Hernández, *Los campos de concentración de Franco* (Barcelona, 2021) p.349.
32. *Hoja Oficial de Alicante*, 28/04/39.
33. In *La Guerra Civil en la Comunidad Valenciana*, Vol. 16. *Exilio y represión franquista* (Prensa Alicante, 2007) p.42.
34. Other sources suggest she was accused, along with three boys, of hanging a propaganda poster on a wall in the town. See for example: *"Fusilaron a una niña de 16 años en Dolores por pegar un pasquín"* in *Información* 17/12/2011.

35. *Derecho penal del enemigo en el primer franquismo* (Universidad de Alicante, 2017) p.164.
36. *Ibid.*, p.237.
37. For more information, see Antonio Maestre: *Franquismo S.A.*, (Madrid: Akal, 2019). The author investigates not only Franco's huge prestige projects, but also the personal fortunes amassed by families that still have an active role in the economy today.
38. *Hoja Oficial de Alicante,* 09/04/39.
39. *The Spanish Face* (Penguin, 1987) p.15.
40. *Ibid.*, p.191.

Chapter 24 *No ha llegado la paz. Ha llegado la Victoria*

1. From Cerdán Tato, *La lucha por la democracia en Alicante* (Madrid, 1978) p.22.
2. *Historia de la Guerra de España*, first published in Buenos Aires. The work was later published under a new title: *Guerra y vicisitudes de los españoles*.
3. From Soledad Fox Maura's foreword to *In Place of Splendour* (London, 2021) p.16. Nancy Johnstone is the author of *Hotel in Flight* (New York, 1940), the owner of the Casa Johnstone in Tossa de Mar, who helped in the evacuation of children to France before the fall of Catalonia. See for example Whitehead, *Republicans and the Second World War* (Yorkshire, 2020) pp.19, 32–33.
4. See for example, a letter from Nora Purcell to an unidentified friend (Carmen): Ref: JLS,998/1,194 in the Archives of the Comunidad Autónoma de la Región de Murcia.
5. *The Last Days of the Spanish Republic* (London, 2017) p.1.
6. See Preston, *The Last days of the Spanish Republic* (London, 2017) pp.35–6.
7. *The Spanish Civil War* (London: Penguin, 1977) p.886.
8. See: Lucas, *The Spanish Pimpernel* (London, 1960) p.254 and Palfreeman: *Aristocrats, Adventurers and Ambulances* (Sussex, 2014) p.192.
9. *ABC* 22/03/1970. This is the only report that I have found that indicates he was in Alicante at his time of death.
10. FO 371/34834/C4225. Courtesy of Peter Anderson. The British Ambassador suggests this is the conclusion of the Spanish Foreign Minister.
11. FO 371/31247/C5250. Courtesy of Peter Anderson.
12. *Ambassador on Special Mission* (London Collins, 1946) p.224. According to a telegram from the acting Consul in Valencia, Apfel was further ordered to pay a fine of 50,000 pesetas: FO 371/31247 C4887, courtesy of Peter Anderson.
13. See the version offered by Sir Samuel Hoare in his memoirs, *Ambassador on Special Mission* (London Collins, 1946) p.223. Also a telegram to the Foreign Office: FO 371/342834 C6672, courtesy of Peter Anderson.
14. *Información* 27/03/09.
15. For more detail, see Evelyn Mesquida, *La Nueve* (Barcelona: Zeta, 2010) pp.259–266.
16. See *Diarios de la guerra civil* (Universidad de Alicante, 2008): entries for 12/03/1939 and 30/03/1936 on p.684 and p.697 respectively. He repeated his innocence in the course of his trial; see *La memoria recuperada. Represaliados del franquismo en la provincia de Alicante* at: https://memoriarecuperada.ua.es/memoriarecuperada_v1/represion/semblanzas/semblanza-eliseo-gomez-serrano/index.html.
17. Marcos González: *La dama roja. Las memorias de Angelita Rodríguez* (San Vicente, Alicante, 2004) p.73.
18. *Diarios de la guerra civil* (Universidad de Alicante, 2008). Annex. p.713.
19. Archivo Represaliados de Alicante, at https://apps.veu.ua.es/archivo_represaliados/records/5690.
20. The story is based on a report in *El País* 15/11/1999: *El último encargo de la guerra civil*.
21. See: Tébar *Derecho penal del enemigo en el primer franquismo* (Universidad de Alicante, 2017) p.177, and Aldeguer Jover and Santo Matas: *Alicante, 1939* (San Vicente [Alicante], 1999) p.61.

22. For a more detailed account, see Tébar: *Derecho penal del enemigo en el primer franquismo* (Universidad de Alicante, 2017) pp.130–31.
23. Biographical notes from Navarro Navarro: *Miguel Hernández* in *La Guerra Civil en la Comunidad Valenciana. Vol.13* (Prensa Alicantina, 2006) pp.124–126. See also: the Fundación Cultural Miguel Hernández: http://www.miguelhernandezvirtual.com/vida/vida.htm (Retrieved 24/01/23) and Diputación de Jaen: https://www.dipujaen.es/microsites/miguel-hernandez/miguel-hernandez-y-jaen/biografia-miguel-hernandez.html. (Retrieved 24/01/23).
24. Biographical notes from: Cornejo, Josefina: *Traduciendo desde el exilio (11): Eduardo de Guzmán*: https://cvc.cervantes.es/trujaman/anteriores/julio_12/18072012.htm (Retrieved 24/01/23).
25. See Whitehead, *Spanish Republicans and the Second World War* (Yorkshire, 2021) pp.91–2.
26. In Fraser, *Blood of Spain* (New York: Pantheon, 1979) p.508. Spaniards have two surnames: their father's and their mother's.

Bibliography and sources

Archives, etc.
Archivo Municipal de Alicante
Archivo de la Democracia (Universidad de Alicante)
Archivo de la Diputación Provincial de Alicante
Archivo Histórico del Ejército del Aire
Archivo Histórico del Partido Comunista de España
Archivo Histórico Nacional
Archivo Histórico Provincial de Alicante
Arxiu/Archivo Municipal Monòver
Arxiu/Archivo Municipal Sant Joan d'Alacant
The National Archives (Kew)
Portal de Archivos Españoles
United Nations Archives
Instituto Alicantino de Cultura Juan Gil-Albert
Modern Records Centre, Warwick University
Real Academia de la Historia

In Spanish (and Valenciano/Catalan)
Azcárate, Manuel: *Derrotas y Esperanzas. La República, la Guerra Civil y la Resistencia* (Barcelona: Tusquest, 1994)
Azcárate, Pablo: *Mi embajada en Londres durante la guerra civil española* (Barcelona: Ariel, 1976)
Bahamonde Magro, Ángel; Cervera Gil, Javier. *Así terminó la Guerra de España*. (Madrid: Marcial Pons, 2000)
Casado, Segismundo: *Así cayó Madrid* (Madrid: Ediciones 99, 1977) [See also the English version: *The Last Days of Madrid* (London: Peter Davies, 1939)]
Cerdán Tato, Enrique: *La lucha por la democracia en Alicante* (Madrid: Casa de Campo, 1978)
Cordón, Antonio: *Trayectoria. Recuerdos de un artillero*. Two editions: *1)* Paris: Ebro, 1971, and *2)* Sevilla: Espuela de Plata, 2008
Domínguez Aragonés, Edmundo: *Los vencedores de Negrín* (Mexico, 1976)
Engel, Carlos: *Historia de las Brigadas Mixtas del Ejército Popular de la República, 1936–1939* (Madrid: Almena, 2005)
Espinosa, Francisco: *La Columna de la Muerte* (Barcelona: Planeta D'Agostini, 2003)
Flaquer Montequi, Rafael: *La opinión pública alicantina durante la Guerra Civil* (Universidad Autónoma de Madrid y Universidad de Alicante, 1994)
García Andreu Mariano:*Alicante en las elecciones republicanas* (Universidad de Alicante,1985)
Gibson, Ian: *En busca de José Antonio* (Barcelona: Planeta, 1980)
Gómez Serrano, Emilio: *Diarios de la Guerra Civil (1936–1939), (Universidad de Alicante, 2008)*

Gutiérrez Rueda, Carmen and Laura Gutiérrez Rueda: *El hambre en el Madrid de la Guerra Civil 1936–1939* (Madrid: La Librería, 2015)
Guzmán, Eduardo (de): *El año de la victoria* (Madrid: Vosa, 2001)
Hernández, Jesús: *Yo, Ministro de Stalin en España* (Madrid: Nos, 1954)
Hernández, de Miguel Carlos: *Los campos de concentración de Franco* (Barcelona: Penguin/Random House, 2021)
Ibárruri, Dolores: *El único camino* (Madrid: Castalia, 1992)
León, María Teresa: *Memoria de la melancolía* (Sevilla: Renacimiento, 2020)
López Fernández, Antonio: *General Miaja, Defensor de Madrid* (Madrid: del Toro, 1975)
Mallol Alberola, José: *La estampida* (Crevillente: self-published, 2000)
Marcos González, María Dolores: *La dama roja. Las memorias de Angelita Rodríguez* (San Vicente [Alicante], 2004)
Martínez Barrio, Diego: *Memorias* (Barcelona: Planeta, 1983)
Moradiellos, Enrique: *Juan Negrín. Textos y discursos políticos* (Madrid: Centro de Estudios Políticos y Constitucionales, 2010)
Moradiellos, Enrique: *Historia mínima de la Guerra Civil Española* (Madrid: Turner, 2016)
Moradiellos, Enrique: See also books in English
Moreno, Francisco: *La prensa en la provincia de Alicante durante la Guerra Civil (1936–1939)* (Instituto Juan Gil-Albert, 1994)
Paniagua, Javier and José A. Piqueras (eds): *Diccionario biográfico de políticos valencianos 1810–2003* (Diputación de Valencia, 2003)
Pacual Devesa, Ángel: *Reflexiones y recuerdos* (Universitat d'Alacant, 2019)
Preston, Paul: *Arquitectos del terror* (Barcelona: Penguin, 2021)
[Preston, Paul: See also books in English]
Ramos, Vicente: *El Teatro Principal en la historia de Alicante. 1847–1947* (Alicante: Comisión de Cultura del Ayuntamiento de Alicante, 1965)
Ramos, Vicente: *La Guerra Civil en la provincia de Alicante. Tomo 1º* (Alicante: Biblioteca Alicantina, 1972)
Ramos, Vicente: *La Guerra Civil en la provincia de Alicante. Tomo 3º* (Alicante: Biblioteca Alicantina, 1974)
Rojo, Vicente (General): *¡Alerta los pueblos!* (Barcelona: Ariel, 1974)
Santacreu, J.M. (Ed.): *Una presó amb vistes al mar* (Universitat d'Alacant, 2008)
Solé i Sabaté, Josep Maria and Joan Villarroya: *España en llamas. La guerra civil desde el aire* (Madrid: Temas de Hoy, 2003)
Tébar Rubio-Manzanares, Ignacio: *Derecho penal del enemigo en el primer franquismo* (Universidad de Alicante, 2017)
Uribe, Vicente: *Memorias de un ministro comunista de la República* (Sevilla: Renacimiento, 2019)
Valero Escandell, José Ramón: *El territorio de la derrota* (Alicante: Col·lecció l'Algoleja, 2004)
Viñas, Ángel and Fernando Hernández Sánchez: *El Desplome de la República* (Barcelona: Crítica, 2010)
Zugazagoitia, Julián: *Guerra y Vicisitudes de los Españoles* Vol. II (Paris: Librería Española, 1968)

Other sources
Abellán, Isabel María: *Isidro* (Murcia: La Fea Burgesía, 2016)
Aldeguer Jover, Francisco and Joaquín Santo Matas: *Alicante, 1939* (San Vicente [Alicante], 1999)

Aub, Max: *El Campo de los Almendros* (Mexico: Joaquín Mortíz, 1968)
Ayuntamiento de Alicante, Patronato Municipal de Cultura, (2005): Martínez Mira, Luis: *Alicante 1936–1939. Tiempos de guerra.*
Campos de concentración de Franco: los últimos supervivientes at: https://www.atresplayer.com/lasexta/programas/lasexta-columna/temporada-11/campos-de-concentracion-de-franco-los-ultimos-supervivientes_614335226584a85ef4703f91/
Causa General. Available online at the Spanish Government's Portal de Archivos Españoles: http://pares.mcu.es/
Canelobre, 7–8, *La guerra en Alicante.* Ed: Francisco Moreno (Instituto Juan Gil-Albert. Summer–Autumn 1986).
Canelobre, 31–32, *Alicante en los años cuarenta.* Ed: Francisco Moreno (Instituto Juan Gil-Albert. Spring–Summer 1995).
Comisión Cívica de Alicante para la Recuperación de la Memoria Histórica: *1939 La Guerra terminó en Alicante* (Alicante: Compas, 2019)
Comissió Llegat Històric: Report on El Poblet published by the Consell Valencia de Cultura 26/05/14
Díez Pomares, Gaspar: *Los bombardeos italianos sobre el País Valenciano durante la Guerra Civil española un estudio fotográfico / The Italian Bombings over Valencia during the Spanish Civil War: A Photographic Study* (Cañada Blanch Centre – LSE). In *Pasado y Memoria. Revista de Historia Contemporánea*, 15, 2016 (Biblioteca Virtual Miguel de Cervantes, 2020)
Excmo. Ayuntamiento de Alicante/Concejalía de Memoria Histórica y Democrática Municipal. Rosser Limiñana, Pablo (coordinator) *Alicante en guerra. De la ciudad republicana de retaguardia y refugios, a la ciudad destrozada, derrotada y franquista. Volumen I*
Festa, 2012 Mira Perceval Verdú and Rico Navarro: *Vicente Amat Furió (1857–1943) su contribución a la historia de Petrer*
Gabarda, Vicent: *Els afusellaments al País Valencià (1938–1956)* (Generalitat Valenciana, 1993)
García Ferrandis, Xavier and Àlvar Martínez-Vidal: *La ayuda humanitaria de los British Quakers durante la Guerra Civil española. (1936–1939): el caso del Hospital Infantil de Polop de la Marina (Alicante.* Published online by *Asclepio* 71(1): https://asclepio.revistas.csic.es
González de Pablo, Mariano: *La Hispano Suiza-Aviación – Guadalajara-Alicante* (1936–1939). Published 31/03/10. At: alicantevivo.org/2010/03/la-hispano-suiza-aviacion-guadalajara.html
La Guerra Civil en la Comunidad Valenciana (Prensa Alicante, 2007)
Mainar Cabanes, Eladi and Robert Llopis i Sendra: *La dimensión internacional de la salida del Consejo Nacional de Defensa, marzo de 1939* in *El pasado que no pasa: la Guerra Civil española a los ochenta años de su finalización* (Universidad de Castilla-La Mancha, 2020)
Martínez Leal, Juan and Miguel Ors Montenegro: *Las cárceles de la posguerra en la provincia de Alicante. Un estudio de la represión franquista* (1939–1945) (Alicante 1994) Archivo de la Democracia. University of Alicante
Moreno Fonseret, Roque (Ed.) *La aviación fascista y el bombardeo de Alicante* (Ayuntamiento de Alicante/Universidad de Alicante, 2018)
Moreno Sáez, Francisco: *Primeros días de la sublevación militar del 18 de julio en Alicante,* article in *Información*, 19/07/2011
Pérez Oca, Miguel Ángel: *25 de Mayo. La tragedia olvidada* (San Vicente-Alicante, 2006)
Pineda Marimón, Paula: *Las colonias infantiles en Sant Joan D'Alacant durante la Guerra Civil Española (1936–1939)* at https://www.santjoandalacant.es/sites/default/

files/2019-10/LAS%20COLONIAS%20INFANTILES%20EN%20SANT%20 JOAN%20Paula%20Pineda%20Marim%C3%B3n.pdf

Quilis Táuriz, Fernando: *Las municipalizaciones durante la Guerra Civil en la ciudad de Alicante: 1936–1939* in Anales de la Universidad de Alicante. Historia Contemporánea. 1984–1985, 3–4: 349–365. (Universidad de Alicante. Departamento de Historia Contemporánea, 1985)

Ramírez Aledón, Germán (ed.) *Bombardeig de Xàtiva 1939* (Xàtiva, 2016)

Ríos Carratalá, Juan A. *La actividad cultural en Alicante durante la II República.* University of Alicante: https://www.cervantesvirtual.com

Rubio, David: alicantepedia.com

Salinas Salinas, Carles *La infància refugiada en les colònies col·lectives de l'Alacantí, 1936–1939.* https://raco.cat/index.php/Rella/article/view/343958/439740

Uviedo Murciano, Olegario: *Yo caí en el Puerto de Alicante* (Valencia, 1983)

In English

Alpert, Michael: *The Spanish Civil War at Sea* (Barnsley: Pen & Sword, 2021)

Álvarez del Vayo, Julio *Freedom's Battle* (London: Heinemann, 1940)

Álvarez del Vayo, Julio: *The Last Optimist* (London: Putnam, 1950)

Anderson, Peter: *British Government Maritime Evacuations in the Spanish Civil War* (War in History, Vol.26 [I] 2019) pp.65–85

Beevor, Anthony: *The Battle for Spain. The Spanish Civil War 1936–1939* (London: Wiedenfeld & Nicholson, 2006)

Bolín Luis: *Spain. The Vital Years* (London: Cassell, 1967)

Bolloten, Burnett: *The Spanish Civil War* (University of North Carolina, 2015)

Butler, Paddy: *The Extraordinary Story of Mary Elmes* (Dublin: Orpen, 2017)

Carr, Raymond: *Spain 1808–1975* (Oxford: Clarendon Press, 1982)

Carr, Raymond: *The Spanish Tragedy. The Civil War in perspective* (London: Phoenix Press, 2000)

Casado, Segismundo. Colonel: *The Last Days of Madrid* (London: Peter Davies, 1939) [see also in Spanish]

Churchill, Winston: *Step by Step* (London: Odhams, 1949)

Cunningham, Valentine (ed): Spanish Front. Writers on the Civil War (OUP, 1986)

Derby, Mark: *Petals and Bullets* (Sussex Academic Press, 2015)

Edwards, Jill: *The British Government and the Spanish Civil War* (London: Macmillan, 1979)

Fraser, Ronald: *Blood of Spain* (New York: Pantheon, 1979)

Graham, Helen: *The Spanish Civil War. A Very Short Introduction* (Oxford: OUP, 2005)

Howson Geoffrey: *Arms for Spain. The Untold Story of the Spanish Civil War* (London: John Murray, 1991)

Jackson, Gabriel: *Juan Negrín. Spanish Republican War Leader* (Sussex Academic Press, 2010)

Junod, Marcel: *Warrior without Weapons* (London: Jonathan Cape, 1951)

Krivitsky, Arthur: *In Stalin's Secret Service* (New York, 1939)

Matthews, James: *Reluctant Warriors* (Oxford: OUP, 2012)

(de la) Mora, Constancia: *In Place of Spendour* (London: Clapton Press, 2021)

Moradiellos, Enrique: *Franco. Anatomy of a Dictator* (London: I.B.Taurus, 2018)

[Moradiellos, Enrique: See also books in Spanish]

Orwell, George: *Looking back on the Spanish War* in *The Penguin Essays of George Orwell* (Penguin, 1984)

Orwell, George: (editor: Peter Davison) *Orwell in Spain* (Penguin, 2020)

Palfreeman, Linda: *Aristocrats, Adventurers and Ambulances* (Sussex Academic Press, 2014)
Preston, Paul: *The Spanish Holocaust. Inquisition and Extermination in Twentieth Century Spain* (London: Harper, 2013)
Preston, Paul: *The Last Days of the Spanish Republic* (London: William Collins, 2017)
[Preston, Paul: See also books in Spanish]
Stewart, Frida: *Firing a Shot for Freedom. The Memoirs of Frida Stewart* (London: Clapton, 2020)
Thomas, Hugh: *The Spanish Civil War* (London: Penguin, 1977)
Vincent, Mary: *Spain 1833–2002. People and State* (OUP, 2007)

Press
ABC
Avance
Bandera Roja
Diario Información de Alicante
El Luchador
El País
Hoja Oficial de Alicante
La Vanguardia
Nuestra Bandera
The Manchester Guardian/Guardian

In other languages
Ciano, Galeazzo: *Il diario del conte Ciano: 7 anni da ministro degli Esteri nell'Italia di Mussolini, agosto 1937–febbraio 1943*

Index

Agost 33
Agudo, Sixto 163, 175, 200
Águilas 155
Aguirre, José Antonio 54, 193
Albacete 15, 17, 20, 44, 75, 76, 110, 133, 135, 162, 198
Albatera 197, 199–200, 203
Alberti, Rafael 112–4, 135–6
Albufereta 154
Alcalá de Henares 19, 105
Alcalá Galiano 120
Alcalde Butler, Vicente 25
Alcoy 15, 27, 64, 85, 144, 169, 171, 182, 201
Alianza de Intelectuales Antifascistas 112–3
Allen, Jay 16, 23
Almansa 15, 170
Almería 9, 55, 64–5, 89, 100, 109, 133, 149
Almirante Antequera 120
Almirante Cervera 37
Almirante Miranda 120
Almirante Valdés 120
Alpert, Michael 7, 120–1, 156
Altea 19
Álvarez del Vayo, Julio 35, 53, 55, 60–1, 68–72, 75, 77, 80–1, 102, 113, 127, 129, 132–7, 193
Anti-Comintern Pact 152
Aragón 6, 20, 58, 83–5, 98, 110, 113, 200
Ashford Hodges, Gabrielle 99, 147
Asociación Española de Mujeres Universitarias 200
Asociación para la Recuperación de la Memoria Histórica 47
Aspe 19
Aub, Max 15, 113, 117
Avance 102, 144
Aviazione Legionaria 20, 30–1, 37, 40, 73

Azaña, Manuel 4–6, 12, 18, 27, 54–6, 86–7, 95–6, 104,109, 115–7, 192
Azcárate, Pablo de 42, 55, 74, 79, 81, 104

Badajoz 99 -100, 150
Bahamonde, Ángel 106, 140, 168
Balas Rojas 19
Balearic Islands 31, 34, 38–40, 45, 73–4, 120
Bandera Roja 20
Barajas 114, 139
Barcáiztegui 120
Barceló Jover, Lt.-Colonel Luis 139–42,
Barcelona, 5–6, 13, 26, 31–2, 35, 44, 53, 56, 69, 73, 76, 78, 80, 84, 88, 89, 91, 95–6, 105, 107, 112, 139, 180, 193, 203
Basque Country 30, 54, 57, 65, 78, 92, 146, 156, 193
Batallón Alicante Rojo 19–20, 198
Battle of Belchite (1937), 57, 113–4
Battle of Guadalajara (1937) 15, 20, 114, 141, 161, 165, 197–198
Battle of Jarama (1937) 15, 20, 102, 161
Battle of Málaga (1937) 20, 64, 86, 100
Battle of Menorca (1939) 73–4
Battle of Teruel (1937–8) 6, 15, 31, 56–8, 113–4, 197
Battle of the Ebro (1938) 6, 15, 31, 45, 51, 56–8, 61, 82, 86, 102, 113–4, 144, 194, 197
Battles of Brunete 6, 52, 57, 102, 114
Baxell, Richard 20
Beevor, Anthony 24, 132, 111, 141, 180–1
Belda, Father 90
Benalúa 14, 16, 23, 182
Benidorm 19, 66–7, 155
Benissa 19
Besteiro Fernández, Julián 104, 106–7, 118, 128–9, 134, 138, 150–1, 162, 194

Bethune, Norman 100
Bilbao 5, 72, 78, 156
Bizerte 121
Blanc, Manuel (Dr.) 40, 66
Blanco, Segundo 112
Bolloten, Burnett 63, 84, 101
Borbón, Don Juan de 105
Brenan, Gerald 88, 98, 187
Buckley, Henry 42
Buiza, Admiral Miguel 52, 74–6, 116–21, 132, 151, 172, 195, 197
Burgos 9, 46, 59, 61, 75, 78, 80–1, 94–7, 106–7, 132, 147–50, 174
Butler, R. A. 44, 46, 73–4, 95

Caamaño, Carmen 164, 182, 200
Cabra 45–6
Cadogan Sir Alexander 81, 94, 101
Cagney, James 90
Callosa de Seguro 23, 27
Calpe 19, 72
Campo de los Almendros 177–8, 181–4, 199–200, 203
Canarias 37
Canary Islands 22, 107
Carbonell, Lorenzo 3, 25, 159
Carlos I (also Holy Roman Emperor Carlos V) 111
Carre Chicarro, Casimiro 14
Carrillo, Santiago 138–9, 144
Carrillo, Wenceslao 128, 138, 148–9
Cartagena 9, 14–15, 37, 55, 71, 74, 76, 110, 115, 118, 149, 194
Cartagena uprising 119–122, 125–7, 132–3, 151, 172
Casado López, Colonel Segismundo 3, 52, 57, 71, 73, 75–6, 80, 88, 102–10, 116–20, 126–43, 146–152, 161–2, 164–9, 172, 194
Castell de Castells 12
Castellón 27, 120, 172, 200
Castillo de Olite 121
Castillo de Peñafiel 121
Catalonia 6, 9–10, 31, 53, 57, 83, 85, 98, 113, 193
Catalonia Offensive 51, 54, 56–9, 70, 75, 82, 86, 92, 102–3, 115, 148, 155, 161, 192, 194

Causa General 24, 27
CEDA 12, 104
Centaño, Lieutenant-Colonel José 106, 147
Cervera Gil, Javier 106, 140, 168
Chalmers, Sir Peter 65
Chamberlain, Neville 51, 61, 74, 79, 94–5, 97–8, 101, 106
Chápuli, Lieutenant-Colonel Fernando 15
Checa, Pedro 136, 139, 143
checas 24, 98
Chetwode Commission 78–9, 88, 106
Chetwode, Lady 80
Chetwode, Field Marshal Sir Philip 78–80
Chilton, Sir Henry 80
Chinchilla 15
Churchill, Sir Winston 27, 70, 83, 86, 94, 97
Ciano, Count Galeazzo 31, 61, 180
Cine Monumental 64, 90
Ciudad Real 162, 176
Claudín, Fernando 136–7, 139, 163
CNT-FAI 16, 26, 60, 63–4, 83, 105, 109, 112, 160
Colectividad Cooperativa Confederal 63
Comisión Cívica de Alicante 47
Comisión Provincial de Abastos 63
Comisión Provincial de Orden Público 25
Comité Agrícola de Alicante 63
Comité Popular Provincial de Defensa 26
Companys, Lluis 54, 193
Condor Legion 21, 30, 42
Consejería Local de Abastos 64
Consejo de Aragón 84, 110
Consejo Nacional de Defensa Junta 104, 127–8, 134, 139–40
Consejo Superior de Menores 16
Conservative Party (of Great Britain) 106
Cooper, Gary 90
Corpo Truppe Volontarie 20, 170–1
Cowan, Denys 80, 88, 106
Cresswell, Michael 46
Crevillente 23, 66
Cuenca 113, 162, 164, 200

Daily Herald 8
Daladier, Edouard 61, 94

Delegación Nacional de Servicios Documentales 153
Deltell Luis 159
Denia 43, 73, 144, 171, 182
Devesa, Ángel Pascual 41, 93, 142
Díaz, José 64, 85–6, 112–3, 139
Dickson, Archibald 155–9, 172, 196, 202
Domínguez Aragonés, Edmundo 128, 149,
Dos Passos, John 81
Durango 100

Eden, Sir Anthony 104
Ehrenburg, Ilya 20, 198
El Día 25
El Luchador 23
El Mono Azul 113
Elche (Elx) 15, 19, 27, 66, 83, 171, 182, 197
Elda 15, 19, 33, 198–112, 114, 116, 120, 127–8, 130–4, 144, 170–1, 182
Elmes, Mary 40, 65–6, 196
Escobar, General Antonio 52, 130
Espinosa Maestre, Francisco 100
Esplá, Carlos 155, 197
Estañ, Lieutenant José 13
Extremadura 55, 99, 111, 130
Extremadura campaigns 15, 51–2, 73, 99, 131

Falange 6, 14, 22, 28–9, 75, 91–2, 105, 154, 185–7, 191, 195, 202
Falcón, Irene 112, 114, 135
Ferrol 45
Fidelman Brodsky Mijailova, Maria 87
Fifth column 26–7, 32, 35, 39, 52, 68, 73–4, 89, 98, 105–6, 108–110, 119–120, 127, 140, 149–51, 154, 163, 170, 194–5, 200
Fifth Regiment 19, 84, 113
Figueras 53–5, 112
Finca La Concepción 117
Finca Pedro José 171
Finestrat 19
Foreign Office (UK) 36, 40, 42, 46, 71, 74, 79–81, 98, 101, 106–7, 121, 127, 137, 156, 159, 162, 167, 169, 192
Franco Bahamonde, General Francisco 3, 5–10, 20, 22, 24, 26, 29–36, 38, 44, 46–7, 51–6, 59, 61, 72–5, 77, 79–82,
85, 89, 91, 94–101, 195, 107, 110, 115–6, 119–122, 125–6, 132–3, 136–7, 139–42, 145–157, 165–82, 185–7, 191–5, 199–201
Fraser, Ronald 68, 164, 175, 185
Freemasons 102
Frente Popular 5, 12–3, 22, 25, 27, 78, 104
Fuente, Ricardo 164

Galán Rodríguez, Colonel Francisco 118
Galíndez, Jesús de 101
Gandia 73, 110, 166–9, 195
García Aldave, General José 13–14, 24, 198
García Lorca, Federico 199
Genoa 114
George VI 104
Gerona (Girona) 114
Gestapo 86, 125, 192–3, 196
Goded, General 6, 13
Gómez Serrano, Emilio 13, 15–6, 34, 41, 53, 60, 67–8, 71–2, 76, 84, 89–90, 92, 101, 118, 138, 141–5, 148–9, 152, 154, 157–8, 170, 173–4, 197
González Beltrán, Alicia 158
González Beltrán, Helia 158
González de Pablo, Mariano 32–4, 171
González de Ubieta, Luis 74
González, Valentín (*El Campesino*) 84, 143
González Marín, Manuel 128
González Peña, Ramón 112
González Prieto, José 143
González Vázquez, Lt. Juan José 28–9
González, Valentin (*El Campesino*) 84, 143
González-Ruibal, Alfredo 52
Goodden, Abbington 107, 127, 165–70
Göring, Reichsführer Hermann 31
Graham, Helen 4, 24
Gramsci, Antonio 113
Granada 19, 45, 52, 111, 113, 199
Grant, Cary 90
Gras Boix, Plácido 111
Gravina 120
Guadalajara 32, 141, 165, 197
Guadix 19
Guardia Civil 13, 15, 24–5, 198, 201
Guernica 30, 47, 100, 197

Guilloto León, Colonel Juan "Modesto" 84, 112–3, 118, 136, 143
Guzmán, Eduardo de 172–3, 175–9, 182–5, 199

Halifax, Lord 42, 55, 74–5, 78–79, 169
Hellín 15
Hemingway, Ernest 81
Henche de la Plata, Rafael 164
Henry, Jules 80
HMS *Boadicea* 65
HMS *Devonshire* 73–4
HMS *Galatea* 167
HMS *Maine* 36, 111
HMS *Nubian* 167
HMS *Sussex* 167
Hernández. Miguel 113, 198–9, 203
Hernández de Miguel, Carlos 182
Hernández Tomás, Jesús 86–7, 116, 120, 126–7, 131, 137, 140, 143, 163
Hidalgo de los Cisneros, Ignacio 16, 110, 112–4, 133, 136, 193
Hillgarth, Captain Alan 73, 121, 153, 167
Hispano-Suiza 32–3, 91
Hitler, Adolf 3, 7, 9, 44, 46, 51, 61, 72, 81, 85, 92, 94, 116, 132, 151–2, 174, 177, 180, 193
Hoare, Sir Samuel 156, 195
Hodgson, Sir Robert 107
Hospital de Convalecientes de Aviación 17
Hotel Samper 14, 24
House of Commons 44, 70, 73–4, 79, 95–6, 101, 137, 169

Ibárruri, Dolores (*La Pasionaria*) 112–3, 126, 134–6, 139, 197
International Brigades 9, 20, 79, 81, 85, 98, 108, 194
Izquierda Republicana 5, 41, 155, 197

Jackson, Gabriel 56
Jaen 162, 165
Johns, W. E. 8
Johnstone, Nancy 194
Jorge Juan 120
José Luis Díaz 14, 64, 85–6, 112–3, 139
Junod, Dr. Marcel 36, 78–9
Junta de Defensa de Madrid 108, 161

Junta de Defensa Nacional 6–7
Junta de Evacuación 166
Junta Local de Defensa Pasiva 34
Juventudes Socialistas Unificadas 19, 84, 138, 161

Kindler von Knobloch, Hans-Joachim 28
Krivitsky, Walter 31–2, 81–2, 87

La Pasionaria see Ibárruri, Dolores
La Roda 15
Largo Caballero, Francisco 6, 28, 53, 64, 87–8, 103, 108, 112–3, 118, 125, 138, 148, 192
Lazaga 120
League of Nations 44, 46, 60, 87
Leche, John 78, 88
Leclerc, General Philippe 196
Lejeune, Major F.B. 42
León, María Teresa 112–3, 135
Lepanto 14, 120
Levante 18, 31, 115, 131, 135, 137, 149, 151, 172
Ley de Represión de la Masonería y el Comunismo 126
Ley de Responsabilidades Políticas 75, 153
Libertad 120
Líster, Enrique 84, 112–3, 118–9, 136, 143
Litten, Dorothy 66
López Fernández, Captain Antonio 57, 69, 76, 131
Los Alcázares 15
Los Llanos 75–8, 88, 108, 161
Luftwaffe 21, 30–1, 42 100

Macdonald, Captain Peter 170
Maciá Rives, Antonio 23
Maciá Rives, José Maria 29
Madrid 3–9, 13, 15–22, 26–28, 30–33, 36, 44, 47, 52–3, 55–6, 65, 68, 71–3, 75–6, 80–1, 86, 91, 96, 99–100, 102–05, 107–114, 116–7, 119, 127–135, 137–44, 147, 149–152, 154, 156, 161–2, 164–5, 170, 180, 191–5, 197, 199–201, 203
Mahon 73–4
Málaga 20, 64, 86, 100, 120, 203
Mallol Alberola, José 154, 171, 182
Mallorca 31, 34, 39–40

Manchester Guardian 81, 105, 135, 162
Mar Cantábrico 120
Martínez Barrio, Diego 14, 53–4, 95–6, 109, 112, 117–9, 161
Martínez Leal, Juan 165
Martínez Monje, General Fernando 13
Martínez Moreno, Lt-Colonel Enrique 15
Matallana, General Manuel 52, 71–2, 74, 109, 116–8, 127–8, 130–1, 147–8, 194–5
Meca, Captain José 13, 15
Mella, Ricardo 83, 89
Méndez Aspe, Francisco 69
Méndez Núñez 120
Menorca 73, 74, 114
Mera, Lt-Colonel Cipriano 105, 128–9, 141
Mercado Central (Central Market) 38–41, 47, 67–8, 91, 202
Miaja Menant, General José 13, 52, 57, 69, 71–2, 74–6, 89, 108, 115–7, 127–8, 131, 134, 144, 150, 161
Miguel de Cervantes 119–20
Milan 144
Milanes, J.H. 107
Millá, Ricardo 64, 143
Millá Santos, Rafael 26, 158
Miller, Mary M. 65
Mínev, Stoyán (alias *Stepanov*) 112–3
Modelo Prison 27, 105
Moix Regàs, José 112
Mola, General Emilio 5–6, 22, 26, 79, 96, 98, 108, 125
Monks, Noel 26–7
Monóvar 19, 110, 133–4, 143, 182, 193
Montaña Barracks 44, 105
Montseny, Federica 57, 63–4, 112
Monzón, Jesús 40–1, 66, 112, 118, 135, 164, 200
Mora, Constancia de la 4, 6, 16–8, 56, 80, 114, 156, 193
Moradiellos, Enrique 10, 126
Moreno, Admiral Franciso, 37
Moreno, Rear Admiral Salvador 15, 121
Morris, Dorothy 35, 65, 67
Motril 52, 111
Mounsey, Sir George 71, 74, 106
Mundo Obrero 103
Munich 8–9, 51, 61, 102, 148

Muñoz Molina, Antonio 58
Muñoz Vizcaino, Lt-Colonel José 171, 197
Murcia 9, 11–12, 15, 25, 35, 64–5, 66–7, 110, 112, 119, 133, 137, 154–5, 181, 196
Mussolini, Benito 4, 7, 28, 31, 44, 46, 61, 72, 81, 86, 92, 94, 113, 116, 132, 144, 151–2, 174, 177

National Joint Committee for Spanish Relief 65
Negrín, Dr. Juan 3, 6, 9, 51, 53–7, 59–62, 68–78, 80–3, 86–88, 91–2, 95–6, 102–3, 106–10, 112, 114–120, 122, 125–7, 129–136, 140, 146, 148, 150–2, 161, 166, 172–3, 192–4, 203
Nelken, Margarita 18, 112
Neva 17
News Chronicle 23
New York Herald Tribune 100
New York Times 161
Nin, Andreu 81, 86, 98
NKVD 81, 86
Non-Intervention 7–8, 35, 44, 60, 74, 79, 81, 87–8, 94, 97, 137, 174, 187
Nuestra Bandera 143, 154
(la) Nueve, 196–7

Oran 135, 155, 157–60, 165, 195
Orihuela 23, 27, 113, 135, 144, 170, 182, 184, 198
Orlov, Alexander 81, 86
Ors Montenegro, Miguel 27, 175, 186
Ortega, José Antonio 10
Ortega y Gasset, José 28
Ortega Gutiérrez, Colonel Antonio 139–41
Ortega Nieto, Cmdr Leopoldo 149–50
Orwell, George 31, 58, 61, 142, 151
Oviedo 45

Palma de Mallorca 40, 45, 121, 153, 203
Palmira 40
Paracuellos 26, 98
Paseo de Soto
PCE 5, 20, 25–6, 62, 64, 66, 77–8, 81–9, 98, 103–6, 109–15, 118, 120, 125–7, 130–1, 133–144, 149, 151–2, 160–1, 164–5, 175, 177, 185, 193, 198–200

Index

Pego 19
Pétain, Maréchal Philippe 101
Picasso, Pablo 47
Pius XI 72, 174
Plaza 25 de Mayo 47
Plaza Balmis 47
Plaza Séneca 34, 47
Plaza de Toros 176, 182
Pollensa 31
Polop 66–7
Popular Flying 8
Posición Dakar 112, 131, 134–5
Posición Jaca 106, 139
Posición Yuste 111, 127, 130–3
POUM 6, 32, 60, 81, 84, 86, 98, 113, 131, 139
Prada, Col. Adolfo 150
Prado Museum 113, 120
Preston, Paul 10, 24, 87, 101, 107, 111, 126, 142, 152, 158, 180–1, 194
Prieto, Blanca 18
Prieto, Concha 18
Prieto, Indalecio 18, 60, 87–8, 118, 132, 136, 143
PSOE 5–6, 12, 18, 26, 57, 60, 64, 78, 82, 84, 87, 102, 104, 112, 118, 125, 138, 155, 159–60, 192
PSUC 85, 112
Puche, José 122
Puerta del Sol 26

Quakers 65–6, 68
Queipo de Llano, General 99, 125

Rabasa 16, 31–3, 91, 134, 154, 161
Rafal 23
Ramos, Vicente 19, 23–4, 38, 148, 154, 158
Reformatorio 23, 176, 198
Regia Aeronautica 30–1, 37, 40, 73–4, 89, 114, 120, 176
Regia Marina 73
Relleu 19
Rey Jaime II 14
Ribbentrop Joachim von, 7
Rivas Cherif, Dolores 18, 192
Roberts, Wilfrid 65
Roberts, Captain William 156
Robles, José 81

Rodríguez, Angelita 175–8
Rodriguez, Melchor 105, 150, 162
Rodríguez Martínez, Manuel 159
Rodríguez Vega, José 164
Rojo, General Vicente 51–2, 54, 56–7, 73, 76, 102, 105, 108–9, 145, 161, 173
Rubio Funes, Major Eduardo 14, 19, 198
Russell Cowan, Howard Denys 80, 88, 106

Sagunto 73, 162
Salamanca 98, 153, 185
San Juan de Alicante 16–18, 24, 37, 66, 110, 164, 171, 200
San Pedro de Cardeña 125
San Rafael 155
San Vicente del Raspeig 32
Sanjurjo, General José 6, 22, 125
Santa Faz 24, 33
Santacreu Soler, José Miguel 27, 91,
Sax 15
Segovia 45
Sella 19
Serrano Suñer, Ramon 29, 75, 105
Servicio de Evacuación de Republicanos Españoles 59
Servicio de Información y Policía Militar (SIPM) 106, 140, 147
Sevilla 5, 45, 99
Siege of the Alcázar 8
Siege of the Montaña barracks 44, 105
Sil 14
Silvestre, Javier 10
SIM, *Servicio de Investigación Militar* 111
Smythe-Pigott, J.R.W. 42
Solé i Sabaté, Josep Maria 30, 46
Son Bonet 31
Son San Juan 31, 73
Speer, George 47
St. Jean de Luz 156
SS *African Trader* 155, 160
SS *English Tanker* 42
SS *Farnham* 42
SS *Gibel Zerjon* 36
SS *Habana* 156
SS *Marionga* 155
SS *St Winifred* 42
SS *Seven Seas Spray* 156
SS *Thorpeheaven* 42

SS *Stanbrook* 95, 155–60, 196
SS *Stanhope* 155
Stepanov, see Mínev
Stevenson, Ralph Skrine 71, 80–1, 88, 106–7, 195
Stewart, Frida 65
Strabolgi Lord 8

Teatro Principal 18, 41, 90, 158, 176
Teruel 6, 15, 31, 56–7, 113–4, 197
The Times 47
Thurtle, Ernest 44
Tigres Rojos 19
Togliatti, Palmiro 112–3, 136, 140–1
Toledo 8, 150, 200
Torrevieja 12, 43–4, 155, 160
Toulouse 69, 70, 136, 196
Tracy, Spencer 90
Tuñón de Lara, Manuel 163–4, 175, 180
Turin 114

UGT 17, 20, 26, 63–4, 84, 90, 104, 128, 138, 149, 164
Ulloa 120
Unamuno, Miguel de 98, 185
Unión Militar Española 161
University Ambulance Unit 65
University of Alicante 155, 175
Uribe, Vicente 63, 72, 103, 109–10, 112, 115–6, 136, 163
Urios Cortés, Emilio 16

Valdés Casas, Francisco 13, 16, 25, 28
Valencia 5, 9, 13, 17, 19–20, 27–8, 31, 37, 42, 53, 55, 71–3, 89, 91, 104, 107–10, 112–5, 117, 119–20, 127–8, 130–3, 142–3, 149–50, 154–5, 163–8, 176, 178, 186, 194–5, 197, 200–1
Valladolid 45, 183
Vallejo Nágera, Antonio 125
Vallelliano, Count 78
Vega Díaz, Francisco 122, 127, 132
Villafranqueza 33, 154
Villajoyosa 12, 18, 43, 155
Villaroya, Joan 46
Villarrobledo 15
Villarroya 30
Villena 15, 144, 170, 182
Viñas, Angel 85, 102, 105
Vincent, Mary 85, 100, 139

Wilson, Francesca 65–7

XIV Cuerpo de Ejército Guerrillero 111, 200
XV Brigade 20

Yagüe, Lieutenant-Colonel Juan 100, 150
Young, Sir George 40, 64–6, 164, 167, 169, 195

Zamora, Ricardo 105
Zugazagoitia, Julián 54, 57, 59, 68, 96, 108, 118, 192